An All Consuming Passion

WILLIAM J. LINES

AN
Origins,

ALL
Modernity,

CONSUMING
and the Australian Life of

PASSION
Georgiana Molloy

ALLEN & UNWIN

First published in 1994
Allen & Unwin Pty Ltd
9 Atchison Street, St Leonards, NSW 2065 Australia

National Library of Australia
Cataloguing-in-Publication entry:

Lines, William J.
An all consuming passion: origins, modernity, and the
Australian life of Georgiana Molloy.

Bibliography.
Includes index.
ISBN 1 86373 553 4.

1. Molloy, Georgiana, 1805–1843. 2. Women pioneers—
Western Australia—Biography. 3. Women botanists—Western
Australia—Biography. 4. Pioneers—Western Australia—Biography.
5. Botanists—Western Australia—Biography. I. Title

994.102092

Set in 10/15 Sabon by DOCUPRO, Sydney
Printed by South Wind Production Singapore Private Limited

10 9 8 7 6 5 4 3 2 1

This project has been assisted by the Commonwealth
Government through the Australia Council.

FOR NED LUDD

Not the first, not the last

CONTENTS

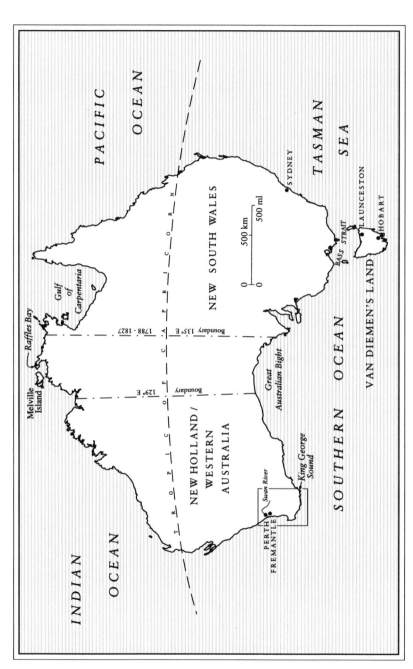

AUSTRALIA 1830

THE SOUTHWEST 1830–1843

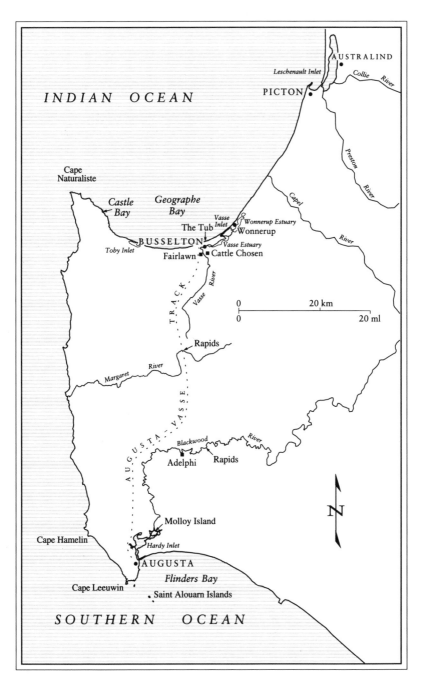

AUGUSTA AND THE VASSE

1

GENESIS

THE EARTH MOVES AND EVERYTHING ON THE EARTH MOVES. Present for millennia, the propelling events and processes continue to occur. But much of the kinesis that actuates planet Earth takes place silently, slowly, an inch at a time, miles below the surface of the earth. These changes occur in millimetres a year, and the sentient creatures on the surface feel nothing move beneath their feet and conclude, therefore, that nothing has happened. Over time, however, coasts recede, deltas form, rivers meander, lakes dry up, continents drift.

But continents, by themselves, do not drift. Crustal segments called tectonic plates underlie and divide the outer face of the planet. Plate boundaries run miscellaneously through continents and down the middle of oceans. Like blocks of ice on a river breaking up in the spring thaw, the large plates on the earth's brittle surface slowly move and jostle one another. Plates move in varying directions and at different speeds and repeatedly collide and join, break apart, and rejoin in different patterns. Plate tectonics, the processes of continental drift, fragmentation, and assembly, have been going on for at least 700 million years and perhaps for more than two billion years. Continents have continually altered their geographical position, their pattern of dispersal, and even their size and number.

Two hundred million years ago, during Jurassic times, the crustal plates pushed all the continents together to form a single supercontinent, Pangaea. Over the next twenty million years, during Triassic times, Pangaea divided into two continents: Laurasia in the north and Gondwana in the south. Soon after the rift with Pangaea these two parts broke again to form new continents. Gondwana split into South America, Africa, New Zealand, Antarctica, India, and Australia.

Australia drifted north. No other continent impeded its passage. In the absence of contact with other landmasses, mountain building in Australia ceased and muted tectonics produced the earth's flattest continent. All across the Yilgarn shield, which covers the western third of Australia, the agents of erosion—wind, water, ice, and snow—began a long, slow, inexorable weathering. Erosion reduced and lowered the land to a nearly flat plain. The detritus from the eroding Yilgarn shield accumulated in large sedimentary basins along the western margin of the continent—a coast of high cliffs, alternating with low sandy dunes, and flanked by a string of offshore islands and fringing reefs. This ancient, variegated shoreline forms the boundary of one of the planet's oldest land fragments.

The earth is 4.5 billion years old. The oldest rocks, 4.15-billion-year-old zircons, crystallised at Mount Narryer in Western Australia's northwest. These crystals formed less than half a billion years after planet Earth began to coalesce. Rocks nearly as old occur at Greenbushes, in the southwest of Western Australia. Life on earth began less than half a billion years later.

The earth's oldest sedimentary rocks, the 3.75-billion-year-old Isua series of west Greenland, record the cooling and stabilisation of the earth's crust. Too metamorphosed (altered by heat and pressure) to preserve the morphological remains of living creatures, these strata nevertheless retain a chemical signature of organic activity. Thus, evidence for life appears in the first rocks capable of providing it.

A billion years of molecular evolution—the weeding out by misadventure of unstable molecular unions—produced a narrow range of cell-like organisms. Animated by rudimentary DNA but without the protection of any kind of nucleus, they survived as small, efficient chemical factories. They fed on a mineral soup of seawater. When they grew too fat they simply divided into more stable proportions.

The earliest life-forms were simple fermenters that harvested natural carbohydrates, such as glucose, from the sea and broke them down for their energy content. But, as earth's early storm clouds cleared and the sun's growing radiation became more penetrating, some bacteria evolved a different process of metabolism. To build nutrient material into living matter, these bacteria used the energy in sunlight to internally synthesise glucose from more abundant, simpler molecules. This process of photosynthesis became the blueprint for almost all future plant life.

Photosynthetic success, however, presaged catastrophe. The explosive multiplication of photosynthetic bacteria released huge quantities of oxygen. Oxygen was a pollutant; it made the atmosphere reactive to organic matter and was poisonous to most life then in existence. Virtually all the existing biota retreated into sediments, stagnant waters, and other environments that provided a barricade against oxygen. But some organisms survived the disaster. The survivors, cyanobacteria—blue-green algae—used oxygen for energy and transformed oxygen's peril into the force of life.

But though the new oxygen-consuming, sea-dwelling organisms adapted to the biologically poisonous nature of their own waste, they had no defence against oxygen's geological impact. Massive erosion from the earth's young landmasses charged the seawater with huge quantities of soluble iron. The iron reacted with the growing volume of free oxygen and the seas began to rust. A rain of iron oxide sediment fell to the sea floor; whole oceans turned red.

For the microscopic life that triggered this chain of events, the deposits of iron oxide came as a suffocating avalanche. By about 1.8 billion years ago, when the seas had eventually been swept clean of iron, much of the early life had disappeared. But in the less crowded waters, more robust organisms appeared. They also produced oxygen and their gas wastes began to move from the sea into the atmosphere.

Part of the oxygen released by bacteria took the form of ozone, most of which concentrated 30 kilometres above earth's surface. The ozone layer scattered the blue light filtered from the sun's spectrum and gave the sky a tinge of blue. Ozone's big molecules also shielded deadly ultraviolet radiation and allowed life to emerge from the shelter of the seas.

For the first four billion years of earth's history, organisms were entirely aquatic. Nothing lived on the land. But the growing stockpile of aerial oxygen and the creation of the ozone shield allowed plants to invade the land and begin a vast expansion of the biosphere. The first terrestrial plants evolved in the Silurian period, some 430 million years ago, when earth was already 90 per cent as old as it is today.

Photosynthesis also produced organic carbon. A tiny fraction leaked into sediments. Plate tectonics transported the sedimentary carbon into the deeper earth. But the movement did not cease once the carbon reached the planet's interior. The buried organic carbon formed a necessary reservoir—continuously replenished and continuously drawn upon. The movement of continents slowly brings rocks back from the interior to the surface, where organisms catalyse a reaction between the uprising organic carbon and aerial oxygen. Without continental drift, the oxygen content of the air would increase to poisonous levels. But with the continuous upwelling of carbon, carbon dioxide is produced again and again and in turn is utilised by the biological cycle. The combined effects of the biological cycle and the rock cycle make the earth habitable.

Each organism, just by living, added chemicals to the environment, the waters, surface sediments, and atmosphere, and removed others. Carbon dioxide, oxygen, methane, hydrogen sulfide, and nitrogen were taken up, transformed, and then returned, on a worldwide scale.

Thus living things did not simply adapt to the vicissitudes imposed by the physical and chemical environment. Organisms modified the environment and actively adapted earth to life's needs. Microbes cleansed the biosphere and kept it fit and nutritious for life. The growth and spread of plants changed the amount of sunlight reflected from land surfaces. Plants massively intervened in the water cycle and drastically changed the earth's environment in favour of conditions that maintained life. The soil, made and held together by plants, began to teem with worms and bacteria and myriad different kinds of beetles that kept the soil fertile and productive. Life itself made the earth fit for life.

Living things even assisted in their own destruction when their individual ends enhanced the community's chances for survival. Cells appeared that underwent reproductive division from DNA coiled within a small membrane sac—a nucleus. Each nucleated cell came with a timed self-destruct mechanism, probably based on a process of genetic error accumulation. After a certain number of divisions, cells begin to show serious irregularities and eventually fail completely. Thus, ageing became nature's normal termination of life.

The organisation of the planet for the self-sustenance of life took vast lengths of time; outcomes were always contingent, never inevitable.

Some 1.4 billion years ago, eukaryotic cells evolved through the physical association of different bacterial, prokaryotic (single-cell) ancestors. Although the advent of eukaryotic cells marked a major increment in life's complexity, multicellular animals did not follow triumphantly. Ninety per cent of earthly time passed before the 'Cambrian explosion', about 570 million years ago, when multicellular animals with hard parts first appeared.

Nor does the course of life from the Cambrian reveal evidence of accumulating excellence. Organic forms were not striving towards a state of perfection; evolution contained no inherent predictability, no progressive imperative. Evolution was neither smooth nor purposeful. Organisms did not arise and prosper because the laws of nature entailed such an outcome as a primary effect. Good design and adaptation to environment arose only as epiphenomena, side consequences of the basic causal process at work in natural populations—the struggle among organisms for reproductive success.

But success did not signal progress. The past was not a preparation for a superior future. The history of life is unprogressive, a story of contingent complexity rather than preplanned harmony. Few contingencies had greater effect on the evolution of life than the five great episodes of mass extinction that punctuate earth's history.

Pangaea provided all life with a single arena for biological competition and only one set of winners in the struggle for survival and reproduction. For 200 million years, reptiles, including the dinosaurs, dominated animal life. When Pangaea broke up, dinosaurs continued their dominance in Laurasia and Gondwana. But for happenstance, their reign might have extended on to the continents that broke out of Laurasia and Gondwana.

At the end of the Cretaceous period, 65 million years ago, a mass extinction annihilated the dinosaurs and their kin, along with some 50 per cent of all marine species. But life, as in each previous extinction, recovered. Gradually, over the course of tens of millions of years, new forms of life evolved to fill the niches emptied during the extinction. The Cretaceous debacle—caused either by the impact of a comet on the earth's surface that blanketed the atmosphere for years with debris and dust and choked off life, or by mass volcanism with similar effects—cleared ecological space for the evolution of large mammals.

Each geographical setting gave room for only a limited number of species. But as continents split into separate landmasses, and smaller continents and islands appeared, so the number of sites where species could form multiplied. The radiation of different species into different niches yielded a steady increase in the diversity of species. And, despite the Cretaceous extinction, the increase in diversity accelerated over the next 100 million years, until the earth contained ten million, or maybe even 100 million, separate species.

Australia's separation from Gondwana coincided with the mass extinction of the Cretaceous. In the absence of reptilian competition, Australia's geographical isolation enabled the evolution of a unique mammalian fauna, the marsupials. For 40 million years Australia's marsupials lived in rainforest that covered the whole of the continent.

Towards the end of the Oligocene, about 25 million years ago, Australia's uniformly warm and wet climate dissipated. Temperature and precipitation regimes fluctuated, storm tracks migrated, seasonality became more pronounced and then less so. Climates moved across the continent over time. Rainforest species retreated to the north and east. Aridity—seasonal, episodic, and chronic—became a regular component of the biological order. Drought-enduring plants, xerophytes, became dominant. Xerophytic survivors included scleromorphs (or sclerophylls), plants characterised by small, tough evergreen leaves that hoarded nutrients and resisted the transpiration of precious water.

During the Pleistocene the oceans rose and fell. Ice sheets on the scale of continents formed and disintegrated. Climates reversed from glacial to interglacial and back to glacial again. A massive wave of extinctions—the most comprehensive since the great Cretaceous extermination—visited the world biota.

In Australia, *Northofagus* and *Podocarpus* retreated before aridity. *Casuarinas* succeeded *Araucarias*. *Eucalypts*, *Banksias*, and other sclerophyll genera thrived. *Eucalypts*, especially, prevailed over the Australian continent to an extent unrivalled by any other plant genus on any other continent. The new floral regime encouraged new fauna and new patterns of biotic interaction. Sclerophyllous plants and sclerophyllous animals became interdependent. Eucalyptus coevolved singular associations with koalas, termites, possums, and parrots.

Aridity shaped the swift and mobile animals of Australia's dry grasslands and parched mallee and selected them for nocturnal life.

Aridity and sunlight also shaped topography and landform, exposed the pigmentation of the raw earth, and bleached the chlorophyll from the leaves of Australian plants. Aridity eroded the earth to rock and sharpened and fractured those features that withstood disintegration.

As sea level changed and changed again, and water inundated the interior plains of the continent, the higher mountains and ranges of the Australian southwest formed islands of biological refuge. Isolation favoured unique evolutionary change and species diversity, especially among plants. When the sea subsided, desert occupied the area once covered by water and the southwest remained quarantined.

Bounded on two sides by ocean and on the third by the vast treeless and waterless Nullarbor Plain, the southwest maintained a distinctive combination of flora and fauna, noticeably Australian but peculiarly southwestern. Its soils leached of trace elements by time and its entropy uninterrupted by glaciation or tectonic activity, the region evolved a high degree of floristic richness and endemism. Over 30 per cent of the total species of *Epacridaceae*, *Myrtaceae*, and *Proteaceae* were confined to the southwest. Up to four-fifths of all the southwest's flowering plants grew nowhere else.

Possessed of a marvellous endemic suite of biotas, the southwest was nevertheless neither irrevocably isolated nor irretrievably separate from the rest of the planet. Life there shared the same atmosphere, the same sun, the same cycles of replication and reproduction as all life. The oceans that touched the southwest also touched other lands teeming with life.

Other landmasses, besides the crustal blocks that became Australia, have also wandered tens of thousands of kilometres over the face of the globe. The patterns and aggregates of continents and oceans and atmosphere, of organisms and evolution, in intricate interdependence, constitute the planet Earth. And this organic cell, this mindless, self-sustaining, spherical orb, moves, and everything on the earth—land and air, water and life, despite accidents of space and time—keeps moving. And the imperative of movement informs the generative purpose of life—to be born and to be born again.

But within the larger system of drifting continents and shifting, uplifting, grinding, cracking landmasses, other phenomena also shape the face of the earth and alter the outcome of life. These phenomena, which happen turbulently and noisily, with smoke and fire, revolution, war, invasion, and economic change, take place on the surface of the earth and on a time scale immensely inferior to the order that originally gave rise to life. But, although of a different temporal order from geological and evolutionary processes, these phenomena shape outcomes that equal, and may exceed, the natural and contingent consequences of continental drift and mass extinction.

For the creatures residing on this planet, the human creatures, millions of them, also move and drift. Driven by fear and curiosity, propelled by conceptions of destiny and hope, humans have travelled singly and in families, in clans and tribes, sometimes as entire nations, out of family homes, across tribal and national boundaries, over rivers and deserts and oceans, through forest and plain, to new continents, eventually to occupy all conceivable habitats upon the face of the earth. And wherever humans moved, they disrupted and displaced the earth: gouged mountains, dredged valleys, created deserts. Wherever humans moved, they disrupted and displaced life: felled forests, altered habitats to favour some species over others, extinguished biotas, poisoned the soil, air, and water, and precipitated the greatest extinction of life since life began. For, unique among species, humans discovered that their true habitat was culture, not nature. And humans became cultural, not natural, beings.

The first human beings to reach Australia arrived at least 50 000 to 60 000 or more years ago. They came from the north, descendants of the *Homo sapiens* who had spread out from Africa into mainland southeast Asia, then onward again, southward and southeast. Over the centuries, island by island, small groups of people moved closer and closer to Australia. On the far eastern horizon they could see land, or smoke from fires indicating land. They pushed on. When they reached the Australian mainland, they encountered the open woodland of the Sahul shelf, the northward continental extension of Australia then above sea level and incorporating New Guinea. The open habitat facilitated movement and dispersal. But neither aridity, nor impenetrable rainforest, nor heat, nor cold deterred their occupation. From the Sahul the aboriginal Australians spread to all parts of the continent, to the mountains of the southeast, to Tasmania (then joined to the mainland), to every section of the coast, and to every acre of the interior. They reached the remote and fecund southwest at least 50 000 years ago.

Wherever they travelled, Aborigines found a hunter's paradise. By the Pleistocene, isolation and evolution had populated Australia with a number of large, defenceless reptiles, marsupials, and birds, rich in protein and fat. The giants included a massive goanna, *Megalania*, six to nine metres long, the *Diprotodon*, browsers of wombat-like build but the size of a rhinoceros, and *Thylacoleo*, the marsupial lion, a leopard-sized predator. Most of the large animals were members of the family of kangaroos and wallabies, the *Macropodidae* (literally, 'big feet'). Giant wallabies, *Protemnodon*, which were larger in size than the largest living kangaroo (the big red, *Megaleia rufa*, which stands up to two metres tall and weighs as much as 90 kilograms), hopped through the forests and woodlands that covered the continent. The largest macropod was *Procoptodon goliah*, a massive three-metre-tall kangaroo with a short, broad face.

Human predators found these creatures easy prey. The cornucopia lasted a long time, but not forever. One-third of the megafauna that existed 50 000 years ago was extinct by 15 000 years ago. The giants had a gigantic thirst, and the drying of the continent at the end of the Pleistocene—not Aboriginal predation—probably caused their demise. The disappearance of lakes and water holes, as well as climatically induced changes in forage, doomed them to extinction.

Over 50 species of large animals became extinct in the Australian Pleistocene.

The comparatively early colonisation of Australia by the Aborigines, and their subsequent isolation, enabled an entire continental human population to bypass the Neolithic revolution that spread domesticated flora and fauna—agriculture—to the Old World. But Aborigines did not need agriculture. Population remained light and food sufficient. Even after the Pleistocene extinctions, Aborigines obtained ample provision from scavenging, hunting, and gathering.

Movement in search of game and plants was not random or a matter of chance. Aborigines did not depend on spearing or ensnaring an animal here and there wherever one happened to be, or on digging out a root here and there wherever one happened to grow. They kept the landscape predictable and productive through the use of fire, and regularly and systematically burned the country—to keep the bush open, to drive animals into traps, and to maintain an environment favourable to their preferred prey. With the coming of the rains, grass, which encouraged game and increased hunting prospects, grew over the burned-out areas. Regular, low-intensity fires also encouraged the growth of certain plants over others, especially certain edible roots and fruits.

The effects of anthropogenic fire, however, were not confined to species immediately useful. Many abundant species of Australian flora tolerate fire, even require a conflagration for their regeneration. Fire had been frequent in Australia even before the coming of the Aborigines, and fire greatly influenced the spread and frequency of flora. Aboriginal fire reinforced tendencies arising from a biotic preference for fire already present in the natural environment.

Australian Aborigines found ways to live companionably with the life-giving earth. They cared for, and loved, the organic suspirations of a fecund world. And, because they believed the land actually participated in human life, they almost dissolved the distinctions between culture and nature, between the human world and the cosmos—almost, but not quite.

All humans live embedded in the passage of time—a matrix open to all possible standards of judgement. All humans experience immanent things that do not appear to change, things permanent and periodic: the cosmic recurrences of days and seasons, natural disasters, and an apparent directionality to life from birth and growth to decrepitude, death, and decay. Australian Aborigines developed their own unique interpretation of these events—an interpretation that formed the basis of their culture.

Aboriginal society was concerned, even preoccupied, with the first and last formula of things. Aborigines sought to understand the ultimate conditions of human being. Like all humans, they responded to an imperative need for an explanation of the continuity between origins and the experiential here and now.

The Aboriginal world came into existence through the actions of spirit Ancestors, the heroes of the Dreaming. During this fabulous epoch, supernatural beings broke through the crust of the earth and emerged on a featureless plain. They lay down to sleep and dreamt of an actions of the next day. One Ancestor might dream of a plain full of kangaroos issuing from himself, who is Ancestor, human being, and kangaroo all at the same time. When he wakes, the Ancestor finds the kangaroos who have crawled out of his armpit while he slept or, alternatively, upon waking, he proceeds to give birth to kangaroos. Dream and actuality are the same.

Through imagination and deed, the Ancestors created all the features and all the life upon the earth. They stocked the land with all the requirements of sustenance, raised up hills and mountains, put spirit-children into the waters, and used wind and song as agencies of will. The task accomplished, the Ancestors ascended into the sky and became constellations, stars, planets, and moon, or entered the earth and became rocks, hills, watercourses, and animals. Thus the universe was filled with evidence of the Dreaming. Every rock, every river, every spring and water hole represented a concrete trace of a sacred journey undertaken in the Dreaming.

Although indefinitely remote, sacred time was not inaccessible. The past was continuously recovered through everyday life and through ritual. When an Aborigine followed the path of an Ancestor, hunted, gathered food, or fired the country, he or she was part of the Ancestor and part of the continuing creation of the land that both existed and was being created. Reactualisation of the Dreaming, in dance and song and everyday life, regenerated life and assured life's continuation.

The Aborigines appealed to no gods, just or unjust, to adjudicate the world. And because they entertained no notion of progress, no thought that the world improved with the passage of time, they made no use of the concepts of favour and destiny. Aborigines were not perplexed by moral dualism. No state of grace or redemption awaited them at the end of life; no expectation of a heaven of reward or a hell of punishment guided their earthly behaviour. No moral issues were involved in successfully reaching the abode of the dead and joining the other spirits. There was no punishment for sins, and the only tests were of an initiatory character. Aborigines neither expected nor sought even a whisper of inner peace and reconciliation. They did not look back to a golden age or forward to an afterlife that would resolve the puzzles of existence.

But the absence of divinity and progress did not leave Aboriginal society without moral compass, subject only to the vagaries of personal whim or influence. Aboriginal society functioned according to a system of obligations and traditions adapted to the biology of Australia. To a much greater extent than other people, Aborigines lived under a government of laws and not of men. The Western concept of law, however, is too restrictive in describing Aboriginal society. Law implies external constraint, whereas Aborigines lived in a society of order, an order wider than law and free from law's coercive, hierarchical, and centralising implications. Aboriginal order was self-regulating and knew nothing of the power of the state, leadership, or justice.

Knowledge of the Aboriginal world took effort and time. Disclosure of sacred history extended over many years. Only step by step did an individual become aware of the greatness of the mythical past and present.

Aborigines lived in small groups. Cohorts were related to one another by language and kinship but not by feelings of tribal identity. And each band, each extended Aboriginal family, inhabited an area of special and personal meaning, inherited from the Dreaming. Campsites, tracks, water holes, lairs, sanctuaries, birthplaces, and landmarks were the means and meaning of life. The manifold forms of eucalyptus, acacia, casuarina, banksia, and thousands of other plant and animal species gave the land a numinous and magical beauty. The land was text and its story told everything worth knowing.

Aborigines traversed the landscape, a grid of Ancestor tracks and sacred sites, not for reasons of conquest, or for the sake of seeing something new, but in order to inhabit their own territory. They travelled in order to stay where they were. The rhythm of Aboriginal life was not interrupted by any memory of having come from anywhere else; rather, existence was amplified by the Aborigines' certainty that they originated from the very soil of Australia. And because Aborigines never gave up their home or left it permanently, they could not conceive of others doing so.

But other people, people who lived on continents and islands far distant from Australia, did leave their homes permanently—to plunder, to proselytise, to seek new lives and settle, to progress, prosper, and get rich. Their destinations included, most especially included, lands already occupied.[1]

2

AUTHORS OF THEMSELVES
IN ALL

FEW PEOPLE HAVE POSSESSED A GREATER PROCLIVITY FOR LEAVING their homelands than the people of Europe. Europeans began to forsake their dwelling places to depart into temporary or permanent exile from the time of the Roman Empire.

By 1800 no territory in the world lay beyond the reach of European governments and business, which found advantage in establishing shop, factory, farm, or prison there. Yet, the numbers of Europeans living outside Europe remained relatively small—in most colonies less than the number of indigenous people. Then came the deluge. In the nineteenth century, European populations increased enormously and tens of millions of people migrated.

In England, especially, population changed utterly. By the end of the eighteenth century the people of England had reproduced themselves up to the level of subsistence. Improvements in the supply of food did not mean that people ate better, but rather that most people ate the same meagre portions. Poverty and misery increased in even greater proportion than population.

In 1801 the first British census recorded a larger population than anyone expected: 10 942 646. Over the next ten years population increased 15 per cent, to over 12.5 million. The country was bewildered by a growth in its own numbers without precedent.

Amidst this flood of humanity, Georgiana Kennedy was born.

She came into the world at her parents' home, Crosby Lodge, near Carlisle, in the north of England county of Cumberland, by the Scottish border. Her Scottish father, David Kennedy, a former military officer, descended from an old border family, inherited estates and lived the comfortable life of a country gentleman. Her mother, Elizabeth, also descended from an old border family and was the only daughter of a former mayor of Carlisle, George Dalton. After her marriage to David Kennedy in 1800 she lived the life of a country gentleman's wife, dutifully bearing heirs. Her first child, a daughter, Elizabeth Margaret, was born in 1801. Georgiana, the Kennedys' second child, was born on 23 May 1805. Three more children followed: David Dalton in 1808, Mary in 1811, and George in 1813.

In the year of Georgiana Kennedy's birth the population of Carlisle numbered less than 11 000. Although a very old, medieval city, Carlisle participated in the great modern changes underway in the English country and town. Cotton spinning and weaving became major industries in Carlisle in the last part of the eighteenth century. The vigour of the trade drew in migrants, particularly Scottish and Irish families. Between 1801 and 1811 Carlisle's population increased by nearly a quarter. The migrant cotton workers crowded into cramped and squalid urban dwellings. Poverty was endemic.

Unlike most of their contemporaries, the Kennedy children did not face the necessity to labour. No hard and exacting toil to procure a sufficiency on which to live overshadowed their lives or blighted their prospects. The Kennedy children were born to a life of upper-middle-class leisure.

But, although privileged by birth, Georgiana Kennedy was born into a Europe at war. At the end of the eighteenth century, through the beginning of the nineteenth century, the ambitions of Napoleon Bonaparte turned the whole continent into a theatre of war. While the conflict did not directly inconvenience the Kennedys, war's energising effects did not leave them untouched. In May 1803, after the fitful one-year Peace of Amiens, Britain and France had severed relations and prepared again for battle. Over the following year Napoleon assembled a massive invasion fleet directed towards England. The British government called for military volunteers, and hundreds of thousands of men responded. Napoleon repeatedly delayed the invasion.

The fear of invasion, which had gripped England for two years, lifted in the first spring of Georgiana Kennedy's life. But there was little summer in England that June and July. Cold, dry winds continued from the north. Towards the end of July, people again began to fear invasion. Reports reached England that the French were in feverish preparation on the opposite coast. As before, however, no invasion came. In October England received the news of Lord Nelson's victory at Trafalgar and of the virtual annihilation of the French and Spanish fleet. Britain gained supremacy at sea. Invasion could now be discounted. The war shifted to the land. In 1807 a British army disembarked in Portugal to expel French forces from the Iberian Peninsula.

Preparation for war always involves more than recruiting soldiers. Before people enter into warfare they first dehumanise those they are intent on eliminating. Suddenly, no calumny was too great to attribute to Napoleon. Press and pamphlet magnified every crime of his career, real or imagined. Accusations against him assumed grotesque proportions. Patriots appealed to every feeling of hatred, scorn, and insular pride that could mobilise the people for battle. Bloodcurdling posters describing the consequences of invasion—universal pillage, women of all ranks violated, children slaughtered, trade ruined, the labouring classes thrown out of employment, famine with all its horrors, despotism triumphant, and the inhabitants carried away by shiploads to foreign lands—appeared on church doors and village trees. During the earliest years of Georgiana Kennedy's life, a parent's warning, 'Boney will come to you!' was enough to quiet any refractory youngster.

Britain remained at war for nine years, as the army, under the command of the Duke of Wellington, slowly pushed the French back into France. The British, like their opponents, like all people at war, viewed their struggle as not only for themselves but also for the whole civilised world. Both antagonists believed they alone represented progress. The French thought the English spiritually decadent, reactionary, and unprogressive for opposing the revolutionary will and the military that enforced it. English power only prolonged the old, corrupt institutions and discriminatory laws that everywhere repressed human energies and preserved inequalities. The war, the French believed, was as much about an idea—the progressive liberation of mankind—as about territorial aggrandisement. War was a test of spirit, of vitality, culture, and life. The English, in turn, believed destiny had bestowed on them the privilege of defending freedom and progress as represented by English law and institutions. Britain stood for stability and responsibility, for teaching the foreigner the rules of civilised social conduct.

During the war years, as Georgiana Kennedy grew into childhood, the English became ever more conscious of themselves as a nation. 'If we are true to ourselves,' Nelson assured his compatriots, 'we need not fear Bonaparte.' Victory at Trafalgar and Wellington's battlefield conquests confirmed Nelson's declaration. Success in war generated a particularly virile patriotism and offered the English a sense of the exuberance, generosity, and specialness of their own history. The period invented the idea of England as mistress of the seas, who held her own against all Europe in arms. Resistance to Napoleon led the English to believe themselves possessed of a genius for cohesion. In the face of danger, an Englishman would always do his duty. The English prided themselves on their inflexible resolve and convinced themselves that if they stood their ground, then tyrants everywhere would bend before the forces of human decency.

Early in 1814 the British pushed the French out of Spain. On March 30, shortly before Georgiana Kennedy's ninth birthday, Paris fell to the allies. When Wellington finally defeated Napoleon at

Waterloo in 1815, the victors knew they had prevailed because their social creed and their political and economic arrangements proved more enduring, proved to be founded more closely on the realities of human nature than had those of their opponents.

The leading men of Britain believed that people, in the pursuit of their economic interests, obey laws of behaviour that establish order in the social world, much as natural laws establish order in the natural world. Adam Smith, in his *Wealth of Nations* (1776), described the most important of these laws as 'the desire of bettering our condition'—a desire that

> comes with us from the womb and never leaves us till we go into the grave. . . . in the whole interval which separates those two moments, there is scarce perhaps a single instant in which any man is so perfectly and completely satisfied with his situation, as to be without any wish of alteration or improvement of any kind.[1]

Self-interest drove the economic machine. Under a system of natural liberty, the market economy, the pursuit of individual interest, resulted in competition. Acquisitiveness, constrained by competition, continuously adapted production to the changing wants of the market. The interaction of supply and demand guaranteed a supply of goods precisely in the quantities society desired and at precisely the prices society was prepared to pay.

More spectacularly, the market system required no intervention, direction, or regulation to bring about the general good. Smith described how the actions of millions of buyers and sellers, each bent on nothing more than finding personal opportunities for exchange, gave rise to a vast system of mutual coordination. Each individual, Smith wrote, 'is led by an invisible hand to promote an end which was no part of his intention'. Unrestrained individual enterprise guaranteed both the wealth of nations and the welfare of individuals—universal material abundance.[2]

But Smith's *Wealth of Nations* was much more than a treatise on economic principles. His book contained a radical message: the ends of life were economic, not spiritual or moral; the purpose of human life was material prosperity. According to Smith, the meaning of human existence lay in the accumulation of possessions. Insatiable desire, formerly condemned as a source of frustration, unhappiness, and spiritual malaise, became instead a powerful stimulus to economic development. In Smith's world, self-improvement assumed the force of moral improvement. The *Wealth of Nations* outlined a history of the gradual economic progress of human society that suggested an indefinite future augmentation of wealth and well-being.

But Smith's insight was incomplete. Avarice needed an ally before the invisible hand and the pursuit of private interest could begin generating wealth. The men of the Enlightenment, the free traders and the free marketeers, found their ally in science, which, starting with Francis Bacon, had believed the natural world to be devoid of any sacred meaning, that it was, in fact, merely a collection of resources to be consumed. This view denied that humans had any relationship to the natural world beyond use and denied that humans had any obligations to other organisms. A world devoid of meaning was a world humans were justified in taming, subduing, and conquering. As one of Smith's disciples wrote: as the division of labour is carried further, 'nature . . . will be more at our command; men will make their situation in this world abundantly more easy and comfortable'.[3]

To compensate for the loss of meaning in the world, the men of the Enlightenment made a grand promise: the pursuit of profit, together with human dominion over the planet, would abolish need, and moral improvement, based on the absence of need, would abolish evil and secure freedom. Progress was that simple.

Smith stated his theme of economic liberty with telling force, with rhetoric and irony, and in a manner that impressed and convinced his contemporaries. His distinctly modern ideas created a sensation. Self-interest, instead of being seen as a daily human temptation, became heroic. People might have their own particular beliefs, but in the market, in their traffic with the world, everyone became subject to one unvarying premise based on a materialist interpretation of life. Moreover, self-interest was progressive; allied to the scientific program to conquer nature, self-interest promised a future without limits.

The *Wealth of Nations* was a prescription for a liberating, expanding, prospering, progressive economy in which the legitimate values and interests of society supported and reinforced each other: liberty and prosperity, the individual and society, industry and agriculture, capital and labour, wealth and well-being. The system required only one innate quality: the 'propensity to truck, barter and exchange one thing for another'.[4]

Although enormously appealing to contemporaries, Smith's theory, apart from his dubious premise that economic motives lay at the core of human nature, contained a major flaw. Private enterprise, the exercise of the propensity to truck, barter, and exchange, required the sponsorship and assistance of government. Market demands did not spontaneously arise; governments had to create, condition, and nurture new economic relations. Most spectacularly, the state consciously and deliberately intervened to change the nature of English agriculture. Between 1796 and 1815 Parliament passed more than 1800 enclosure bills. Their passage constituted a highly visible interference in the economy with highly visible consequences. The privatisation of once-common land created a commercial agriculture, destroyed subsistence farming, and drove a rural labour force into industrial employment and the army.

During the first decade of Georgiana Kennedy's life, under the stimulus of the Peninsula War and the sponsorship of the state, the multitude of private economic preoccupations quickened. British manufacturers called into existence a vast working population to supply every manner of article to continental countries too busy in mutual slaughter to be able to make for themselves. Industrial workers crowded together in urban squalor. Industrial towns grew so fast that they became almost overwhelmed by congestion, smoke, and filth. Men, women, and children laboured long hours for minimal wages.

Growth of population, as well as changes in agriculture and industry, sundered the old social economy. Factory products intruded into everyone's lives and became the chief articles of commerce. Everywhere, down to the smallest country towns and villages, shops—specialised or general—supplanted the peddler, the itinerant tradesman of the fairs, and the ancient custom of making clothes at home.

The destruction of traditional trades and ways of work and the dissolution of the conventional bonds of masters and workers shattered old forms of community and fraternity. Economic revolution mobilised British society and left the population footloose and dislocated. The growth of industry gave rise to a new sense of creation and self-sufficiency and to a new culture no longer dependent on the past, composed of individuals who no longer felt dependent on others.

Britain became a land bustling with transients. Displaced persons left their place of birth in search of new opportunities and prospects. Country people moved to the new industrial towns, and great numbers of vagrants wandered the English countryside looking for unskilled rural work, making ditches, cutting drains, and carrying loads for masons. In Scotland, Highlanders moved into the lowlands, and lowland Scots—mechanics, peddlers, and merchants—moved into England. Enclosure, urbanisation, and industrialisation produced swarms of Britons no longer bound to villages and no longer born to clear identities.

The Industrial Revolution also gave rise to new ways of thinking about the world. For 2000 years after Plato's *Republic*, people's expectations of a better worldly order were based on the possibility of altering social relationships. But the Industrial Revolution promised a far more luxurious estate. Happiness depended upon sustained mechanical and technical progress—a paradise of expanding needs and satisfactions. Advances in production, trade, and technology meant increasing and unprecedented control over nature. Mechanisation mastered natural forces that people felt had hitherto mastered them. Technical advance generated enormous pride and confidence in human capacity. People no longer felt as dependent on the natural world as had previous generations.

The effects of human culture and industry became ubiquitous. Human presence was felt over the entire earth. The Industrial Revolution confirmed the idea of progress, strengthened belief in the rationality of self-interest and profit, and accustomed many people to see triumph everywhere.

But not everyone rejoiced. War on the Iberian Peninsula kept food prices high, and five times during the war the harvest failed. Though the rich and middle classes suffered little, and certainly the Kennedys felt no imposition, working people—those who depended solely on wages and lived largely on bread—faced starvation. Many called for an end to this endless war. Radical criticism of aristocratic privilege grew. The opposition complained loudly against the cost, mismanagement, and waste of life on the peninsula.

At the height of the continental blockade, in 1809 and 1810, when Napoleon sought to close Europe's ports to everything Britain made or British ships carried, ruin spread among merchants. Factories closed and employers dismissed workers. Whole populations became deprived of the wherewithal to buy. After a wet summer the harvest failed again and the price of food soared. The workless and working poor appeared on the point of riot.

Workers objected not only to unemployment but also to new manufacturing machines that made them redundant. They responded with direct action aimed at machinery held to be obnoxious. The first outbreaks of machine breaking occurred in Nottinghamshire in March 1811. More organised, disciplined outbreaks followed in November, led, according to government spies, by a Ned Ludd.

Midlands Luddism died away early in the new year, but machine breaking spread to Yorkshire—the county neighbouring the Kennedys' home county of Cumberland—during March and April 1812.

Factory owners and the governing class saw the sabotage as a threat to the new industrial order and to private property. They demanded strong action. By the summer of 1812 military officials had deployed no fewer than 12 000 troops in the disturbed counties, a greater force than Wellington commanded on the peninsula. Even so, further Luddite-inspired machine sabotage broke out in Lancashire the following March and April. Government repression continued, and harsh reprisal, show trials, capital punishment, and transportation eventually brought machine breaking to an end.

Some Britons recognised the Luddite revolt as a protest against modernity and industrialisation. Lord Byron chose the subject as the topic for his first speech to the House of Lords. He pleaded for compassion in dealing with the captured Luddites and argued that the workers were right: the best solution to the problem of labour replacement was to scrap the new machines. He wrote to Lord Holland, leader of the Whig opposition in the House: 'However we may rejoice in any improvement in ye arts which may be beneficial to mankind we must not allow mankind to be sacrificed to improvements in Mechanism.' Besides, the new machines produced shoddy goods, fit only for export and the mill owners' profit.[5]

Despite worker unrest the war was enormously expansive and profitable. Although the 22-year struggle cost Britain £700 million, the war doubled the country's export trade and trebled revenue. The end of the war, however, brought an end to big wartime production. British firms collapsed by hundreds, workers were dismissed by scores of thousands, farmers went bankrupt, and rural labourers became paupers. Soldiers and sailors, who had done what the nation needed but who were wanted no longer, were demobilised. They flooded the labour market, wages fell, and unemployment increased.

Between 1815 and 1820 social turbulence and discontent among rural labourers, industrial workers, and the unemployed seemed to threaten the whole fabric of society—the economic order as well as the Constitution. Strikes, protests, and riots terrified property owners. Although the Luddite revolt had been suppressed, the whole of the manufacturing districts of the north and Midlands again seemed engaged in a gigantic conspiracy against progress and profit.

Once more, however, a unified and determined governing class contained the rebellion. Authorities suspended habeas corpus, banned the sale of radical literature, broke up political meetings, and jailed, hanged, or transported strikers and agitators.

Some property owners and their apologists saw the uprisings in terms of deluded people led astray by dangerous agitators. Other commentators detected a more fundamental underlying cause—surplus population. By the end of the second decade of the nineteenth century, no one could doubt the growth of British population; population was not merely growing, but growing extraordinarily fast. From 12.5 million in 1811, the people of Great Britain increased to 14.3 million in 1821.

An ever-growing population seemed a burden. High unemployment following another economic crisis in 1825 confirmed the view that Britain suffered a population surfeit and that the growth of population constituted a major menace. Emigration offered the only possible relief.

In 1826 Parliament appointed a committee to assess the evidence for a redundant population in Ireland and the Scottish Highlands. Witnesses argued in favour of government subsidies to encourage the emigration of the surplus population, and the hearings helped change people's minds about emigration. The act of leaving one's country to settle in another became acceptable, even patriotic.

A national system of emigration, however, proved unnecessary. Voluntary emigration made projected government schemes redundant.

By the time of the 1826 parliamentary hearings, Britons had already acquired an inextinguishable yearning to leave home.

Many of the Britons who departed the overcrowded country for the burgeoning cities did not stop there. They kept on moving, left Britain entirely, and migrated overseas. Opportunities had never been better. Fares, especially across the Atlantic, were cheap, as little as £10 after the Napoleonic Wars and becoming cheaper. By 1830 the cheapest fare from England to New York had dropped to as little as £5.

All over the world, Europeans were conquering wilderness: in the pampas of South America, in the Mississippi Valley and Canada, in the Himalayas and the Andes, and in the Australian bush. As they conquered, they claimed. Never before had so much cheap land become available. People of Europe found the lure irresistible. Large-scale emigration started the year after Waterloo and increased steadily. Huge numbers of men, women, and children began to move from the Old World into the new settlements on the edge of the wilderness or even directly into the wilderness itself. Thus began the greatest population movement in history.[6]

Most migrants left in order to better themselves. Some left in order, in the words of a contemporary, to escape 'from the vulgar sarcasms too often hurled at the less wealthy by the purse-proud, commonplace people of the world'. But whether impelled by necessity or lured by settlement propaganda, the number of emigrants steadily increased throughout the 1820s. Individual need and individual enterprise re-peopled the world outside Europe.[7]

The majority of migrants crossed the Atlantic, the short and safe route to the promised land of North America. A few, more intrepid or more foolhardy, took the much longer and more perilous journey to Australia. Georgiana Kennedy was among those audacious few.[8]

3

THE LANGUAGE OF
HEAVEN

BRITAIN EMERGED FROM THE NAPOLEONIC WARS A DEEPLY RELIGIOUS
nation. Moral earnestness had increased. Though still a cruel and
violent people, the first generation of postwar Britons was concerned
just as much to point to moral progress as to focus attention on
continued wickedness.

The source of national devotion—the precepts of British Prot-
estantism—derived from the authorised translation of the Bible. The
words of the King James Version of the Gospels, heard week after
week in church or chapel and studied at home, in company or in
private, formed the mould of people's minds. Christianity and the
Bible supplied the only comprehensive system of thought of which
most people were aware. The Old and New Testaments supplied the
only philosophy or ethics easily available, the only cosmology or
ancient history. People accepted the Bible as a true account of the
human condition. Christian teaching intruded into all exhortation
and instruction and even into what was read or seen for pleasure.
Biblical phrases strayed into everyday speech and biblical symbolism
supplied subjects for many of the engravings and oleographs people
hung in their houses.

This fashion for seriousness and ardent devotion, for sobriety
and solemnity, swirled around the young Georgiana Kennedy. Of all
the Kennedy siblings she was the most affected by the religiosity of

the times. A very earnest young woman, she found her brothers and sisters frivolous.

In 1821 David Kennedy died in a hunting accident. Mrs Kennedy retained Crosby Lodge but two years later moved the family to Rugby, in the industrialising English Midlands. Eighteen-year-old Georgiana was unhappy in her new home. She detested the new world of the English town. After the placid seclusion, harmony, and rural quiet of Crosby Lodge, she found Rugby an abode of noise, disorder, and impropriety. She later attributed all the subsequent family misfortunes—the waywardness and licentiousness of her brothers and sisters—to the bad influence of Rugby. In the meantime, she began quarrelling with her siblings, who found her tiresomely pious. To avoid domestic unpleasantness, she spent long periods away, staying with religious friends.

In 1827 Georgiana's older sister, Elizabeth, became engaged to the Reverend John Besly. Georgiana strongly disapproved, disliked Besly, and sought to persuade everyone of the inappropriateness of the match. Her advocacy, however, was unavailing. For the sake of peace, the family agreed Georgiana should leave Rugby to live with her Scottish friends, the Dunlops, at Keppoch House, on the 340-acre Dunlop estate in Dumbartonshire, northwest of Glasgow.

At Keppoch House Georgiana Kennedy again found elegance, propriety, regularity, harmony, and friendship. She was particularly close to the three Dunlop daughters nearest her own age: Mary, Margaret, and Helen. Their older brother John was prominent in the temperance cause in Scotland. The four young women admired his zeal and became fervent participants in the religious revival then animating Scotland.

With the Dunlops, Georgiana Kennedy embraced Presbyterianism and eschewed a sensual and self-indulgent emphasis on the external. Too great an immersion in the material world necessarily implied a neglect of the internal matters of conscience and spirit. One's thoughts must be directed inward to the state of one's soul.

Kennedy and her friends lived consciously under the eye of their maker and fixed their thoughts on the account they would one day be called to render. In preparation for that time, life's central task was to come to terms with conscience, emotions, beliefs, and aspirations.

But Kennedy's outlook was not shaped entirely by biblical scripture. She had other interests. The daughter of country gentry, she was educated in the manner of a gentlewoman. She learned the arts of pleasing men, and her tutors imparted skills regarded as distinctly and admirably feminine: French and English, piano, singing, sewing, composition, fine handwriting, and an appreciation of poetry. As expected of all literate people, she read and absorbed Shakespeare, Thomas Gray, and John Milton.

But neither religion, nor superior education, nor class, nor aspirations protected Georgiana Kennedy from exposure to the brutality, wretchedness, degradation, and heavy drinking that characterised much of public and private life in Britain during the first three decades of the nineteenth century. Despite the growth of sentiment and refinement among the middle class, many people lived brutal and nasty existences. Drunkenness was widespread and evident in most of the streets and marketplaces. Violence for many Britons was a matter of habit, and casual and calculated violence, assaults, and muggings were common.

Violence was not confined to criminal activity. Popular tastes were coarse and pleasures callous. Crowds delighted in the fighting and torturing of animals. Ox driving, cock fighting, and the baiting of badgers, bears, and bulls were all legal. People also approved of and applauded fighting between human beings—violent and damaging forms of wrestling, cudgel play, or prize fighting with bare fists. Boxing was the national nursery of manliness. People scorned softness; flogging was common. Even at the elite Rugby School, where Georgiana Kennedy's youngest brother, George, was enrolled, ten-year-old boys were whipped from their beds in the small hours to take up duties for their seniors. The list of capital offences was long, and hangings were a popular public spectacle.[1]

Amidst public and private violence and in the general tumult of postwar life, religious revivalism flourished. Distressed Britons turned to revitalisation movements, which offered to provide a more satisfying life out of what many saw as the ruins of the present: endemic political unrest, enfeebled social bonds, and baseless moral codes. People responded eagerly to preachers imbued with strong missionary zeal. A great revival of enthusiastic religious feeling swept Britain. Evangelicals preached conversion from indifference to lively faith, from moral apathy to earnest endeavour after righteousness, from callous selfishness to care for others in Christian charity. Evangelical preaching stressed the great Christian doctrines of sin, grace, and redemption.

By coupling virtue, piety, the work ethic, and human progress with salvation, and associating idleness and dependence with sin and damnation, evangelical belief became the necessary religion for the Industrial Revolution. No other belief or established religion was considered capable of withstanding diligent, persistent evangelical onslaught.

The most powerfully eloquent evangelical preacher of the postwar period was Edward Irving. Irving was born in 1792 at Annan, Scotland, across the border from the Kennedy family home in Cumberland. While at Edinburgh University Irving befriended a fellow theology student, Robert Story, who, in 1815, was appointed assistant minister at Rosneath, a parish that adjoined Keppoch. Irving and his close friend Thomas Carlyle took walking tours through the Scottish Midlands and sometimes called in at Rosneath. Story became Rosneath's ordained minister in 1818 and in 1824 he became engaged to Georgiana Kennedy's close friend, the nineteen-year-old Helen Boyle Dunlop.

Irving, like Story, opposed the narrow, gloomy, Calvinist religiosity that had characterised Scottish belief. He craved a religion of the heart and despised the bibliolatry of an era that he felt honoured the letter rather than the spirit of the Scripture. Irving preached during a period of great change in sensibility. Inspired by the Romantic movement, people began to value personal truth and emotion. Irving responded to this desire for a more concrete and living faith, mystical and majestic, with passion.

While Robert Story ministered to his necessarily small congregation at Rosneath, Edward Irving preached to the nation. Irving's evangelicalism created a sensation, and during the 1820s he assumed a commanding presence in the country's religious life. Over six feet tall, with long flowing hair and always dressed in the best of fashionable taste, Irving cut a striking figure. His vigorous good looks complemented his ardent preaching. Outgoing and enthusiastic, Irving possessed an extraordinary capacity for self-dramatisation that he revealed in his preaching, his missionary work, and his heightened rhetoric about his own and his nation's Christian destiny.

In 1822 Irving left Scotland to preach in London. His eloquence transformed his original small and poor congregation at Hatton Garden into a large and rich one. After George Canning, the British foreign secretary, referred in the House of Commons to one of Irving's addresses as 'the most eloquent sermon I have ever heard', the young preacher quickly became popular. His sermons attracted the most distinguished members of London society. The curious crowds returned again and again, fascinated by his magnificent appearance and his earnestness, his extravagant mode of address, and by the strange beliefs to which he gave utterance. Carriages and pedestrians blocked the roads to Hatton Garden for miles; early arrivals waited in long queues for admission. Sunday after Sunday a thousand people assembled to hear Irving expound for three hours at a stretch on sinfulness and the need for immediate redemption. He warned his listeners of the imminence of the day of judgement.[2]

Irving's self-possession and assurance contrasted with the perplexity and uncertainties that afflicted his friend Robert Story. Even at Divinity School Story had never shared the evangelical fervour so pronounced in Irving. In 1825, burdened by doubts, debt, and ill health, Story called off his engagement to Helen Dunlop. He felt unprepared for marriage. But after attending a religious assembly in England in 1827 he regained his health and his faith and freed himself of all financial encumbrances. He returned to Rosneath a religious enthusiast and became active and energetic in the cause of temperance and was vigilant in denouncing drinking. He now felt ready to marry and he and Helen Dunlop resumed their engagement. They married at Keppoch in September 1828. Story was 37 years old and his bride was 23. After the marriage Georgiana Kennedy came to live with the Storys at Rosneath. There she participated in the life of the parish.

The Reverend Story constantly challenged his parishioners to emulate the virtues of the sixth-century ascetic Modan, patron saint of Rosneath. According to Story, St Modan lived frugally and rejected the adventitious advantages of riches and royal descent. Content with bread and water drawn from a spring, he never imbibed wine or ate flesh and passed his days in poverty and obedience until he became a warrior of religion and a model of life in the ways of truth, virtue, and holiness. Story exhorted his congregation to consider the worthiness of St Modan's life:

> By the gravity of his manners and the austerity of his life, all could see the purity and modesty of his character. By chastity he banished sensuality from the hearts of many of the sons of iniquity. He cast down anger by patience, he extinguished envy by love, he prostrated pride before humility, he overcame sloth by diligence and prayer, and subdued every vice by its opposite virtue.[3]

Although Georgiana Kennedy took no monastic vows, her move to Rosneath was almost a retreat. Only 700 people lived in the entire parish and society was limited. Out of necessity rather than conscious emulation of St Modan, families lived plainly and frugally. Even household bread was a rarity; instead, people ate scones and oatcakes.

The climate was too wet for most grain crops, but trees grew well and landowners enclosed large portions of their estates for plantations of larch, spruce, and silver firs.

Kennedy lived with the Storys at Rosneath Manse, the minister's house attached to the church. The manse and the church were very plain buildings. Church seats were of rough deal and the floor was earth. A gallery ran around three sides of the interior and the pulpit stood between two windows near the manse. The walls were plain and, though whitewashed, grew green with damp and mould.

Story conducted the Sunday service, both summer and winter, from noon to 3 p.m., permitted no interval, and expected the congregation to remain seated. Outwardly subdued, he was nevertheless a strict disciplinarian and publicly rebuked those who sought to slip away unnoticed during a pause. He opened with a psalm, then a long, full prayer, a reading from the Bible followed by an exposition of the passage, another psalm and a shorter prayer, then the sermon. He then read another prayer and concluded with a psalm. Afterwards the collection plate was passed around.

But if people's material and religious life in Rosneath parish was plain and austere, the natural surroundings were neither. Situated between the peaceful waters of the Gareloch and the more turbulent broad estuary of the Clyde, Rosneath lies on a peninsula that stretches for about fourteen kilometres from Highland moors to rich pasture. The pellucid waters of the Gareloch abounded in salmon, herring, whiting, and haddock. Water herons, several species of gulls, and curlews moved along the shores and moors of Rosneath. Dunlins, dotterels, wild ducks, geese, and sandpipers gathered along the shores and skimmed the surface.

Garden species of fuchsia, arbutus, myrtle, and peach trees grew along the shores of the Gareloch. Hillsides of turf, bracken, and heather sloped down to the rugged shore. Rich and perfumed copes of rhododendron, spruce, and pine flourished in the peninsula's moist climate. Oak, ash, and birch grew indigenously and the humid, mild climate gave rise to a profusion of ferns and mossy plants. Owls and larks, thrushes, blackbirds, robins, bullfinches, chaffinches, greenfinches, linnets, cuckoos, wood pigeons, and starlings and other song birds thrived in the peninsula's woods and heather.

Early in 1828, the year of the Storys' marriage, Edward Irving visited Scotland and addressed crowded congregations day after day in St Cuthbert's, the largest church in Edinburgh. In June, at Robert Story's invitation, Irving preached at Rosneath. The small church could not contain the overflowing audience. Irving spoke from a wooden outdoor pulpit set up under a tent. He spoke extempore, as was his practice, and astonished and thrilled those present by his weird and dramatic oratory.

Irving continued his preaching around Scotland and late in the summer returned to Rosneath. Again, from under the rich sycamores and blossomed laurel of the churchyard, he addressed a large gathering. He proclaimed the Second Coming of Jesus Christ, spoke of the Apocalypse, and prayed fervently for God's direct intervention in the world. He exhorted those imbued with the Holy Spirit, as seen at Pentecost, to come forth. His oration stirred the whole neighbourhood. Miraculously, those very phenomena he had prayed for, the signs of the coming king—glossolalia and faith healing— began to appear. In March 1829 Mary Campbell, an invalid from Row on the Gareloch, began speaking in an unknown tongue. Shortly afterwards two brothers in the neighbourhood began performing miraculous healing feats.

Irving returned to Scotland in May of 1829. Thousands and thousands of people came out to hear him as he toured parishes, speaking for hours each day. In June he visited Rosneath and, as before, spoke outdoors to a large assembly.[4]

Irving's flamboyance contrasted with the simple, if prolix, preaching of the earnest Robert Story. Nevertheless, Story now shared his friend's enthusiasm for ecstatic conversion. He revered revelation and prophecy and encouraged the revival atmosphere at Rosneath.

The brief and blameless life of an invalid farm girl, Isabella Campbell, Mary Campbell's older sister, moved Story to write *Peace in Believing*, a memoir of Isabella's rapt and ecstatic communion with God.

Campbell had died, aged twenty, of tuberculosis in 1827. Throughout her long illness she evinced an intense preoccupation with preparing for death. Stories of her communion with her Heavenly Father and of her marvellous spiritual insight circulated widely. To all appearances she had led a pious childhood, yet she felt that her early youth was a period of utter vanity. Any youthful concern she had had about the state of her soul was light and trivial. She was convinced that had she died then, she would have gone to a place of torment. The body, she believed, was an infamous receptacle of pollution and impiety. She prayed for continuance of life only so that she might be better prepared to meet her God.

In his preface to *Peace in Believing* Story wrote that those who find that the story 'of a soul delivered from conscious guilt and fear is the most intensely affecting, will find in this record of peace and joy, of holy living, and triumphant dying, abundant occasion for solemn and delightful mediation'.[5]

Readers instantly found the story inspiring. Isabella Campbell displayed the traditional characteristics of a Christian heroine: sickly, enfeebled, dying. Indeed, her debility was the chief part of her attractiveness. Six thousand copies of the memoir sold in a few weeks and several further editions were published. *Peace in Believing* circulated widely in Britain and North America and drew many visitors to Fernicarry, opposite Rosneath, to see the scene of Isabella's life and her surviving sister, Mary. Story paid the proceeds of the book, over £600, to the Campbell family.

Under Story's influence Rosneath Manse became a centre for Church of Scotland revivalism. While she lived there Georgiana Kennedy met some of the leading exponents of pietistic faith. She was receptive to their advocacy, and religion became her total response to life. The Divine informed her in an active sense, not limited to impersonal and abstract concepts. She developed a feeling of what God might effect. Faith in God, she believed, granted the believer a spiritual life that survived the ruin of the visible universe.

But faith in the immaterial posed difficulties. Those who aspired to otherworldliness still had to account for the fact that there was a this world to be escaped from. Different generations dealt with the problem differently. In medieval times, theologians simply dismissed this world, the material world, as an illusion. Only spirit mattered. But ever since the time of Francis Bacon, discoveries in natural history revealed greater and greater realms of worldly existence. The corporeal world was a fact far too insistent to be disproved by simple denial.

In the eighteenth and early nineteenth centuries, religious people sought a reconciliation between this world and the next through the precepts of Natural Theology. The most popularised Natural Theology was that of William Paley (1743–1805), archdeacon of Carlisle, whose book *Natural Theology* was originally published in 1802 and reprinted almost annually well into the nineteenth century. According to Paley, any examination of a plant or an animal revealed various structures or contrivances that enabled it to survive and propagate its species. These contrivances were so elaborate that they could not possibly have been the product of mere chance; they must have been designed by the Creator.

Organic creation thus became a theatre for the observation of Providence in action. Part of the purpose of nature, then, was to let humans know He exists. Thus the message of the majesty and wonder of God's revelation could be read not only in the inspired writings but also in His book of nature. As the pages of a book are opened to reveal its contents, so the open book of nature revealed God's presence. And, like the books of the Bible, study of nature lifted the mind towards the worship of God.[6]

Most theologians agreed; the study of natural history brought man nearer to God. Accordingly, clergymen recommended nature study to country gentlemen as a healthy alternative to books and the bottle. Middle-class women, who enjoyed a comparable level of leisure, were also urged to become involved. Botany, in particular, became a familiar pastime for ladies and gentlemen. They roamed the fields and woods of Britain in search of examples of design in the contrivances of nature, contrivances functioning exactly as God designed.[7]

Georgiana Kennedy shared the general enthusiasm for natural history. At Crosby Lodge she and her mother had kept a large garden. Gardening stimulated an interest in botany in general, which she developed further at Keppoch and Rosneath. While she lived frugally and plainly in Scotland, she and Mary Dunlop nevertheless delighted in country walks, horsecart rides, and botanical rambles. These expeditions compelled the young women to harmonise their other-worldliness with this world. As they strolled over heaths and moors by sedgy pools and running waters, and through woods of oak, beech, walnut, Spanish chestnut, and planes, they could no longer maintain that the genuine and the truly good were entirely antithetical to everything found in the natural world. Some accommodation had to be reached. The world they discovered through their senses possessed substance and realness.

The discovery was potentially subversive. Some people who observed and scrutinised the world around them could not help but notice that the natural world had a life of its own, independent of human needs. Christianity, however, taught that God had made the world for mankind. All other species were subordinate. The biblical account of creation proved that the Garden of Eden was a paradise in which Adam had God-given dominion over all things. Mankind's ascendancy was central to the Divine plan. Georgiana Kennedy in Scotland did not question the Divine plan.

Part of the Divine plan, another accommodation necessary with this world, was marriage and family. In May 1829 Georgiana Kennedy passed her twenty-fourth birthday, unmarried and seemingly without prospects. In contrast, Helen Dunlop had married the previous year and Kennedy's sister Elizabeth was engaged. Their fiancés were older men, both of them ministers. Georgiana Kennedy delighted in family life and wondered about her own future. But life at Rosneath restricted her exposure to eligible men. She maintained, however, a friendship with an older man, a family friend outside the circle of Scottish Presbyterians in which she moved, the 48-year-old Captain John Molloy, known as 'Handsome Jack' among his fellow officers in the Army's Rifle Brigade.

Kennedy and Molloy had been acquaintances for many years. Military postings around the British Isles kept Captain Molloy from prolonged and intimate contact with the Kennedy family but he and Georgiana Kennedy corresponded regularly. Kennedy's letters eagerly acknowledged their friendship but she remained correct and formal and her prose betrayed no intimacy.

In December 1828 Captain Molloy wrote to Kennedy that he and the Rifle Brigade had been posted to Canada. He assured her that he was not perturbed by the prospect of a long sea voyage across the Atlantic. In the meantime, as a token of their friendship he sent a present of a cabinet. Kennedy protested at the captain's generosity, which, she wrote, 'if I had had any idea of, I would have endeavoured to prevent'. After the receipt of his letter she had read in the newspaper that the Rifle Brigade was not going overseas after all. She hoped the report was correct, for however cavalierly Captain Molloy might regard the journey, she could not bring her 'untravelled mind to regard so long a voyage so lightly'. Besides, she declared, there were personal reasons for rejoicing in the Rifle Brigade's home detention: 'As I always have, and always shall consider you are one of my greatest friends, I should be glad to retain you on this side of the Atlantic.' She devoted the rest of her letter to news of upcoming marriages and reflections on the pleasures of family life. She concluded, 'I shall at all times be much gratified at hearing from you, and I hope you will occasionally favor me.'[8]

Molloy favoured her more than Kennedy dared hope. In July 1829 he wrote again. He proposed marriage.

John Molloy was born in London on 5 September 1780. He was schooled at Harrow, then under the charge of the young and liberal headmaster Joseph Drury. Drury had abolished the birch and introduced a system of education that gave Harrow a degree of celebrity it had never previously known. Young aristocrats thronged to the school and enrolments flourished. Under Drury's tutelage, Molloy's fellow alumni included four future prime ministers: Lord Goderich, Sir Robert Peel, Lord Aberdeen, and Lord Palmerston.

Molloy, however, did not follow his peers into politics. Early in his teens he joined the navy. But the navy did not suit him and in 1807 he obtained an army commission, in the flamboyant 95th Brigade, as a second lieutenant.

The 95th was formed in 1800 and soon become famous as the Rifle Brigade. Riflemen were dressed in distinctive dark green jackets with black facings and armed with a straight grooved rifle, the Baker. They were trained in marksmanship and to fight not as the rest of the army, in a rigid line, shoulder to shoulder, but in loose formation, every man using his own wits to make the most of cover. The Rifles' informal method of combat devastated the serried ranks of the French during the campaigns of the Napoleonic Wars on the Iberian Peninsula. But the Rifles always fought in the front in an advance and in the rear in a retreat and suffered an appalling number of casualties.

Constant exposure to danger, as well as the soldiers' independent form of engagement, produced a feeling of solidarity. The Rifles quickly became one of the most popular regiments and, unlike the rest of the army, never suffered a shortfall of volunteers. A recruiting poster for the Rifles proclaimed: 'The bloody, fighting Ninety Fifth—the first into the field and the last out.' The Regiment stood out in its own opinion as well as in others', and a greater number of chronicles of the Rifle Brigade's deeds appeared after the war than for any other unit of Wellington's army.

In 1808 Molloy joined the brigade on the Iberian Peninsula. He was 28 years of age, ten or more years older than most of his fellow officers of his own rank, who had joined in their teens. Molloy arrived in time to participate in the first British victory of the Peninsula campaigns.

On 21 August 1808 Wellington defeated the French at Vimiera. The battle, like the greater war, was a personal affair. Officers fought alongside their men, shared the mud and the blood, and engaged hand to hand, using the cold steel of sword, lance, and bayonet. Like all Peninsula battles, Vimiera was sudden, exhausting, short, and bloody. Clouds of smoke from cannon and musket slowly drifted over the battlefield. Horses, riders, and infantrymen lay bleeding and screaming or dead in the trampled mire. The survivors slipped and slid through the mud and blood and gore. 'It seemed,' wrote one of Molloy's men, 'hell upon earth.'[9]

After the battle Molloy lay injured on the field. He survived only because of an exceptionally strong constitution. British army surgeons operated with knife and saw and probe, without anesthetic and without sterilisation. Half the battlefield wounded died from loss of blood, or from gangrene or tetanus.

Images of hell and the presence of death and horrible injury did not generally disillusion, however. Most war memorialists ascribed clear and usually noble causes and purposes to accidental, confusing, or demeaning events. To themselves, and to the credulous, they conveyed a satisfying, orderly, and even optimistic and wholesome view of catastrophic occurrences. War, after all, provided participants with the most vivid experiences of their existence. One of Molloy's men later wrote that he enjoyed life more on active service than ever after, and Molloy's brother officer John Kincaid found death on the field 'a scene of extraordinary and exhilarating interest'.[10]

For Kincaid, military life consisted of colourful uniforms, spectacular battles and sieges, and, above all, romantic adventure. Confronted with brutality, violence, cruelty, and carnage, he represented the war as a frolicsome romp through Portugal and Spain, a succession of amorous liaisons with dark-eyed Spanish women. Indeed, soldiers had always conflated sexual conquest and war. Kincaid observed:

> Whether in love or war, I have always considered that the pursuer has a decided advantage over the pursued. In the first, he may gain and cannot lose; but, in the latter, when one sees his enemy at full speed before him, he has such a peculiar conscious sort of feeling of being on the right side, that I would not exchange places for any consideration.[11]

The commingling of sex and war contrasted with the usual war-induced habit of dichotomising. The Napoleonic Wars habituated participants to seeing the world in dualities, as either one thing or another. The binary perspective—the dichotomy between the righteous side and the enemy, between liberty and tyranny, between progress and reaction, between victory and defeat, between civilisation and barbarism—stemmed from the adversary proceedings that war accustomed in its participants.

In 1809 Molloy became a full lieutenant, in charge of a full company. His men admired his command. Rifleman John Harris described Molloy as 'as fine a soldier as ever stepped, and as full of life in the midst of death'. Molloy proved a cautious officer and Harris recalled him checking the recklessness of some charging troops with the order, 'Damn you! Keep back, and get under cover. Do you think you are fighting here with your fists, that you are running into the teeth of the French?' Cautious but not diffident, Molloy always proved attentive to his troops' welfare. Years later Harris recalled gratefully how, when another officer, in the midst of a fatiguing retreat and late at night, haughtily ordered him to mend the officer's boots, Molloy intervened and asked the officer to cancel his order.[12]

Admired by his men, Molloy also enjoyed the respect and companionship of his fellow officers. He became special friends with

Lieutenant Harry Smith. They had a good war. Possessed of a devoted sense of Englishness, Smith kept a pack of hunting dogs and, between battles and during the severe winter months when both sides withdrew from the soggy battlefields, he and Molloy went coursing hare and hunting fox. When not fighting or hunting, the two men, like their fellow officers, danced and sang and drank with the young women of the villages and towns through which the army passed. After the siege of Badajos in 1812, two highborn young Spanish women, fleeing from British pillage and rapine, sought Smith's protection. With Molloy as witness, Smith immediately married the youngest, the fourteen-year-old Juana Maria de los Dolores de León, a lineal descendant of Juan Ponce de León, the discoverer of Florida. Like the other wives and mistresses of the officers and men, together with prostitutes and a great ragged train of animals, baggage, carts, and provisions, Juana Maria followed the army from battle to battle. After Napoleon's abdication in 1814 the British occupied Toulouse, and for three months Molloy and Harry Smith and his wife shared a commandeered chateau, where they enjoyed the services of a French cook.

But not everyone savoured such good fortune. The Spanish response to the French invasion—guerrilla warfare—provoked brutal reaction and sanctioned brutal reprisal. Combatants refused to discriminate between soldiers and civilians. Civilians were regularly violated and massacred. Troops considered rape and pillage the reward for victory and the compensation for defeat. Harsh measures—deserters were summarily shot, looters hanged—did little to instil discipline among rampaging troops. Officers too helped themselves to whatever they found on their advance or retreat: food, horses, goods, women, and liquor. Troops especially prized liquor. Heavy drinking was normal in the Peninsula army and most soldiers drank to excess; many drank themselves to death. Not a drinker but not a teetotaller either, Molloy did not object to his soldiers drinking.

Although he declined to hunt on Sunday, he enjoyed good living; he was no prude.

In July 1814 Captain Molloy quit his dalliance in the Toulouse chateau and returned with his regiment to England. Peace lasted less than a year, however, and in June 1815 Molloy joined Kincaid and Smith at Brussels, as part of the great army assembled under Wellington for the Battle of Waterloo. In the one-day engagement, French casualties amounted to between 30 000 and 40 000. Allied dead and wounded numbered 23 000, including 15 000 British, or a third of the British army. Among those who fell and lay wounded on the battlefield overnight was Lieutenant Molloy. But again, with the aid of a strong constitution, he survived and returned to England.

With the final defeat of Napoleon, Kincaid reflected, 'We had been born in war, reared in war, and war was our trade; and what soldiers had to do in peace was a problem yet to be solved among us.'[13]

Molloy decided to stay in the army. He liked the military. When he later reminisced over the incidents of the war, he recalled encounters with the French and their poor aim, the songs of the Spanish women, the troops and officers at plunder, and the bearing and command of Wellington. The war, in memory, became an exciting, even romantic, time.[14]

After the war Molloy remained on active duty with the Rifles and received postings all around the British Isles. From 1819 to 1820 he served at Glasgow, then left for Belfast and served in Ireland. In 1823 he commanded his unit against agrarian rioters known as 'Whiteboys' and 'Ribbonmen', members of a secret organisation—anti-Protestant and anti-landlord—that flourished in Ireland as a result of the postwar agricultural depression and the famine conditions of 1817 and 1818.

In August 1824, while on active duty, Lieutenant Molloy gained promotion to captain. Promotion had come slowly. His friend Harry Smith had gained his captaincy in 1812 and his majority in 1826.

By 1829 Molloy was 48 and still a captain. He had spent his entire adult life in the military. Prospects for further promotion appeared negligible and he began to investigate opportunities in civilian life. He asked his military colleagues for suggestions. Major Smith told him about a veteran of the American War of 1812, Royal Navy Captain James Stirling, who had recently returned from a survey of the west coast of New Holland and had proposed to the Colonial Office a new Australian colony headquartered at Swan River. Captain Molloy decided that life in the new colony provided precisely the opportunity he sought.

4

CARPE DIEM

CAPTAIN STIRLING WAS NOT THE FIRST ENGLISHMAN, NOR THE FIRST European, to explore the coast of Western Australia. From at least 1616, Portuguese and Dutch sailors, en route to the Indonesian archipelago, had touched on the west coast of the land they knew as New Holland. The first Englishman, William Dampier, arrived off the coast in 1688. The reports and several shipwrecks connected with these voyages made the west the best known of all Australia's coasts—and the least interesting. Sailors depicted the land as forbiddingly barren, sterile, and dangerous. High cliffs alternating with low sandy dunes that were flanked by a string of offshore islands and fringing reefs made all approaches hazardous and difficult. Rivers appeared infrequent, small, and, from the sand bars that closed many of their entrances, unnavigable. Vegetation was stunted, sparse, dull green in colour, and as unattractive as it was unfamiliar.

The inhabitants of New Holland, visitors observed, were primitive in the extreme: ugly, stupid, naked, and possessed of the most rudimentary material knowledge. They made no use of the land beyond the simple gratification of hunger and thirst. Of the Aborigines, William Dampier wrote:

> They are the miserablest people in the world. The Hodmadods
> [Hottentots], though a nasty people, yet for wealth are gentlemen
> to these . . . and setting aside their human shape, they differ but

little from brutes. Their eyelids are always half closed to keep the flies out of their eyes . . . So that from their infancy being thus annoyed with these insects, they do never open their eyes as other people: and therefore they cannot see far. . . . They had great bottle noses, pretty full lips, and wide mouths. . . . They are long-visaged, and of a very unpleasing aspect.[1]

By 'miserable' Dampier meant unfortunate and wretched. He pictured a people doomed to eternal hardship in an inhospitable land. His description was a catalogue of deprivation, insufficiency, and inadequacy. Although most of his judgement was based on conjecture rather than direct observation, his widely publicised comments prejudiced British opinion for the next several hundred years.

While the British clung tenaciously to their preconceptions concerning the Aborigines, one man did succeed in changing the perception of the land of New Holland as barren, unattractive, and unsuited to colonisation. Born in Drumpellier, Scotland, in 1791, James Stirling entered the Royal Navy as a first-class volunteer at age twelve in August 1803. He first saw action off Cape Finisterre in 1805 against the French and Spanish fleet assembled to thwart the British during the Peninsula campaigns. Later he participated in naval operations off the coast of South America. He enjoyed the patronage of his uncle, Rear Admiral Charles Stirling, and advanced rapidly through the ranks. At age twenty he received command of the ship *Brazen*, with which he harried American shipping in the Gulf of Mexico during the War of 1812 between Britain and the United States.

In 1818, following the demobilisation of the military at the close of European hostilities, Stirling received promotion to captain, was relieved of his duties, and placed on half-pay—a form of retirement. He had no qualifications for shore employment. Over the next few years he toured Europe and mixed in polite society. In 1823 he married Ellen Mangles. Only sixteen years old, she was the daughter of James Mangles, a wealthy country gentleman. The Stirlings toured

Europe and on their return lived at Woodbridge, the Mangles family home near Guildford, Surrey. James Stirling's father-in-law was High Sheriff for Surrey and a director of the East India Company, which held far-reaching and profitable monopolistic powers over trade in the Indian Ocean.[2]

The collapse of family businesses in the financial crisis of 1825 severely reduced Stirling's income. Fortunately for him, renewed French naval activity had prompted the British government to mobilise mothballed ships, and Stirling returned to the active list on full pay. Early in 1826 he took command of H.M.S. *Success*.

The British government and Australian colonial authorities suspected the French of planning to colonise lands in the Pacific and the Antipodes. To forestall French claims to any part of the continent of Australia, the British government and the governor of New South Wales posted preemptive military garrisons to the north and south. But the settlement at Melville Island, in the north, had been badly situated and was failing. In May 1826 Captain Stirling sailed out of Portsmouth for Sydney, with orders to confer with Governor Ralph Darling about transferring the Melville Island settlement to a more suitable site, which Stirling was to choose. Stirling, however, after consultation with his father-in-law, had his own plans for Australia.

Only six days after he arrived in Sydney, Stirling presented Darling with a well-prepared, artful document proposing a visit to the coast of New Holland. With James Mangles's extensive interest in the East Indies in mind, Stirling argued that the direction and velocity of winds in the Indian Ocean greatly favoured the establishment of a settlement at Swan River to support Indian Ocean trade. He recommended that a British officer—himself—investigate whether the hitherto inadequately explored area contained sufficient good soil and fresh water to support a settlement and provide safe anchorages for naval and merchant vessels.

Stirling proved persuasive. He had the advantage, however, that his listener was receptive to the idea of a west coast settlement.

Teritorially ambitious, Darling had extended the western boundary of New South Wales to the 129th degree of east longitude when he became the colony's governor in 1823. But the boundary was still a thousand miles from the western shores of the continent, and Darling wished to extend British national sovereignty over the whole of Australia.

In November 1826, shortly before Stirling's arrival in New South Wales, Darling sent Major Edmund Lockyer and a small detachment of convicts and soldiers to establish a base at King George Sound on the southwestern coast. The King George Sound settlement, however, still left most of New Holland unclaimed, unexplored, and vulnerable to French territorial encroachment. In this context, Stirling's proposal for a Swan River exploration perfectly matched Darling's ambitions. Darling immediately gave the captain permission to sail to the west coast to ascertain whether the region was suitable for settlement. Stirling left Port Jackson on 17 January 1827 and the *Success* anchored off Rottnest Island, off the coast from Swan River, on 5 March.

From 8 to 16 March, Stirling, botanist Charles Fraser, and sixteen others explored the Swan River aboard a rowboat. A smaller party made a brief survey of the Canning River, a major tributary of the Swan. Stirling spent another five days surveying Cockburn Sound, the waters enclosed between the coast to the south of the mouth of the Swan River and Garden Island, several kilometres off shore. On 22 March, just seventeen days after he arrived, he left.

Contrary to the observations of every sailor before him, Stirling concluded that 'Swan River appears to hold out every attraction that a Country in a State of Nature can possess. . . . I am therefore of the opinion that it ought to be immediately retained.' He was also favourably impressed with the natives and wrote, 'They are active and hardy in habit and seem to possess the qualities usually springing from such habits; Bravery, Vivacity, and Quickness, and a Temper alternating between kindness and ferocity.' He did not think they would prove an obstacle to settlement.[3]

On his return to Sydney, Stirling wrote to Lord Bathurst at the Colonial Office that he had discovered a premier site for settlement. The Swan River region contained a magnificent harbour, abundant fertile soil, and an expansive potential. 'The country is more valuable for that which it might produce,' he suggested, 'than for its actual productions.' The land was parklike, and with an average 'ten trees to the acre', a settler could 'bring his Farm into a state of immediate culture'. Cattle might graze on the plentiful natural grasses and a shipbuilding industry flourish because of the variety and extent of timber. Moreover, Swan River settlement would assure the China traders of a safe and easily approachable anchorage, where they would find refreshment and goods for trade. Stirling recommended himself as the superintendent of any such establishment. Governor Darling supported Stirling's application and described him to Bathurst as a very zealous officer who, from his conduct and character, would be 'well qualified for the situation he is desirous of obtaining'.

Unfortunately for Stirling, his glowing Swan River reports and recommendations necessarily reached England without his commanding presence. He still had to complete the task that had first brought him to Australia. For the remainder of 1827 he was engaged in moving the Melville Island settlement to another site at Raffles Bay. In his absence the British government was unpersuaded about Swan River and found no compelling reason to sponsor settlement there. Officials agreed that occupation of New Holland would be uneconomical. In May 1828, when Stirling returned to England, he found the prospects of settlement almost negligible.

Undaunted, Stirling was determined that Swan River would be settled. Brash, and confident in his own abilities, he was certain that events could be manipulated to favour his plans and advantage. To further his cause, he took quarters in London close to the Colonial Office, where he hoped to exercise his considerable persuasive powers. Although he received a sympathetic hearing, he found Colonial Office officials 'trembling at the thought of increased expenditure'. When neither government nor the East India Company appeared willing to bear the expense of sponsoring a colony at Swan River, Stirling quickly devised another basis for settlement.

Stirling proposed the formation of a private association of investors, which, granted a proprietary charter by the British government, would settle Swan River at private expense. He persuaded a group of speculators, including Thomas Peel (cousin of the then home secretary, Robert Peel), Sir Francis Vincent, Thomas Potter Macqueen, and Edward Schenley, to form the Swan River Association. In exchange for a grant of four million acres of Swan River land of their own choosing, the investors proposed to send 10 000 settlers to Western Australia to raise cattle, horses, and pigs, and grow cotton, tobacco, flax, sugar, and other export crops suitable to the climate.

The government rejected the proprietary charter idea. Stirling was undeterred; he believed promotion could overcome any opposition. He immediately began a campaign of recruitment and pamphleteering to attract emigrants and generate interest in a colony at Swan River. Stirling realised that success depended upon the creation of demand. If enough people were convinced that their interests would be served by a new colony in Australia, then the Colonial Office would have no choice but to sanction such a colony.

Fortunately for Stirling, the post–Napoleonic War years provided unprecedented opportunities for the expression and promotion of opinion. Increased literacy and wider dissemination of the printed word enabled people to articulate their ideas and manipulate those of others on a wider scale than ever before. The proliferation of daily newspapers (in 1830 London alone had seven daily morning papers and six evening ones), provincial and Sunday papers, religious and secular journals of every description, weeklies, monthlies, and the great quarterly reviews (*Edinburgh*, *Westminster*, *Quarterly*) gave an enormous stimulus to the language, the play of mind, the passion of polemic, and the value of publicity.

Publicity already favoured Australian colonies. In the early years of the 1820s, prospective British emigrants began to view Van Diemen's Land as a desirable destination. Only a trickle of free settlers had migrated there in the decade and a half since the establishment of a penal colony on the Derwent River in 1803, but in the four years after 1817 the free population doubled. Emigration followed the declaration of generous Colonial Office offers of land and the appearance of favourable articles in English periodicals. In 1822 the *Quarterly Review* described Van Diemen's Land as 'England with a finer sky, with less of its winter frosts and of its autumnal and spring moisture, where all the fruits and vegetables of an English country garden are raised without difficulty'.

In 1823 Australia received more favourable publicity when Commissioner J. T. Bigge made public his reports. Appointed by the Secretary of State for the Colonies to inquire into conditions in the Australian colonies, Bigge was enthusiastic. He predicted the establishment of a prosperous pastoral society based on the exploitation of convict labour. Bigge's report sped the flow of applications for land. A growing number of English farmers, facing heavy financial loss and ruin, came to look on the antipodean penal settlements as their salvation.

But for every prospective migrant who viewed Australia favourably, many more were repulsed. Middle-class people, especially, considered convict colonies irredeemably corrupt and no place for respectable persons. The prospect of a convict-free settlement at Swan River changed their minds.

Press discussion of Swan River began in mid-August 1828. At first, reports focused chiefly on Stirling's negotiations with the Colonial Office. Within two months the first press accounts of Swan River itself, and the possibility of a settlement there, appeared in print.

These reports were all sympathetic and, in fact, reflected Stirling's own enthusiastic assessment.

While the press campaign stimulated public interest in Swan River, personnel changes in government further advanced Stirling's cause. Sir George Murray, a family friend of the Stirlings, replaced William Huskisson as secretary to the Colonial Office in May 1828, and Horace Twiss, another family friend, became parliamentary under-secretary. Stirling reminded the government that, in the face of continuing inaction, New Holland was anyone's land. While the British equivocated, some other nation, maybe France, might annex the territory. In his negotiations Stirling relied on the psychology of panic. His confidence was not misplaced.

By October 1828, John Barrow, first secretary of the Admiralty, and formerly opposed to Stirling's proposals, had become convinced of the necessity of a Swan River settlement. Barrow was an imperialist who believed that law and civilisation were coterminous with British authority and that to extend the third was to promote the first two. Law and civilisation must advance and could not be delayed. Accordingly, Barrow urged the government to dispatch, at once, a warship to the west coast of New Holland, to take possession, to commence surveys, and to make arrangements for the reception of settlers. A few days later Sir George Murray issued instructions to the Admiralty to carry out the necessary preparations for taking possession. On 14 December 1828 Captain Charles Howe Fremantle left Portsmouth aboard the navy ship *Challenger* with orders to formally annex the whole of New Holland west of the 129th meridian. Although about to acquire 2.5 million square kilometres of new territory, the British government still had no definite plan or policy for settlement.

In the meantime, Stirling's press campaign and his entrepreneurial activities on behalf of Swan River generated such widespread excitement that support for the proposed colony appeared overwhelming and success seemed assured. Inquiries about Swan River inundated the Colonial Office. Interested individuals submitted their own schemes for colonisation.

On 25 December the government advised Stirling of Captain Fremantle's departure. Stirling also learned of the imminent release of regulations setting the conditions of Swan River settlement and of the government's decision to make him a free grant of 100 000 acres in the new colony, to be chosen wherever he desired. In addition to his free grant, Stirling also won his case for independence. From the time of his first proposal, Stirling had argued that the future colony answer directly to London and not be a dependency of New South Wales. The Colonial Office agreed and appointed him commander of the settlement.

On 12 January 1829 the government issued a set of 'Regulations for the Guidance of those who may propose to embark, as settlers for the New Settlements on the Western Coast of New Holland'. Nine paragraphs in length, the regulations had grown out of the Colonial Office's rejection of the demands of the Swan River Association.

First, they dealt with the only original would-be investor still interested in Swan River, Thomas Peel. To avoid charges of political jobbery and nepotism, the regulations limited Peel's grant to one million acres. He could claim the first 250 000 acres on the arrival of his first 400 sponsored settlers.

For other intending migrants, whose ambitions were only slightly less grand than Peel's, the regulations appeared unbelievably generous; the possibility of obtaining a large landed estate appeared almost limitless. The regulations promised grants of land to any party that emigrated, in a proportion of not less than five female to six male settlers. Acreage received depended on the amount of capital (liberally defined) colonists were prepared to bring to the colony, at the rate of 40 acres for every £3. Capital was considered to consist of goods, stock, and equipment but also included servants. The regulations estimated the expense of taking a labourer to New Holland at £15, and thus anyone sponsoring a labourer received a grant of 200 acres. At these rates land worked out at one acre for every 1s 6d invested in the colony—the cheapest land at the most generous terms available anywhere in the world.

The publication of the regulations and the ensuing publicity generated a national obsession with emigration to Western Australia. Swan River became all the rage. Contemporaries termed the infatuation 'Swan River Mania'.

The mania did not spring from acts of government alone. For the government that saw the need to make living room in Britain by sending British people overseas declined to assist in the recruitment and transportation of emigrants. Officials left that potentially profitable undertaking to the invisible hand of the market, or rather, to a highly visible body of land speculators, merchants, shipowners, and their agents. These interested individuals gave the regulations unprecedented publicity.

Entrepreneurs competed fiercely for passengers. To induce migrants, agents and ship charterers disseminated and embellished the favourable press reports, extended descriptions of Swan River to the ultimate limits of credibility, and emphasised the incredible cheapness of the land. They passed out pamphlets, settlers' guides, and other forms of propaganda, which depicted Swan River as a bucolic wonderland where industry and virtue would inevitably be rewarded. More literature, all of it favourable, appeared about the proposed settlement at Swan River than heralded the beginnings of any other Australian colony. The new colony, the propagandists stressed, was to be a colony of free settlers, without the corrupting presence of convicts that had so tainted society in New South Wales and Van Diemen's Land. Swan River sounded too good to be true; by comparison, no other portion of the habitable globe seemed worthy of notice. Nevertheless, plenty of people were willing, even desperate, to believe that their prospects would be bettered by migrating to Swan River.

The sudden fashion for Swan River particularly appealed to many 'persons of respectable connections'. Through the operation of the rule of primogeniture, Britain had a surplus of dispossessed younger sons, many of them military officers on half-pay. In the convict-free colonies they saw a chance of becoming what, but for elder brothers, they thought they already were: landed gentry. According to a sympathetic writer who married a younger son, these men left Britain as a matter of necessity, for they could not

> labour in a menial capacity in the country where they were born and educated to command. They can trace no difference between themselves and the more fortunate individuals of a race whose blood warms their veins, and whose name they bear. The want of wealth alone places an impassable barrier between them and the more favoured offspring of the same parent stock.

The writer, herself an emigrant, continued: 'Few educated persons, accustomed to the refinements and luxuries of European society, ever willingly relinquish those advantages, and place themselves beyond the protective influence of the wise and revered institutions of their native land, without the pressure of some urgent cause.'[4]

Pressed by the perceived urgency of their own cause and swayed by the publicity and propaganda, hundreds and hundreds of Britons decided to take the opportunity to better their condition by embarking for Swan River. On 7 February 1829, Stirling, his officials, a detachment of the 63rd Regiment, and the hopes of many of Britain's younger sons sailed from England aboard the *Parmelia* and *Sulphur*. Within a few months thirteen more ships, with nearly 1500 passengers, left for Swan River.[5]

Stirling arrived off Garden Island in the *Parmelia* on 1 June. Only a month earlier Captain Fremantle had hoisted the Union Jack on the south head of the Swan River and, in the name of the King, taken possession of the whole of New Holland. A few days after Stirling's arrival, the *Sulphur* sailed into Cockburn Sound. The settlers disembarked on Garden Island, quickly assembled bush huts, and took shelter. Few, at first, felt any inconvenience. Spirits were high and dinner parties frequent. Settlers dined on roast swan, kangaroo, wild duck, and black cockatoo.

Meanwhile, Stirling, who believed he had ample time to prepare for the reception of migrants, gave priority to surveying Cockburn Sound. Within a month, however, the first migrant ship, *Calista*, with 47 settlers, sailed into view. Next day, 6 August, the *St Leonard* appeared off the coast. The ships' unexpected arrival caught Stirling unprepared. He hastily transferred part of the makeshift Garden Island colonial headquarters to the mouth of the Swan River, at the newly named settlement of Fremantle, where the colonial surveyor, John Septimus Roe, began surveying. On 11 August Stirling, most of the colony's officials, and some of the newly arrived settlers rowed twelve miles upriver from Fremantle to examine the site of the future colonial headquarters. Next day Mrs Dance, the wife of an officer, cut down a tree to celebrate the foundation of Perth, the capital of the colony of Western Australia. Roe began marking out allotments, but before he had finished, the *Marquis of Anglesea*, with 73 settlers aboard, arrived, and he returned to survey town lots in Fremantle.

By mid-September the situation was chaotic. No rural land had been surveyed, let alone transferred to private ownership. The majority of the 215 settlers, government officials, and their families huddled in tents on the barren coastal dunes at Fremantle, exposed to the full blast of the still-frequent westerly gales. To establish claims for land, colonists had to produce their capital and unload goods, workers, and livestock for inspection and itemisation. Many ships' masters proved uncooperative and simply discharged cargo onto the open beach. Surf damaged the goods, and waves washed some goods out to sea. The disembarkation, tethering, and corralling of animals proved especially troublesome. Stock wandered around camp or strayed into the bush. Disembarkation activity exacerbated sandhill erosion, and sand became a byword for Fremantle. Blowing sand made living conditions unpleasant, and sand fleas bit constantly. Settlers became discouraged and confused. On 3 September a violent storm damaged all seven ships now riding at anchor and completely wrecked the *Marquis of Anglesea*. Winds tore through tents, and rain spoiled provisions and possessions. To meet the shortfall in food, Stirling sent the *Parmelia* to Java to purchase stock and provisions.

In mid-September the ships *Amity*, *Calista*, and *St Leonard* left the colony for England, via Sydney, carrying news of disorder. In the meantime, conditions grew worse. Winter squalls gave way to summer heat, sand fleas, flies, and mosquitoes. Scurvy broke out, ophthalmia afflicted many, and poor hygiene and crowded living conditions caused an epidemic of dysentery.

Moreover, despite the regulations that codified the British government's intention to balance the sexes in the new colony, more men than women emigrated. The disadvantages of the imbalance quickly became obvious, at least to single men. A man needed a female companion if he was to subdue the wilderness. One migrant wrote to his brother, 'You know not how we male settlers miss the assistance of a woman to wash, cook, and sew for us.'[6]

Lieutenant W. H. Breton, who arrived at Fremantle in October, reported that many Swan River colonists

> had quitted England with the most visionary notions imaginable, and, on the demolition of their airy castles, which vanished within a few hours after they had landed, they left the place in disgust, with heavy complaints of deception, and then strove to assuage their choler by striving to make it appear far worse than is actually the fact.[7]

Expectations, of course, had been a necessary part of the decision to emigrate. But the reality of Swan River bore no resemblance to the land of milk and honey many settlers had anticipated. Colonists had been led to believe, or let themselves believe, that good land extended from the coast to the mountains and stretched far to the south and north in an immense fertile plain. They found instead a coast flanked by sand dunes and covered with a thin layer of stunted vegetation. Sandy soil extended well inland, beyond the site of Perth. Only a few fertile areas existed, in narrow stretches along the upper reaches of the Swan and Canning rivers. Settlers quickly found that Stirling's and botanist Charles Fraser's original reports about the Swan River area were incorrect, if not bogus. The land was more thickly wooded, the soil not as fertile, and the fertile soil less abundant than had been portrayed.

Many settlers lost heart. Discouraged, they fell into idleness and drinking. T. B. Wilson, who visited the colony in October, wrote that at Fremantle, people 'chiefly employed themselves in smoking cigars, drinking brandy-and-water, and abusing Mr Fraser'.[8]

Bona fide settlers were not the only ones clamouring for land. All the colony's naval and military officers felt entitled to grants. In addition, Stirling was committed to assigning hundreds of thousands of acres to people who had not yet left England. And everyone wanted land along the Swan River. The floodplains contained the only good land so far reported, and the river offered the only means of transport.

Just as Captain Fremantle, when he claimed Western Australia for Britain, had acted on behalf of a government that assumed the land was empty and therefore required neither conquest nor treaty, so Stirling proceeded to act in a similarly cavalier fashion in dispensing land to private owners. His largesse was astounding. On 28 September 1829 he led a party of settlers to the junction of the Swan River with Ellen Brook. As they worked downriver, Stirling allocated grants, personally marking trees to distinguish boundaries. He took care to ensure that each block was long and narrow, stretching back from the river, so as to provide as many settlers as possible with river frontage on which they could erect landing ramps. In three days he distributed 95 504 acres to 21 grantees, six of whom were government officials.

The grants were woefully insufficient. Settlers still clamoured for land. T. B. Wilson observed that crowds surrounded Stirling wherever he went. Each settler pleaded his case for land and each assured Stirling that his own case was worthier than any other. Inevitably they were disappointed, for:

> All the land on the banks of the Swan, of which these emigrants had heard such flattering accounts, and of which they naturally expected to obtain a slice, after having come so far for that purpose, was already, and, perhaps, improvidently given away.[9]

Stirling's preemptory distributions were not enough to satisfy the land hunger or mollify disappointed settlers. The surveyor-general and his assistants were unable to survey land quickly enough to accommodate the demand, and settlers were unable to move onto their rural properties. Colonists gave up in disgust. By the end of 1829 one-third of the passengers who had arrived on the *Calista* and *Marquis of Anglesea* had left—either returned to Britain or gone on to the eastern colonies. In December 1829, when news of conditions at Swan River reached Sydney, the *Sydney Gazette* predicted:

> Depend upon this, that the very instant the first account of the disasters reaches London, the whole will fall to the ground—the speculators will abandon the project—the ship owners pocket the money—the captains laugh at the folly, and the poor deluded sufferers either starve—be at the mercy of the Governor for returning home—or come out here for something like a habitable place to exist on.[10]

Reports of the colony's affairs reached London on 24 January 1830. As the *Sydney Gazette* had predicted, mania gave way to antipathy. The news from Swan River led to the cancellation of voyages and discouraged many potential settlers who were awaiting firsthand information before making their decisions. Emigration to Swan River declined dramatically after February 1830. Half a dozen ships en route were diverted from Western Australia. By early 1830 emigrants and shipowners were in accord: the new colony offered neither adequate soil to support a large population nor adequate anchorages to protect vessels.

Emigrants en route knew none of this, and for the time being, settlers continued to arrive. The bad news came too late to alter Captain Molloy's emigration plans, which he put into effect about the time Stirling and the first colonists arrived at Swan River.

5

GODSPEED

CAPTAIN MOLLOY DID NOT INTEND TO EMBARK ON TAMING A
wilderness single-handed, without female companionship, without a
woman to wash, cook, sew, and bear children for him. In July 1829
he asked Georgiana Kennedy to marry him and to venture with him
to the new colony at Swan River.

Kennedy found Captain Molloy's double proposal especially
challenging. Marriage alone was an astonishingly serious commitment, but the additional prospect of travelling to and settling at Swan
River required even greater resolve. To leave Scotland, to leave
Britain, she had to break defining bonds, sever friendships, and
abandon a sense of place. Leaving was so final, so severe, almost
impossible to contemplate, inconceivable to her 'untravelled mind'.
Yet, no matter how secure, how settled and comfortable Kennedy
found life at Rosneath, she could still perceive a need for escape, an
urge for self-definition through detachment from the familiar. After
all, once before she had separated herself from the intimate yet
confining circle of her family, from her siblings and her mother. And
if she could dissociate herself once, she could depart a second time.
She discussed her decision with Helen and the Reverend Story. She
told them of her reluctance to leave and of the little time she had
to consider the consequences. Captain Molloy wanted to marry and
leave as soon as possible. Kennedy replied promptly and unequivo-
cally: she accepted his proposition in full.

Earlier in 1829, before his marriage proposal, Captain Molloy had discussed business prospects at Swan River with Captain Marshall McDermott of the 8th Foot, Captain Francis Byrne of the Rifle Brigade, and George Cheyne, a Scottish merchant. The partners agreed to purchase a ship, load it with trade goods (primarily prefabricated housing materials and boats), sail to the new colony, and become traders. By April, the arrangements had fallen through. Captain Molloy lost heavily, but each of the former partners remained committed to emigration. McDermott decided to continue the speculation separately, Cheyne decided to pursue merchandising, and Captains Molloy and Byrne decided to become farmers. They sought passage aboard one of the many ships advertising for Swan River passengers.

The two captains turned to the charterer Hamilton Collins Sempill. Urbane and unprincipled, Sempill aimed to profit from the enthusiasm for emigration. At the outbreak of Swan River Mania he arranged to charter a ship to take settlers to the colony. His handbill advertising lauded Western Australia's attractions, the abundant wild game, the attractiveness of the land regulations, the area's potential for commerce, the 'finest climate in the universe', and the fertility of the soil. Coast and rivers 'literally teem with fish', while proximity to the Cape, Mauritius, Timor, India, and New South Wales 'must open a door for commercial enterprise of vast magnitude'. The Swan River settler, Sempill promised, would not 'have to wage hopeless and ruinous war with interminable forests and impenetrable jungle, as he will find prepared by the hand of nature extensive plains ready for the ploughshare'. Moreover, Swan River was to be a colony of free settlers. The immigrant would not be without the comfort and protection of British institutions,

> nor hardened in his heart by the debasing influence of being obliged to mingle with, and employ those bearing the brand of crime and punishment; and as no convict of any description of prisoner will be admitted into the Colony, those who establish

property and families will feel that their names and fortunes cannot be mixed hereafter with any dubious ideas as to their origin.

When arrangements for Sempill's first ship, the *Lady Campbell*— 'the finest vessel afloat', due to sail 15 June—fell through, he immediately chartered another, the *Warrior*. Although the ship changed, Sempill's huckstering did not. 'The southland is a truly blissful place,' he declared:

> Its climate is temperate; it never experiences rain storms or gales
> . . . It contains no flies, caterpillars or any other sort of insect
> and one never catches sight of spiders, snakes or any other
> venomous beast. In a word, it is a country which encompasses all
> the delights which are absent in the other parts of the world and
> is exempt from all the inconveniences which are to be found
> everywhere else.[1]

As soon as Captain Molloy received Georgiana Kennedy's acceptance he approached Sempill about passage aboard the *Warrior*. He requested the best accommodation the vessel could offer and paid £1000 for a first-class cabin for two in the stern under the poop deck. The fare included meals and wine. Sempill promised the ship would sail at the end of August. Captain Molloy promptly engaged sixteen servants, bought horses, pigs, sheep, and cattle, farm tools and equipment, and enough provisions to last a year or more. At the end of July he left London for Rosneath.

On Thursday, 6 August 1829, Captain Molloy and Georgiana Kennedy were married. Robert Story performed the service. Marriage ceremonies at Rosneath were usually boisterous affairs, but the Molloys elected more sober celebrations and left Rosneath on Saturday. They took a cart to Portkil and there, on the banks of the Clyde, bade goodbye to their Scottish friends before boarding a small packet boat down the Irish Sea to Liverpool. From Liverpool they took a coach to Coventry, where Georgiana Molloy's mother sent a carriage to bring them to the Kennedy home at Rugby. Presents from the

Kennedy family and friends awaited them. Georgiana Molloy received several packets of flower seeds and, from her mother, yucca lilies. After a three-day valedictory, the couple left for lodgings in London.

The torrent of change—marriage, leave-taking, travel, frenzied preparation for emigration, and the prospect of a long sea voyage—unsettled the new Mrs Molloy. She grieved over the break with family, friends, and place, but she sought and found solace in her religion. Three weeks after her marriage she wrote to Mary Dunlop, 'I feel very low when I look back on all I have left—but my chief Friend and Father will never leave nor forsake me.' For every discontent, she found an answer in the Bible. For every doubt and misgiving, the gospels provided serenity and reassurance; so did routine and occupation. Molloy believed time spent dwelling on one's losses was time wasted. Presbyterians kept busy. At her London lodgings Molloy instituted morning and evening prayers. But the outward appearance of observance was insufficient; religion demanded active propagation. Molloy had a duty to spread the gospel, and she spoke to each of the newly employed servants about their beliefs.[2]

Practical matters also required attention. Georgiana Molloy needed clothes for the colony, clothes useful and lasting. London was the centre of fashion, but Molloy was not distracted by frivolous and indiscriminate passions. 'My gowns,' she wrote to Mary Dunlop, 'are all very plain without anything but hems and tucks . . . and my bonnets cottage shape with X ribbons.' As well as eschewing ostentation, Molloy expected to employ her leisure time in the colony in an appropriate pedagogical manner. She hoped to be able to botanise, to collect and classify those floral contrivances in nature that reflected the greater glory of the Creator. To aid in her collecting, she bought a large *hortus siccus*—a bound book of stiff pages for the arrangement and storage of dried plants.[3]

After Georgiana Molloy bought and packed her clothes and some few domestic purchases, her husband arranged for a miniaturist to paint her portrait. Captain Molloy was pleased with the result, which he described as 'a lively representation of her visage'. His wife sat for her portrait in a dark gown, tight-waisted and bodiced, low-cut, with wide, full sleeves. Despite the distortions common in portraits of the time—elongated neck and rounded jawline—her face revealed several distinguishing features. She dressed her thick hair, gathered from a low hairline, high on her head. From the top, garlanded with pink and blue flowers, two large ringlets trailed down her cheeks and framed her face. Her heavy-lidded and long-lashed eyes looked straight ahead, slightly to the left of the viewer, intelligent, unequivocal, and unembarrassed. Her pursed lips gave a Madonna-like hint of a smile. Altogether, she projected a composed and determined confidence. Only 24, and just married, her self-assurance permitted no doubt that she would persevere, no matter what lay ahead.

Molloy had never previously visited London, and her stay exposed her to a degree of depravity and squalor that horrified her. She had never seen so much drunkenness, wretchedness, and display of wealth; she had never witnessed such allurements and such yielding to temptation. She would resist, however. Her unadorned wardrobe and her fearless portrait indicated her determination not to give 'way to the vanities in this truly depressing London where I never dreamt of such dreadful vice and search after unsatisfactory things'.[4]

London was the centre of empire and the capital of the first industrial nation. The smoke of a million coal fires poured from a million red and brown chimney pots and hung as a sulphurous smog over the city, shut out the sun, killed vegetation, and blackened the mud in the streets with tar. Coaches and wains, sheep and oxen, and multitudes of people rushing on business, buying and selling, filled the streets. Scores of waifs scrambled to gather horse, sheep, and cattle manure and other detritus into bags to earn a penny or two. Prostitutes, pickpockets, hawkers, mendicants of every degree—one multitudinous crush of humanity—assailed the visitor.

A great world of shipping plied the Thames and congested the middle of the city. So many ships crowded the river and docks that some waited months for a quay at which to load and unload. Coal dust enveloped the whole port, but tourists flocked to the docks to gaze at the activity and wealth. Piles and piles of goods sat on the wharves and spilled out of overflowing warehouses full of stores and produce from all over the world.

Amidst the pandemonium the Molloys found at least one comfort—Edward Irving. During their London stay they called on him several times. He evinced great interest in their venture, and one Sunday after a private counsel they went to his church. He prayed publicly for their success and likened the newly married couple to Abraham and Sarah in the land God had allotted them. He prayed also that they might reach that other promised shore that God had ordained for them for Eternity.[5]

The Molloys heard Irving preach at his new but less successful church at Regent Square. The fashionable flock that had filled Hatton Garden now stayed away. For there was a dark side to Irving. When he had taught at a boys' school in Kirkcaldy he had beat his pupils so severely that, even in those severe times, many parents and other teachers disapproved. At Hatton Garden his prolixity and prophecies brought ridicule as well as admiration, and he became the subject of violent lampoons and angry leading articles. He was unpopular with his clerical contemporaries—Presbyterian, Anglican, and Methodist. They found the passion and rashness of his preaching disturbing. Some congregants thought his bearing artificial, strained, and pompous. He radiated distrust. Walter Scott found him unctuous and said Irving reminded him 'of the devil disguised as an angel of light'.[6]

Church authorities disclaimed much of Irving's preaching. He had publicly proclaimed the controversial opinion that the body of Christ was sinful, mortal, and corruptible, and by 1829 accusations of heresy threatened his status as a clergyman in the Church of Scotland. Throughout the year of the Molloys' departure, hostility to Irving's understanding of the human nature of Christ continued to grow in England and Scotland. But, faithful to her own beliefs, none of the controversy perturbed Georgiana Molloy.

She had never entirely embraced the revivalist Christian phenomena that later proved Irving's downfall. Faith healing, automatic writing, and glossolalia possessed an energy and a disparity of ethics and rationality altogether too anti-intellectual for Georgiana Molloy. Acceptance of ecstatic Christianity required a kind of incredulity she lacked. Moreover, although she believed in the transitoriness and vanity of earthly life, and although she respected and admired Irving, she did not share his sense of imminent end. Otherwise, she would not have contemplated emigration. To voluntarily leave one's home country required optimism, or at the very least, a belief in the future.

Molloy, however, did share something of Irving's zeal. Like him, she was part of the evangelical Protestant tradition that emphasised passion rather than sentiment, the centrality of the personal drama of conversion and salvation (in which each soul has a unique destiny), and that stressed a prophetic stance vis-à-vis a sinful world. Accordingly, Molloy occupied her time in London not only in preparing for her earthly journey but also in spreading the word of God.

Molloy discovered in the city that despite the overlay of religion in much public life, a great many people in Britain had had no religious instruction and no contact with any Christian body. To evangelists this was a source of endless despair. Molloy's proselytising made her acutely aware of the large areas of heathendom all around her. Convinced of the necessity of a worshipful attitude in all areas of life, she felt an obligation to make converts and seized every opportunity to do so.

She lent her husband's valet, Elijah Dawson, her copy of Robert Story's *Peace in Believing*. She was delighted that Dawson liked the story of the young woman who became a temple of faith, belief, and holiness, and she allowed him to lend the book to a friend. She was also gratified to learn that Dawson enjoyed the daily prayers. Dawson's wife of three months, Anne, however, was less worshipful and less believing. She confessed to Molloy her unhappiness and her doubts about being accepted of God. Molloy interpreted this disclosure as an opening for conversion. She asked her friends in Scotland to pray for her so she might obtain His assistance and 'an increase of light to aid me in the direction of these poor people'.

Secular affairs, however, overshadowed all attempts at conversion. Within days of their arrival in London the Molloys realised that Sempill could not keep his promise of a late August departure. Because of their responsibility for sixteen servants, stock, and equipment, they found the delay inconvenient and expensive. They decided to leave London and wait for the *Warrior* at Gosport, near Portsmouth, the ship's final embarkation port. A month after settling in London they boarded an overnight coach to Gosport and took up residence at Brockhurst House.

In the meantime, Sempill had succeeded in attracting a full complement of 166 passengers to the *Warrior*. Many began assembling at Portsmouth. The day after she arrived at Gosport Georgiana Molloy met her husband's army colleague, the 30-year-old Captain Francis Byrne, and his 21-year-old wife, Matilda. The Byrnes were also staying at Brockhurst House. Like Captain Molloy, Captain Byrne had paid Sempill £1000 for a first-class cabin aboard the *Warrior*.

Georgiana Molloy was especially curious about Captain Byrne's wife. Because of her marital status, age, and class, Matilda Byrne appealed to Molloy as the one passenger she might befriend. From London Molloy had written to Byrne about the prospects for their religious life in the new colony. She found her reply unsatisfactory and was apprehensive lest 'Mrs Byrne [prove] much the woman of the world'. For while Byrne expressed the hope that 'we shall be able to preserve that reverence which creates happiness when Vice is unknown and to attend properly to the salvation of our souls', she also declared that a piano was indispensable to the comfort and pleasure of the settlers. Molloy found such aspirations frivolous and distracting from more serious pursuits. She feared for the worst but suspended judgement until she met Matilda Byrne in person.[7]

At Gosport, however, she discovered other aspects of Byrne's character of which she disapproved. She thought the younger woman 'quick and abrupt', flirtatious, and 'unquiet with a bustle—her petticoats in the air and two very pretty legs and feet protruding beyond them'. She discussed Byrne's vanity and lack of seriousness with Captain Molloy. He counselled patience and suggested that exposure to Molloy's more sedate and steady character would moderate Byrne's coquetry. Molloy hoped so and agreed that, despite her faults, Byrne was 'good-natured'. And, she reported triumphantly to her friends in Scotland, Byrne acceded 'instantly to my wish of having Prayers morning and evening'. These sessions disappointed Georgiana Molloy, however. Her husband, she remarked critically to Helen Story, *read* the prayers; no ritual or mystery interrupted his ramble through psalms and hymns. She preferred prayers conducted extempore—free speaking denoted greater sincerity.[8]

The day after she reached Gosport Molloy commenced a religious dialogue with Captain Byrne. She told him that the only way of ascertaining 'our having the right Belief' was assurance that Christ was the saviour. On subsequent meetings she spoke of no other subject to either Captain Byrne or his wife. Shortly, she began to perceive the effectiveness of her ministrations. She succeeded, she noted approvingly, in so unsettling the captain's wife that Mrs Byrne rose early every morning to commit her feelings to paper and 'has been weeping copiously these last three days and her eyes are now quite swollen'. The Byrnes, however, resented Molloy's unceasing hectoring, and by the time the *Warrior* left England the two couples were barely on speaking terms.[9]

Bad feelings and stiffness in behaviour did not deter the energetic Georgiana Molloy. Although she ceased preaching to the Byrnes, she found other opportunities for conversion. While shopping in Gosport she discovered that the woman from whom she was buying sewing

materials was Jewish. Molloy believed the Jewish religion was inferior, preparatory to a future, more perfect revelation. Jews, she had
learned, had a congenital hardness of heart that precluded them from
believing in a suffering Messiah. She had been told that their received
opinions were so absurd and impious, their rites so unmeaning and
frivolous, their ceremonies so minute, punctilious, silly, and contempt-
ible, and often so revolting and execrable that any account of them
would surpass credibility. She had, therefore, never learned what
exactly they were.

Molloy, however, refused to accept that Jews were irredeemable.
Accordingly, she opened a conversation with the Jewish haberdasher
by telling the woman of the debt Christians owed the Jews. She then
questioned her about Christ. The woman said the Messiah would
come, but He had not yet come. Molloy disagreed and told her that
Christ would not come again as Saviour but as Judge on those who
did not believe in Him as the Redeemer. The woman reiterated her
confidence in her own belief and faith, to which Molloy replied, 'My
dear woman, I devoutly pray the Light of the Gospel may break in
upon your hardness of heart and enable you to see you are one of
Christ's Redeemed sinners.' Molloy continued the harangue, and the
woman broke into tears. Molloy now took the opportunity to warn
her of the danger she was in until she accepted Christ as her Saviour.
She promised to return with more good news the following week.[10]

On their first Sunday at Gosport the Molloys walked to an
outlying small country church. The clergyman, an old man according
to Georgiana Molloy, chose as his text the biblical injunction that
husbands love their wives as themselves and that wives, in turn, revere
their husbands. To Molloy's disquiet, the minister explained the
matrimonial state exclusively in terms of duty and obligation. He did
not mention passion, and spoke only of formal and specific requirements that couples must always observe, and described love as a
matter of mutual taste. Molloy disagreed; she believed that love—

romantic love and true love—was founded on manner, appearance, and passion.

Molloy judged the old minister's discourse 'a dreadful tissue of folly'. She preferred the preaching style of the Reverend Robert Story, who emphasised love, compassion, and forgiveness. She was also disposed to the passion of Edward Irving. Both preachers appealed to individual conscience as much as to doctrinal authority. Individuals had the ability to feel what was right and to see what was true. Both preachers stressed lyrical passion, sincerity, and spontaneity. Their preaching encouraged disputation between the romantically inclined congregants of the nineteenth century and the austere and rational theology of the eighteenth century. Accordingly, Molloy felt no inhibition in criticising the old Gosport preacher.

Weeks passed. By the end of September the *Warrior* had not even left Gravesend on the Thames, and dissatisfaction with the grasping, fraudulent charterer Sempill began. Thomas Hapgood, whose son was about to embark, wrote to Horace Twiss at the Colonial Office to complain that the *Warrior* was so overloaded and unseaworthy that the government would not certify it as fit for convicts. Steerage passengers, including his son, had been relegated to berths in dark dormitories of bunks ranged end to end with no ventilation. Sempill's 'avarice', Hapgood continued, 'has been so great that he has not even left a table, or a space, for the steerage passengers to mess or take their scanty allowance of food, but are compelled to take it on their knees, their chests, or on the Ground'. He demanded government intervention. The government, however, was not persuaded. Ministers and officials held to the presumption that private pursuit of maximum individual gain would maximise public welfare. Any order issued to Sempill to correct the ship's deficiencies would constitute an unwarranted interference with trade and obstruct the flow of emigrants.[11]

Early in October the principal surveyor of the Thames police cleared the *Warrior*. The ship left Gravesend and sailed for Portsmouth. Some steerage passengers had boarded the ship in London, but most passengers waited to embark from Portsmouth.

Despite the long delay, expectations remained high. The prospect of Swan River continued to excite, and while the emigrants mourned departed family, friends, and country, they also looked to the future. Assembled at Portsmouth and stripped of their friendships and daily routines, the emigrants confronted the questions of who they were and why they were travelling. Given the circumstances—the length and discomfort of the voyage ahead, the unreliability and meagreness of the information concerning Swan River—the fact that Sempill readily obtained a full complement of passengers indicated the perceived severity and helplessness of contemporary social conditions. Migrants had to be highly gullible or enormously optimistic and motivated to commit to such a speculative and risky undertaking.

Among those prepared to take the risk were the brothers John, Charles, Vernon, and Alfred Bussell. Their father, the Reverend William Marchant Bussell, the Anglican minister at Saint Mary's, Portsea, Hants, had died in 1820, leaving a wife, six sons, and three daughters. His estate was inadequate for the support of a young widow and nine children. But on his death, friends, parishioners, and relatives raised £3000 for investment in government securities issued to meet the public debt. Trustees settled the income, 3 per cent, on Bussell's widow, Frances Louisa. The dividends, together with a small annuity from an insurance policy taken out by her husband, enabled her to provide for the education of her sons.

The eldest, John Garret Bussell, was on a scholarship at Winchester School at the time of his father's death. He later won a scholarship to Trinity College, Oxford, and two years later, a second scholarship. He graduated with a bachelor's degree in 1829 and sought ordination in the church. His brother William, the second eldest, entered the Royal College of Surgeons, Lenox joined the navy, and Charles, Vernon, and Alfred attended Winchester School.

The family expected the girls, Mary, Frances (Fanny), and

Elizabeth (Bessie) to marry well. In the meantime, they received their education at home, an education suited to acquiring the domestic and social arts best calculated to please men.

Charles Bussell spoke with a stammer, a social handicap that he felt acutely all his life. His estrangement from society precluded a professional career or, indeed, any occupation involving constant and painful contact with strangers. He preferred his own and his family's company. In 1829 he was about to take up law studies when the publicity surrounding the plans for settlement in Western Australia attracted his interest. Of all the Bussell family members, Charles regarded the prospect of emigration and the seclusion of self-reliant settlement with the most favour. But the allure of Swan River was not confined to Charles.

John Bussell viewed life as a 'wilderness of anxiety and hope'. His chief anxiety was shortage of money and his fondest hope was to secure a good income. During the summer of 1829, on the Isle of Wight, John Bussell met Captain Molloy, who told him of his determination to seek his fortune at Swan River.[12]

At the same time as Charles and John became interested in the Swan River Colony, the family's chief trustee, Captain Robert Yates, RN, began favouring emigration as a solution to the Bussells' financial difficulties. Yates, who, like Captain Molloy's advisers, was a fellow officer and friend of James Stirling, thought the prospects at Swan River excellent. By early August the family agreed that the new colony provided them with their best chance for prosperity. Eventually all but William would emigrate. In the meantime, Mrs Bussell appealed to John to abandon or postpone plans for ordination and lead three of the brothers on a pioneering party to Swan River. When the Bussells' cousin Capel Carter assented to providing financial guarantees, John agreed to go.[13]

The Bussells expected the *Warrior* to sail on 1 September and began hurried preparations. John went to London to purchase goods, while the rest of the family sought to put as much capital together as possible. Charles wrote to Capel Carter to assure her that haste did not presage abandonment of traditional family frugality: 'You may be inclined to think this a foolish precipitation but in addition to the numerous advantages we shall enjoy from the seasonableness of the time of our arrival, we shall have our land attached to us at a more advantageous rate than if we should go later.' Delay would bring wasteful dissipation of capital.[14]

But with the continued delay of the *Warrior*, the Bussells feared this might happen anyway. Eventually they received notice of a definite sailing date and, in mid-October 1829, John Bussell, 26, Charles, 19, Vernon, 16, Alfred, 14, and their servant, Edward Pearce, also 14, assembled at Portsmouth, ready to embark. To save money, the economical Bussells booked a tiny cabin in steerage. Their goods and capital stock entitled them to a grant of 5500 acres.

The Bussell entitlement represented just one-fifth of that of the wealthiest migrant leaving aboard the *Warrior*, James Woodward Turner. At 49 years of age Turner was also the oldest passenger. He had lived in London all his life, where, for 30 years, he worked as a surveyor and builder. Except for his trade, Turner started most things late. He married for the first time at 30, and when his wife died, after giving birth to seven children, he married her sister, Maria, who bore him another son. He travelled frequently. Business took him all around England and to France.

Perhaps mobility unsettled him, for despite a lucrative business and a family, Turner was restless and dissatisfied. Relative affluence and relatively advanced age had not inoculated him from the discontent then prevalent in England. Success had not banished the feeling of confinement or the anxiety for immediate happiness he had once thought was restricted to the poor and the young. Turner wanted change; he longed to be a landowner—a large landowner—and a country gentleman. In 1829, during the mania for Swan River, he saw his chance. In August he wrote to the Colonial Office to inquire about land and colonisation at Swan River. The reply, a copy of the land regulations, finally persuaded him to act. On the last day of the month he booked passage on the *Warrior*. In September he sold his business, purchased goods and material worth thousands of pounds, and engaged three families and several single men as servants and labourers. He embarked his children and servants at London. On 14 October he and his wife arrived by coach at Portsmouth.

The *Warrior*, which took a week to sail from London, reached Portsmouth early on a cold and windy Friday, 16 October. The ship lay at anchor, with sails furled, in the crowded harbour half a mile out from the docks. Small boats plied between the anchored ships and the shore.

On Saturday—a fine and mild day—Turner vacated his shore lodgings and came on board the *Warrior*. Other passengers began loading their goods. Captain Molloy and Captain Byrne superintended the rounding up of their cattle and livestock, embarked them in boats on loan from the local Marine Artillery, and took them out to the *Warrior*. Next day Captain Molloy's valet, Elijah Dawson, took the family luggage aboard. Dawson had remained a loyal servant. The others felt no such obligation. The Molloys had arrived in Gosport with sixteen servants, but the long delay caused many to lose enthusiasm for emigrating. Half of them deserted.

On Monday the Molloys and the rest of their servants, now numbering five adults and three children, prepared to embark. Like the other passengers, they were rowed across the harbour to the *Warrior*. At the ship's side, sailors lowered a chair attached to ropes into the waiting boats and hauled the passengers one by one onto the deck.

Once aboard, Captain Molloy discovered that Sempill, 'in direct breach of agreement', had removed his cattle stalls from the hold so as to provide more room for cargo. Reerected on deck, the stalls occupied an 'ill selected and perilous situation'. Georgiana Molloy shared her husband's discontent. She began a journal and noted that she found her 'cabin crammed with luggage' and the people on board 'most ordinary'.[15]

When James Turner moved in with his family he found his first-class cabin crowded, confused, and dark, with 'filth and dirt in every hole and corner'. Nevertheless, he considered himself lucky. He was, he noted, 'a very little fellow, with a very small wife', in a relatively large cabin. Other passengers were more constricted and uncomfortable. He also noted, with foreboding, the insufficient water, indifferent wine, and inadequate food provided by Sempill for the long voyage to the Cape.[16]

The Bussells found their cabin located under the animal stalls Sempill had erected on deck. 'Huge drops of the effusions of swine and cattle' leaked through the decking, and the pounding of hooves continuously sounded overhead.[17]

Over the next few days, space aboard ship became ever more circumscribed as more passengers embarked with their goods: barrels of pork; wrappers of ham; cases of cheese and biscuits; bags of salt, sugar, rice, and flour; sacks of currants, raisins, suet, and smoked red herring; casks of coffee, tea, oatmeal, barley, and salted butter; hogsheads of brandy; puncheons of rum; trunks of bedding, linen, clothes, and shoes; chests of hats, caps, and bonnets; packages of soap, candles, and medicines; crates of books, stationery, and cutlery; boxes of tools, ironmongery, and building materials; packets of seeds; plant cuttings, shrubs, earthenware, furniture, and saddlery. Emigrants also embarked six pianos and sets of strings and a menagerie of live cargo, including 50 pedigree dogs, several pens of fowl, sheep, goats, and pigs, two milk cows, and three thoroughbred horses. Captain Molloy tethered his thoroughbred stallion next to the Turners' cabin; the horse's stomping and knocking about kept them awake at night and disturbed them through the day.

Inconveniences, however, were not at first taken too seriously. Excitement prevailed over foreboding, and the bustling crowd entered into a festive spirit. Each day passengers gathered on deck to play

music, sing, and dance. Those with guns found amusement in shooting at the seagulls that flew about the ship and floated on the water.

Passengers had no real idea of their destination. Speculation was
rife and wildly imaginative, stimulated by press reports that referred
to Swan River as a new land of Goshen—a biblical reference to the
land of plenty. Fiction and fantasy became even more fused with fact
when John Barrow, secretary to the Admiralty and a government
expert on the Southern Hemisphere, suggested that New Holland be
named Australia Hesperia, a name linked with Hesperides, the Greek
equivalent of an earthly paradise. Hesperia was also the homeland
sought by Aeneas in Virgil's *Aeneid*, a story familiar to all educated
Britons, about a man who undertook a journey out of obligation and
whose life was ruled by his sense of duty to his gods and his family.
But, unlike the ancient hero compelled by the Fates, the *Warrior*
passengers travelled of their own volition; theirs was a free-enterprise
journey. Nevertheless, the identification of Swan River with Hesperia
added to the exhilaration of departure. Emigrants wanted to believe
the hyperbole even while they suspected exaggeration. To subdue his
growing excitement, the sober James Turner reminded himself that
he was not 'going to a land flowing with Milk and Honey'.[18]

6

PASSAGE

ON FRIDAY, 23 OCTOBER 1829—A COLD, OVERCAST, WINTRY DAY, A portent of a ferocious winter throughout Britain—the *Warrior* weighed anchor. Winds were slight, however, and the ship made slow progress. Georgiana Molloy sat at her cabin window wondering 'if I should ever again see England and what changes time will have effected'. Other passengers shot sea birds or danced on deck. In the evening a breeze sprang up and took the *Warrior* out of Portsmouth harbour and past the Isle of Wight. Passengers hoped the ship would call at Plymouth, to enable the dispatch of last-minute letters, but the wind freshened overnight and the ship sailed rapidly down the channel. Plymouth fell astern, the coast of Devonshire receded, and the *Warrior* put into the Atlantic Ocean. Ahead lay a void of space and time. Behind lay their only certainty, England, which, in another 24 hours, would be invisible, perhaps forever.[1]

On Sunday the passengers assembled on the quarter deck. Captain Stone read the church service and Sempill read a sermon—an address to persons embarking or commencing new worldly pursuits. James Turner and other serious-minded listeners concurred on the appropriateness of the subject.

For the first few days at sea passengers continued rearranging their cabins to make habitable space. They stowed necessities close at hand and secured other goods against the unsteadiness of the ship.

Landlubbers, however, found no prophylactic against the ocean swell; once in the open sea, and driven by a rising wind, the *Warrior* began to lurch and roll, strain and creak. The majority of passengers became dreadfully seasick.

Four days out, Matilda Byrne organised a dance on the poop deck, to which she invited cabin passengers and the genteel from steerage. The Bussells accepted but found the promised entertainment lacking. Charles noted, 'There was a lack of those two most essential prerequisites in such cases—ladies and music.'[2]

Georgiana Molloy did not attend Byrne's dance. In fact, since the *Warrior* had sailed she had hardly been out on deck at all. Now two months pregnant, she suffered from morning sickness. And although her cabin under the poop deck enjoyed the freshest air on ship, she fell seasick the morning after the ship's departure. Nausea compounded her distress and she remained sequestered.

The day after the dance, a ship appeared on the horizon, bearing down on the *Warrior*. Passengers lined the decks straining to see and pronounced the intruder an armed and dangerous pirate. All hands prepared their weapons and ammunition, but the suspect ship quickly passed astern. Nevertheless, the thought that an adversary might seek to sack the *Warrior* panicked passengers into proposing defensive measures. The solution adopted appealed to male vanity and provided an opportunity for the display of male braggadocio. The captain called a general muster of all rifles, guns, pistols, and other weapons. Male passengers drilled on the quarter deck and, according to sceptical James Turner, 'talked of deeds of valour to be done'.[3]

Feelings of solidarity, even in the face of a common enemy, did not last long, however. Unity could not prevail given the different motives and expectations and the mixture of credulity, earnestness, and avariciousness among passengers. The *Warrior* did not convey to Western Australia, in uniform mass, the moral verities and social disciplines of evangelical religion and the drive of progress. Rather, the transfer of such a cross-section of British society took the worthy as well as the raffish and libertarian, London's dissolute as well as their pietist, sober superiors. All of them, however, the best and worst, emigrated to improve their prospects; some aspired to riches, the rest, at the very least, aspired to substantial betterment of themselves. Families with children, servants, and responsibilities mixed with intemperate single young men fired with the hope of making an easy fortune in the land of promise. There were also class differences. The 479-ton *Warrior* crammed together labourers, tradespeople, ex-military officers, and the resentful younger sons of gentry or near-gentry, who felt themselves unjustly deprived of the inheritance to which birth and education had entitled them. 'Such are the men,' Charles Bussell observed, 'whom Sempill has flattered himself with the idea of cheating.'[4]

Passengers who felt defrauded began to protest. Arguments over Sempill's inadequate provisioning broke out. Detractors cited his Scottish nationality as an explanation for his great parsimony. On 31 October an Irish passenger threatened to throw Sempill overboard. The Scots came to Sempill's defence and Captain Stone intervened before a fight erupted.

The commotion on deck and the widespread rancour disturbed the ailing Molloy. She felt, she noted, 'worse than ever I was in my life'. But she and her husband had other problems. Their stallion had fallen over and could not get up. Captain Molloy arranged to support him in slings and occupied himself in reinforcing the disintegrating horse stalls. Sheep and pigs had died and the cows no longer gave milk. Captain Molloy spent most of his time caring for the surviving animals. Sempill's niggardly husbandry arrangements vexed Captain Molloy and he complained to his wife of the charterer's negligence.[5]

Dead animals were mourned not only for their economic loss but also because their passing seemed a portent. While alive, they had formed a link of association with home. Each death, however, deprived the owner of one more material connection to England.

As the *Warrior* plunged south the weather warmed and became unsettled. In the first week of November the ship encountered boisterous seas and contrary winds. Passengers who were not seasick before became seasick now. Sheep, pigs, and chickens continued to die.

On 7 November passengers drew up and signed a protest, which they read to Sempill. Petitioners felt that besides his contractual commitment, Sempill had a moral obligation to provide decent and adequate provisions. They hoped formal complaint about his scrimping would shame him and cause him to change his conduct. But Sempill was shameless; he had no intention of increasing either the quality or quantity of rations. His responsibility began and ended with the calculation of profit and loss. He stood to make £10 000 from the voyage of the *Warrior* and he saw no reason to jeopardise that profit by providing more or better provisions.

A few days after he received the passengers' petition Sempill cut potable rations, restricted water to the children only, and limited adults to one glass of porter a day. Later he tried to limit the daily ration of wine to one-third of a bottle each. Loud arguments broke out and disgruntled passengers verbally abused him. A gentleman, noted Charles Bussell, would find such treatment intolerable; 'he, however, with the greatest *magnanimity* sits and hears and bears every insult'. Sempill pleaded depleted stocks; his wine reserves lay under twenty tons of cargo.[6]

After nineteen days at sea Georgiana Molloy began to feel better. Fine weather during the second week of November induced her on deck. She mixed with other passengers, who found her venturous and full of spirit. She initiated conversation and talked of literary subjects, the Romantic poets, and the beauty of nature.

To the Bussell brothers, Georgiana Molloy had seemed something of a mystery. Now they met her for the first time. Her eloquence charmed them and Charles Bussell thought she possessed 'all the air of a lady well born and well bred'. Her presence on the *Warrior*, he felt, was 'quite an acquisition to our society'. Nineteen-year-old

Charles thought Molloy's romanticism indicated an innocence in the ways of the world, but this provided for 'a great deal to interest about her'. Molloy, in turn, thought the Bussells 'very nice young men and the most gentlemanly on board'. Charles paid a similar compliment to Captain Molloy but found him rather old for so young a wife.[7]

But while Bussell was preoccupied with contemplating Captain Molloy's age and wisdom, other passengers had reached the limit of forbearance over conditions aboard ship. Arguments were now daily occurrences. On 9 November Charles commented that, as a consequence of the continuing dissatisfaction, 'a row now appears to be brewing'. Next day he remarked, 'A party spirit is beginning to show itself pretty strongly among the passengers.'[8]

Sempill provided steerage passengers with bread, salt, beef, salt pork, tea, sugar, peas, and oatmeal, as well as bedding. They ate where they could. First-class passengers fitted out their cabins with their own bedding, linen, and furniture and usually stocked a private larder. They dined with the captain but were just as dependent on the charterer for provisions as steerage passengers. When Matilda Byrne invited John and Charles Bussell to dinner in the captain's cuddy, the brothers found the food 'shabby' and the wine 'execrable'.[9]

Many passengers sought to distance themselves from the shipboard quarrels and feuds. A piano in the Turners' cabin provided the setting for nondisputatious musical gatherings. Other passengers removed themselves from the conflicts by continuing their dancing, singing, and music making on deck. The feuding parties, however, remained sultry and temperamental. Lieutenant De Burgh, a leader of the anti-Sempill faction, was frequently drunk.

On 14 November—a hot, windless day—Captain Stone ordered the sailors to take up the goods from the hold and liberate Sempill's wine stocks. Calm weather continued and the *Warrior* drifted listlessly. Now in low latitudes, passengers remarked on the suddenness of the sun's rise and setting, so unlike the lingering dawns and prolonged twilights of Britain. Hot weather forced the shedding of heavy English clothes, and the heat became the main topic of conversation. According to James Turner, 'the prospect of a never-ending voyage' made some passengers irascible and they readily sought quarrels. Others amused themselves by shooting at the dolphins playing about the ship.

On 18 November a breeze sprang up, the ship moved forward, and passengers saw their first land in four weeks—the mountains of the Cape Verde Islands (Ilhas do Cabo Verde), a ten-island volcanic archipelago belonging to Portugal, 480 kilometres off the West African coast. The excitement of sudden change and unwonted novelty after weeks of 'the boundless space of the ocean' brought all passengers on deck.[10]

Most passengers had read about, but had never seen, mountains. They belonged to a generation that believed that mountains and ocean were the two grandest phenomena of nature. Under the influence of the early nineteenth-century Romantics, mountains had become, in the imagination, temples of nature built by the Almighty. Mountains were places of spiritual refuge, of withdrawal; mountains were seats of the gods, where humans might encounter divinity and be transfigured.

As the *Warrior* drifted towards the Cape Verde Islands, curious passengers crowded the decks, passed telescopes from one to another, and gazed in awe as the clouds occasionally dispersed to reveal peak above peak at heights they found almost inconceivable. Previous generations had believed that mountains were monstrous excrescences on the original smooth face of nature, but not the *Warrior* passengers. As Charles Bussell noted, the mountains of the Cape Verde Islands were 'indeed a beautiful spectacle and were so regarded by all the passengers high and low'.[11]

Georgiana Molloy joined the sightseers. The mountains reminded her 'of dear and bonny Scotland' and she remained on deck all day. Along with other passengers, she looked at the mountains with eyes trained by Byron, Shelley, and Wordsworth, all of whom exalted high places. Sensitive to the archetypal mystery of mountains, the deep compelling call they exerted, she continued looking through the night and into the morning, hoping for a view by moonlight. But the moon did not rise until late morning and she retired ungratified.[12]

Ever since Molloy broke with Matilda Byrne her own immediate concerns—accentuated by seasickness and compounded by advancing pregnancy—had been paramount. For the first time in her adult life the needs of the flesh took conscious precedence over those of the spirit. She lacked both energy and inclination to proselytise. Instead, she concentrated on seeking relief from the discomfort of her sickbed and sought solutions to the recurrent problem of personal cleanliness. Moreover, realisation that her body contained a future life forced her to reconsider the superiority of spirit over flesh. The desire to save her own soul was now coupled with a need to safeguard her own body. Faced with the responsibility of nurturing and suckling life, a mother could not accept Christian admonitions to flail the body. Such injunctions seemed somehow less urgent, less pressing, irrelevant, even wrong. But religion's claims did not end with the body.

Although Molloy's Christian religion focused on the implications of temporality—finality and death—it did not exist as a mere commentary on ordinary life. Religion promised immortality, and evangelical Christianity, in particular, promised a direct and living engagement with that immortality. While Molloy rejected most of the supernatural claims of the ecstatic divines, she embraced the possibility of the development of a sense of life encompassing and superseding her own. For Christianity had never entirely banished the pagan belief that life on earth was sacred and that the interpenetration of moon and earth, of sun and earth, of soil and organism were all essential to livelihood. Molloy's improved health and the sight of land provided an opportunity to contemplate these wider spiritual possibilities. Her all-day and all-night vigil on the deck expressed a longing to live in such a numinous world, in which forests, hills, rocks, water, and mountains were alive and hallowed.

Awe, compounded of mingled terror and exultation, was once reserved exclusively for God. But the Romantic movement, the first outcry of protest against the modern world, transferred awe to God's sacred creation, nature. Romanticism, in opposition to contemporary utilitarianism, celebrated a world independent of human needs and use, yet one to which humans were still morally accountable.[13]

Awe, then, was an appropriate response to the mountain splendour of the Cape Verde Islands. But as the *Warrior* slowly drifted towards the shore, passengers began to note the land's obvious desolation. The islands, Charles Bussell wrote, were 'without a vestige of vegetation'. To people accustomed to the green fields of England, the novel sight of an utterly sterile country possessed an unexpected grandeur. But the grandeur was not natural. The Islands' barren, black lava slopes arose not just from their volcanic origin. Decades of deforestation, farming, and grazing had destroyed the original vegetation; severe soil erosion then laid bare the volcanic slopes. In the landscape of the Cape Verde Islands, the Swan River migrants had their first encounter with the biologically impoverishing consequences of human settlement.[14]

Neither the great relief of sighting land after weeks of the sameness of unbounded ocean nor the balmy weather pacified relationships between feuding groups on board. Indolent young men, drunk on spirits and confrontational by disposition, lounged about and congregated on deck. On the afternoon of 19 November, as the ship lay becalmed, a general melee broke out. The ship's captain and officers moved in to break up the fight but were struck down and beaten. The sailors rushed forward on behalf of their officers, and the servants of several of the passengers joined in. Nonparticipants eventually accomplished a separation of the pugilists. Loud abuse and death threats continued throughout the evening.[15]

The Bussells stood aside during the fighting. Captain Molloy supported authority. He noted tersely in his diary that 'a great tumult took place in the evening and much danger apprehended'. His wife recorded the scene more vividly as 'a complete time of blows, imprecations, terror and sickness'.[16]

For the Molloys the fight distracted attention from a more serious concern: the poor health and continuing mortality of their animals. Exposed on deck, the horses, sheep, pigs, and chickens suffered terribly from the rolling of the ship, confined stalls, unaccustomed heat, and inadequate feed and water. Within a few weeks of putting to sea they had begun to die. Pigs and sheep were now dying daily, and on the day of the great fight Captain Molloy noted, 'We lost another of our sheep.' Georgiana Molloy had brought along a hive of bees, and when her health allowed she checked their condition and hoped they would survive the voyage. Animals belonging to the other major stockholders on board, James Turner and Captain Byrne, were also dying.[17]

On the day after the great fight Captain Stone assembled all steerage passengers on deck, read ship's regulations, and prohibited them from gathering aloft the main mast. In the meantime, he intended to divert the *Warrior* to Praia, on the main Cape Verde island of St Jago (São Thiago), where he resolved to take the disputants before the British consul. The weather frustrated his determination, however. The ship sat becalmed, within sight but not within reach of the islands, for two days before an afternoon breeze on Sunday, 22 November brought the *Warrior* into Porto de Praia.

Next morning, before breakfast, several small boats came out to the ship. Island peddlers, who made a precarious living selling oranges, lemons, coconuts, pineapples, bananas, and eggs to passing ships, tried to gain the decks. Passengers bargained eagerly for the desperately wanted fruit. Most had never tasted bananas. The Bussells considered the pineapples inferior to those grown in English hothouses.

Meanwhile, Captain Stone went ashore to lay his charges and

bring the troublemakers before the British consul. He called several witnesses, including Captain Molloy, who testified against Lieutenant De Burgh. Convicted of striking ship's officers and of mutinous conduct, De Burgh was sentenced to be left behind on St Jago. One of the convicted Irish participants entered a bond of £100 to preserve the peace.

Passengers not involved in the fracas spent their time ashore buying wine and fresh fruit to compensate for the deficiency of Sempill's victualling and to ward off incipient scurvy. The Bussell brothers took the occasion—their first-ever excursion in a foreign land—to compare themselves with the inhabitants and note the superiority of English men and English society. Unfamiliar surroundings gave them a heightened sense of being British.

One evening a group of the *Warrior*'s passengers gathered outside English Mary's Hotel and the ship's bugler played 'God Save the King'. Those assembled considered the tune especially inspiring and Charles remarked how, 'In this anthem, doubly beautiful in a foreign land, every Englishman with head uncovered joined most fervently while a number of natives looked on in stupid amazement.' Not only were the locals unable to appreciate finer feelings of patriotism but they were also, Charles noted, ignorant of the virtue of industry. He could 'not have imagined that there lived upon the face of the earth a nation who passed their time in such utter indolence'. Nor could he understand how people lived without the motivation to improve and accumulate; he noted in astonishment and disgust, 'Subsistence is all they appear to desire.' John Bussell, less prepared to be amazed than his younger brother, and less inclined to description, dismissed the island's inhabitants as 'black ruffians jabbering away in unintelligible language'.[18]

Georgiana Molloy longed to go ashore and enjoy the same freedom of movement as the male passengers. Her husband, however, warned her that there were sights that would disgust her, as many of the island's inhabitants 'were nearly naked and very dirty'. Moreover, he told her, none of the other ladies planned to venture ashore. To preserve solidarity and decorum, she elected to stay aboard.[19]

Convention did not deter the lively Matilda Byrne, who spent two nights on the island. She had grown fond of De Burgh and after his sentencing she began pleading with the British consul to allow him to continue his passage. She nearly succeeded in changing the consul's mind when Captain Stone became aware of her intervention. He immediately announced the *Warrior*'s departure, hastily rounded up the passengers, and hurriedly embarked. Early on Wednesday, 25 November, the *Warrior* weighed anchor, unfurled sails, and caught a steady wind south. Movement and the exile of De Burgh did not, however, lessen shipboard tension. Bickering and factional animosity continued.

From the very beginning of the voyage Georgiana Molloy conceived a dislike for Matilda Byrne that grew in intensity with each passing day. She refused to speak to Byrne and noted maliciously that because of Byrne's behaviour—fraternising with De Burgh—the other ladies had avoided her company. Molloy also refused to eat in the cuddy, owing to Byrne's presence. She did not regret the loss of society, for she found the noise and conversation at dinner 'too annoying'. At the Cape Verde Islands, however, 'from the absence of the "disrespectable" ', she dined in public.[20]

As the ship plunged south the sun rose higher in the sky and air temperatures increased. Cabins became rank and began to stink. A putrefying odour rose from stale cabins, old and new vomit, sweaty bodies, damp beds, sticky sheets, unwashed clothes, chamber pots, and sour and rotten food. Fitful attempts at personal hygiene failed to inoculate passengers from the stench of adjoining unaired cabins; all felt the discomfort caused by the lack of general cleanliness in cramped quarters.

An excess of modesty prevented both men and women from bathing properly. Men, however, managed better than women. Standards of decency allowed them to shed more clothes, and since custom gave them priority on deck in the morning, they were able to strip almost naked and splash one another with water before the women appeared. Women and children were unable to enjoy a similar frolic.

Whenever it rained and the ship remained steady, passengers quickly set out dozens of pails, basins, jugs, and mugs to collect fresh water. They then threw their dirty clothes on deck, stamped on them, and washed them. Later, hundreds of shirts, shifts, napkins, gowns, skirts, and trousers hung from the fore and main shrouds and all the fixed ropes of the rigging.

After leaving the Cape Verde Islands the *Warrior* encountered the equatorial doldrums. An alternate succession of calms and squalls beset the ship. 'Rig out' and 'close up' were the orders shouted across decks. Georgiana Molloy stayed in her cabin, enervated by the heat, ill and weak, incapable of exertion, barely able to write in her journal. She lay on her berth thinking of Scotland and of her friends at Keppoch and Rosneath and imagined herself enjoying country rides in the cool Scottish air on a horse-drawn cart while sitting on a plank of wood or a bag of straw. She imagined summer shadows falling rapidly across hillsides and the waters of the Gareloch, and pictured winter snow sprinkled on the firs and pines and mantling distant summits. She recalled the thickets of rhododendron, laurustine, and jessamine that, on the mild Rosneath Peninsula, bloomed as late as December.

But despite immeasurable homesickness, Molloy did not think of returning. The *Warrior*'s coactive track down the English Channel, across the Bay of Biscay, around the Horn of Africa, and south, towards the equator, precluded regress, and Molloy accepted her commitment—to her husband, to emigration—as an irrevocable choice. Her Bible and her religion valued travel as an explication of human fate and necessity. But Molloy, along with the other migrants, also saw travel as an expression of freedom and an escape from necessity, towards a chance to determine her own future.

The violence of seasickness also formed a barrier to returning. By the time she had reached the Cape Verde Islands, Molloy had resolved never again to undertake a sea voyage and later told her mother never to expect to see her in England.[21]

Changeable weather after the Cape Verde Islands affected James Turner's rheumatism, and he retired to his cabin suffering from lumbago. The Bussells, although they berthed in steerage, considered themselves distinct from steerage class and physically segregated themselves from the other, rowdy passengers. When weather permitted they took refuge among the rigging of the main top deck. They read Shakespeare and Byron and borrowed botanical books from Georgiana Molloy. Molloy, during the periods when she felt 'tolerably well', played chess with female friends and read the poetry of Robert Burns and Oliver Goldsmith. On Sundays she heard Bobby and Charlotte, two of the young children of her servants Robert and Ann Heppingstone, read from the Bible.

Seven days out from the Cape Verde Islands, on 1 December, Sempill cut daily water rations by one pint. Passengers protested loudly but Sempill was impervious to all remonstration. The Bussells shared their ration with their dogs and worried about the animals' survival.

Some relief from shipboard tedium and tension occurred during a boisterous and alcoholic celebration of crossing the equator on 10 and 11 December. Passengers who bribed sailors escaped tarring and feathering, but most everyone participated in the water ceremonies. Molloy avoided a drenching; her husband covered her with a tarpaulin. In contrast, Matilda Byrne, Molloy noted with satisfaction, received five whole buckets of water. According to Charles Bussell, two-thirds of the ship's company were drunk by midnight.[22]

The wind now blew strongly and the ship made steady progress. Notwithstanding the colds many developed following the dowsing, passengers found the forward movement exhilarating. On 23 December the *Warrior* crossed the Tropic of Capricorn, the wind freshened, and the ship plunged forward at ten knots. Wrangling persisted, and although all passengers exchanged Christmas greetings on 25 December, many complained that the meagre food allowance prevented them from celebrating in true British fashion. Nevertheless, 'all the gentlemen', according to Molloy, 'except my husband and the mate were very merry'. No fights broke out, and six days later, on 31 December, the ship's company began celebrating the New Year. People sang and danced and drank on the poop deck. Morning hangovers did not deter the celebrants, who continued merrymaking until 2 January.[23]

Favourable winds prevailed. A sow gave birth to piglets and then died. Two ewes lambed and all survived. The weather turned cold and stormy. The ship rolled before gales, spray lashed the deck, and the ship sailed so close to the wind that many passengers feared it would capsize. As the Cape of Good Hope drew near, passengers longed for land and yearned for fresh provisions.

On 12 January, twelve weeks after leaving Portsmouth, the *Warrior* reached Cape Town, the capital of the British colony in South Africa. In 1806, during the Napoleonic Wars, the British government had taken possession of the former Dutch colony at the Cape of Good Hope. Britain's aim was commercial and strategic. The Cape was a naval base on the sea route to India, the East, and Australia. Too arid to tempt many British immigrants, the colony was governed by men who had fought together during Wellington's Peninsula campaigns.

At Cape Town Captain Molloy introduced his wife to several former comrades from the Rifle Brigade and their wives: General Sir Lowry Cole, governor, and his wife, Lady Frances Cole; Colonel John Bell, colonial secretary, and his wife, Catherine Bell; and the dashing, vain, and reckless Colonel Harry Smith, quartermaster general, and his wife, Juana Smith. As Captain Stone planned to keep the *Warrior* in port a week or more, Colonel Smith invited the Molloys to stay at his residence. The Byrnes, however, were already Smith's guests, and Georgiana Molloy refused to stay under the same roof as Matilda Byrne. Instead, the Molloys took lodgings in town. But, overawed by Colonel Smith and won by his charm, they could not resist his entreaties to dine almost every night at his house.

Captain Molloy and the colonel revisited their Peninsula leisure activities and went out hunting deer and antelope. Georgiana Molloy enjoyed the company of her new friends. Juana Smith played guitar 'divinely' and copied out and presented Molloy with several of her favourite tunes. Molloy also found the Cape coastal vegetation—succulents, wildflowers, grasses, heathers, bulbs, waterplants, flowering shrubs, and herbs—a delight: in her experience, a botanical domain without compare. She visited gardens and found several blooms to admire, despite the scarcity of blossoms at the height of the Cape summer. She quickly identified her favourites, and before she reembarked she bought a supply of seeds, including oleanders, Cape gooseberries, and a pink lily, the watsonia.

Most *Warrior* passengers remained accommodated aboard ship throughout their stay at Cape Town. Many wrote letters so as to catch the ships bound for England. The Bussells went shooting, but without the assistance of a guide of the calibre of Captain Molloy's Colonel Smith, they saw very little game. Those who could afford to purchased provisions and stock for Swan River. Captain Molloy replaced the pigs and sheep he had lost; James Turner bought two horses, one cow, sixteen sheep, six chickens, seven pigeons, and one rabbit.

Warrior passengers were, of course, curious about Swan River and sought news of the fate of those who had preceded them. They could not believe what they heard. They were told that the Swan River Colony had failed, that masters and servants were living in wretched conditions bordering on starvation, that grants remained unoccupied, and that absentees had received all the best land. Many of the emigrants dismissed these reports. They had invested too much to turn back now. Their voyage, their undertaking, was conclusive.

They convinced themselves that the rumours were untrue, or at most, exaggerated. John Bussell questioned the credibility of the propagator of the information, a Cape merchant, whom he accused of having a conflict of interest since the merchant encouraged settlers to stay at the Cape. He assured his mother in a letter that he and his brothers remained sanguine about their prospects at Swan River. Captain Molloy also questioned the reliability of the sources and thought the reports of disaster exaggerated. Others, however, were discouraged. Six of James Turner's eighteen servants deserted him.[24]

Georgiana Molloy was now more than five months pregnant and Catherine Bell urged her to remain at the Cape until after her confinement. Bell warned her that otherwise she would arrive at Swan River in a 'desolate state'. Molloy, however, could not be persuaded to stay and later told her family, 'I was determined to follow my husband under all circumstances.'[25]

On 25 January 1830, as the *Warrior* prepared to depart, Molloy wrote a hasty and brief letter to Helen Story. She apologised for her long silence but pleaded sickness. She gave her remembrances to all at Rosneath and confessed to homesickness but claimed she had no regrets about emigrating. Indeed, she urged her friends to follow her and her husband, either to the Cape or to Swan River. As for the rumours about Swan River, she did not dwell on them and noted only that 'The accounts of the new Colony are varied.' In any case, she was not about to return to Britain. If the bad news turned out to be true, then she and her husband might consider settling at the Cape. As for her husband, the new bride claimed satisfaction. 'Molloy is a dear creature,' she wrote, 'and I would not exchange him for £10 000 per annum and a mansion in a civilised country.'[26]

On 26 January the *Warrior* left Cape Town for the final part of the voyage to Swan River and dipped down into the Southern Ocean, the longest stretch of unbroken water on earth. Opened up by the fragmentation of Gondwana, the Southern Ocean extends continuously around the planet, between South America, South Africa,

Australia, and Antarctica. From small irregularities and disturbances in the surface waters, waves develop and grow with the strength and consistency of the wind. Powered by constant westerly winds, the Southern Ocean current becomes incessant. The waves never dissipate but instead form a long, low swell that moves steadily eastward, around and around the world. The current and the westerly winds favoured the *Warrior*'s course. With studding sails, low and aloft, the ship scudded steadily east.

On board, among the passengers, the steady tempo of unceasing motion and the absence of incident discouraged description. Captain Molloy and Charles Bussell discontinued their journals. Georgiana Molloy wrote less, as did the conscientious James Turner. What comprised the vast bulk of travel at sea remained unrecorded: the rocking, swooping, flowing, and streaming of the wind and the ship; the hypnotic, ever-moving but persistent pattern of the surging and cresting waves; the changing forms of clouds and light; the routines of passage and working a ship, going about, making the reach.

Dissatisfaction with Sempill remained, however. The supply of provisions grew even worse. The mutton that Sempill had bought at Cape Town proved diseased, and passengers subsisted on salt pork and rice. Fodder for the stock was inadequate, and sheep and lambs continued to die. All the bees in Molloy's carefully tended hive were eaten by moths.

Georgiana Molloy, less sick than previously, nevertheless fell several times on deck and down stairs, owing to the roughness of the passage. Although bruised and shaken, she began making baby clothes. Her maid, Anne Dawson, whose own pregnancy was a little more advanced than Molloy's, continued to suffer from seasickness.

Irish and Scottish passengers kept up their quarrel, but as Swan River drew nearer, the emigrants began to think more and more about the colony ahead and to consider the rumours they had heard at Cape Town. To reassure themselves, they read and re-read the early optimistic accounts of Swan River published in England. But they could not banish entirely all forebodings. What if the rumours were true, or even half-true? New plans would have to be made. In accordance with the general rule of travel—that the purposes and motives of a journey change and accrue in its course—many migrants began contemplating the possibility of bypassing Swan River altogether. As unsatisfactory as they found Sempill's charter, disembarkation at Swan River might prove worse than staying aboard the *Warrior* for Hobart and Sydney. In the meantime, all waited expectantly for New Holland.

Long before they sighted the Western Australian coast, passengers could smell the continent. Up to 150 kilometres out to sea, an aromatic odour as of spicy flowers alerted them to the proximity of land and terrestrial life. They smelled bushfire smoke and a volatile and pungent admixture of eucalyptus, acacia, melaleuca, casuarina, leaf and mould, bark, wood, and blossom—the odour of decay and the scent of the living world. They smelled and breathed a wild continent, not an uninhabited wilderness but an inhabited wild place, where biological processes continued unbridled, relatively free of human interference.

On 12 March 1830 the *Warrior* reached the Western Australian coast and anchored in Gage Roads, between the mouth of the Swan River and Rottnest Island. Next day the ship anchored off Fremantle. Intense expectation prevailed among the passengers, and they crowded on deck, intently looking towards the shore. Perceptions of the new country differed. Some saw a scene thickly wooded with trees and shrubs of the most beautiful foliage, one complete mass of verdure. Others saw nothing but sand, sand in every direction as far as the eye could reach, sand so dazzlingly white that children thought it snow and wondered why the trees were green.

7

TO THE BUSH

EARLY ON THE MORNING OF 13 MARCH 1830, AS THE *WARRIOR* LAY
at anchor off Fremantle, an offshore breeze blew. The fresh air carried
an overwhelming smell of land. Passengers wished themselves ashore.
But five months aboard an unhappy ship did not end easily. Fremantle
boasted neither wharf nor jetty, and even though the *Warrior* dropped
anchor as close to the entrance of the Swan River as the shallow
water allowed, off-loading took effort and ingenuity.

To disembark, passengers assembled a small flotilla of boats,
flats, and rafts on which they loaded themselves and their cargo. As
they lowered the animals from the ship to the smaller craft, several
fell in the water and drowned. Captain Stone and charterer Sempill
considered their contract terminated and did little to assist. They
exercised scarce supervision or care over unloading. Sailors tore open
the large packages, conveyed the goods to shore, and threw them on
the beach, often at widely dispersed locations. Stores got wet and
spoiled, some washed into the sea, never to be recovered. Settlers
had to carry or drag their possessions from the beach, up and over
steep dunes, and through ankle-deep sand to the Fremantle camp.
Weakened stock found little grass and only brackish water. Settlers
fed them oatmeal, peas, and biscuits. But without pens to hold them,
distracted animals bolted, including one of James Turner's two horses.

Turner found that Fremantle 'was composed of a good number

of miserable looking tents, most of which were grog shops; however, to tell the truth, these said shops were very good things as I got some bread and cheese & Porter in one of them, half an hour after I landed'.[1]

Most colonists from the *Warrior* were too busy, at first, to voice any disappointment with Swan River. Visitors were not so reticent. Mary Ann Friend arrived in the colony a month earlier than the *Warrior* passengers and found the Swan a very poor river, barely navigable in places, and possessed of an extremely narrow entrance, at times impassable and dangerous. She thought Stirling's report of 'beautifully undulating and thinly wooded' land generally true but the soil was nothing but sand. Settlers, she noted, complained of government neglect and of inequitable disposal of land. They resented the fact that absentees and military officers had first choice. Meanwhile, they sat and brooded. 'There appears a great want of energy on the part of the settlers,' Friend wrote. 'Melancholy appears to pervade all classes and great dread is felt lest there should be a scarcity of provisions.'[2]

James Turner found the despondency a spur to action. To keep his servants from the temptations of the disheveled and drunken camp at Fremantle, he decided to establish a separate camp a quarter of a mile up the river. He piled his goods on a raft that he dragged through the water to a spot above the high-water mark. Here he erected his prefabricated house and his servants pitched their tents. Around his encampment he stashed all his gear and tethered and yarded his animals: horse, cow, sheep, goat, pigs, chickens, pigeons, and one rabbit.

The Bussell brothers knew themselves to be less vulnerable to temptation than Turner's servants and so chose to stay in the main Fremantle camp. They pitched their tent by the river, among the cluster of half a dozen wooden buildings, bush huts, and scores of tents that formed the settlement. Around the centre pole they stashed their guns: three double barrels, two single barrels, and three rifles.

From the ceiling they hung four brace of pistols and two cutlasses. A slab of wood supported by three desks sufficed for a table. For chairs they sat on upturned buckets and saucepans. Their dogs, forbidden entrance, crowded around the opening.[3]

The Molloys decided to leave Fremantle altogether and proceed directly to Perth. The day after the *Warrior* dropped anchor they boarded a boat for the 22-kilometre trip upriver.

Georgiana Molloy's first and lasting impression of the new country was of the unbounded, generous profusion of trees, trees everywhere, trees that were always green, so many trees as to form 'an unlimited extent of dark green woods', wild, huge trees, 'trees of full growth with branches untroubled by the storm and unpruned by man', trees that made the Swan River 'beautifully wooded to the water's edge with both copse wood and magnificent old trees', and trees so luxuriant the soil must be fruitful from the 'immense timber growing from it'.[4]

At Fremantle Molloy had made a quick botanical examination of the shrubs and trees but the season was summer, she wrote, and she found no flowers, though she thought 'some of the trees almost aromatic'. Perth, she discovered, was a 'thicket of low shrubs, Grass Plants, 10 feet high and palms'.[5]

Unlike Fremantle, however, Perth boasted a cleared, though sandy, main street, St George's Terrace. Eucalyptus trees shaded a sidewalk on one side, where public notices and printed newspapers affixed to the tree trunks flapped in the morning and afternoon breezes. Coffee and grog were available from several tents. A few prefabricated buildings served as dwellings and offices. A timber-framed church, walled and thatched with rushes, stood at one end of the street. The parade ground of the 63rd Regiment stretched out next door. The soldiers pitched their tents next to a spring, a favourite camping site for the local Aborigines, who called the area *Mooro*. The colonial secretary's house, a wooden building with shingled roof, stood further along St George's Terrace, on the side where the ground sloped down to the river. The governor's temporary residence, a large wooden building, stood at the other end of the street.

The Molloys fitted easily into Perth society. Most government officials were retired naval or army officers who had either known each other in England or had friends in common. Many, like Captain Molloy, had young wives, most of them Georgiana Molloy's age. Ellen Stirling, the governor's wife, was 22, the colonial secretary's wife, Caroline Brown, was 23, as was the surveyor-general's wife, Matilda Roe. The Molloys stayed in a succession of officers' houses and enjoyed a variety of Australian food, including, Molloy told her mother, kangaroo, parrot, crayfish, and crab.[6]

Perth was the colonial headquarters, and immigrants who wanted land had to come to the government camp to register their names, obtain permission to settle, and apply for a grant. Settlers from the *Warrior* quickly learned from their Fremantle neighbours that all the land in the vicinity of the Swan and Canning rivers had been allotted. Anxious to press their own claims, they hastily followed the Molloys upriver. James Turner found the trip enchanting and later wrote, 'We were quite astonished at the splendid scenery on both sides of the River, although the soil is nothing but a white sand. The foliage of the trees was exquisite, and together with the many beautiful turnings in the River, one might fancy themselves in a fairyland.'[7]

At Perth the colonial secretary, Peter Brown, told settlers to submit an account of all the goods they had imported, the value of which would be applied towards a grant of land. Brown confirmed that most of the land in the vicinity of Perth, including all the good agricultural land, was claimed. He advised settlers, however, that superior land lay to the south, which, at that moment, Governor Stirling was exploring.

Stirling had always evinced interest in the land along Geographe Bay, to the south of Perth. Even though he had not actually landed there during his 1827 exploration of the west coast, he believed the land held great promise.

In November 1829, in response to the growing land shortage at Swan River, Stirling appointed surgeon Alexander Collie and Lieutenant William Preston in charge of an expedition down the south coast to Geographe Bay. During their two-week boat trip they explored Peel Inlet, as well as the Vasse and Leschenault estuaries. They discovered two rivers, afterwards named by Stirling the Collie and the Preston. They found the land around the estuaries covered in grass growing over a deep soil. The expedition also encountered large numbers of Aborigines, of whom Collie and Preston wrote, 'All their intentions seemed friendly, and their character unsuspecting and fearless.'[8]

Expedition members also noted the region's prolific wildlife. In fact, most observers were struck, as by revelation, by the almost immeasurable fertility of animal life in the southwest. One expedition member later reported tens of thousands of black swans, which rose and darkened the sky for a distance of eight to ten miles. Indeed, the southwest wetlands harboured the most abundant populations of waterfowl in Western Australia. At the end of summer, when inland waters dried up, enormous numbers of waterfowl migrated to the perennial wetlands along the coastal plains. Large nesting colonies of black swans and pelicans formed in the winter. The Vasse, Leschenault, and Murray estuaries supported tens of thousands of swans and even greater numbers of ducks, which fed on the flourishing marine life.

The concentration of birdlife and other plentiful foods attracted the Aborigines. Swamps provided abundant freshwater tortoises, crustaceans, and frogs. Zamia palms and *Haemadorum* roots grew prolifically on the stable dunes, edible rushes grew in the swamps, and *Dioscorea* (yams) grew in the alluvial soils. As Collie and Preston confirmed, the coasts were the most densely populated areas of the southwest.

Collie and Preston also noted the concurrence of fire and

Aboriginal habitation. From the sea they saw many bushfires, 'a circumstance,' they remarked, 'which assists in explaining the so frequent burnt appearance of the trees and shrubs in Western Australia; we have no doubt they owed their production to the natives'. Indeed, the Aborigines were habitual users of fire; they regularly set fire to the land to extract their means of existence. Aboriginal fire, in fact, had created the grasslands around the Vasse, Leschenault, and Murray estuaries on which kangaroos flourished and that Collie and Preston so much admired.[9]

The expedition's favourable report induced Stirling himself to embark on a more detailed exploration of the Leschenault–Vasse region in March 1830. At Leschenault Estuary, Lieutenant Preston, J. S. Roe, the surveyor-general, and his assistant, John Kellam, journeyed inland. Roe recommended settlement. He wrote of 'open plains, covered with grass, and thinly scattered with trees', of land 'of equal value to the agriculturist and grazier', and of undulating country 'well clothed with grass and timber'. Although the party met no Aborigines, Roe noted, 'The traces of them were evident and numerous in many places.'[10]

Stirling returned to Perth on 18 March, shortly after the *Warrior* settlers arrived. On 22 March a government notice appeared that gave details of Stirling's exploration and declared the area open for selection. Stirling claimed there was now no excuse for colonial idleness. His discoveries to the south were an opportunity for industry, enterprise, and intelligence:

> The country inland from Port Leschenault, as far as it has been seen, offers fertile soil, and good stock stations. The climate is decidedly cooler than in this district; and, judging from the quantity of grass, and the verdure of the foliage, it appears to sustain a dry season not so long in duration as that experienced in this quarter. For these reasons, the Lieutenant-Governor recommends it to the notice of settlers . . . who will do wisely to make an early selection.[11]

He did not intend, Stirling warned, to open up any more districts for selection and settlement. Leschenault was the settlers' last choice.

To confirm the wisdom of his own recommendation, Stirling immediately took up a large grant for himself. The agent for the absentee landlord, Colonel P. A. Lautour, selected another 103 000 acres. Other large grants quickly followed. But settlers camped in Fremantle, even those who had selected Geographe Bay land, declined to move to Leschenault. Stirling next tried to interest the newcomers from the *Warrior* in Leschenault. He told them he was going to establish a military post there and so they would be well protected. They too declined his offer. Most still hoped to find land closer to Swan River.

Many had given up, however. Scarcity of good land and the idleness and despondency at Fremantle and Perth confirmed many *Warrior* passengers' worst fears about Swan River. Although most had originally intended settling permanently in the new colony, fewer than half actually did so. Notwithstanding continuing complaints about Sempill's conduct, the rest chose to reembark on the *Warrior*, which left for Hobart and Sydney on 15 April.

Those who remained in Western Australia were still sanguine about their prospects and hopeful that they would soon obtain land. In the meantime, they had other concerns to attend to. The long sea voyage and monotonously limited diet had left many suffering from scurvy, plagued by dysentery, and ravenously hungry for fresh meat. The men took enthusiastically to hunting, but they found the wildlife already depleted.

When Stirling first explored Swan River in 1827 he reported seeing large colonies of seals all along the coast. In particular he noted a large colony that inhabited the rocks and beaches around the mouth of the Swan River. During May 1829, while Captain Fremantle took possession of Western Australia, his crew hunted the seals for oil in such numbers that the population soon dwindled. The first settlers finished off the survivors and extended the hunt up and down the coast. In less than a year they extirpated all the local seal colonies. They then turned their guns against the swans, ducks, kangaroos, wallabies, and any other creatures that might provide food or good sport.

On account of the popularity and frequency of hunting, dogs fetched high prices, and settlers recommended that future emigrants bring out trained dogs. 'For there are a multitude of ducks and swans shot in the rivers and lagoons, and cannot be got at for want of a good water-dog,' wrote one migrant. The colony also wanted fast dogs 'to overtake the kangaroo for it bounds along at an astonishing rate'. Migrants hunted with such avidity and lack of discrimination that observers soon complained of the rapid depletion of wildlife. By the time the *Warrior* arrived at Swan River, the new colonists had reached an already impoverished land.[12]

Nevertheless, hunting continued. The possibility of extermination did not diminish the glee with which hunters stalked the ducks, swans, and pelicans of Swan River, or the kangaroos and wallabies of the plains. Hunters likened their pleasure to the delight of boys in England shooting their first woodpigeon or lying in ambush behind a hedge for an old crow.[13]

Colonists hunted not only for food and sport but also to affirm their new freedom from the restrictive and discriminatory game laws of Britain. There only gentry could hunt; laws reserved game for their exclusive use. At Swan River anyone with a cache of firearms, a pack of dogs, and a horse could appropriate, without restriction, wild creatures as game. At Swan River guns made everyone equal, at least among men.

But while immigrants needed only a gun to claim wildlife, only those with capital could claim land. Once settled, the *Warrior* passengers began to inventory their goods and stock and to apply for land grants. James Turner calculated his total outlay at £1800 and on 5 April applied for a grant of 25 026 acres. But the government recalculated his capital stock and awarded him a grant of 5000 acres less than he claimed. Nevertheless, he remained a potentially very large landowner, especially in comparison to other *Warrior* immigrants. A few days after Turner received notice of his grant, Captain Molloy received permission to select 12 813 acres, based on an outlay of £961. John Herring, a working man, who had left his wife and children in England, received credit for £57 10s and a grant of 766 acres.

Claims remained notional, however, when there was no worthwhile land left to select, certainly none at Swan River. The Bussells and Captain Molloy soon confirmed their lack of choice when, accompanied by Governor Stirling, they examined land in the vicinity of Perth. Their excursion took them into what settlers were already referring to as 'the bush'. 'Bush' derived from the Dutch word *bosch*, acquired at the Cape Colony and generalised from its original meaning as 'woods' into a generic description of unreclaimed land. The term signified the natural state of the country, whether covered in trees, shrubs, grass, or even barren soil. At Swan River, bush mostly included trees. In either case, the definition served to separate settlers from their surroundings.

From the earliest days of settlement, the British accepted the distinction between their own presence and nature, or the bush. A visitor to Fremantle in October 1829 thought settlement efforts so far had been puny but nonetheless sufficient for definition. He found Fremantle 'a mere encampment . . . consisting entirely of sand, and the "bush" or forest, extends to within a very short distance of it'. A sylvan border of darkness defined the limits of civilisation, of economic activity.[14]

Swan River settlers thought of Perth and Fremantle as bounded by wilderness. They saw forest trees at the edge of clearings as the advanced lines of the vast wilderness that lay beyond. 'From out of the depth of those woods,' wrote one settler who shuddered from the foreignness of the bush, 'rose the occasional shrieks of an owl, or other night bird, and at intervals the long dismal howl of a wild dog.' Colonists used the term 'bush' to denote land that lay beyond their cultivated and tamed boundaries. The bush lay outside of civilisation; the bush was country yet to be possessed and made useful.[15]

Captain Molloy was bewildered in the bush. He could not make up his mind. Without an agricultural background he was unable to judge land quality and therefore remained undecided about where to select his grant. Stirling, who entertained grand ambitions for expanding Western Australian settlement, took the opportunity of Molloy's indecision and agricultural inexperience to urge him to consider settling in the south. When Captain Molloy and the Bussells balked at the idea of taking up land on Geographe Bay, Stirling, notwithstanding his commitment of only a month earlier to open no more land after Leschenault, suddenly became enthusiastic about the country at Flinders Bay, near Cape Leeuwin, on the extreme southwest corner of the Australian continent.

Although Stirling had never actually seen the land around Cape Leeuwin, sealers who called at Fremantle reported the existence, near the cape, of a large inlet and river. Other observers reported land on the southern coast as 'fit for all rural purposes'. Stirling needed no further convincing. He was not bothered by any necessity for consistency in argument or commitment. Constancy applied only with respect to ambitions for himself and the colony of Western Australia. He believed in whatever was necessary at the time and to this end he devoted his whole attention. When so engaged he could be extraordinarily persuasive. Accordingly, he told Captain Molloy and the Bussells that the Cape Leeuwin district was attractive and boasted a sheltered port and a good river. Furthermore, if they should settle there, he promised government assistance in shipping, improvements to the port, and protection against the natives.

Georgiana Molloy was quickly convinced of the advantage of such a move. Perth, like Fremantle, was plagued by flies, fleas, and mosquitoes. Molloy found the insects so unrelenting she could not sleep till morning. The water gave her dysentery, while the heat made her 'quite delirious'. Now in the ninth month of her pregnancy, she was increasingly distressed and felt she was 'losing health and strength hourly'. The south promised a cooler climate and freedom from insects. The governor and Ellen Stirling urged her to prevail upon her husband to relocate. She agreed and 'earnestly persuaded Molloy to go at once thither'.[16]

The omens for a successful confinement at Swan River were not good. A high rate of mortality, particularly among children, struck the colony in the first several months of 1830. Debilitated scurvy sufferers succumbed to dysentery, which spread even among the relatively healthy. Pregnant women and young children were most prone. Matilda Byrne's two-year-old daughter, Selina, died at Fremantle in April. A month later the Byrnes' other daughter, three-year-old Fanny, also died. In February Ellen Stirling had given birth to a son, William; he died two months later, also of dysentery. On 24 April Molloy's maidservant, the debilitated Anne Dawson, gave birth to her first child. The baby died four days later.

In the face of Swan River misery and land scarcity, Captain Molloy and the Bussells agreed to move south. They realised, however, that they could not settle Flinders Bay alone. Shipboard life, while productive of dissension for some, had forced on many passengers the recognition that their own fate was entwined with that of others. Accordingly, Captain Molloy and the Bussells approached fellow *Warrior* passengers James Turner and John Herring and urged them to consider joining in pioneering the new settlement. The parties arranged to charter the *Emily Taylor*, captained by James McDermott, to take them south. Turner, who had the largest amount of goods and the greatest number of family, servants, and stock, furthermore agreed to pay nearly half of the £200 chartering cost. Captain Molloy and John Bussell paid £55 between them, Herring contributed a little, and Stirling agreed to make up a government party for the balance.

Everything the settlers had unloaded from the *Warrior* in March—goods, stock, machinery, provisions, and household effects—they now reloaded onto the *Emily Taylor* in the last week of April. All were eager to leave, the Bussells in particular. John and Charles Bussell believed that time was money: every hour wasted in idleness or in unnecessary delay would inevitably be attended with loss. They were convinced that if their labours were retarded or the sowing of their seed postponed to an unseasonable period, they would suffer privation and inconvenience.

On 29 April 1830 the *Emily Taylor* left Fremantle and sailed down the coast past Cape Naturaliste and around the surging seas of Cape Leeuwin, where the Indian and Southern oceans merge. Here in February the *Cumberland*, bound for Swan River from Van Diemen's Land and loaded with stock and trade goods, had floundered and was wrecked. The *Emily Taylor*, however, passed on round the Cape, tacked east, negotiated the string of rocks and rocky islets teeming with seals and known as the Saint Alouarn Islands, and sailed into Flinders Bay. The settlers travelled blind to the south. No one, including Stirling, knew anything about the Flinders Bay region. But this did not worry the irrepressibly optimistic governor.

Few founders of British colonies so intimately allied themselves with the success of their schemes as James Stirling. He was the instigator of the Swan River Colony, the first governor, and a pioneer landowner. He was an empire builder and he saw the expansion of settlement to Flinders Bay as a necessary and inevitable result of the decision to colonise Western Australia. His enthusiasm, force of personality, and self-assurance sustained the hopes and buoyed the spirits of those aboard the *Emily Taylor*.

On 2 May the ship anchored in Flinders Bay outside the entrance to a large inlet, the embouchement of a river. The next day Stirling, a party of officers, and the three principal settlers went ashore to examine the surrounding country. Stirling named the inlet Hardy Inlet, after Thomas Hardy, one of Nelson's officers at the Battle of

Trafalgar; he named the river the Blackwood, after Henry Blackwood, another of Nelson's officers. Over the next three days the explorers took daily boat trips around Hardy Inlet, inspected the shore, and determined a site on the western shore, just inside the mouth, for the township of Augusta. Surveyor-general J. S. Roe and Governor Stirling believed this location possessed 'excellent soil, plenty of good water, a pleasant aspect and easy access in moderate weather to the anchorage and to the interior country'.[17]

Stirling's coxswain, John Boultbee, who accompanied the governor during his explorations of the southern coast, including the highly lauded Leschenault Estuary, was unimpressed. Boultbee had spent time in temperate New Zealand; in comparison, the west coast of Australia seemed dismal indeed:

> From the very first time I saw the land from Cape Leeuwin to Swan River, I had a poor opinion of it, and whoever says there is anything promising in it, is a liar. It is a dreary, sandy, barren looking hole. . . . The coast is full of dangerous reefs and rocks. The fresh water scarce . . . in short, the whole is unpromising.[18]

Augusta, however, was different from the rest of New Holland. The mild climate and relatively heavy rainfall encouraged the growth of forest—heavy jarrah forest, a mixture of jarrah (*Eucalyptus marginata*) and marri (*E. calophylla*). Trees grew to the water's edge from the surrounding plains, in lavish abundance. The forest supported a dense understory of shrubs and ground plants, including colourful creepers, orchids, and other flowering plants. At various places the jarrah forest gave way to thickets of huge karri (*E. diversicolor*). Among the tallest trees in the world, karri's smooth white trunks rose with little taper to 60 metres before reaching the first branch; crowns often topped 80 or more metres. Karri forest had once extended over the entire southwest, but increasing aridity confined the species to pockets. Jarrah, tolerant of lower rainfall and poor soil and generally more adaptable than karri, can grow as either a small mallee or a giant forest tree. Special roots sink deep into the ground to tap water and enable jarrah to grow and flower during the long, dry southwest summer.

The Augusta settlers were, on first sight, pleased with the forest. They believed that trees grew only in fertile soil; the big trees and thick undergrowth of Augusta promised great agricultural potential. Stirling encouraged this belief. He never doubted the fecundity of his Australia Hesperia and found ample confirmation of his wisdom in choosing Hardy Inlet as a site for settlement. He found that the Blackwood ran north for fifteen miles, then east for ten miles. Good timber covered the banks. Exemplary land extended everywhere. 'The best soil, the finest blue gum and some good grass are to be found on the hilly land, but even on the rest of the land there is generally food for cattle, and on the downs skirting the coast very good sheep pasturage,' he reported. In short, Governor Stirling found perfect conditions for a contented, prosperous community.[19]

The settlers decided to stay. Having come so far at such expense, they had little choice. And, in prudent anticipation of trouble, they decided to stay together. As Vernon Bussell later explained, 'None of us wished to divide our force, so we took small grants on the place fixed for the town.'[20]

After the preliminary inspections, and mutual compliments regarding Stirling's sagacity in choosing Hardy Inlet and the settlers' wisdom in accepting his recommendation, disembarkation commenced. Settlers experienced the same unloading difficulties as at Fremantle. The *Emily Taylor* stood offshore while the ship's crew lent little assistance. The shortage of small vessels extended the discharge of cargo over four days. On 6 May the ship's boat began ferrying passengers to shallow water, from where they waded or were carried ashore, clutching the smaller animals, chickens, and rabbits. Horses and cattle made their own way through the surf and over the rocks onto the beach. James Turner used the raft he had built at Fremantle to fetch machinery, merchandise, and general stores, which the settlers then dragged across the sandbar mouth of the inlet to the white sand beach of the western shore. Here, at the end of the first day, they pitched tents, lit fires, and ate a meal of damper, pork, biscuits, and cheese, and drank tea and wine. They were excited by the prospects and promises of independence and felt confidence in their own energies and abilities. Even the stiff, cool westerly wind that heralded the start of winter felt exhilarating. They looked with pleasure on the shrubs and trees, the broad expanse of the inlet, and the numerous birds overhead.

Settlers had already begun the process of possession. Before they could truly call the land their own, the newcomers had to symbolise it, acquaint themselves with it, and name its recognisable features. Stirling obliged this necessity when he bestowed the names of English heroes on the surrounding landscape. These names—Blackwood and Hardy—rendered the strange, invaded, and newly claimed land familiar.

To make the land further habitable, settlers also had to demarcate the forest and bushland with familiar notation—chains, squares, perches, rods, and acres. Before he left on 12 May, Stirling instructed surveyor John Kellam to commence immediately a preliminary survey. But this survey might take months and in the meantime the settlers needed somewhere to settle. Captain Molloy, James Turner, John Herring, and the Bussells had already pressed Stirling with their impatience for land. Accordingly, he duplicated the peremptory, cavalier, and bountiful approach to apportioning land that he had adopted at Swan River: he walked along the beach of Hardy Inlet and marked out rough grants, extending from the water's edge into the forest. He allotted twenty acres to Turner, fifteen acres to Captain Molloy, ten acres each to the Bussells and Herring, and smaller blocks to Captain McDermott and to Kellam. He instructed Kellam to incorporate these initial grants into his larger survey and to remember that James Turner, Captain Molloy, and the Bussells had been promised first choice when the surveyed country was finally opened for selection.

Stirling left a small detachment of sailors under the command of Lieutenant Richard Dawson, to provide protection until the soldiers stationed at the unoccupied Leschenault Estuary could be moved to Augusta. For his last official act, Stirling presented Captain Molloy to the 52 settlers as their resident magistrate, to adjudicate among them and to represent them in their dealings with government.

Molloy's military service, however, ill-prepared him to direct or control the free-enterprising spirit that actuated the Augusta settlers. Although, like an army, settlers were intent on conquest and domination, they did not need military discipline to accomplish their goals; military subordination was incompatible with free colonisation. Individual desire for improvement provided all the direction necessary to engage in battle against the bush.

8

WILDERNESS

WITHIN DAYS OF GOVERNOR STIRLING'S DEPARTURE FROM AUGUSTA, winter rains began along the southern and western coasts of Western Australia. Settlers found scant protection in their tents. English canvas, exposed to Australian weather, to the sun, wind, and rain, soon dissolved and became frayed, tattered, thin, absorbent, and punctured. For the time being, however, the Augusta colonists had no other shelter.

On 24 May 1830, as the rain beat down from the west, Georgiana Molloy's labour began. She lay on a wooden plank in a cold and leaky tent, at the edge of the sodden forest, above the white sand beach, in agony. She did not know what assailed her but told her husband she had never been in so much pain in all her life. Captain Molloy called their servant, Ann Heppingstone, who recognised that her mistress was about to give birth. Captain Molloy left the tent. Twelve hours later the final labour began. Heppingstone fetched a box for Molloy to kneel on. Despite the umbrella her servant held over her, rain splashed Molloy's face as she delivered her baby on the ground. Heppingstone picked it up, roughly tied off the umbilical cord, and wrapped the child, a girl, in flannel. But the baby, Elizabeth Mary, was weak, had difficulty eating, lost weight daily, developed blisters and skin rashes, and died nine days later.[1]

To lose a newborn in the company of friends and familiar

surroundings was difficult enough, but Molloy faced the sad loss of an innocent child in the midst of a fearsomely remote and hostile world. She had accepted pain and risk to her own life to carry on the family and could hardly bear the death of her firstborn. Her body had told her that this child was the truest part of her and now it was lost.

Within weeks Molloy wrote to her mother with details of Elizabeth Mary's birth and death. Nearly three years later she would still recall the devastation the child's death brought her in an alien and repellent land. The wilderness of her surroundings accentuated her loss. She found the claustral forest impenetrable, physically and mentally. Not a single feature offered her imagination any purchase. In October 1833 she wrote to Helen Story, who had recently lost a child of her own, to offer condolences:

> I was indeed grieved my dear Nellie, to hear of the poor infant's demise for your sakes, not for its own. I could truly sympathize with you, for language refuses to utter what I experienced when mine died in my arms in this dreary land and no one but Molloy near me. . . . I thought I might have had one little bright object left to solace all the hardships and privations I endured and have still to go through.[2]

For Molloy the untamed, anonymous Australian bush was inexpressible. Only familiar surroundings afforded language and comfort. To articulate their place in the wilderness and to mitigate its indifference to their hopes and longings, she and her husband buried Elizabeth Mary in a grave sown with English clover and rye grass. This condolent scene evoked wonted images of Britain, although the exiled grave looked, in Georgiana Molloy's mind, 'so singular and solitary in this wilderness, of which I can scarcely give you an idea'.[3]

But Molloy's alienation from the new world could not be total; she had to concede something to her surroundings. When she laid Elizabeth Mary in her coffin she placed 'some little blue [native] flowers on her body'. And after she had planted the grave with hyacinth, she and her husband built a bower of bush twigs over which she trained some native creeper, which, she noted to her mother, 'in this country are very numerous'.[4]

Within two weeks of her child's death and burial, Molloy began her garden in the Australian bush. She had the labourer, James Staples, dig a patch of ground behind her tent, in which she planted jasmine, white lilies, bulbs from the Cape, seeds from England, and the yucca lilies from her mother.[5]

Meanwhile, settlers began settling. Captain Molloy directed surveyor John Kellam to mark out the boundaries of the town blocks, while landowners and their servants dug wells, cleared scrub, and worked to secure more permanent shelter, stockade their animals, ponder tree-felling techniques, and prepare vegetable gardens.

Captain Molloy began work on a small two-storey building with a veranda on a site with an imposing view up the inlet and less than 100 metres from the water's edge. To preclude the spread of fire, he copied the common colonial practice of setting the kitchen a little apart from the main building. Another exterior room housed the Molloys' principal servants, the Dawsons.

James Turner also started a two-storey house, but bigger than the Molloys', with a cellar and more rooms. He called his residence Albion, after the Roman name for Britain, which alludes to the white cliffs of Dover. He was pleased with his situation and although he felt he had never worked harder in his life, he claimed to enjoy good health.

Turner's servants put up huts and sheds but with the increasing cold and perpetual rain, they started grumbling. The married couples, in particular, saw little point to their labour as employees. They envied Augusta's several small independent settlers, whose establishments on small plots of land left vast areas unclaimed, and they felt that the country afforded them opportunities as well. They began to think they might do better on their own.

John, Charles, Vernon, and Alfred Bussell commenced their colonising with a vegetable garden. They planted seeds of radish, melon, cabbage, and carrot, and sets of potatoes brought from England, but found the soil rocky and unpromising. The potatoes failed. 'We have a crop of marbles rather than potatoes,' John reported three months later. Under the supervision of their more practical neighbour John Herring, the brothers put up the frame of a house and thatched the roof with rushes, which grew abundantly around the inlet. From constant pulling on the twine while tying the rushes to the roof battens, John Bussell badly injured a tendon in his finger and ceased work for seven weeks. Meanwhile, his brothers built a large farmhouse chimney with stone dug from the garden and carried to the house in a wheelbarrow. As an allusive acknowledgement of their proximity to the house of Resident Magistrate Molloy, the Bussells named their establishment Datchet, after Datchet in England, near Windsor, the home of the royal family. With the winter rains falling harder and harder, they pitched their porous tent under the thatched roof and interrupted house building to concentrate on tree removal.

For the British, trees, more than any other element of the landscape, were an index of soil quality. Short, straggly trees indicated poor, deficient soil; immense trees indicated immense fertility. And, because Augusta grew such an abundance of mighty forest trees, the settlers concluded that the soil possessed tremendous riches.

Since Mesolithic times, human progress in Britain had depended upon grubbing up and demolishing the trees that originally covered much of the land. The process accelerated in Neolithic times, when stone axes made felling trees more efficient. Clearing continued under the Romans, Saxons, and Danes. By the time of the Domesday Book, no more than 20 per cent of the country remained wooded. By the late thirteenth century, most of today's human settlements had been established, yet clearing continued. Forests became fleets of ships and agricultural clearings. In the sixteenth century, iron smelting used prodigious amounts of wood. Whole forests were felled to make charcoal fuel. The extension of empire devoured the land and the wild animals that once dwelled there.

By 1700 only about 16 per cent of England and Wales supported woodland. But British civilisation, like all civilisations, never recognised limits to its needs. By 1800 there were no more than two million acres of forest left. By the end of the Napoleonic Wars, England had been stripped almost completely of native woodland. A land of field, park, copse, plantation, and, in many parts, hedgerow timber, England possessed singularly little forest, natural or cultivated. Culture had remade the land into a human artefact.

Few regretted this development. The transformation of the English countryside symbolised and epitomised the triumph of man over nature. Progress from forest to field marked the course of civilisation. Early nineteenth-century Britons viewed forest as synonymous with wildness and danger. Forests were an abomination. Civilisation existed in opposition to forests; civilisation was incompatible with an aboriginal environment. Only in leaving and destroying forests would people find civility.[6]

'Human industry,' proclaimed the English writer William Howitt in 1838, 'has appropriated everything; fire, air, earth, everything is subjected, everything is tamed. The forests have ceased to be impenetrable; the rivers to be wild torrents; the mountains themselves to be savage.' For Howitt, the anthropomorphised British countryside smiled like a garden beneath the triumphant effect of British tillage. The disappearance of the forests gave vivid evidence of the progression of England in power and population.[7]

The Augusta settlers thus came from a long tradition whereby to cut down a tree was to strike a blow for progress. Under the regime of the axe, the forest, with its thickets and unreliable pathways and its unpredictable and dangerous inhabitants, would be domesticated. Allotments, clearings, houses, and fences would instil civic order. But for progress to triumph, the Augusta settlers had to clear

away 'trees of stupendous magnitude and great hardness'. Few
entered into the task with greater enthusiasm than the Bussells.[8]

Although, at least from a distance, Charles Bussell thought the
unbounded forest partly attractive, he wrote that it was 'almost
incredible that so fair a portion of the earth should have remained
so long uninhabited, save by its wretched aborigines'. He found the
prodigious tangle of life and death not only physically disruptive—'an
almost impenetrable undergrowth . . . and trees, which had been
blown over by the storm or prostrated . . . by the white ant,
obstructed our path at every turn'—but also psychically threatening.
The Bussell brothers were distressed to find how different the timber
was from that which grew in England; they were astonished at the
'amazing magnitude' of the trees and they feared the untamed bush.
Charles proposed a remedy: 'Nature has been permitted to run to
waste, and man, not to mention his fairer partners, is sadly wanted
to correct her too great luxuriance.'[9]

In practice, Charles's antidote to nature's wanton prodigality
amounted to felling trees. And, at least during the first few months
of settlement, the Augusta immigrants were willing and eager. Settlers
found themselves, in the words of a Swan River contemporary,
possessed of

> an emulative feeling [that] stimulates the natural industry of his
> constitution. The rattling clank of a neighbour's axe, the crashing
> fall of a heavy tree, seem to demand responsive exertions on his
> part, and give rise to an energy which quickly rouses within him
> the spirit of active labour.[10]

When they began clearing, settlers hoped that by cutting a few
roots, a strategically selected tree would topple and bring down its
neighbours. This approach failed; more direct methods proved just
as unproductive. An English axe made no impression upon the forest
giants. Half a dozen men laboured two or three days to fell, dig up,
and cut up a single tree. The slow and heavy work 'of subduing a

land into a garden' frustrated feelings of accomplishment. For the most part, however, settlers remained sanguine.[11]

At the end of August 1830, H.M.S. *Sulphur* sailed into Flinders Bay. A detachment of soldiers, under the command of Lieutenant D. H. McLeod, disembarked to replace the naval force temporarily stationed at Augusta in May. A medical officer, Dr Charles Simmons, also disembarked. In addition, the ship carried government dispatches and official notification of Captain Molloy's appointment as resident magistrate at a salary of £100 a year. Molloy acknowledged his assignment and sent the governor an optimistic report on the state of the settlement, noted measurable advance in forest clearance and the cropping of 'about 7 or 8 acres of ground', and praised nature's largesse. 'We have good water and abundance of fish,' he wrote. He added that he and Mrs Molloy looked forward to a future visit from Stirling and his wife, who would, he guaranteed, dine on produce from the Molloys' own garden. Notwithstanding nature's abundance and the productive art of farming, Molloy took the precaution of obtaining provisions from the ship.[12]

By the *Sulphur* the Bussells received a package of magazines and letters. John Bussell took the opportunity to write to his mother and report cautiously on the family's 'commencement of colonization'.[13]

For James Turner, communication meant combat. Ever since he left Fremantle for Augusta, Turner had been determined to challenge the government over the inadequacy of his 20 026-acre grant. He believed the colonial authorities had undervalued his capital worth and deprived him of 5000 extra acres. By the *Sulphur* he wrote to Stirling to ask him to restore this deducted land. Turner also claimed entitlement to an allotment next to the town spring and he requested Resident Magistrate Molloy to acquaint Stirling with his claim. To his brother in London Turner recounted his past and current misfortunes and difficulties but predicted progress and future comfort.[14]

Captain Molloy expected another ship in six weeks' time, but the vessel never arrived. Supplies of flour ran low and the resident magistrate ordered the settlement on half-rations of bread. Rationing lasted only three weeks, however. In November the schooner *Eagle* put in at Flinders Bay and Molloy bought another five hundredweight of flour. In a long letter to the colonial secretary he wondered if he had been acting rightly as resident magistrate. He felt uncharacteristically inadequate and confessed, 'I have been placed in circumstances which my former life supplies no example to guide me.'

Captain Molloy had spent his entire adult life in the military, under the command of, and exercising, military authority. Augusta's civilian population, however, rejected military discipline. Captain Molloy was exasperated to discover that he lacked both control over the ambition of the masters and sanction against the recalcitrance of the servants. Settlers had come to Australia to exercise self-interest, not self-restraint, and they resented authority. Masters felt entitled to government assistance without obligation, while servants quickly discovered that Australia lacked the foundations of authority of the Old World—the traditions of Church, class, and established property relations. The compulsions to labour for a master no longer existed; servants became less diligent and more assertive.[15]

In Britain the one relationship that connected precapitalist and capitalist society was that between master and servant, between superior and inferior. British theologian William Paley counselled the poor that servitude was the divinely ordained natural order of things, the best of all possible worlds, and the greatest source of happiness. To perpetuate this beneficial hierarchy, the possessing class in Western Australia imported its own servants.[16]

But in Australia, servants, like their masters, wanted independence. Masters accustomed to command were shocked to find that servants behaved as equals. James Turner's servants talked of leaving him. The Molloys' servants also wanted land of their own. Even the Bussells' fourteen-year-old servant boy, Edward Pearce, proved unwilling. Charles wrote, 'We have found Pearce almost everything that is a bad, a lazy, shuffling, pilfering scoundrel. To be plain, a complete townbred blackguard.'[17]

Restlessness among the servants reflected the restlessness that drove their masters to Western Australia in the first place. Emigrants with capital left to escape from a capitalist, industrialising Britain. They hoped to find in the Swan River Colony an arcadian idyll of landed gentry waited on by servants. They believed, with Paley, in social hierarchy. But they also trusted in the modern faith of self-interest. And a static society could not coexist with a society dedicated to the pursuit of self-interest. The pursuit of self-interest required and generated mobility, and mobility undermined Providentially allotted roles in life. Consequently, Australian colonial life bore no resemblance to an imagined arcadian England. The bush yielded no meek and orderly tradition of village labourers, tenant farmers, and respected squirearchy. Achievement depended upon individual effort and, even more crucially, as settlers quickly discovered, upon government support.

By the end of 1830 most Augusta settlers saw evidence of progress; almost all of them were out of tents. Turner's large house stood on the slope of the hill above and behind the Molloys'. The Bussells, John Herring, John Kellam, George Chapman (another independent settler), and Dr Simmons each had a wattle-and-daub cottage marked by rough clay chimneys. More modest huts housed the labourers and their families. Space had been cleared in the midst of forest. Belled animals wandered among the buildings and around the tangle of broken branches, prostrate tree trunks, and raw stumps. Rough wooden fences enclosed vegetable gardens and selected stock. Fences also protected, divided, distinguished, and abstracted the activities of the civilised Augusta settlers from nature.

Government, masters, and servants agreed that individual and collective progress and prosperity depended upon the subjugation of the bush. The conquest of the southwest of Australia began when the colonists bestowed the names of British national heroes on the river and inlet where they settled. Next, the contrived structures and allotments of the settlement received an imported nomenclature. In naming their establishments Albion and Datchet, James Turner and the Bussells imposed approximate analogies to elsewhere. Yet, amidst a cartography of misplaced metaphors, the settlers remained unsure how to view their surroundings. 'This place is beautifully picturesque,' John Bussell wrote to a fellow Oxford graduate, 'but so wild, so savage.'[18]

Bussell and his correspondent understood 'picturesque' to mean those irregular details, rough surfaces, and coarse textures in nature and art that pleased the eye with their chiaroscuro. Picturesque also described any scenery capable of assuming the form of pictures. A picture, in turn, was an object, an object that people stood before and looked at. The observer of picturesque scenery stepped back, detached and disinterested, or at least viewed the scene with a detachment that would be inconceivable if the viewer believed the surroundings possessed by spirits. Picturesque nature, then, was an object that existed apart from, and outside of, people.

Bussell distinguished picturesque landscape from wilderness, though the distinction was not always clear. Wilderness, like picturesque scenery, was an object, different chiefly in that in wilderness, space failed to congregate into picturesque forms and nature failed to speak, failed to provide even the minimum elements of scenery. Wilderness was a state of mute externality. John Bussell and his fellow settlers found Australian nature both picturesque and wild. In both cases, nature remained an object.[19]

But if John Bussell found the land wild and savage, and picturesque on occasion, he found the land's inhabitants entirely odious. In Australia, he wrote, 'Man [Aborigines] alas! is more uncultivated than all.'[20]

Initial contact between the Augusta settlers and the local Aborigines was uneventful. The settlers saw their first Aborigines two weeks after they landed, when a party of natives appeared on the opposite shore of the inlet. Later, contact was closer. 'They are quite strange,' Georgiana Molloy wrote to her mother, 'but always have evinced a friendly part towards us in the way of peace.'[21]

First contact was peaceful partly because it was infrequent, owing to the fact that the settlers landed in May, the start of winter, when Aborigines generally moved inland to escape the heavy rain and damp of the coast. But peace also reigned because the southwest Aborigines, the Nyungar [the people], could not imagine their land was being invaded.

In the Nyungar universe, everything was related. The world was not divided, as it was for nineteenth-century Europeans, between the observer and the observed, between picturesque landscape and wilderness. The world was whole and had been sung into existence by Dreamtime Ancestors. Nothing happened without a reason, without an explanation rooted in the Dreaming. Thus, to explain the settlers' sudden appearance, the Nyungar quickly came to believe that the colonists were the returning spirits, or reincarnates, of Nyungar dead. They welcomed their relatives back to the world and did not object to sharing the land.

At the time of first settlement, Nyungar guides courteously showed the *djanga* [the dead] a spring of fresh water. And through gesture, mime, and demonstration, they sought to reinstruct them in the ways of living off the land. Settlers learned how to kindle a fire by rapidly twirling a piece of the stem of the *Xanthorrhoea* plant (grass tree) within a hole cut in another piece. Dry material taken from the withered seedhead and placed around the point of contact would soon begin to smoke and then ignite.

Despite Nyungar practical advice and peaceful behaviour, John Bussell remained suspicious and apprehensive. 'There is something that makes one shudder,' he wrote, 'when one crosses unawares in his path, the naked "Lord of the forest".' For the most part, however, Bussell and the other settlers chose to suspend any admission of Aboriginal presence; they wanted to apprehend a country waiting for their own occupation. Therefore, in their minds, the land was empty. The land belonged to the colonists by virtue of their nationality; Britain was the first European power to lay claim to Australia's vacant western third.

Bussell gave voice to this assumption of *terra nullius* in a letter he wrote to a friend in England. To dramatise his own unique historical presence, he quoted the first two lines from Aeschylus's *Prometheus Bound*:

> Here we have reached the remotest region of the earth
> The haunt of Scythians, a wilderness without a footprint.[22]

Uninhabited wilderness, however, was hardly an accurate description of the wild, inhabited land of southwest Australia, where the footprints of thousands of generations of Aborigines had left the region crisscrossed with tracks. By the time British settlers founded Augusta, southwest Australia was already a highly cultivated region. Forty to fifty thousand years of Aboriginal occupation had created trails and water holes, yam grounds, and kangaroo grazing grounds; Aboriginal fire had created the country the settlers found so picturesque and so desirable. Nevertheless, like Prometheus, the settlers believed they had their own historical destiny, a path of possession, expansion, and liberation. Their purpose in coming to the southwest was occupation, ownership, and personal aggrandisement.

But by the end of 1830, owing to the incompetence of surveyor John Kellam, no settler had actually taken land outside the Augusta townsite. Kellam spent the winter building his hut and did not commence surveying until September. Four months later Resident Magistrate Molloy announced land open for selection. No one rushed to make a claim, however. After the struggle against the trees on their relatively small town lots, settlers were reluctant to assume larger commitments. They hoped, instead, to find more tractable land elsewhere. In the meantime, domestic and other distractions kept settlers preoccupied.

Four months after the death of her firstborn, Molloy was again pregnant. She did not, however, carry this pregnancy to term. On a hot night in December, while her husband and the colonial surgeon, Dr Simmons, were away in the bush, she 'was taken,' she later told her family, 'as in labour'. She felt 'as faint as death and in agony'. She could not call out and 'did not know what was happening'. Next morning Anne Dawson found her exhausted and soaked with blood. In silence and alone, Molloy had suffered a miscarriage. She laid herself up in bed for three weeks.[23]

By the end of the year, food supplies had again run low, vegetable gardens had not produced as expected, and the absence of shipping had left a shortage of flour, sugar, salt, tea, and meat. Captain Molloy rationed government stocks; to supplement their meagre allowance, settlers began spending more and more time in the bush, hunting. Fish swarmed in the river; ducks, herons, and swans abounded on the water. Catching the fish and shooting and retrieving the birds took time, however, and the birds, at least, soon grew shy of men with guns. Kangaroo flesh still tasted unusual, although settlers quickly learned to make a broth from the tail. Kangaroo hunting also took stealth and time. The problem of food temporarily diverted attention from land occupation.

From the time of their disembarkation at Augusta, the colonists knew of more open country along the coast at Geographe Bay, 80 kilometres to the north. Surveyor Kellam had accompanied the Collie and Roe expeditions to the Leschenault and Vasse inlets in November 1829 and March 1830, and he told the Blackwood settlers that the land there was superior to that at Augusta—at the least, less wooded. This observation, in particular, excited those with land to select.

For the moment, settlers remained clustered among the trees around Hardy Inlet. But the Bussells, less patient and more aspiring than their neighbours, began looking for less forested land beyond Augusta. During the first few months of 1831, John Bussell embarked on several exploring trips up the Blackwood River and beyond. In

March 1831 he, Charles, and Lieutenant McLeod rowed up the Blackwood and at various landing spots took short excursions into the bush. Aboriginal fires burned on both sides of the river—'a true picture of the realms of Pluto and the stygian stream', John Bussell thought. As the flames crackled and glared all around, Bussell chose the peninsula he planned to claim as part of his grant. He did not, however, regard the selection as permanent.[24]

Later in March, Bussell, with two Aboriginal guides, and John Dewar and Andrew Smith, indentured servants to James Turner, left Augusta to walk to Swan River. The party kept to the coast and lived largely on bush food procured through the help of the guides. Bussell kept an exploration journal and noted the coincidence between what he regarded as good country and fire. On the second day out he 'passed over better land . . . [which] had been lately burnt'. The next day he travelled through 'superior [country] undulating with fine valleys covered with silky grass . . . many excellent situations for farms well cleared of timber', and observed, 'the whole of the country . . . has been burnt'. He shortly after passed through the area around the Vasse estuary, but whether out of a desire to keep the information private, or because he fully expected to see what he saw and therefore found it not worth comment, Bussell did not record, at least on this expedition, his impressions of the open, grassy country.[25]

Bussell's reticence was unusual; other explorers who passed through the Vasse country were profuse in their praise of what they found.

In April 1831 Lieutenant William Preston, in charge of an exploring party travelling by sea and land from King George Sound to the Murray River via the Vasse, arrived at Augusta. Preston was impressed with the settlement and 'astonished to find so much had been done by the labouring classes in building their cottages and clearing their grants, and they all appeared perfectly happy and contented'. But contentment was not general. The more ambitious settlers wanted more land, more easily worked. As Preston prepared to depart, Charles Bussell and Lieutenant McLeod asked if they could accompany him as far as Geographe Bay, in order to examine the intervening country.

Like most early expeditions, the Preston party carried little or no water. They depended on rivers and swamps, but mostly, since they navigated via Aboriginal tracks, they sought replenishment at native wells. The *bidi* [Aboriginal path] that Preston followed passed by the best watering holes. Two days from Augusta, the party reached the edge of the Vasse plains. Here, at the end of the day, Preston found Charles Bussell so overcome by fatigue he recommended that Bussell and McLeod not continue with the main party. They parted next morning. Preston pushed on to the coast and lauded what he saw: the area around the Vasse contained 'the *finest land* I had yet seen in the colony. Settlers near this country can never want hay and food for their stock. The grass was thick, from three to four feet high.'[26]

Without having to say so, Preston knew the reason for the country's highly desirable appearance. He felt no compulsion to remark that the country was made accessible and traversable by Aboriginal fires. Preston was an experienced explorer for whom only unburnt country was unusual.

Within a year of the establishment of the Augusta settlement, John Bussell decided that the future lay not among the heavily timbered shores of Hardy Inlet but on the grassy, open, and well-maintained plains of the Vasse. Shortly after his March 1831 trip he again travelled northward from the Blackwood at Augusta along a route further from the coast and that followed, he hoped, 'as near as possible the direction of the future road' to the Vasse. He made notes of the best travelling country and avoided 'the bush, where unburnt, luxuriant'.[27]

But settlement at the Vasse would have to wait. The Bussells could not yet afford to leave the Blackwood region. In the meantime, however, they decided to relocate their homestead nineteen kilometres upriver, to a promontory John Bussell had claimed in March. They called the new grant Adelphi, from the Greek word for 'brothers'.

John Bussell gave cousin Capel Carter several reasons for the brothers' move. First, he disparaged the lack of ambition among the Augusta settlers who, he felt, were content to 'linger about the mouth of the river devoting themselves to the culture of small allotments'. His own aspirations could not be satisfied in such a complacent and limited society. He preferred his own company and that of his brothers to membership in the struggling community at Augusta. Second, isolation would reduce expenses. Distance from overpopulated Augusta would enable the brothers to procure more game, upon which they now depended. Lastly, the struggle against the rock and heavy timber of Augusta was futile; labour would yield a greater return on the less heavily forested land at the Adelphi.[28]

In July 1831 the Bussell brothers rowed up the river and claimed 40 acres at the Adelphi. Experienced now in the skills of colonisation, they erected their first hut in three weeks, raised a post-and-rail fence of split jarrah across the half-kilometre-wide neck of their peninsula, dug a well, made paths through the bush, and then extended their cottage into a four-room house with a drawing room and kitchen. John Bussell built a separate cottage for himself and his library. The work afforded greater satisfaction than labouring at Augusta, and the Bussells looked with pleasure at their progress and at 'the forest by degrees levelled to the ground'.[29]

Shortly after the Bussells moved from Augusta, George Chapman, now joined by his brothers James and Henry, claimed 3000 acres upriver from the Adelphi. The Bussells' Augusta neighbour, John Herring, claimed a grant nearby. Carpenters George Layman and John Cook, both of whom arrived in Augusta early in 1831 under contract to build military barracks, also wanted land, and they too took up grants along the Blackwood.

While the men on the Blackwood worked to claim land, extend their boundaries, build empires, and push back the walls of nature,

Georgiana Molloy accustomed herself to domestic labour. The Molloys had arrived at Augusta with five servants, but a few months later Robert Heppingstone, his wife, Ann, and their four children decided for independence and settled on their own town lot. The Molloys retained only the services of Elijah and Anne Dawson and labourer James Staples. Georgiana Molloy found Anne Dawson an unwilling maid and, in her stead, assumed the major responsibility for cooking, washing, and cleaning. She also took over the dairy. She churned the milk from two cows, pressed the sweet curd to the bottom of the cheese pan, boiled the whey for making whey butter, pressed the curd into cheese vats, placed the new cheese in the press, salted and turned it. She performed all these tasks by hand and found her daily life a sluggish routine that rewarded her with only torpor of mind.

Molloy continued to teach Bobby and Charlotte Heppingstone till, she told her mother, she 'found my other necessary occupations encroached on'. The eight-year-old Charlotte, however, stayed with the Molloys, for 'She works very well, indeed better either than her mother or Mrs Dawson.' Charlotte, Molloy hoped, 'will prove a reward to me in my riper years'.[30]

Daydreams afforded Molloy greater immediate relief. As she stood at the washtub, she thought of Rosneath and the Scottish countryside and nurtured a memory of violets and primroses. In contrast, her surroundings at Augusta offered her nothing on which to feast her imagination. From her house she looked out over Hardy Inlet to the undifferentiated blue-green forest that appeared unbounded, without limits, unimaginable, unknowable, and therefore suspect. Molloy shared John Bussell's ambivalence towards her surroundings. Augusta was beautiful and picturesque but also wild, savage, and uncompromising. The land needed taming, reshaping into recognisable and familiar forms. The Australian landscape was implausible and lacked all the allegories of life—Northern Hemisphere seasonality, deciduous trees, cultivated land—so cherished by an outlook shaped by the Romantic poets.

A flower garden, however, could start the process of reclamation, of redemption. Domesticated flowers were emblematic, comforting, and soothing. A well-ordered, regulated, and colourful garden set amidst the disorderly and monochromatic bush would provide an imaginative escape. Happily for Molloy, the seeds and cuttings she had planted in June throve in the damp Augusta soil and, by the time of her first Australian spring, were in flower.

But even the solace of a garden could not erase entirely Molloy's loneliness and isolation. No one at Augusta shared her religious interests. Although John Bussell had studied for the ministry, he belonged to the Church of England and disdained the appeal to the emotions of the Scottish revival. Moreover, Molloy's Augusta neighbours attached little importance to matters of the spirit, nor felt any urgent necessity to prepare for the next world. Their robust materialism distressed her.

Incessantly, insidiously, however, this world, the material world, constantly demanded Molloy's attention. The death of her firstborn and her subsequent miscarriage did not deter her or her husband from procreation. When she settled at Augusta, Georgiana Molloy embarked on a course of childbearing that lasted the rest of her life. In February 1831 she became pregnant for the third time.

9

SPIRIT AND NECESSITY

GEORGIANA MOLLOY'S THIRD PREGNANCY COINCIDED WITH THE second growing season at Augusta. The quickening of life within mirrored the increase of life in the outside world. With the coming of the winter rains in 1831, Molloy's flower garden flushed with life. Her garden, like all gardens, represented the threshold of the feminine mystery of birth and death, the site of renewal and decay, of giving and taking life. In stricter Christian teaching, the garden possessed significance as a place for spiritual reverie, a reminder both of Eden and of Christ's agony at Gethsemane. As a paradigm of life, the garden united genesis with death. Gardening was the one form of labour necessary even before the Fall, for when God put Adam in the Garden of Eden, He required him 'to dress it and to keep it'. This injunction created the idea that it would be possible to return to a state of prelapsarian grace by the cultivation of the soil.[1]

But cultivators were divided. The vegetable garden and the flower garden represented two fundamentally opposed ways of using the soil. In the vegetable garden, the gardener used nature as a means of subsistence; the garden's products were to be eaten. In the flower garden, the gardener sought to create order and aesthetic satisfaction and showed respect for the welfare of the species under cultivation. Molloy's flower gardening, her devotion to a fundamentally unproductive pursuit, distinguished her from her colonial neighbours. In fact, she told her mother she was 'the only Lady in the colony possessing a flower garden'.[2]

The practical Bussells, in particular, did not flower garden; they preserved a strictly utilitarian attitude towards the soil. The soil yielded either vegetables or grain or fodder but never beauty alone. While they often commented on Molloy's attachment to flowers, in all their voluminous writings about their lives as settlers, the Bussells never mentioned her garden. For Molloy, in contrast, her garden quickly became one of the main topics of her correspondence.

Differences in outlook did not, at least at first, cause dissension. On the contrary, the Bussells considered themselves fortunate to have the Molloys as their neighbours and co-colonists. Charles Bussell thought Captain Molloy 'a gentlemanly, good natured kind of man'. And when Captain Molloy advanced the Bussells stores on credit from government stocks and took responsibility for their servant, Pearce, when they could no longer afford to provide for him, John Bussell praised Molloy as 'really a most estimable man, but for him, I should be in a most unpleasant situation'. Of Georgiana Molloy, Charles wrote, 'She is perfectly ladylike and yet does not disdain the minutiae of domestic economy, an indispensable accomplishment in a settler's wife.' The Molloys did, however, belong to that group of settlers John Bussell disparaged as lingering 'about the mouth of the river devoting themselves to the culture of small allotments'.[3]

As resident magistrate, Captain Molloy had little choice but to stay at the township. He was not as mobile as the Bussells. Unlike the young, vigorous, and self-reliant brothers, the 50-year-old Captain Molloy was ill-disposed to periods of heavy physical effort and had to rely on the reluctant and scarce labour of others. Moreover, since his salary as resident magistrate and his military pension placed him in a comfortable financial position, he felt no urgency to select his 12 800-acre entitlement. He could afford to linger and so did not follow the Bussells' initiative in selecting land up the Blackwood. For the time being, he remained attached to his fifteen-acre Augusta town allotment.

The Bussells did not envy him, but they did wish to emulate at least one aspect of Captain Molloy's colonising experience. They quickly learned that the best, indeed the only, way to prosper in the new land was to follow the practice of the leading men of the colony and secure a remunerative government appointment. Although, like the colony's leading men, the Bussells were Tories and were, theoretically at least, in favour of minimum government, they understood the great benefits bestowed by a government sinecure. A cash income would serve as base capital from which investments could grow. Accordingly, Charles Bussell applied for the position of storekeeper at the settlement. Captain Molloy recommended the appointment and in 1831 Charles became Augusta's storekeeper at £60 a year. The brothers now had a steady income. Charles, however, had to stay at his post in Augusta.

During the first half of 1831, as Georgiana Molloy passed her first and second trimesters of pregnancy and tended her flower garden, the Bussells dreamed of war against the bush. By July, John, Vernon, and Alfred Bussell and the boy, Pearce, had moved onto the land at the Adelphi. Several other settlers prepared to follow the Bussells up the Blackwood. Those who remained at Augusta townsite continued working their lots. Prosperity seemed assured and in July Captain Molloy wrote to the colonial secretary to report progress and 'a degree of activity, confidence and industry among this increasing settlement'.

By 'activity' Captain Molloy meant male activity, the only kind of activity men considered worth reporting. Male confidence and male industry were the only legitimate measures of progress. Additionally, adventure and misadventure among the men of Augusta comprised the settlement's chief topics of interest and conversation.

During a severe July gale, high waves at the mouth of Hardy Inlet capsized the Bussells' rowboat. John and Vernon were washed overboard. They swam against the ebb tide to a sandbar. Afraid of being washed out to sea, they remained on the bar for several hours, up to their middles in water and encircled by sharks. Finally, the incoming tide enabled them to swim to shore. The boat was irretrievably lost, but next day John discovered another boat drifted ashore from the barque *Nimrod*, from India, which had anchored in Flinders Bay. The captain and passengers attended church service at the settlement. Later, John and Vernon, Lieutenant McLeod, and the settlement's new surgeon, Alfred Green, dined on board.

John and Vernon's mishap, the *Nimrod*'s visit, and the socialising that followed added colour and excitement to life at Augusta. John Bussell wrote of the shipboard dinner: 'Everything here is Indian or Chinese, Arabs standing behind your chair with their swarthy visages and many coloured habiliments. I find great amusement in obtaining an insight into the various manners of mankind.'[4]

The various manners of mankind failed to amuse Georgiana Molloy or relieve her loneliness. The settlement's male-initiated kinesis left her feeling solitary and remote. She did not seek the company of the other women at Augusta. Like them, she laboured at domestic work, but she had literary, religious, and botanical interests they did not. Furthermore, class differences kept the small community strictly segregated.

Nevertheless, Molloy began to identify with her chosen home and she shared the community's wish that outsiders form a good impression of Augusta. Settlers were proud of their efforts and even thought themselves morally superior to settlers at Swan River. Early in 1831 John Bussell wrote to Capel Carter that despite the hardships of life in the southwest, he was glad he had left Swan River. In settling Augusta, he told his English cousin, 'We have avoided a Rif Raf gentry or set of sharks and avid plundering monopolists and a debauched and discontented accumulation of labourers.' For proof of their progress, even of their superiority, the Augusta settlers solicited favourable comments from their infrequent visitors.[5]

133

Few visitors indulged the settlers with praise more willingly than Governor Stirling. Wherever he went in the colony—and he travelled extensively—Stirling presented a front of unassailable optimism and good cheer. Accompanied as often as possible by his young, attractive, and popular wife, he visited all the scattered settlements by turn. At each he artfully managed to convey to individual settlers that they merited his special interest and personal advice. He complimented each on his industry and commended the potential of his land. On 2 November 1831 he brought the good news to Augusta.

Stirling arrived on the *Sulphur* accompanied by his wife, Ellen Stirling, the colony's surveyor, J. S. Roe, and a visitor from India, recuperating in Western Australia, Colonel Hanson. The party dined at the Molloys'. Georgiana Molloy conversed with Colonel Hanson, who patronisingly described her as 'a very interesting young woman [who] complains sadly of solitude'. He dismissed her discontent as querulousness and refused to take her isolated circumstances seriously. He predicted her loneliness would soon end. 'As she appears to be in the way "Ladies wish to be who love their Lords," she will not be long without occupation,' he wrote. The nine-months-pregnant Molloy showed the visitors her blooming flower garden, her most tangible accomplishment after eighteen months' residence at Augusta. Hanson viewed the variegated scene indifferently and wrote, 'Mrs Molloy's garden abounds with the choicest flowers; but I am sorry to say I am unable to describe them more particularly than that they are all of them very fragrant and very beautiful.'[6]

In contrast to her first pregnancy, Molloy did not spend her third pregnancy aboard ship, restricted to a diet of salt meat and biscuits, constantly sick, confined, and suffering from scurvy. She had enjoyed a robust nine months in the 'heavenly clime' of Augusta, active about her house and garden and sustained by fresh food. A few days after the departure of the Stirlings, Molloy's labour began. On 7 November she gave birth to a strong and healthy daughter, Sabina.

The only untoward aspect of the birth, Molloy confided to her mother, was the afterbirth's lateness in coming away. Alfred Green, the attending physician, was worried and suggested an examination. Molloy thought Green incompetent, and his possible intervention frightened her. To be touched by Green, she told her mother, 'was so disagreeable to my feelings'. Molloy 'prayed most fervently to be relieved', fell into a deep sleep, and twelve hours later the afterbirth was discharged naturally.[7]

In Britain new mothers of Molloy's social class engaged wet nurses to breastfeed their babies. In Australia wet nurses were unavailable and Molloy fed Sabina herself. Previously when Molloy had thought about motherhood, she had not envisioned breastfeeding. Nevertheless, despite social disapproval of middle-class breastfeeding, at least in Britain, Molloy did not feel ashamed. Indeed, she took pride in an act that she saw as obviously self-reliant. She wrote to Margaret Dunlop, 'I need not blush to tell you I am, of necessity, my own nursery-maid.'[8]

By the time Molloy gave birth to Sabina, she retained the help of only one female servant, the sullen Anne Dawson. So besides breastfeeding Sabina, Molloy washed, scrubbed, and cleaned by hand, sewed and mended clothes, and cooked. She also attended to the clerical duties attached to her husband's position as resident magistrate. In November 1831, however, Governor Stirling appointed George Earl clerk to Captain Molloy. A linguist, writer, and adventurer, Earl took care of the considerable amount of paperwork that even a settlement as small as Augusta generated: statements of accounts for building, public accounts, provisions accounts, bills for the payment of the detachment of soldiers at Augusta, and salary abstracts.

Molloy enjoyed motherhood. She delighted in Sabina's every facial expression, every gurgle, every wave of her hand, and every kick of her legs. Pride and vanity she knew were perilous and subversive states of mind, but her daughter was still her pride and she took unabashed pleasure in the child's health and growth. In early March of 1832 the Stirlings again visited Augusta and Molloy extracted from Ellen Stirling the compliment that Sabina 'was the largest and finest child in the Colony'.[9]

With the sense of belonging and responsibility that a child brings, Molloy began to survey the world around her. There was much to discover. By the time Sabina was six months old, another winter had begun. And winter in the Australian bush, unlike winter in northern climates, brought into active life not only vegetation but many dormant and aestivating organisms as well. With the first rains, frogs appeared and croaked and bellowed all day and into the evening. Tadpoles swarmed in puddles and pools. As winter drew on, floods rinsed the Blackwood with fresh water and swept saltwater species into the sea. Mussels and crustaceans tunnelled the banks and the bush flushed with new growth: creepers, shrubs, and trees sprouted new shoots, seeds germinated. Molloy's garden plants also pushed out new shoots and formed buds.

Within the colony Molloy remained singular in her interests in gardening and botany, but many people in Britain shared her preoccupation. Popular gardening developed as a reaction to industrialisation. As factories spread over the countryside and people crowded into metropolitan areas, British town dwellers expressed their nostalgia for country life through their urban gardens. A vision of a country cottage, vine-covered, with hollyhocks, honeysuckle, and an apricot tree growing in nearby profusion, became the epitome of human felicity. But if a country cottage lay beyond the means of most people, a suburban flower garden was an acceptable substitute. In the early nineteenth century, small-scale domestic flower gardening became one of the most characteristic attributes of British life. Although flowers still held emblematic meaning as symbols of purity, beauty, and the shortness of life, people grew them chiefly for aesthetic pleasure. Flowers bespoke refinement and sensibility; gardens spread a taste for neatness and elegance. Honeysuckle around a cottage door was not just picturesque: it was also a sign of the sobriety, industry, and cleanliness of the inhabitants within.

As a refugee from an industrialising England, Molloy carried the prevailing passion for flowers with her to Australia. By the spring of 1832 she had a well-established garden of British, South African, and Australian flowers. This cultivated, domestic space provided reassurance and a sense of rootedness. She felt free and confident, at last, to write about her surroundings. In November 1832 she wrote enthusiastically and buoyantly to her previously estranged sister, Elizabeth. From her secure home in the bush she wrote of English gossip, her hopes for a piano, her child's birthday, and baby clothes. The outside, however, still remained suspect. From the sanctuary of her bounded Eden she surveyed the undifferentiated bush and recoiled with distaste:

> This is certainly a very beautiful place—but were it not for domestic charms the eye of the emigrant would soon weary of the unbounded limits of thickly clothed dark green forests where nothing can be descried to feast the imagination and where you can only say there must be some tribes of natives in those woods and they are the most degraded of humanity.[10]

But if the bush as a whole remained indescribable and unknowable, the bush's particularities began to be accessible. The freedom and courage Molloy's garden of exotic flowers gave her to express homesickness also drew her outward. For despite floral allusions to Britain and her former life, Molloy's plants grew in Australian soil, under Australian sun, enclosed by Australian bush. For all its repugnance, the view of the dreadful forest wrought a kind of awakening that made Molloy increasingly aware of the limitations of solitary introspection and appreciative of the pleasures and possibilities of the larger world.

Most Christians treated nature as an elaborate text composed of fixed lessons in morality. Many clergymen believed gardening was an activity that brought the gardener nearer to God, an activity appropriate for 'studious persons that have a taste for beauty and order'. But a subversive pagan theme intruded into this Christian pedagogic paradise. Paganism held that *this* world was beautiful too; behind its tangle, sorrow, and decay lay intelligence and goodness. Gardens complemented the pagan message, for gardens affirmed organic life. A garden supported real nonhuman organisms with their own self-determined existences.[11]

But gardens, especially gardens in the wilderness, also attracted other living creatures unaffiliated with God's grand design for humans. Molloy's garden in the midst of the bush attracted Australian birds. Their colours mesmerised her; she found them 'most brilliant in plumage' and to her sister she described the various birds that flew into her garden, including 'a small bird called the Australian robin with shining black back and head, and the breast of a very bright scarlet. Also a little bird of a complete blue colour all over resembling Smalt or Cobalt, with short green wings.' 'These little creatures,' she continued, 'seem quite delighted at the acquisition they have made in our emigration.' Molloy seemed, perhaps, not so much describing the birds' pleasure as her own.[12]

From the vantage point of her veranda she discovered not only the birds' 'perfect symmetry of form' but, on stepping into her surroundings, she commenced an exploration of the country's botany as well. Amidst what she had previously thought of as undifferentiated sameness, she uncovered difference. Strangely enough, plants that produced 'numerous kinds of leaves [bore] identical flowers'. She also discerned various flowers that were 'exceedingly small but beautiful in colour'. She discovered blossoms with 'powerfully sweet' fragrances, 'some like may, some like bergamot'. And although she could only describe and not yet name, she now recognised several distinct flowering species: a vine, common in the tangled undergrowth of the karri forest, with a great splash of gorgeous purple-blue flowers that appeared in mid-winter (*Hardenbergia comptoniana*), a shrub with leaves she likened to a holly (*Hovea chorizemifolia*), and a shrub, common in the jarrah forest and coastal woodlands, that she discovered possessed a scent like allspice or clove and that also bore purple flowers (*H. trisperma*). But Molloy did not just observe. She picked wildflowers and dried them but discovered that when dried, 'their exquisite colour fled'. She also started collecting seeds, feathers, and other natural curiosities to send her mother and sister.[13]

As she contemplated her freshly discovered surroundings, Molloy rejoiced in the decision to leave Britain. In Western Australia, 'We are freed from many unpleasant circumstances now existing in Britain,' she wrote to her sister. For whatever their difficulties—the battle against the trees, painfully slow progress in establishing agriculture, shortages of labour and supplies, and the infrequency and inadequacy of communicating with family and friends in Britain—settlers did not easily forget why they had emigrated. Industrialising Britain generated uncertainty, chaos, and social disintegration. Besides, on a practical level, colonists simply could not afford to look back. Embellished recollections of a former life of comfort and luxury among friends produced only discontent and unhappiness. They could afford to look only towards their future.[14]

But if colonists remained physically separate from their former homes and thankful for their emigration, they maintained other tangible and irrevocable links. Early nineteenth-century Britons were products of a written culture with a long, self-conscious historical tradition. European culture had produced an enormous and rich quantity of literature and history of art, expressive of an enormously diverse range of human experience, and with ancient antecedents. Educated and serious-minded persons like Georgiana Molloy and John Bussell sought and found authority in the written word. Discursive prose allowed them to think and reflect, to contemplate and learn.

People read not just for amusement or as a diversion. Earnest people looked on reading as mental instruction. John Bussell's colonial library contained works by Homer, Thucydides, Livy, Tacitus, Sophocles, Aeschylus, Xenophon, Horace, Quintilian, Lucretius, and Juvenal, as well as *Plutarch's Lives*, William Mitford's *History of Greece*, Nathaniel Hooke's four-volume *Roman History*, Charles Rollins's *Ancient History*, David Hume's *History of England*, Tobias Smollett's *History of England*, and Edward Gibbon's *Decline and Fall of the Roman Empire*. English literature and philosophy also filled Bussell's shelves, and he kept copies of Edward Malone's edition of *Shakespeare*, the novels and poems of Walter Scott, Noble's *Memoirs of Cromwell*, John Locke's *Essay on the Human Understanding*, and Bunyan's *Holy War*, as well as Byron, Gray, and Wordsworth. These ancient and modern authors provided Bussell with courage and power and the rhetorical means to apprehend and ultimately conquer a new country. The books, in their quantity and diversity, created a feeling of strength, permanence, and indestructible continuity. Bussell regarded his collection as a fortification, as personal armour. 'I clasp them as the old Greek did his personal shield,' he told his cousin.[15]

Georgiana Molloy's library, in contrast to aspiring clergyman Bussell's secular collection, was mostly religious. She allowed herself no time for secular books. Besides the texts she brought to Australia, relatives and friends continued to send her the latest religious tracts. Her sister Mary sent her a copy of the Scottish poet Robert Pollok's religious poem, *The Course of Time*, first published in 1828. Prolix, discursive, and seriously and earnestly morally correct, the book proved enormously popular and reached its fourth edition in 1828, its ninth in 1829, and its 25th in 1867. The 78 000th copy appeared in 1868. Molloy read *The Course of Time* avidly, finding in the blank verse a meal of healthful, useful, and thoughtful pedagogy. She recommended the book to Helen Story and described Pollok's eschatology, after her third reading, as 'delightful'.[16]

Pollok constructed *The Course of Time* as a meditation upon human destiny, damnation, and deliverance. In the course of ten long chapters he traced man's ascent from a corrupt, decayed earth to renewed and everlasting life. Pollok exhibited a medieval outlook on time, a preoccupation with eternity, and an obsession with the final judgement, 'the final doom of man'. Like St Augustine, Pollok considered time as something that resided in the soul, and he sought to divert readers from the utter folly of pursuing earthly schemes to happiness. The consequences of such distraction were disastrous. The quest for earthly pleasure brought ruin and damnation. Only through the knowledge offered by the Bible could man transcend the vanities and trifles of material existence and find true happiness.

But Pollok did not disdain corporeity entirely. He glorified the felicity of rural solitude and especially the bliss of motherhood. To women he offered the solicitude of domestic contentment:

> . . . Her house
> Was ordered well, her children taught the way
> Of life, who, rising up in honour, called
> Her blest. Best pleased to be admired at home,
> And hear, reflected from her husband's praise
> Her own, she sought no gaze of foreign eye;
> His praise alone, and faithful love, and trust
> Reposed, was happiness enough for her.[17]

Pollok's view of women duplicated that of Milton, to whose verse Molloy was especially attached. Milton expected a woman to act as an unquestioning executor of her husband's ideas. In *Paradise Lost*, Molloy's favourite poem, she read the familiar praise of submissive domesticity:

> . . . for nothing lovelier can be found
> In Woman, than to study household good,
> And good works in her Husband to promote.[18]

In the nineteenth century all educated people read Milton; they relished his elevation of mind, sonority of language, and relevance. His readers assumed he was talking about them in his poems *Paradise*

Lost, Paradise Regained, and *Samson Agonistes.* In these works Milton promised that, although life was difficult, God was a loving God and there was a Redeemer. But Milton was also a puritan and considered love good only insofar as it stabilised marriage and the family and was founded on reason. He valued austerity, rationality, and control. Overt passion was bad. Passion distracted man from his God-given tasks of making money and improving his own position. And nothing distracted man so much as woman. For Milton, woman was liar and cheat, a seductive siren who could not keep a secret once she had managed to winkle it out. Woman was a wicked, sensual snare laid for men.

Molloy did not reject, at least consciously, this misogyny. She did not even detect the hatred and distrust of women that pervaded the verse of Milton and Pollok. She accepted faithfully the advice of her male superiors concerning woman's proper role. But the assumption of domestic chores and of wifely duties at Augusta did not bring the spiritual repose Milton and Pollok promised. Molloy remained dissatisfied. Her husband's praise was insufficient. Her reading and seeking disclosed the profound unease that disturbed her life. Self-examination revealed an attachment to a world she knew was corrupt and decayed. 'I cannot help looking at myself,' she confided to Helen Story, without discovering that

> I am not exalted enough from the world to look only to where I know my peace lies. I ask myself if I possess the Fruits of the Spirit—Love, Joy, Peace. No, no, no. St. John says, 'Try the spirits whether they be of God.' But I would write volumes for I have no Physician here to apply to, and really long and pray for some faithful minister.[19]

Unfortunately for Molloy's peace of mind, no one at Augusta, in their scramble to clear and build, to sow and reap, shared her preoccupation with religious grace, and she found no one in whom to confide. She looked in vain for a confessor under whose guidance she might be nurtured and strengthened in the ways of God. Instead, she suffered disquietude and painful fluctuations of mind.

Captain Molloy did not share his wife's convulsion of piety. Although he dutifully observed the Sabbath—as resident magistrate, he had ordered community observance from the beginning of their arrival at Augusta—and read prayers and a sermon, the quest for spiritual enlightenment did not consume his waking moments. Unlike his high-minded, devout wife, he spent his leisure time reading for pleasure. He did not feel compelled to seek peace in believing. Instead, he enjoyed the flippant and jocose reminiscences of the Peninsula War by his fellow officers. He read Jonathan Leach's *Rough Notes of the Life of an old Soldier* and John Kincaid's *Adventures in the Rifle Brigade*. Molloy disparaged her husband's reading habits, as she herself 'read only books relating to religion'. She especially objected to Kincaid's book, partly because her husband told her it contained an occasional 'damn'. But perhaps she was also repulsed by the unabashed, crude masculinity of Kincaid's overwhelmingly male world. She stated flatly, 'I do not intend to read it.'[20]

Any deviation from religious pursuits brought on an uneasy conscience, and she wrote, 'I confine myself chiefly to [religious] books for my conscience seems to say when reading others, "Is your peace made with God?" ' Molloy's troubled conscience assured her that no, her peace with God was not yet made. The object of life, she knew, was to prepare for death, when the faithful would ascend to renewed and everlasting life. But she did not feel prepared.[21]

Pioneering, meanwhile, required a commitment to the temporal world. Building a home and making a living in the bush required faith in the idea of earthly improvement. In practical matters, immigrants had to abandon preoccupations with eternity. After all, colonists lived in the expectation that future earthly years would bring improvement over the present ones. Otherwise, why continue to struggle?

But this necessary obsession with the material world proved

vexatious for Molloy. Focus on the here and now subverted attention to the possibilities of eternal rapture with God. Molloy's religious thought was at variance with the imperatives of existence at the edge of the southwest Australian forest. She could not avoid concessions to worldly matters. Life in the bush demanded daily participation; domestic chores and child care took all her time. Moreover, Molloy was not indifferent to the interval chiefly occupied by drudgery—as she frequently described her domestic work. For the sake of the temporal world, Molloy dated her letters, kept a diary, and shared her husband's colonising hopes and plans, which exalted the importance of worldly time.

Was it possible to find a balance between this world and the next? Molloy's reading suggested only a very painful answer. Along with many Christians of her time, Molloy was fascinated by John Sargent's *A Memoir of Rev. Henry Martyn, B.D.* Like Pollok's poem, Martyn's life was dedicated to the advocacy of the superiority of spiritual knowledge. Born in 1781, Martyn studied for Anglican Holy Orders at Cambridge. He joined the East India Company, as chaplain, in 1805 in Bengal, where he evangelised among the natives and oversaw translations of the Bible into the vernacular. He died of the plague at Tokat, Persia, in 1812, aged 31.

His career of selfless devotion created a profound impression on his contemporaries. Sargent's *Memoir*, first published in 1819 and chiefly a diary of Martyn's missionary years, ran through ten editions before 1837. The book's rapid sale evidenced the deep interest of the Christian world in his life. Although singularly unsuccessful in converting the heathen, Martyn's failure seemed only to further excite the admiration of his contemporaries.

Evangelising subjected Martyn to severe trials of faith and patience. He avoided earthly happiness and pleasure in order to achieve a higher state. He aimed for complete abstraction from the vanities of the world and wrote, 'Mere earthly affections are weakened by time and absence; but Christian love grows stronger as the day of salvation approaches.'[22]

The existence of a world of sinners, unrepentant and indifferent to Christian entreaties, caused Martyn great anguish. Convinced that the day of death was better than the day of one's birth, Martyn prayed to his God, 'O hasten the day when I shall leave the world to come to thee; when I shall no more be vexed, and astonished, and pained, at the universal wickedness of this lost earth.'[23]

Martyn's life was a religious version of the sentimental, mawkish romances popular at the time—tales of a moral innocent abroad in a corrupt world. Like the Christian heroine Isabella Campbell in Robert Story's *Peace in Believing*, Martyn was not at home in the world. He could not compete with its rampant energies. Molloy identified with that role. Like Martyn, she was repelled by a sinful world. She longed to withdraw from the dark atheistical state that surrounded her. In the meantime, she lived amidst infidels.

To reassure herself of the righteousness of her own life, Molloy deplored the indulgent proclivities and preferences of others at Augusta. She found plenty of behaviour to censure. The military garrison brought a rougher element into the small community. Soldiers sought amusement in drinking and were unenlightened by the Sabbath observances they attended under orders. They and their wives refused to take Captain Molloy's Sunday sermons seriously. 'All is heard as if not heard,' complained Georgiana Molloy, 'and the soldiers' wives, who are compelled to attend or to go without their rations, very often quit the service in the middle of it to hold their inebrious orgies.'[24]

But if the conduct of others, particularly those who belonged to the lower classes, provoked the ire and condemnation of Molloy, other colonists were not so preoccupied. Molloy's neighbours had migrated to Australia to prosper materially, not to improve morally, and their concerns focused on the profitability of land, not on the upholding of Old World virtues. In the new world of Australia they anticipated wringing human plenty from the wealth of nature. Moral improvement would follow automatically.

1 0

A WORLD OF READY
WEALTH

FROM THE MOMENT THEY ARRIVED IN WESTERN AUSTRALIA, THE
Bussell brothers never passed a single instant perfectly and completely
satisfied with their situation. They were perpetual seekers of alter-
ation and improvement. Even as they began the development of their
land at the Adelphi, John, Charles, Vernon, and Alfred continued to
venture after property elsewhere.

In November 1831, after only five months at the Adelphi, John
Bussell's restlessness drove him to the Vasse again. He travelled with
the soldier Kenny and Augusta's new surveyor, R. Edwards. Kenny
had been with the Preston expedition the previous April and both
he and Edwards had accompanied Stirling's original Vasse exploration in March 1830. Bussell depended for his direction less on his
well-travelled companions, however, than on the Nyungar, whose
tracks had left a *bidi* that led straight from the Blackwood to the
Vasse country.

Soon after leaving the Blackwood, Bussell's expedition made a
good quick march 'over country clean burnt'. Next day Bussell found
'the best land I had yet seen, a rich red loam, it had been recently
burnt, and was therefore free from a woody bush and covered with
a herb much resembling clover'. Although Nyungar fire had removed
obstructing undergrowth, the way around other obstacles required
more explicit Aboriginal direction. On the banks of a seemingly

impassable river in flood, the party met an old man who obligingly pointed to the best crossing place.

When Bussell reached the Vasse he rejoiced in a country 'so clear that a farmer could hardly grudge the fine spreading trees of the red and white gum and peppermint the small portions of ground that they occupied only to ornament'. Such splendid country could not remain unoccupied for long, and Bussell predicted an imminent flow of population towards this prospect, away from the Blackwood.[1]

What John Bussell found so appealing had been, like the picturesque scenery at Augusta, created by the Nyungar. The Vasse plains were not naturally open and grassy but had been cultured by the careful and systematic use of fire. Although resident in the colony less than two years, Bussell certainly understood the purpose of Aboriginal fire. He clearly recognised the concordance between the open, grassy country he coveted and the open, grassy country produced by Aboriginal burning.

Burning was not an incidental activity of Nyungar life but an intrinsic part of normal existence. The Nyungar used fire as an aid to hunting; animals could be speared or clubbed as they broke cover to escape the flames. Firing the bush also served longer-term interests. After a fire, vegetation regenerated and the sweetened grasses attracted kangaroos. Fire also encouraged the regrowth of edible plants, such as bracken roots, young leaves, shoots, and yams, or *djubak*. Regular and conscious firing of the bush suppressed the invading scrub and kept the most-used areas of the southwest clear of undergrowth and small timber, and open for the free movement of people and large animals. Settlers found that country sympathetic to Aboriginal travel and food gathering and covered with grass for kangaroos was equally accessible and attractive to European agriculture and European stock.

Blackened tree trunks and open woodland were not the only evidence of a ubiquitous Aboriginal presence at the Vasse. Nyungar footsteps were everywhere. These too were useful. To extend his exploration, John Bussell followed the 'native paths which traversed these lawns in every direction'. Bussell did not travel unobserved. Vasse Aborigines were well aware of the strangers' intrusion. Near the mouth of the Vasse River, three men approached the party. In hopes of humouring them, the explorers demonstrated the magic of a flint firelock and produced a spark. Bussell, for whom skin colour and appearance represented real and discrete biological difference, observed:

> The countenances of two of them were certainly ugly and brutal enough: but the third had a sprightly air and good humored expression unaccompanied with that revolting laugh, which is so general with these savages. His hair [was] matted with peculiar taste into strings resembling spun yarn and bound up close displayed a head of true Caucasian proportion, with a facial angle less acute than is often observable in the European.[2]

Despite revulsion at the men's ugliness, Bussell felt prudence demanded peace. He wanted to ensure 'that the population about to flow towards the Vasse' met a friendly reception. With himself as paragon, he hoped his interlocutors would circulate a favourable report on Europeans among their kinsfolk. To determine whether the Vasse natives had anything in common with those of Augusta and might thus prove as tractable, Bussell obtained a number of words of vocabulary. The result, he gratefully reported, 'struck me as a considerable evidence of connection existing between them and the savages of Cape Leeuwin'. Indeed, the fact that the Aborigines had any language at all surprised Bussell. From his reading of the English theologian William Paley, he expected the savages of Australia to be without speech. He reported, however, that 'that certainly is not the case'.[3]

Although Bussell discovered that Aborigines used nouns and named objects, he still did not believe they possessed a grammar. He believed the semantic constructions of so rude and simple a people were inartificial and elementary in the extreme. It was not credible that savages should have refinement of phrasing.

Most Western Australian observers shared Bussell's depreciatory view of Aboriginal language. At Augusta, King George Sound, and Swan River, settlers collected word lists but compiled no extended texts recording what Aboriginal speakers used the words to articulate. Colonial glossarists did not expect to find subtlety and complexity of expression and therefore did not listen for it. Lack of interest in the country's indigenous inhabitants translated into indifference as to what Aborigines actually had to say. Queries about names of objects characterised the method of interrogators more used to taking than talking. Collecting words betrayed no sympathy with occasion and context. Real acquisition of language presupposed amicability or at least, interaction. Cordial relationships were essential for the learner to obtain any fluency. But the settlers had neither the inclination nor the time to cultivate real friendships with Aborigines, whom they regarded as little above brute creation.[4]

All indigenous Australians, including the Nyungar, used vocabularies of at least 10 000 words—about the size of the working vocabulary of any member of any language group anywhere in the world. Subtle and intricate grammars characterised all the approximately 200 distinct languages spoken by the Aborigines of Australia. Words inflected for case, tense, and mood in a manner reminiscent of Latin and Greek. Aborigines made semantic distinctions and ingenious contrasts that related directly to physical and social aspects of their lives. Since affective relationships, not economics, were central to Aboriginal life, Aborigines drew upon an enormously rich vocabulary to describe the network of relationships in which their lives were embedded. Specialised verbs existed for referring to the satisfaction of social obligation that depended on specific kinship ties. Language also contained rich classes of adjectives that described physical properties of things, types of skill and mental attitudes, feelings and propensities of people. Classes of adjectives also applied to the inclinations and characteristics inherent in all life, not just human life. Verbs were similarly expressive. A series of Nyungar verbs, for example, applied to different kinds of spearing, depending on whether the spear was held on to or let go, whether the target could be seen or not, and whether the activity took place by day or at night, using artificial light. Aboriginal languages contained far fewer generic terms than European languages, however. Aborigines valued allusive speech in certain social contexts, but when speaking of objects, they esteemed explicit description. Among the Nyungar, for example, a snake would always receive its species-specific name; the generic term, snake, would apply if the observer noticed only the tail and could not identify the species.[5]

Aided by their keen interest in language matters, the Nyungar did most of the learning that took place between themselves and the southwest settlers. The Nyungar initiated communication and quickly acquired elements of English. In early 1831 John Bussell noted that coastal Aborigines already used the word 'woman' for 'the name of their female'. Bussell was puzzled by this use of English, which preceded the Augusta settlement. But from early in the century, Aborigines had had contact and confrontation with the sealers who hunted among the abundant seal colonies along the south and west coasts and who abducted Aboriginal women for use as concubines and labourers. Growing Nyungar knowledge of the British invaders was not reciprocated.[6]

Besides yielding their women, under threat of force, to marauding sealers and acting as willing guides and unwitting hosts to insistent settlers, the Nyungar also furnished a scale by which colonists could measure their own civilised achievements. The bias of progress led nineteenth-century Britons to view the past as ever more inadequate the further back one went. As Aborigines represented the most fundamental state of human existence, they also represented the most inferior. Therefore, each encounter with the Nyungar provided settlers with an occasion to reflect on British superiority.

Vernon Bussell once witnessed an altercation among the natives, during which a woman was hit. He subsequently reflected on his own advanced moral state and observed, 'I could not help thinking how differently we, who have been debarred from female society so long, would have behaved.' Only under the shield of nineteenth-century British Christianity were women safe from insult, degradation, and slavery.[7]

Vernon always felt superior around Aborigines and was often flippant and patronising. He also found them intensely irritating. He resented his dependence on their knowledge and skills. Once, in search of stray cattle from the Adelphi, while guided by the brothers Wooberdung and Gahpot, Vernon camped with a group of his guides' extended family. Bussell distributed rations to his guides but gave none to his hosts. Gahpot, as obliged by Aboriginal custom, shared his flour and damper among his kin. Bussell objected to this further distribution and castigated Gahpot.[8]

The Bussell brothers shared Vernon's disgust at seeing precious provisions distributed among undeserving Aborigines. Indefatigable workers, they expected everyone about them to be so too. They had learned frugality in the exacting years after their father's death and they sought to instruct others in the same lessons. Industrious, clearheaded, sensible, and efficient, the Bussells could not abide Aboriginal detachment from the world of things and material aspiration.

Aborigines placed no value on the abstract or the deferred. Objects they could not use or make useful, other than sacred objects, had no value. Settlers could not understand how a people without desire could feel sufficient. According to the creed of self-improvers, the purpose of the needs of the body, of desires, was to rouse the spirit and make it capable of progress. Thus progress was innate, built into the human constitution. Among Aborigines, however, desire for progress seemed deficient. Indeed, colonial linguists held that the Nyungar did not even have expressions for wishes or wants.[9]

But the lack of understandable motivation and material desire was not a problem confined to Australian Aborigines. The contrast between the seeming satisfaction of native peoples everywhere and the energy and restlessness of industrial Britain preoccupied nineteenth-century British imperial planners and theorists. Classical economists could not believe that people who possessed no wealth and little opportunity or inclination to truck and barter were happy. Only hard work and economic exchange could make the lazy inhabitants of the New World content. Indigenous people, however, lived on the produce of the land and had nothing to trade in return for all the goods that British exporters were frantic to sell them. Thomas Malthus argued:

> The greatest of all difficulties in converting uncivilized and thinly peopled countries into civilized and populous ones, is to inspire them with the wants best calculated to excite their exertions in the production of wealth. One of the greatest benefits which foreign commerce confers, and the reason why it has always appeared an almost necessary ingredient in the progress of wealth, is its tendency to inspire new wants, to form new tastes, and to furnish fresh motives for industry.[10]

Western Australian settlers understood that civilisation was characterised by discontent, myriad wants, and a progressive, improving outlook. In contrast, Aboriginal composure and lightness of touch in dealing with the surrounding world represented barbarism.

Settlers, however, had not come to Western Australia to convert the heathen. Migrants wanted land, and colonists supported whatever pretense was necessary to secure what they must have.

In claiming the whole of New Holland for Britain, Captain Fremantle had thereby turned all the inhabitants of the west coast into British subjects entitled to the full protection of British law. But settlers were unprepared to accept Aborigines as subjects entitled to rights, particularly the right to their own soil. Settlers preferred to justify Fremantle's annexation and their own subsequent occupation on the principle that the land was originally unoccupied. The Aborigines, therefore, did not legally exist—a fiction that settlers managed to maintain even in their personal letters and journals.

Aboriginal presence was only incidental, when not ignored entirely. Aborigines appeared in journals, diaries, and letters only insofar as they successfully aped European cultural norms and commanded the rudiments and rhetorical occasions of English speech. Wooberdung, Gahpot, and their relatives appeared in Vernon Bussell's letters only when they rendered useful assistance as guides, or because they were annoying, and because they spoke English. To the rest of Aboriginal life, to the great bulk of what really mattered to the Aborigines, Vernon Bussell, like other settlers, remained wilfully ignorant.

And what really mattered to the Nyungar, as for all Aboriginal Australians, was the land. Unlike the settlers, who anticipated change, transformation, and increase, the Nyungar looked on their country as already abundantly stocked with the means of life. Although they experienced periods of hunger and scarcity, the Nyungar boasted of the plenty with which the Ancestors had endowed them. To commemorate their Ancestors' fecundity, they called their country *Bibbulmun*—the land of many breasts. They knew exactly what their land produced, the proper period for seasonal produce, and the best times for hunting and gathering. Normally they procured a sufficiency with minimum effort. One local observer conceded that, 'In all ordinary seasons [Aborigines] can obtain, in two or three hours, a sufficient supply of food for the day.'[11]

According to the Nyungar, the land gave so generously because of the essential kinship of all life. The natural world was a myriad of living things in social union. People were related to, and dependent upon, innumerable beings, extending in a web of reaction to every human action throughout the world. Each man and woman knew his or her kin among the animals, trees, plants, and stars, and their

duties towards them, and acted out their parts at dances and ceremonies. Reciprocity was the order of the universe, and all Nyungar
activity attested to the land's organic entity.

Travel, in particular, simultaneously affirmed and implanted
meaning in every physical feature of the terrain. The Nyungar were
always moving, an ebb and flow, up and down, from the coast to
the inland, from the estuaries to the bush, according to the seasons,
the ripening fruits, and the migrations of birds and animals on which
they depended for food. No boundaries, geographical or conceptual,
hindered physical or emotional movement. Travel consisted of visiting
a sequence of known places via a grid of familiar Ancestor tracks
and sacred sites. Travel renewed contact with the deeds of the
Ancestors commemorated in each uniquely and precisely named
locality, resting place, riverbend, swamp, and water hole, each and
every hill and shoreline. Travel instilled a sense of place and a feeling
of belonging.

No such familiarity aided the first settlers. The migrant invaders
undertook explorations into unknown land, into a fearful environment without place names. The southwest became comprehensible
and tame only after the Bussells and their fellow explorers applied
their own names and grids to its features. The Nyungar had named
the land, invested each rock and tree and animal with spiritual
significance, in order to inhabit it. The settlers named the land,
bestowed their own names on the rivers and estuaries, in order to
possess and conquer it.

Whereas the settlers believed that landscape features were nothing but natural forms—hills were hills and rivers were rivers—the
Nyungar understood such undulations as signs, evidence that something happened long ago, something mysterious and momentous.
Independent nature did not exist in the Nyungar world. The Nyungar
language contained no word for nature. To the Nyungar, nature as
understood by the settlers—an external realm, part of God's creation
but nonetheless separate from people—was an absurdity.

For example, the Nyungar had their own explanation for the origin of the crimson-flowered creeper (*Kennedia coccinea*) that Georgiana Molloy discovered growing so profusely in the karri forest. In the Dreaming the unhappily married Yoondalong eloped with her lover, Boojin. Yoondalong's husband gave chase. The pursued couple ran through the forest, where Yoondalong cut her foot on a rock. The couple eventually escaped, but all along the route they had travelled, a creeper sprang up, reddened by the blood that had flowed from Yoondalong's foot.[12]

John Bussell saw no such affiliation. For him, the land was mute. Indeed, when Bussell marched through a landscape that, to him, appeared all the same, he described the prospect as one where 'the face of nature . . . exhibited little change'. Even though he meant this metaphorically, to the Nyungar his description would still have made no sense: the land did not materialise as an object face that wore an independent visage. Only the all-encompassing Dreaming existed. The Dreaming placed an interdependent construction on the landscape. The Dreaming gave cohesive meaning to the world and turned the landscape into a mythical topographical map.[13]

In order to claim the land as their own, to wrest it from the Nyungar, the settlers had first to redefine and rename the landscape. Thus, John Bussell did not undertake his excursions out of curiosity, or even to discover, but to impose a nomenclature on, and to take possession of, a land he already knew existed. He understood that possession involved enclosing the coveted land in a net of familiar association. To take possession, he had to erase Nyungar meanings. To take possession, he had to destroy the Dreaming.

Exploration civilised a country by translating it into English and into familiar cultural paradigms. John Bussell civilised the southwest by assigning his own analogies and metaphors. His classical education equipped him with the means to reinterpret the country in recognisable form. Features of the land and incidents of travel reminded him of scenes from the classics, and he recorded these perceived affinities at length.

During his trip to the Vasse in November 1831, the sight of his companions kindling a fire and preparing food reminded Bussell of a scene from the *Aeneid*. He noted Virgil's Latin verse in his journal and then, 'for those whose memories fail to recall one of the earlier lessons of the grammar', he offered a free and colourful translation:

Achates from the flints mysterious springs

Strikes out the latent spark, then careful brings

This fuel dry, and as it glows receives

The lambent flame in grass, and burnt leaves.

Each hand is ready for the approaching feast

One flails the hide, and bares the beast.[14]

On the banks of the Vasse River, near where he had interrogated the three Aboriginal men who had approached his exploring party, Bussell discovered 'a spot that the creative fancy of a Greek would have peopled with Dryad and Naiad and all the beautiful phantoms and wild imagery of his sylvan mythology'. Elsewhere, he found flowers that though 'perhaps not precisely the same that characterize an English meadow, they were not the less beautiful in appearance'. He recognised, or thought he recognised, clover, buttercup, and marigold. He found their proximate familiarity and literary association auspicious. He extended the Greek motif at length and on one evening described the party's bivouac as a 'procoenium'—a reference to ancient Proconnesus, an island in Propontis, now called Marmara, and a source of black-streaked marble—where, at sunset, the camp fire was to 'yield the light that the fading orbs of Heaven deny'.[15]

John Bussell's letters and journals reflect an intercourse with literature common among educated people of the time—instinctive and unapologetic, indeed, shameless. Lurking behind his words is the presence of Homer, Virgil, Horace, Milton, and Shakespeare. The traditional emblems of British civilisation—stars, moon, the heroes of the *Iliad* and the *Aeneid*, pastoral flowers—are intact and generative. Bussell offered his quotes and allusions not only to parade his learning. He understood that the new country, his new possession, had to be just as much a rhetorical construction, a product of language and culture, as a deeded, certified, bounded object.[16]

But Bussell was not the first European explorer to bestow names on the southwest, or the first to explore the Vasse region. On 27 May 1801, 29 years before the British settled Augusta, Captain Nicolas Baudin, in command of the French ships *Geographe* and *Naturaliste*, sighted Cape Leeuwin. Baudin sailed north for about 100 kilometres, rounded a cape he named Naturaliste, and entered a bay he named Geographe.

On 4 June Baudin put ashore at an inlet, where he saw an Aborigine up to his waist in water, spearing fish. The man retreated to the top of a sand dune, from where he began to shout violently at the French to go back to their ship. When the French advanced, the man vanished into the bush. Baudin concluded the place was 'much frequented' and noted the many signs of human habitation: large cooking sites, wells that provided the French with fresh water, fishtraps, and 'well-worn tracks'.[17]

French explorers in Australia, unlike British explorers, were eager to make contact with the native inhabitants. The French Enlightenment had stressed human equality and taught that 'men differ only in the ideas they form of happiness and the means which they have imagined to obtain it'. The French believed in the universality of human behaviour and feeling. Differences between people were only modifications produced by climate and social organisation. No impassable barriers existed between the progressive and the stationary people of the earth. French explorers sought to confirm these presuppositions and hoped that an examination of aboriginal life would answer philosophical questions concerning the nature of civilisation and its effects on human behaviour. They wanted to resolve the question of whether people untouched by civilisation were naturally good and naturally happy. The British evinced no such curiosity. Utterly convinced of the superiority of their own civilisation, they already knew the answer and entertained no doubts.[18]

In contrast, for Baudin and the expedition's scientists, everything they observed confirmed the essential humanity of the Aborigines. In Van Diemen's Land the expedition's botanist, François August Peron, became interested in a seventeen-year-old girl, Oure-Oure, who, Peron noted with evident delight, was 'not in the least aware that her nudity could be thought immodest'. The British, whether actually titillated or not by such exposure, usually recorded nudity with disapproval.[19]

The Van Diemen's Land Aborigines were also interested in the French. A group of male Aborigines gathered around a party headed by Peron and urged them to strip, so as to determine their sex. When one young sailor obliged, he not only satisfied Aboriginal curiosity about gender, but

> suddenly exhibited such striking proof of his virility that they all uttered loud cries of surprise mingled with loud roars of laughter which were repeated again and again. This condition of strength and vigour in the one among us who seemed least likely, surprised them extremely. They had the air of applauding the condition as if they were men in whom it is not very common. Several of them showed with a sort of scorn their soft and flaccid organs and shook them briskly with an expression of regret and desire which seemed to indicate that they did not experience it as often as we did.[20]

Perhaps, in recording this incident, Peron meant to boast of French potency in comparison to that of Aboriginal males. Whatever his motivation, Peron was not ashamed of the encounter. British explorers were far more inhibited. When Captain Fremantle visited Swan River in 1829 and his men faced a similar Aboriginal request to strip, they refused, because, Fremantle reported, they 'had too much decency to think of satisfying [native] curiosity in that particular'.[21]

The unconcerned frankness with which Aborigines treated bodily functions shocked the British into silence. Much of what Aborigines said and did overstepped the threshold of British delicacy and therefore remained unrecorded. The personal habits of Aborigines, their differences in colour, odour, and cast of countenance distressed the British settlers, who chose to ignore particularities and focus instead on derogatory generalities. They expressed their discomfort towards the unembarrassed and uninhibited Aborigines with such adjectives as 'barbaric' and 'uncivilized'.

Baudin admired Australian Aborigines. He found them strong and vigorous, with healthy, well-set teeth and lively eyes. His visit to Geographe Bay, however, proved less fruitful of the kind of felicitous encounters that occurred in Van Diemen's Land. Local Aborigines avoided the French, and the expedition suffered a fatal accident. A boat capsized and one of its crew, the seaman Vasse, was swept away. In memory, Baudin applied Vasse's name to the river flowing into the inlet where the expedition had first landed and had seen such abundant evidence of Aboriginal occupation.

The Augusta settlers had read of Baudin's landing in Geographe Bay and believed the Aborigines had killed Vasse when he washed ashore, or that he had lived with them a while and then been killed. In either case, the story served almost as a creation myth, or at least as a narrative relevant to the land the settlers wished to occupy. Vasse's supposed death at the hands of the Aborigines confirmed British prejudice that the natives were innately savage and treacherous.

After his rhetorical possession of the Vasse country in November 1831, John Bussell made more formal annexation. Upon his return to Augusta he applied for a grant of 3573 acres on the right bank of the Vasse River. He received authorisation to occupy the land the following July. He celebrated the prospect of possession in verse:

The kangaroo is in the swamp,
    The wild man in his cell,
And heavy rise the vapours damp
    And brood o'er yonder dell.

We'll fill our cups, and sing our song
    Before we sink to sleep,
Our dogs shall then the drear night long
    Their faithful vigils keep.

No lurking savage shall assail.
    To-morrow, with the day,
O'er stream, savanna, hill and dale
    Our compass points the way.[22]

The land to which Bussell's compass pointed, the free land he appropriated, was free and productive not because it was empty or virgin or free for the taking. The Aborigines, at least, knew it was none of these things. The land appeared free—without cost—because natural abundance offered rewards to British enterprise incommensurate with the effort expended in achieving them. Unexploited natural abundance was the central meaning of the settlers' economy. Unexploited natural abundance drew John Bussell to the Vasse. He found there a country with 'fields of grass . . . waving like corn'. The beckoning grass was an invitation to profit. The Vasse country, he concluded, 'appeared almost a paradise to those long accustomed to the dense forests of the Blackwood'.[23]

Bussell and other British settlers subscribed to the suppositions of the classical economists and believed in the labour theory of value. Every economic good acquired its worth only to the extent that human labour was expended in producing it. Settlers believed their labour alone would convert the southwest into valuable property. But the fertility of the soils, the availability of timber, and the presence of water had far less to do with human labour than with the autonomous ecological processes that people exploited on behalf of the human realm, a realm less of production than of consumption. Prosperity was contingent not upon hard work alone but upon the fact of bountiful nature—soil, forests, plains, plants, rivers, and a climate that enabled people to sustain themselves in plenty.[24]

The Bussells were optimists, and optimism—an untenable philosophical position but a necessary one for those attempting the impossible—was reassuring, deterministic, and enduring. In 1830 the brothers had regarded forest as the true indicator of soil fertility and desirable land. The difficulty of clearing and the poor yield of Blackwood soils soon disabused them of any notion that Augusta would make the family wealthy. Family optimism, however, proved immutable. By the end of 1831 the Vasse's parklike landscape had replaced the karri and jarrah forests as the ultimate measure of beauty, fertility, and wealth. Prosperity, the brothers were certain, would soon follow.

The karri and jarrah forests of the southwest made the Bussells uncomfortable; the Vasse, in contrast, appealed because of its openness. Whenever they travelled from Augusta, they always felt elated and gratified as they emerged, after two or three days' journey through claustrophobic wooded country, onto the Vasse plains. Open regions marked a threshold. On a plain, settlers could survey the land and determine the boundaries and extent of their possession. In a forest, overall views were impossible and trees appeared without limit. Vernon Bussell, in the midst of clearing at the Adelphi, predicted 'there are such quantities of [timber in the forest] that we may burn for everlasting and there still will be enough to supply the world for ever'. In fact, the ruin of the karri and jarrah forests took less than three generations.[25]

John Bussell did not intend that he and his brothers should labour alone at the Vasse. Even the independent Bussells recognised that for organised social life, for markets, and for labour, people needed the presence of others. John Bussell was sure that most of the other Augusta settlers would follow the brothers' initiative in taking grants at the Vasse. Indeed, his Vasse reports created a sensation among the settlers at Augusta. As they approached the second anniversary of their arrival in Western Australia, progress against the Blackwood forests seemed painfully slow. If less wooded land, free for the taking, existed elsewhere, then they would leave.

1 1

BLUNDERING PLOUGH

NO IMMEDIATE EXODUS FROM AUGUSTA FOLLOWED JOHN BUSSELL'S report of the bountiful plains of the Vasse. In contrast to the unbridled circumstances of their arrival at Swan River in March 1830, colonists were now settled. Houses, gardens, stock pens, wells, and clearings fixed them in place and represented investments in labour, time, and money. By 1832 few Augusta settlers could afford to move again. Two years' struggle against the bush had left them impoverished.

Few ships arrived in Flinders Bay and provisions were always short. When a vessel did arrive, Captain Molloy and James Turner were able to buy stocks of food, but the Bussells, even with Charles's income as storekeeper, were constantly short of money. Expected remittances from England never arrived. In the face of penury they borrowed from government stores and depended on the generosity of Resident Magistrate Molloy to extend them credit and lend them powder and shot so they could hunt.

Each settler took the shortage of shipping and communication personally. Absence of letters from home caused doubt about the strength and constancy of friends' and families' affections. Even the steadfast John Bussell despaired. In December 1831, after a year and a half of no news from England, he wrote to his cousin in exasperation, 'If a letter is not already on its way from some member of the family I must conclude, and a sad conclusion it will be, that I have been the subject of neglect, and from a quarter whence I hope perhaps I deserve other treatment.'[1]

Letters were on their way but did not arrive until March 1832, when the colonial schooner *Ellen* called. The *Ellen* also brought a passenger whose intentions caused excitement and gossip. James McDermott, former captain of the *Emily Taylor*, had returned to Augusta to marry James Turner's daughter Ann. McDermott faced a rival suitor. Alfred Green, the surgeon, had courted Turner aboard the *Warrior* and again at Augusta. Turner, however, hastily chose the captain. McDermott was considerably older than his bride, and Georgiana Molloy considered the match loveless; in her opinion Ann Turner married to escape an unhappy home life. In a letter to Helen Story she described the bride's circumstances:

> She was a Miss Turner, a neighbour of ours, the eldest of nine children . . . Mr Turner unfortunately married his first wife's sister by whom he had one child, the subject of much jealousy from its mother's foolish affection. And I believe had her home been happy, Miss Turner would never have married one whom she had neither time nor opportunity to be attached to.[2]

After Magistrate Molloy married the couple, the newlyweds left Augusta to settle at Fremantle. There, Ann McDermott discovered that feelings of despondency and abandonment were not confined to remote Augusta. Swan River settlers also felt neglected by the government and people of England. They too suffered shortages. Provisions were so depleted by December 1831 that Stirling had sent H.M.S. *Sulphur* to Van Diemen's Land for supplies.

In the meantime, colonists began spending more and more time in the bush, hunting. Hunters quickly depleted local game. As early as January 1832, upper Swan settler William Shaw noted that, as a consequence of relentless hunting, 'Animals and Birds are become extremely scarce.' And, in proportion to the disappearance of their traditional food sources, chiefly kangaroo, Swan River Aborigines began taking pigs, spearing sheep, and stealing from vegetable gardens. Some settlers recognised equity and justice in the exchange. Appeals to principles, however, did not compensate for lost property. Settlers demanded retaliation. A group of settlers at Guildford, on the upper Swan, called on Stirling to take strong action to protect property; otherwise, the settlers warned, they must abandon the colony.[3]

Settler George Fletcher Moore was so agitated by the thefts and the killing of his pigs that he recorded in his diary, 'My warlike propensities are so much excited that I am . . . preparing to watch and attack the natives, and kill, burn, blow up, or otherwise destroy the enemy, as may be most practicable.' He doubted, as some claimed, that the civilising process would convince Aborigines 'of the evil of their pig-killing ways'.[4]

At Augusta supplies fluctuated between sufficiency and scarcity. The *Ellen*'s March visit had temporarily relieved the situation. The Bussells received building materials (window frames and doors), clothes, books, preserved foods, salted meat, and a fishing net. By May, however, provisions were short again, and the start of winter rains made game harder to find.

Towards the end of May John Bussell wrote, 'We have for the last month been reduced to the greatest extremities.' Fortunately, the fishing net 'proved an instrument in the hands of Providence to save not only ourselves but many of our fellow colonists from absolute starvation'. The Bussells rarely lent their property, but the situation became so dire that John Bussell allowed the married men of the settlement to use the net without his superintendence. Single settlers and soldiers used the net under his supervision. In all cases he expected users to pay him one-third of the catch.[5]

At the end of May H.M.S. *Sulphur* returned to Western Australia from Van Diemen's Land and called in at Flinders Bay. The ship carried goods from England addressed to Western Australian settlers but originally sent to Van Diemen's Land. The Bussells received another shipment of windows and doors, as well as old clothes—all rotten—and a bundle of cash. They regretted a lack of shoes but otherwise provisions seemed adequate and John Bussell optimistically predicted, 'We shall not want again, our own produce will supply us next season.'[6]

The *Sulphur* returned to the Swan River settlement early in June. The ship's arrival failed to provide significant relief or generate Bussell-like optimism. Although settlers were certain that ultimately Western Australia would prosper and benefit the mother country, they perceived the present home government as indifferent, even hostile, to the Swan River settlement. But unless England extended substantial help, and soon, the colony could not continue and would not achieve its vaunted potential. Colonists called on Governor Stirling to return to England to plead the colony's case.

Stirling was a man only momentarily daunted by bad news or setbacks. He quickly recovered his confidence and could always put an optimistic gloss on any event. In his mind the colony always stood on the threshold of rapid growth and prosperity. Confident of Western Australia's ultimate success, he therefore accepted the settlers' request to put the colony's case before the British government and, in July 1832, sailed for England.

Meanwhile, settlers at Augusta began turning their land grants into specific land claims. In February 1832 James Turner applied to select his grant of 20 026 acres around the shores of Hardy Inlet. Owing to shipping delays, eight months passed before he received notice of permission to occupy his selection. By then, October 1832, Captain Molloy had decided to select most of his grant at the Vasse. He asked John Bussell to lead a survey expedition to the Vasse before selection. The Bussell party made a quick trip and returned to Augusta by 6 November. With the map drawn up by R. Edwards, Captain Molloy left for Perth a week later. He applied for 12 400 acres on the right bank of the Vasse River and sought the balance of his grant, 413 acres, at Augusta.

Captain Molloy chose as the major portion of his Augusta selection the island at the head of Hardy Inlet, at the point of embouchement of the Blackwood River—land he already occupied. As early as June 1832 he had directed his labourers to clear the island, plough, and sow. Augusta settlers referred to the island as Molloy Island, but Captain Molloy asked the surveyor-general to change the name to Dalton Island, after Georgiana Molloy's brother. The new name was not accepted and Molloy remained the island's name.

The island, however, already had an identity. For tens of thousands of years, the Nyungar had named the southwest, had systematically classified the natural world, and assigned an Ancestral spirit to every physical feature of the land. But the Christian God-given act of naming enabled the British settlers to erase those meanings. God gave Adam in Eden the privilege of naming the animals and plants. Although none of the Augusta settlers yet imagined themselves in Eden, the unwritten shape of the new country appeared like the world before things had been tagged with names—like John Locke's *tabula rasa*. Through the bestowal of their own names, and through deeded possession, the settlers implanted their own meanings on the terrain. They made the soil, rivers, and forests the scenery, the backdrop, for their own story, a drama animated by self-interest and underwritten by private property.

Although Captain Molloy had his name bestowed on the major island of the Blackwood River, James Turner had made the largest actual claim in the Augusta area. In October 1832 Turner wrote to the colonial secretary and the surveyor-general. He acknowledged recognition of his selection at Augusta but he reminded the government of his claim to a further 5000 acres. The provision and employment of Turner's numerous family and even more numerous retinue of servants required a strong and immediate commitment to

Augusta. He thus resented his neighbours' growing enthusiasm for the Vasse. He felt betrayed. With a large inventory of buildings, fences, and gardens, he could not so easily move his establishment. Nevertheless, he thought he might select his 5000-acre additional entitlement at the Vasse, and in November 1832 he journeyed north to inspect personally the much-discussed country.

Captain Molloy returned to Augusta, from Perth, in mid-December. Government had approved his application for land at the Vasse, and a week later he rode to the Vasse to inspect his selection. On his return he told his wife that the Bussells were right, the Vasse was 'a most pleasing country and answering with truth to the description given of its park-like appearance, with long waving grass and abounding also with kangaroos'.[7]

In January 1833 Captain Molloy took another trip to the Vasse. As he left, Georgiana Molloy took to her bed from exhaustion. When her husband had left for Perth in October she had again taken over his duties as resident magistrate. The government clerk George Earl had left in March 1832 and Molloy had had to resume clerical duties. In her husband's absence she wrote his letters, issued rations, and supervised the unloading of ships. In addition, she directed the farm's labourers and tended to domestic chores and needlework for herself, her husband, their daughter, and their servant. She was still breastfeeding Sabina, now fourteen months old. 'I have not even time to say my prayers as I ought,' she confided to Margaret Dunlop. 'This life,' she continued, 'is too much for dear Molloy and myself. And what I lament is that, in his decline of life, he will have to lead a much more laborious life than he did in one and twenty years' service. He does not despair, but I never knew anyone having his losses to bear—but who would?'[8]

In November 1832 Molloy had written a resilient, cheerful letter to her sister, celebrating Augusta's 'heavenly clime', singular botany, bird life, and the joys of motherhood. She had, however, conceded that her husband's farming pursuits yielded far less satisfaction. He had suffered 'heavy and frequent losses in stock'. An expensive cow in calf died when it fell on a slope and strangled itself on the tether. 'We have besides,' Molloy continued, 'lost twenty-five pigs, goats, sheep without number and Jack the pony.' 'Animals,' she concluded, 'are bad property to begin with; they require constant attention, if not, they stray away.'[9]

Servants were another irritation. In fact, the family's happiness and serenity depended on the character and attitude of their servants. After nearly two years in Western Australia, during which time the Molloys saw most of their servants leave, Georgiana Molloy told her sister, 'If a perfect absence of grief or pain constitutes happiness we certainly ought to posses it, for our lives are only now and then interrupted by the remissness of domestics.'[10]

In January 1833, in the middle of summer, enervated by heat and overwork, Molloy wrote to her friend Margaret Dunlop and unburdened herself of all the felt hardships of colonial life. 'My head aches,' she stated at the conclusion of her letter. 'I have all the clothes to put away from the wash; baby to put to bed; make tea and drink it without milk as they shot our cow for a trespass; read prayers and go to bed, besides sending off all this tableful of letters.' She felt acutely homesick and wrote, 'I cannot contain myself when I think of the past.' Loneliness compounded the pain of exile, and she challengingly asked her correspondent, 'How would you like to be nearly three years in a place without a female of your own rank to speak to or to be with you whatever happened.'[11]

Loneliness did not disturb the self-sufficient and future-oriented Bussells. Although the brothers longed to see the rest of their family, they expected reunion to take place in Australia. In the meantime, they had to prepare the way. Their future, John Bussell was certain, lay at the Vasse. But as they expected the imminent arrival of sisters Fanny and Bessie and brother Lenox, John, Vernon, and Alfred stayed at the Adelphi, where they might better receive their siblings.

By the end of 1832, after nearly eighteen months on their

2000-acre Adelphi grant, and despite almost constant labour, the three brothers had managed to clear only about five acres. Although proud of their accomplishments—'the forest by degrees levelled to the ground, a good garden rising, paths made to the most frequented parts instead of the thick jungle that used to be, and a good well of water'—the labour expended seemed inordinate for the return. Even to burn a tree trunk and stump took immense effort. The fire-tender had constantly to replenish the kindling stacked against the burning log; fires blazed a week to ten days before the wood was reduced to ash. Once cleared, the Australian soil proved impoverished, and crops failed. The brothers looked enviously at the Vasse. 'What a pity we did not know of that country before,' Vernon wrote. 'How much labour it would have saved us! No trees to get up, the land rich, bearing nothing but grass. In fact, it resembles an English park, only instead of deer, you see an abundance of kangaroo. You can not imagine anything more beautiful.'[12]

Vernon was less impressed by King George Sound, which, from curiosity, he had visited aboard the *Ellen* in November 1832. Jurisdiction over King George Sound and the town of Albany had passed to the colony of Western Australia in 1831. A few settlers from Swan River took up grants, and Stirling appointed Alexander Collie the first government resident. Lieutenant McLeod, formerly in command of the soldiers at Augusta, replaced Collie in November 1832.

Officially the settlements of Augusta and King George Sound were thriving and the settlers content. Captain Frederick Irwin, lieutenant governor in Stirling's absence, visited both outposts in February and March of 1833. He reported to Stirling that

> the persons located at each of these settlements are perseveringly engaged in prosecuting the various and appropriate pursuits of a Settler's life,—are apparently contented with their prospects in the Colony,—have continued without intermission to preserve the most amicable intercourse with the neighbouring Aborigines and have found their respective climates remarkably healthy.[13]

171

George Fletcher Moore, who accompanied Irwin, detected a rather different attitude at Augusta; restlessness was everywhere. 'Most of the colonists here,' he noted in his diary, 'speak of going to settle at the Vasse where they can procure sheep, the land there being described as open and grassy.' Moore considered walking to the Vasse from Augusta but concluded the trip would be pointless; there was little left to discover, as the country was 'so recently explored, and so well laid down in charts, it did not possess sufficiently the interest or novelty to induce us to take a step'.[14]

Irwin and Moore brought news that the Bussell sisters, brother Lenox, and two maidservants, the young Emma Mould and 65-year-old Phoebe Bower, had arrived aboard the *Cygnet* at Fremantle on 26 January 1833. John Bussell immediately took passage to Fremantle and arrived on 8 March. His sisters found his appearance changed, and Fanny described him as 'rather barbarous, but quite poetical, in large canvas trousers made by his own hands, a broad-leather belt, hair and beard both long and moustache enough to give a bandit look'.

Fanny Bussell's pleasure at seeing John, and her romantic delight in the pioneering idea, were tempered by a suspicion that Emma Mould was pregnant. She wrote to her mother, 'It is now generally understood that Emma is in the family way. From her conduct since we left England I see little reason to doubt it.' Although she had been in the colony only ten weeks, Fanny had already discerned one of Australia's distinctive characteristics: servants behaved differently than in England. She warned her mother, 'We ought to have had more than a vague hint of Emma's real character, nothing but annoyance and anxiety have accrued from our connection with her. You must conceive the annoyance of servants here, expensive wages, and consummate impudence.'[15]

At Swan River John Bussell bought provisions and stock, which, together with two cows shipped out from England, he loaded aboard the colonial schooner *Ellen*, bound again for Augusta. The *Ellen* left

Fremantle in the middle of April and anchored in Flinders Bay on the twentieth. Passengers disembarked onto the beach. A half-mile-long path led to the houses of the three main families at Augusta: the Molloys, the Turners, and the Bussells. 'Mr Green escorted me to Mrs Molloy's,' Fanny noted in her diary. 'It was nearly dark but I could perceive that the river was broad and beautiful and the country more richly wooded than the English imagination can conceive.'[16]

Molloy had eagerly anticipated the arrival of the two Bussell women. 'I feel towards them like sisters,' she told her mother, 'from the affection and friendship that has always existed between us and the brothers.' She hoped they would find common interests. She greeted the party at her door, and Fanny recalled, 'Mrs Molloy came out to receive us with her little Sabina in her arms, looking so youthful and interesting. Her home is very comfortable and she is so active.' Unable to accommodate the sisters in her own house, Molloy had prepared a nearby building for their occupation. The arrangements delighted Fanny, who described to her mother how 'nicely' Molloy had 'fitted up' the house with 'a French bed and all sorts of land comforts. A vase of sweet mignonette upon the table and your picture, my own Mother, were its ornaments, and a large wood fire blazing on the hearth cast a cheerful light around.'[17]

That evening Molloy hosted a small reception party for the new arrivals in her sitting room. At the conclusion of the evening, Fanny and Bessie, too excited to go to bed, joined their brothers at the family's Augusta house, the Datchet. 'There,' Fanny wrote,

> among casks and barrels of all descriptions we found them seated round something by courtesy called a table, a lamp fed with pork slush, a huge chimney in which a wood fire was blazing, eating rashers of salt pork and pancakes, without either the adjuncts of knives, plates or forks. Two hammocks suspended from the roof completed the picture which Bessie compared to a bandit's cave.[18]

Although it was late, the moon—rising above the dark line of forest that fringed the western shore of Hardy Inlet—and the star-filled sky seduced them outdoors. Fanny and Bessie proposed a walk along the forest-fringed beach, splashed and shadowed by moonlight. Under southern skies, Fanny reflected on the enormous travel-induced changes in her life over the previous ten months and the attainment, at last, of her final destination. 'It is here,' she concluded, 'that one sees the magnificence of emigration. At the Swan, European comforts and luxuries have already robbed this life of all its wildness and grandeur.'[19]

The reality of immigration for women—bondage into domestic service—quickly diminished any initial expansiveness female immigrants felt for the new colony. During their nearly three years in the bush, the brothers had neglected their domestic arrangements and now stood in sore need of female ministration. Their English blankets had disintegrated, and flour and wheat sacks formed their bedding; their boots had decayed and fallen away; their clothes, ripped and torn, had rotted. In their stead they had sewed crude trousers and shirts from canvas. These responsibilities, and more, they now relegated to their sisters and female servants. Molloy was sure the sisters would 'make their brothers happy and comfortable, a thing men never are without families'.[20]

After two weeks at the Molloys', Bessie went up the river to the Adelphi, with Emma Mould, to housekeep. Mould, the Bussells discovered, was not pregnant. They believed she had feigned the condition to induce a man to marry her and thus free herself from domestic service. The family decided Mould should serve at the Adelphi, away from the temptations of Augusta—men. Fanny stayed at the Datchet with Phoebe Bower, to look after Charles, to sew and wash his dirty clothes by hand, to cook and bake bread, and to clean. Later, Phoebe joined Bessie and Emma at the Adelphi.

At first acquaintance, Fanny had described Georgiana Molloy as 'active'. But she was also unwell; strenuous and continuous occupation had left her enfeebled. In May Molloy weaned Sabina, who, during the first difficult days and nights, slept under Fanny's and Phoebe's care at the Datchet. Captain Molloy was also unwell. Fortunately the Molloys had recently engaged two servants, Frederick and Kitty (Mildred) Ludlow. Although crippled and sickly, the 30-year-old Kitty could sew and baby-sit Sabina. The Ludlows had lost their house in a fire that Molloy blamed on Frederick Ludlow:

> Kitty's husband, not by any means a good character, in a state of intoxication set fire to the house and Kitty was nearly in flames, but seizing her crutches escaped. She then came to me for an Asylum and said it had been her dearest desire for some months to be in my service.[21]

But Molloy saw the ailing Kitty Ludlow as more than just a servant; she fixed on her as a necessary subject for conversion and discussed the woman's case with Margaret Dunlop and Helen Story. 'Kitty's life is very precarious,' she wrote, 'but I know she has no right idea of her state of acceptance with God.' Following Henry Martyn's example, Molloy felt obliged to exhort and persuade and to attend to her servant's spiritual welfare, to seize every opportunity of doing good by spreading the knowledge of the truth by conversion. But she found Kitty Ludlow, like most of the labouring classes in the colony, resistant to upper-class preaching. 'If you tell them here,' she lamented to Helen Story, 'of the merits of their Saviour's Atonement they will say, "I suppose you are what they *call* a *Wesley* or *Methody*." '[22]

But Molloy persisted and lent Ludlow her copy of Robert Story's *Peace in Believing*. The book, however, 'did not seem to affect her'. Ludlow did not identify with the brief and blameless life of Isabella Campbell, nor see any point in emulating Campbell's piety and mortification. Campbell thought of herself as a 'sinful worm', a state she believed was necessary for redemption. Ludlow, already burdened by a surfeit of humiliation and affliction, rejected Campbell's recommended path to salvation. The idea of obtaining grace through abject abnegation, through the acceptance of one's personal wickedness and unworthiness, did not appeal.[23]

Molloy's failure to convert Kitty Ludlow, as well as preoccupations with her own troubled spirit, did not cause her to neglect her garden or other worldly concerns. By their third season at Augusta, the settlers had decided that June was the proper time to sow wheat. Previous crops, however, had been diseased and stunted and had yielded poorly. Molloy decided on the prophylactic of a brine bath for the seed wheat. She instructed Elijah Dawson on the precautions to take before he sowed the wheat on the hillside behind the house. She also asked labourer James Staples to dig a garden and sow vegetable seeds in a plot next to the house. Molloy herself sowed Cape peas and other flower seeds sent from the Cape Colony by Colonel Harry Smith. At either end of the veranda she planted nasturtium. Winter's stormy weather, however—wind, rain, and cold—curtailed her gardening and brought on rheumatism in her arm.

The Molloys no longer confined their pioneering to their lot at Augusta. Every few days Captain Molloy and Frederick Ludlow, or Dawson, or Staples rowed up Hardy Inlet to Molloy Island, to clear and plough and erect buildings. John Bussell was also active and mobile and made frequent trips down the river from the Adelphi to obtain supplies and to superintend the Bussells' scattered projects. He often dined with the Molloys.

Such activity conferred direction and purpose on the settlers' laborious undertakings. Progress was tangible. The conquering of virgin land was real and assumed an almost sacred aspect. The newly arrived Bussell sisters shared their brothers' acute consciousness of the virginity of the wilderness and of their pioneering roles as conquerors. On 21 June 1833 Fanny Bussell recorded in her diary, 'The banks of the Blackwood were first invaded by the plough share. The iron entered into its bosom for the first time.'[24]

Fanny Bussell's comment reflected an inchoate and atavistic sense of earth as a benevolent female, a gesture to an ancient, pre-Christian anthropomorphic ideal. But Fanny's identification of the earth with a woman's body also reflected and reinforced her and her sister's own submissive role in a society dominated by men—her brothers. Additionally, identification of women with nature and, by implication, of men with culture, also served to justify the power of men and their machines over the land.

Neither ploughing nor domestic labour, however, proceeded uninterrupted. The vagaries of pioneering life continually upset even the best-planned colonial activities. Stock frequently strayed into the bush and settlers often spent days in search of lost cows, pigs, and sheep. Inept in bushcraft, settlers enlisted the aid of Aborigines, whose quickness of sight and hearing made them invaluable as guides and trackers. Aborigines could follow tracks, imperceptible to the settlers, over grass or leaves or even bare rock. They could recognise individual footprints, and an unerring sense of direction served them even in districts in which they had never before been.

When stock went missing, the Bussells called on Wooberdung and Gahpot, who willingly tracked stray cattle in exchange for flour and other provisions. In June and August 1833 Wooberdung and Gahpot tracked the Bussells' cow, Yulika, and calf and recovered the calf. They also found the government bull and heifer, missing for some months from Augusta.

Wooberdung and Gahpot offered to track and guide not only for food. They acted out of curiosity, from a spirit of adventure, and for amusement. Like other Aboriginal guides and trackers, they found the settlers' seriousness enormously entertaining and settler concerns and priorities almost unbelievably trivial. Possessed of a language rich in ironic idiom, the Nyungar made especial fun of the Britishers' lack of irony.

As guides to exploring parties, Aborigines enjoyed travelling over unknown and distant ground, touching trees and objects hitherto known to exist in name only. Their memory treasured a detailed recollection of the various incidents and scenery along the route: the killing of a kangaroo, the capture of a cockatoo, the sight of a bullock, and the antics of the *djanga*—the dead—the Nyungar name for the settlers. The Nyungar were great lovers of gossip and scandal, and guides and trackers, as well as Aboriginal workers, later recounted their stories to appreciative audiences around camp fires.

While the vagaries of pioneering life often provided amusement for the Nyungar, the settlers, necessarily, took their own lives very seriously. During the winter of 1833 rain fell throughout August and September. On a wet September Friday the thirteenth, a saturated mud wall and fireplace adjoining the Molloys' house collapsed. At first the Ludlows, sitting nearby, dismissed the noise as falling rain. When Frederick Ludlow realised the wall was giving way, he pushed his crippled wife down the stairs and outside, before making his own escape.

The collapse of the wall, of several tons of clay and rock, rushes and wooden spars, shook more than the ground and nearby buildings. The ruin, the narrow escape of Kitty Ludlow, and the imagined escape of Sabina, who usually sat on Kitty's lap at that time of day, completely unnerved Georgiana Molloy, who reported furniture 'smashed to atoms' and rent into 'shivers', iron utensils 'broken to pieces'. She feared losing another child and invented lurid images of Sabina's possible fate. 'What dreadful spectacles would flesh and blood have presented,' she conjectured. Several weeks later she confessed she still could not reflect on the incident 'without emotion mingled with amazement'. 'Everytime I embrace Sabina,' she wrote to Helen Story, 'I felt how different it might have been—that instead of a dear little child, blooming with health and rosiness, she might have been a mutilated pallid corpse.' Molloy was especially troubled by the thought that the near miss meant inadequate mothering. 'What would my feelings have been,' she asked, 'if I had sent my dear little child into the midst of [the scene of the accident].' 'I tremble and wonder,' she wrote as she reflected on the transience of life. She was convinced the Almighty had spared Sabina's and Kitty's lives and felt humbled before His grace and inadequate in her gratitude. Although John Molloy gave thanksgiving at the service on the following Sunday, she asked Helen Story to do the same at Rosneath.[25]

During the evening following the accident, Augusta's surgeon, Alfred Green, drunken and delirious, entered the Molloys' house. Although she 'was not much alarmed', Green's condition caused Molloy to 'grieve' on the state of 'great intemperance' that prevailed at Augusta and on 'the open state of regardless wickedness that I have gone through and that still reigns'. She counselled Green next day, 'but I fear without hope of amendment'.[26]

The building's collapse, widespread drunkenness, and her loneliness made Molloy long for Rosneath more than at any time since she had left Britain. Time and distance combined to leave a single idyllic image of her former home. She imagined Ayrshire roses entwining poles at the end of the manse garden. 'Oh my dear and lovely Rosneath—my heart bleeds when I think of all the happy, celestial days I spent there and all the violets and primroses are fresh in my memory.' For the first time, she admitted misgivings about her emigration. She felt 'exiled' in Australia, told her mother, 'We never should have left England,' and confided to Helen Story, 'I wish we had taken a den at Rosneath to be next to you, my dear, kind Nelly and Mr Story.'[27]

But Molloy knew such wishes could never come true. Even as she regretted coming to Australia, she and her husband enlarged their commitment to the colony. Captain Molloy believed his major grant at the Vasse would, at last, prove the means to landed independence. Georgiana Molloy, though she shared her husband's hopes, found more immediate satisfactions than those offered by the promise of landownership. Gardening and child rearing, nurturing and preserving life, formed bonds of place and of belonging that mere private property could never confer.

The Molloys felt duty-bound to accept all the children God might send them. They believed the number of offspring measured the success of a marriage. A large family guaranteed continuity. Procreation was the sole justification for the sexual act. For as long as a woman breastfed, however, lactation prolonged postparturition amenorrhoea (cessation of menstruation) and thus prevented ovulation and conception. But within four months of weaning Sabina, and shortly after Captain Molloy returned from an inspection of his grant at the Vasse, in September 1833, Georgiana Molloy became pregnant again.

Conception coincided with the return of spring and the blooming of Molloy's flower garden. She began to think of accessions and wrote to her sister Elizabeth, 'You could not send old Georgy a greater treat than some seeds, both floral and culinary.' In return, she promised Australian seeds. She also wanted fruit trees, 'for Sabina rarely ever tastes anything but hard salt meat'. Live plants, she suggested, could survive the sea crossing. The Bussells, she noted, recently received some fig and grapevine cuttings, wrapped in tanner's bark and tightly enclosed in a metal container, with shoots three and four inches long.[28]

The Bussells' cuttings were not destined to be planted at Augusta, or anywhere else along the Blackwood, however. On the night of 5 November, at the Adelphi, after John had departed downriver, Alfred had gone to bed, and Bessie and Lenox sat reading in the main room, Emma Mould calmly announced a fire in the kitchen chimney next door. Bessie and Lenox went outside to look and saw the chimney ablaze and the flames leaping to the rush roof of the main building. They quickly decided the fire was too advanced to fight. Bessie rushed in to save the encyclopedias, while Lenox and Alfred pulled out the piano, tables, chairs, and medicine chest. All the Bibles and editions of Byron were saved. Emma Mould cleared everything out of the kitchen. Phoebe Bower was 'active beyond compare'. As flames tore across the rush roofs, Emma, Bessie, and

Lenox tossed out bedding and clothes, and Alfred ripped out the windows—with their precious glass—but could not save the doors. Lenox threw the gunpowder into the bush and saved the silver, mirror, and sheet music. They salvaged much, but lost shoes, clothes, books, sewing materials, tools, building materials, and their commitment to homesteading on the Blackwood.[29]

The next evening the Bussells departed the Adelphi forever. Bessie, 'accompanied by Phoebe and Emma, our pigs, poultry, cats, dogs, cockatoo and pigeons, Mr Green, John, Alfred, Lenox and Vernon for our crew and the two boats in tow, very deeply laden', described the trip downriver:

> It was a lovely balmy moonlight night and when we contrived to banish from our minds that we were going to leave the place that had formed so delightful a home, and the home, too, where we anticipated the meeting of so many dear relations who would have looked round on all the improvements with such wonder and delight, when we had contrived to forget this and had looked our last look I sang *Fleur de Page*.[30]

At Molloy Island the Bussells, with Captain Molloy's permission, liberated their animals and pitched a tent for Phoebe and Emma. They wanted Phoebe to look after the stock. They wanted Emma kept from the temptations of the town; as Bessie explained, she 'would rob us so at Augusta where she might find receivers for her stolen goods'.[31]

From Molloy Island the Bussells rowed across Hardy Inlet to Augusta. They stored their wine and piano at the Molloys' house. 'You may well conceive my gladness at this acquisition,' Molloy wrote to her sister when the piano was unloaded in her sitting room, 'as I have not heard the sound of music for four years. Sabina at first was a little afraid, but in an hour soon overcame it. She seemed to think it was an animal, and insisted on tying a piece of cord round one of its legs—hearing us speak of the legs of the piano.'[32]

John Bussell quickly decided the fire was a stimulus to further and more profitable pioneering. He later wrote to his mother, 'You will hear this accident bewailed by others as a calamity. To you who are accustomed to acquiesce in the decrees of providence, it will appear a seasonal stimulus to efforts in a more favourable field.' He explained the new opportunity more fully to Capel Carter:

> The Adelphi's distance from Augusta, the troublesome navigation by which it must be approached, its heavy timber, invincible shade so pernicious to crops, but more than all, [our possession of] the most beautiful grant of land in the whole colony on the Vasse river, lead me to think that the fire is not such a misfortune as first sight would estimate it. A rolling stone, they say, collects no moss, but from the first time I found this fine tract of country, I was impressed with the conviction that the sooner we commenced our labours on so fair a field the better—a spot where more was done by the benignant hand of Nature than years, I may say centuries, could effect in these wooded districts.[33]

Contrary to John Bussell's impression, nature had not laboured alone at the Vasse. Aborigines had taken advantage of biotic predispositions in Australian flora—chiefly, affinity for fire—to turn the Vasse into Bussell's 'fine tract of country'. But Vasse Aborigines remained ignorant of the Bussells' intentions. They found inconceivable the notion of strangers coming and claiming land. They knew the land was not free for the taking; it was already fully occupied. Augusta Aborigines, however, had realised the settlers had come to stay. They learned that the Europeans' presence disrupted the landscape and interfered with traditional food gathering. What Aborigines in either place still did not understand was the vision of empire, markets, and triumphant self-interest that inspired the emigration from Britain to Swan River, from Swan River to Augusta, and from Augusta to the Vasse.

12

POSSESSION

GEORGIANA MOLLOY OFTEN BOASTED OF THE TRANQUIL RELATIONS that prevailed between the settlers and the Aborigines. In a November 1833 letter to her sister she wrote, 'The natives are very fond of all the settlers at Augusta and we live on the most peaceful terms.' She contrasted this situation with that at Swan River where, 'from the indiscretion of several persons and particularly their servants, [the Aborigines] are hostile'. But at Augusta, through mutual goodwill, amity—not enmity—prevailed. Local Aborigines affectionately referred to her as 'King-bin' and to her husband as 'King Kandarung'.[1]

In 1833 Molloy befriended the man Gyallipert, an Aborigine from King George Sound, who, in 1832 at the behest of Albany Resident Magistrate Alexander Collie, had sailed to Perth to conciliate the settlers and local Aborigines. On a second voyage in March 1833, Gyallipert and his companion, Manyat, decided to stay at Augusta. Molloy found that Gyallipert spoke 'tolerably intelligible English' and she told her mother that he exhibited 'great confidence' towards her and Captain Molloy. She supplied Gyallipert with flour, which he kneaded into damper and baked on her griddle. With her permission he also cooked goanna and other game in the Molloys' kitchen. In exchange, he and other Aborigines brought her possum, 'a delicate food, the flesh as white as rabbit but much better of flavour', fish, which she gave Sabina and which she was 'thankful for', and other bush foods. Gyallipert entrusted her with his spears; local Aborigines gave her knives and waddies, and once, Mabin, an elder, presented her with a bundle of emu feathers, covered with red earth. Molloy found the presentation both curious and beautiful and forwarded the feathers to her sister.[2]

Although Molloy found the Aborigines 'indescribably dirty' and 'quite naked, except a kangaroo skin they wear as a sort of cloak', she did not fear them, either for herself or her daughter. The Aborigines were, she wrote, 'delighted with Sabina'. The child played with Aboriginal children, learned their dances, and was not 'the least alarmed at their black figures and rude voices'. Nor did physical contact cause alarm. Once, 'an old native woman seized Sabina by the leg and embraced it, without producing the slightest emotion or fear'. Nevertheless, there was occasional tension.[3]

One morning early in February 1834, about twenty Nyungar men and women gathered at the Molloys' house. Captain Molloy was at Swan River on business, and six-months-pregnant Georgiana Molloy was alone with Sabina and the Dawsons. Aborigines regularly assembled on the Molloys' veranda and normally Georgiana Molloy paid them no heed. This time, however, she perceived her visitors wanted the potatoes from the vegetable garden. She signalled for them to retreat but they refused to leave. Two men began to play with Sabina, whom Molloy held in her arms. Molloy did 'not like their manner', told them to 'Ben-o-wai' [be gone], and called Elijah Dawson. One of the men flourished his club and threatened Dawson, who turned pale and withdrew.

The man with the club and another man then 'took hold of Sabina's legs and shook their spears at me', Molloy later wrote. 'I was afraid to show fear and smiled. The tall man, perceiving that I was not intimidated, cut the air close to my head with his wallabee stick. I stood it all, taking it as play, but I heard the whizzing stick and expected either Dawson, the child or I should be struck.' She called on the wavering Dawson to stand his ground, while a native,

> seeing that I cared not for his manner drew a piece of broken glass bottle close to my cheek. I smiled and trembled, and said, 'Dirila', or glass, meaning that I knew they used it for sharpening their spears. He rubbed his fore-finger in his hair until it was covered with the fat or red earth with which they rub themselves and poked it right into my face. This I could not stand and, but for Sabina, I should have knocked his insulting hand away.

Molloy attempted to evade the man but he kept following her. She told Dawson to call the dogs, but 'not one of them would even bark'. In the meantime, the other Aborigines kept pointing to the potatoes and Molloy kept indicating her refusal. She knew they were aware of the lethal power of firearms, so she laid out her husband's pistol and rifle for everyone to see; 'they one by one dropped off and went over to the Miss Bussells'.[4]

At the Datchet, Fanny and Bessie were alone. Fanny noted the Aborigines 'seemed well aware of our un-protected situation'. They demanded 'bread in a tone of great authority and even pointed a spear, evidently with the intention of alarming us'. To Bessie's repeated admonition to 'Ben-o-wai', one boy shook his fist; the others ignored her. Dawson, who had been sent over by Molloy, 'at length succeeded in getting them off the grant and very glad we were to see the last of our troublesome guests'.[5]

After the group had gone, the sisters discovered three glass salt cellars missing. They assumed the Aborigines had taken them to make spear points. Fanny reported the theft to Molloy, who immediately ordered the soldiers out in pursuit. She commanded them 'to use no violence'. After a short chase the soldiers seized and searched several women, from whom they recovered the glass. The soldiers then made the women kneel and threatened them with their bayonets.[6]

Two days later most of the Aborigines returned to the settlement.

This time they brought a number of recently killed wallabies and gave one each to the settlers, a gesture which, Molloy wrote, 'we accepted as a peace offering'. She claimed she never again saw the man who threatened her and Dawson.[7]

When Captain Molloy took passage for Swan River early in December 1833, Georgiana Molloy expected him to be gone three weeks. He was detained, however, and the new year came without his return. More weeks passed and Molloy began to find her husband's absence 'agonising'. Meanwhile, she assumed his resident magistrate duties and oversaw the operation of the house and farm as well. 'Many events have occurred since he went,' she told her sister, 'which have loudly called on me to act a more conspicuous part than I could have desired, knowing my inefficiency.' She continued this theme of personal inadequacy in a later letter to Helen Story: 'I felt severely as all the agricultural and harvest business devolved on me a very important personage.'[8]

In January Molloy's servant Kitty Ludlow, 'deranged and her diseased frame so appalling that no one could go near her but her husband', died on Molloy Island. In Molloy's opinion, Frederick Ludlow had been an unsatisfactory husband, who offered his wife little solace or comfort. He was, she wrote, 'an iniquitous wretch who, the instant life had fled, came down to Augusta about his own concerns and publicly expressed his joy at her decease'. But Molloy had other concerns besides Frederick Ludlow's callousness: Kitty Ludlow did not have a good death. She died uninterested in consoling herself with God. Molloy worried about the woman's spiritual repose. At the time of death, Kitty was, Molloy wrote, 'in a most dreadful state, not only from bodily suffering, but in perfect indifference as to her future state and I fear now for the eternal consequences'.[9]

The heat of summer caused the body to decompose rapidly and made a prompt burial essential. Molloy travelled to the island and conducted the funeral service at night, by torchlight. Kitty Ludlow's 'poor frame,' she noted, 'was so highly decomposed, it made two of the bearers ill for some days'.[10]

After the funeral Molloy turned to the harvest and organised the labourers to cut and stack the wheat. She noted proudly that, owing to the brine treatment she had insisted on for the seed wheat, the Molloys' crop 'proved the best in the settlement . . . the other settlers' wheat was much more smutted and full of darnel [weeds]'. Afterwards, she ordered a troop of soldiers to Molloy Island to guard against Aboriginal theft and instructed Dawson to yoke the oxen and begin ploughing for the next season.[11]

Late in January, 'when I was almost dead with expectation, the *Ellen* arrived. I set off in the cart, left Sabina asleep in her cot and when I got to the landing place, was told Captain Molloy had been prevented leaving Perth . . . I returned very much disappointed.' Her disappointment caused her to reflect that pioneering was not as attractive or romantic as she had imagined from Scotland. The reality of life in the Australian bush betrayed the pastoral ideal. At times Molloy believed the whole undertaking had been a terrible mistake. She wrote to her sister, 'We have drunk many dregs since we embarked on this fatal Swan River expedition, fraught with continued care and deprivations.'[12]

At other times, however, Molloy could be quite gay. Although the *Ellen* had not brought her 'much loved one', she nevertheless proposed a dance for the ship's captain, the Bussell sisters, Charles Bussell, and other passengers. She and Bessie Bussell took turns at the piano while the others danced, waltzed, and sang. According to Bessie, 'Biscuits, melons and wine were handed round and we were very merry.'[13]

Despite the appearance of companionship and jollity, Molloy was disappointed with the Bussell sisters. At first she found them 'truly good tempered young women', but she had not been able to establish the intimate friendship with them she had hoped for, and relations remained formal. Although most settlers recognised and accepted their mutual dependence, the Bussells strove to distance themselves from others. They always looked first to their own family and regarded outsiders warily. They accepted Molloy's hospitality and gifts but made no return. She found them 'as perfectly selfish and inconsiderate as any people I ever knew' and confided to her sister:

> They are genteel nice people and that sort of thing—but terribly *close-fisted*, which gives us the idea that they belong to the *Take All* family, as we have on several occasions been most liberal to them. Yet they are not ashamed of receiving everything and you will hardly believe they have made no return; nor have Molloy or myself ever broken their bread.[14]

For fear of giving offence Molloy asked her correspondents to keep this opinion confidential. The Bussells, however, cared little what others thought of them. They were preoccupied with their own affairs. At the end of January, as native fires burned in the bush around Augusta and along the Blackwood, John, Vernon, and Alfred camped at the Adelphi and brought in their last harvest. They then began preparations for their departure to the Vasse.

In the meantime, Molloy waited for her husband to return. 'Although I felt uncomfortable at Molloy's prolonged absence,' she wrote,

> I had so much to do I was a stranger to ennui. . . . In the evening, after the heat of the day, I would daily sit on the beach on a line with Cape Leeuwin watching the running bar and the ever agitated waves of the Southern Ocean. Dearest Sabina would be picking up cuttle fish bone (and rubbing it together with a nutmeg grater) with which these shores abound. We repaired thither with great constancy, hoping, perchance, to discover the masts of the vessel that was to bring back dear papa.[15]

Molloy also passed the time reading. For the first time since her arrival in the colony, she read a nonreligious book, *Sir Edward*

Seaward's Narrative, by Jane Porter. Because of its seeming verisimilitude, the book made a great sensation when it first appeared in 1831. Porter claimed to be only the editor of the genuine journal—an early eighteenth-century account of a young couple's shipwreck on a deserted Caribbean island, of the dangers they faced from pirates and Spanish man-o-wars, their discovery of treasure, and their establishment of a flourishing colony under the British flag.

The *Narrative* painted a sweet picture of conjugal bliss and domestic contentment. Sir Edward's companion was simultaneously sagacious muse, exemplary friend, and obedient wife. Together they learned the value of partnership and mutual assistance. Happiness was found not in possessions (although they became rich) but in togetherness. Sir Edward's wife was always a source of support and cheer, a companion in all necessary labour, a moral agent who gently admonished her husband and warned against the sin of pride and the danger of vanity.

The Seawards lived their life wholly in the presence of God. Even in the midst of shipwreck, they kept the Sabbath. Mrs Seaward's favourite book was *Paradise Lost*, and the Seawards compared their lot to Milton's description of the sweet innocence, and therefore perfect felicity, of humanity's first parents in the Garden of Eden. They considered their island an earthly paradise and took seriously their duty to care for it, 'to dress it and keep it'.[16]

Molloy admired the Seawards' homespun achievements. She told Helen Story that the *Narrative* was 'a delightful book and one much suited to this strange life'. She was enamoured of the story and went on living in it because the *Narrative* gave a glimpse of a heartbreaking perfection that the settlers of Australia's southwest could never attain.[17]

Early one morning in March, Molloy heard a ship's gun sound in the bay, 'and shortly after dear Molloy appeared in his rifle jacket looking quite fat from the gentlemanly life he had been leading at Perth'. He had been absent nearly three and a half months. He promised his wife he would never leave her again, 'unless it is to enrich ourselves and procure more comforts than we have hitherto enjoyed'.[18]

In April Bessie Bussell wrote to Capel Carter to inform her of the brothers' imminent departure for richer and more comfortable fields. 'Vernon, John and Lenox are going to commence colonization anew on the banks of the Vasse,' she wrote. 'The country is a beautifully undulating grassy lawn. The river is small in comparison to the Blackwood, very deep with very high banks and full of fish. Kangaroos are seen in herds, which accounts for the natives being so numerous. I hope they may be as harmless as the local tribes.'[19]

The Augusta Aborigines, however, while generally averse to violence, were no longer as sanguine about the newcomers. Their invaded country no longer yielded as much traditional food, and they had acquired a taste for the exotic substitutes of the settlers, especially flour. Early in April Aborigines broke into the Augusta store and took 150 kilograms of flour. Several soldiers gave chase and captured a young girl, whom they took hostage back to Augusta. Some Aborigines followed and indicated they would exchange the stolen flour for the girl. After the girl had been returned, John, Lenox, and Charles Bussell armed themselves and went in pursuit of the rest of the band. The Bussells and some soldiers surprised a group in the middle of making damper. The Aborigines fled before shots were fired; the Bussells destroyed the food and gave up the chase.

The incident confirmed the Bussells' distrust of Aborigines. They determined in future to respond promptly and severely to Aboriginal transgressions and promised themselves to apply this policy at the Vasse.

A few days after the chase, on 13 April 1834, the *Ellen* anchored in Flinders Bay. John Bussell, his four brothers, Phoebe Bower, Elijah Dawson (loaned by John Molloy for six months), and independent settler George Layman, together with sufficient provisions and equipment to start colonising the Vasse, embarked. The *Ellen* sailed the party round to Geographe Bay and landed at Vasse Inlet on 18 April.

Incapable of true pioneering, of conquering true wilderness, and defeated and frustrated in their attempts to transform the forest along the Blackwood, the Bussells were nevertheless capable and energetic opportunists. They found the Aboriginal-made landscape of the Vasse irresistible. To stay at Augusta and ignore the wholesome grasslands at the Vasse was, in their minds, a perverse rejection of the bounty of Providence. And the Bussells never doubted that Providence, in supplying pastures of natural grasses and cleared land, had an eye to the family's future prosperity. Expropriation, however, required Aboriginal acquiescence.

The Bussells' priority at the Vasse was water. They knew the existence, but not the location, of Aboriginal wells. In the course of disembarkation, some Aboriginal men appeared on the beach. The Bussells made signs for water and mimed the action of drinking. The Aborigines understood, and one of them led Alfred, Lenox, and Dawson to a well. The well served the party's needs for the next several days as they sorted their goods and searched for homesites. John Bussell celebrated the friendly reception in verse:

> Welcome as a lover to the maiden's eye
> Passed a wild native in his own wild land,
> His friendly guidance shewed the spring hard by
> We filled our pails to cheer the thirsty band.
> With curious glance, our goods around he scanned
> Where they lay spread between us and the sea
> Nor grudged our habitation on the sand
> Nor frowned to see our tent beneath his tree
> The earth he held alike to self and stranger free.[20]

The next day, brothers Henry, James, and George Chapman, independent settlers from Augusta, and a party of soldiers, who had travelled overland, arrived. The Bussells assigned the soldiers to guard the stores while they began a detailed exploration. The Chapmans searched for land around the inlet. The Bussells walked and rowed— in a boat named after their mother, Frances Louisa—up the Vasse River and dug several wells. But saltwater filled every excavation. One evening, by chance, they discovered a native well that yielded, according to Lenox, 'very good water'. He remarked, 'We were very glad of it and made up our minds to remove our things up to it the next day.'[21]

The need to meet immediate material wants, to clear, build, plant, and sow, occupied much of the brothers' time. They quickly erected four huts of wattle and daub, vented by chimneys of mud and rushes. Their imaginations, however, were never circumscribed by their labour or their physical surroundings, the Australian bush. They revered ideas of empire and civilisation, which superseded their locality and time. During their designated rest periods, they read books. Under a tent of sail canvas and by the light of a slush lamp, Vernon read Shakespeare and John studied Edward Gibbon's *The Decline and Fall of the Roman Empire*. The great events these chronicles narrated gave the Bussells a sense of identity and shared destiny. Through their own discovery, occupation, and exploitation of the land, they were helping to bring Australia into history and the marketplace.

Australia's indigenous inhabitants, in contrast, occupied the land in a way antithetical to visions of empire. The Aborigines did not understand, could not understand, and were not permitted to understand the vision of empire behind the market, the vision of progress and prosperity that lay behind settler restlessness. Like human beings everywhere, Aborigines quarrelled, mostly over relationships; feared the dead; distrusted and maligned their neighbours; fell in love when not permitted, and stole others' husbands and wives against the prohibition of the elders. But unlike the British, Aborigines lived by precepts inherited from the Dreaming and by consensus within the great net of life that held them. They had no need for government or for hierarchy of command; the only rank they recognised was earned by age and degree of initiation. They did not desire possessions and never felt any necessity to leave their own country. And, in common with Aborigines throughout Australia, the southwest Nyungar had never known purposeful invasion. The sudden appearance and undivided determination of the British immigrants were incredible.[22]

Despite the wealth of their own cultural background, the Bussells were incapable of appreciating the depth and breadth of Aboriginal culture. Nor did they care to. They found Aboriginal life inaccessible: it was oral rather than written and technologically satisfied rather than technologically restless. Aborigines belonged to a culture with at least 50 000 years' experience of living with the land. A culture that old lay beyond European comprehension. Most Europeans of the Bussells' generation accepted the Mosaic chronology literally; the earth was only 6000 years old. To book readers like the Bussells, Australian Aborigines existed outside history, outside the literate circle that began with the Pentateuch. Illiterate and ignorant, Aborigines were incapable of thought and were, in fact, subhuman.

Self-conscious pioneers, the Bussells were acutely aware of their own unique historic role. They dedicated themselves to documenting and recording their colonising efforts to tame the land. Lenox kept a detailed journal of the brothers' first months at the Vasse, Alfred wrote a long account of the landing, John celebrated the events in verse, and they all wrote letters. Aware of the importance of documentation, Fanny and Bessie made copies of these written records, stored the originals, and sent the duplicates to relatives and friends in England.

The Bussells preserved their voluminous correspondence and journals as a record and measure of their progress. Their own written testimony reveals steady progress at the Vasse. Within six weeks of landing, the brothers had erected four huts, laid out a garden, felled trees, built fences, and designated future pastures and croplands.

Although Phoebe Bower undertook all the cooking and washing at the Vasse, she was largely absent from the brothers' accounts of Vasse pioneering. They concentrated instead on their own more significant and worthy male efforts. They now considered themselves experienced and self-sufficient pioneers. Alfred noted how much better prepared they were than at their first landing at Swan River, 'for our hands were not, as then, totally unaccustomed to labor, nor our minds as resourceless in difficulty'.[23]

As John Bussell implicitly recognised in his verse paean to Aboriginal hydrography, colonial resourcefulness consisted chiefly in the knowledge of how to exploit Aboriginal Australia. Nyungar tracks directed the Bussells' explorations; Nyungar campsites, wells, and water holes provided the sites for their homesteads; Nyungar yam grounds became their gardens and arable fields; and Nyungar hunting grounds inspired the Bussells with visions of future sheep pastures and meanwhile supplied them with the game necessary to supplement their meagre rations. As John wrote to his mother, 'The produce of the chase is one of the main attractions of our new abode. It completely supplies our family in animal food, so that on our first planting our feet on the sod we found more done for our subsistence than our long residence on the Blackwood had effected.'[24]

Early in May, after only a few weeks at the Vasse, Charles Bussell fell ill and returned overland to Augusta. He quickly recovered. Within a few weeks of his return he got family servant Emma Mould pregnant. Also in May the *Ellen* anchored in Flinders Bay, and Fanny and Bessie dispatched the first accounts of their brothers' Vasse colonisation to England.

The *Ellen*'s arrival prompted Georgiana Molloy to conclude the letter to her sister Elizabeth that she had begun the previous November. Unbeknown to Molloy, Elizabeth had been dead for over a year, since March 1833, but the news did not reach Augusta until September 1834. In the meantime, Molloy wrote, 'I expect my confinement every hour, I may say moment.' Molloy was apprehensive; she had been unable to obtain a midwife. 'The only woman I can engage,' she lamented, 'is herself also in expectation—Mrs Dawson, my servant, perfectly inexperienced.' Dawson's only qualifications as a midwife were her gender, her proximity, and her own fertility.[25]

Captain Molloy added a postscript to his wife's letter and assured Elizabeth, 'We are all in very good health,' and joked:

> We are not much richer than we were on leaving England beyond the possession of some miles of wild Country to which I have not as yet been able to establish a good title as the periodical conflagrations that take place in this country [consumed] the original patent from the Emperor Kandarung—we live a very original kind of life of the pastoral order. My little daughter thrives on it, is very lively and entertaining.[26]

Whatever the truth of Georgiana Molloy's estimation of Anne Dawson's competency, she misjudged her own pregnancy. She did not give birth for another month. With Alfred Green in attendance and the pregnant Dawson as midwife, Molloy gave birth to her third daughter, Mary Dorothea, on 16 June 1834. Labour was brief but 'the after birth as usual,' she wrote to her mother, 'was more than 12 hours in coming away, and at last was brought away per force'. Green, in deference to Molloy's abhorrence at physical intimacy with him, instructed Dawson on the placenta's removal. 'And much credit she deserves,' commented Molloy, 'for although a most uncomfortable operation, it was not painful.' Dawson gave birth shortly after, also to a girl, Mary Ann.[27]

Molloy quickly found that another child produced a 'multiplicity of business' and wrote to Helen Story, 'I have not only to nurse and carry her about, but all my former occupations to attend.' Domestic labour and sleepless nights of nursing made her weary and thin, but she could still laugh at herself and added, 'I am overwhelmed with too much labour and indeed my frame bears testimony to it, as I every day expect to see some bone poking through its epidermis.'[28]

While Molloy coped with her newborn, Governor Stirling returned to Western Australia. He reached King George Sound on 21 June 1834, after nearly two years in England. Although he had received a knighthood, the British government had largely ignored his pleas on behalf of the floundering colony. Stirling had argued that lack of population and capital operated against Western Australia's success. R. W. Hay, the under-secretary for the colonies, replied that the character of the emigrants, rather than the paucity of their numbers, constituted the chief drawback to the success of their undertaking. Land speculation and greed, not lack of capital, was ruining them. The government disclaimed responsibility for a private enterprise settlement that had originated as a concession to individuals induced by various accounts to settle at Swan River. Those who emigrated had done so at their own risk and had been warned they ought not look for any assistance from the government stores beyond a very limited period. Consequently, the British government was not prepared to increase general expenditure. Government did, however, sympathise with the settlers' fears regarding their protection and agreed to increase the size of the colony's military detachment.[29]

Stirling did not limit his appeals to government. He sought a larger audience and arranged with a London publisher, Joseph Cross, to publish *Journals of Several Expeditions Made in Western Australia, During the Years 1829, 1830, 1831, and 1832*, as an advertisement for the colony. Two accounts by John Bussell, one of an expedition along the Blackwood and the other of his November 1832 exploration of the Vasse, were included. In the preface Cross wrote that the book had been compiled as an encouragement to emigration. The narratives collected revealed the existence in Western Australia

> of many extensive and fertile districts . . . Occasionally extensive
> forests of noble timber encumber the surface, and sometimes single
> trees, in all the luxuriance and pride of natural beauty, so decorate

1 *Georgiana Molloy, 1829.*

2 *Crosby Lodge, Cumberland, 1810—the Kennedy family home.*

3 *Keppoch House, Dumbartonshire, Scotland. Georgiana Kennedy lived here with the Dunlops after estrangement from her family.*

Top: 4 *Helen Dunlop Story;*
below: 5 *Reverend Robert Story.*

6 *Reverend Edward Irving. Charismatic and of striking*
appearance, Irving created a sensation in 1820s England and
Scotland with his flamboyant and exaggerated preaching.

7 *Ruins and graveyard of Rosneath Church, Rosneath, Scotland. Georgiana Kennedy lived and was married here before leaving for Western Australia with her husband in 1829.*

8 *Arrival at Augusta, May 1830. Settlers used small boats and a raft, built by James Turner while at Fremantle, to tow supplies and equipment through the shallow water of Hardy Inlet to the proposed settlement at Seine Bay. The forest at this time grew to the water's edge.*

9 *Hardy Inlet, Augusta, c. 1837. Painted by Thomas Turner, this view shows Albion, home of the Turners, on the far left among the trees. The Molloys' house is to the right of centre, while the Bussells' house, Datchet, is between them.*

10 *South-southwest view across Seine Bay, Hardy Inlet, to Augusta, 1838. This view shows the Turner, Bussell, and Molloy residences, the entrance to Hardy Inlet, and, on the far shore, the barracks beside the flagstaff.*

11 *Albion House, Augusta, 1836. Built of bricks brought out from England, Albion House sits to the right among the trees. The Molloys' house is to the left, down towards Hardy Inlet. The Bussells' house lies in between. The work of clearing has commenced. A jumble of tree trunks and branches litters the foreground.*

12 *Albion House, Augusta, c. 1840s. Comparison of this picture with the same view above reveals much more cleared land and more buildings and fences erected.*

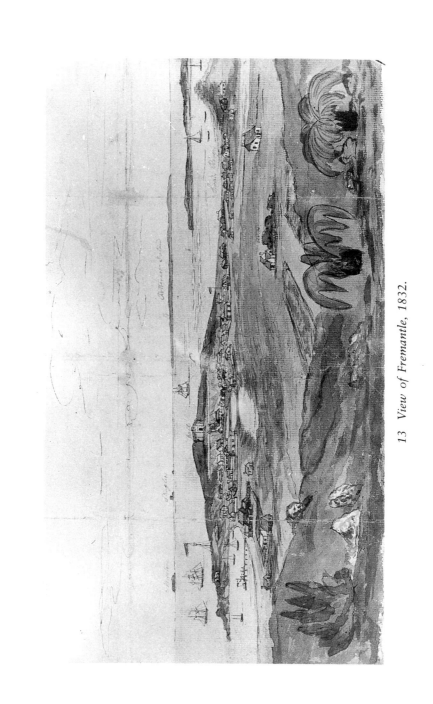

13 *View of Fremantle, 1832.*

14 Cattle Chosen, the Vasse, 1835. The main house, centre, was a two-storey wattle-and-daub building with a clay floor. The cottage near the vegetable garden was the first to be built.

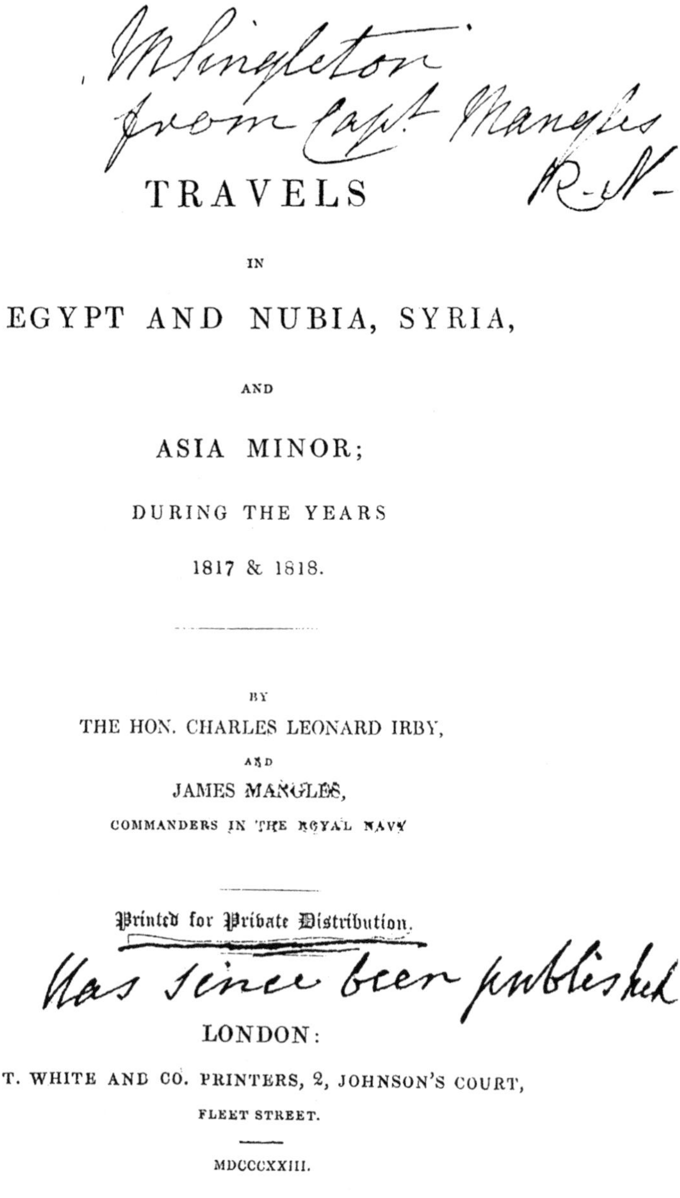

M. Singleton
from Capt. Mangles R.N.

TRAVELS

IN

EGYPT AND NUBIA, SYRIA,

AND

ASIA MINOR;

DURING THE YEARS

1817 & 1818.

BY

THE HON. CHARLES LEONARD IRBY,

AND

JAMES MANGLES,

COMMANDERS IN THE ROYAL NAVY

𝔓rinted for 𝔓ribate 𝔇istribution.

Has since been published

LONDON:

T. WHITE AND CO. PRINTERS, 2, JOHNSON'S COURT,

FLEET STREET.

MDCCCXXIII.

15   Inscribed title page of a copy of James Mangles's Travels.

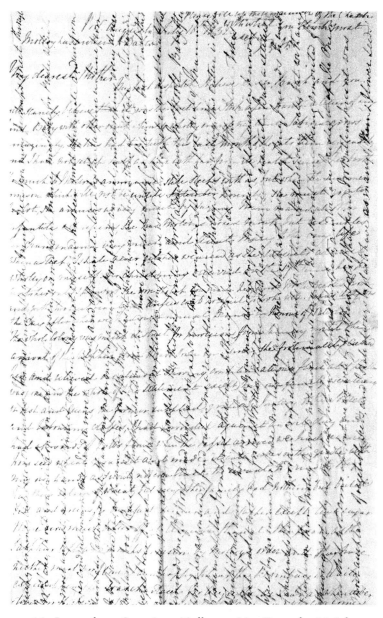

16 Letter from Georgiana Molloy to Mrs Kennedy, 16 July
1832. To save paper and postage, Molloy commonly
'crossed' her letters: she wrote down the page as normal,
then turned the paper and wrote across the previous writing.

Top: *17 John Bussell, c. 1850;* below: *18 John Molloy in old age.*

the scene, that the landscape resembles the spacious park of some wealthy proprietor, rather than a sylvan solitude in a newly discovered world.

The colony's greatest want, Cross argued, was labour: 'Without a large supply of labour, or some obedient power, improvement and civilization must stand still.'[30]

Winter storms stranded Stirling at King George Sound for seven weeks. During the delay Stirling realised that the colony had not advanced since the second year of settlement. Improvement and civilisation stood still; Western Australia remained a collection of isolated and disorganised settlements with little communication between them. No roads connected the settlements and no markets existed to encourage commerce. The population was too small and too scattered to generate local trade, and yearly exports amounted to less than £900. Isolation and an inadequate population generated a feeling of vulnerability and a fear of organised attack from Aborigines.

Settler paranoia reflected a complete misunderstanding of Aboriginal social organisation. The British imagined they faced organised opposition and thought in terms of Scottish clans or American Indian tribes under councils of war. But the Nyungar lived without chiefs or even hierarchy of authority. No structure existed to negotiate treaties or organise Aboriginal people under leaders. Not only did settlers misunderstand the Aborigines and project onto them the organisation of traditional enemies but they also did not even appreciate their own superiority. The invaders possessed a preeminence in social cohesiveness as well as in weaponry. United by a single purpose—to possess and prosper—they were better organised for conquest than the Aborigines were for defence. Moreover, British culture was characterised by immense confidence in its own centrality, by a political organisation based on command and submission, and by a willingness to use coercive violence on both strangers and fellow countrymen.

The Nyungar, in contrast, at least around the settlements, had become dependent on the settlers for flour, biscuits, salt pork, and beef. While some individuals were hostile towards the settlers' usurpation, others cared or thought little about the matter. They cared only about the kangaroo and other game becoming alarmingly scarce. Otherwise, Nyungar remained absorbed in their own preoccupations. They had families, sacred traditions to uphold, and all the minutiae of daily life to contend with. They were utterly unprepared for war.

The settlers—steeped in the traditions of conquest, inspired by legendary heroes, and led by Napoleonic War veterans—thought obsessively in terms of war, of offence and defence. They clamoured for action against the Aborigines, who, in Stirling's absence, and propelled by hunger, had made increasing claims on settler food stocks. When he reached Perth in August 1834, Stirling found food stocks so depleted that he reinstated rationing. Settlers supplemented their supplies with game from the bush.

Under the impress of competition for their traditional food sources, Aborigines turned increasingly to the exotic supplies of the settlers. In April 1834 members of the Murray River cohort boldly raided a flour mill in South Perth. They and other Nyungar continued to take stock and harass stockkeepers throughout 1834. Settlers feared mass attack, and Stirling wrote, 'If they [the Nyungar] had the inclination and the power to combine their efforts, it would be useless to attempt to maintain our conquest with our present numbers.'[31]

Stirling's initial impressions of the Aborigines, at least officially, had been favourable. 'They are active and hardy in habit,' he wrote during his exploring trip to Swan River in 1827, 'and seem to possess the qualities usually springing from such habits; Bravery, Vivacity, and Quickness, and a Temper alternating between kindness and ferocity.' He added one cautionary note: 'They seemed angry at our invasion of their Territory.' With settlement, opinions changed. The once-respected, once-active and hardy people became lazy, indolent, and treacherous, and in need of correction and punishment. Soon after he returned to Perth from England, Stirling organised a corps of mounted police to deal quickly and severely with Aboriginal depredations.[32]

Late in October 1834, in retaliation for the raid on the flour mill in April, Stirling led the corps—an armed and mounted party of 25 police, soldiers, and settlers, including Waterloo veteran Captain Richard Meares—from Perth to the Murray River. Stirling knew that the Murray people frequently camped by the river, at a site they called Pinjarra. Stirling wanted Pinjarra for a military post, the first of several garrisons he planned along a proposed road to Albany. Early on the morning of 28 October the corps surrounded a band of 70 to 80 men, women, and children camped on the river's bank. The avenging party began firing and caught the sleeping group in a deadly crossfire. The shooting continued until some twenty or more Aborigines lay dead; an uncounted number of bodies floated downstream.

Settlers quickly applauded the massacre. Different accounts circulated through the colony. Some chronicles put the number dead at 35. But though they disputed the details, settlers concurred that the rout effected the pedagogic goal of teaching the natives a salutary lesson. G. F. Moore, who received a personal account of the attack from the governor, commented:

> The destruction of European lives and property committed by that tribe was such that they considered themselves quite our masters, and had become so emboldened that either that part of the settlement must have been abandoned or a severe example made of them. It was a painful but urgent necessity, and likely to be the most humane policy in the end.[33]

The massacre also boosted confidence in Stirling's leadership, and settlers felt affirmed in their own claim to the land. British ascendancy now seemed assured, and settlers celebrated the 'Battle of Pinjarra' in music, song, and poetry.

The Augusta settlers shared the general colonial fear of Aboriginal combination. As a defence against possible Aboriginal attack, Captain Molloy recommended that Vasse grants be concentrated. The government agreed, and in April 1833, when John Bussell received permission to occupy his Vasse grant, the surveyor-general told him that land had been assigned 'with a view to [settlers'] mutual support and protection against the native population in that district, which appear very numerous and may possibly become troublesome'.[34]

Although they received Aboriginal help, not hindrance, when they occupied their Vasse grant, the Bussell brothers continued to anticipate trouble, especially when they discovered that the grassy, fertile Vasse supported a much larger number of Aborigines than they had originally thought. The land was not as free as they wished. In October 1834, seven months after the brothers' occupation, John Bussell journeyed to Swan River to ask Governor Stirling for more military protection. Bussell's visit coincided with the Battle of Pinjarra, and Stirling, pleased with the success of his own policy of firmness against the Aborigines, readily agreed to the request. He ordered two more soldiers to the Vasse. The tiny settlement now had five full-time sentinels.

Despite the victory at Pinjarra, the small number of British settlers in Western Australia still caused concern. By 1834 the immigrant population was decreasing. In 1829, during the first six months of settlement, 1125 settlers arrived. In 1830, 635 arrived but in 1831, arrivals dropped to 179. Only fourteen arrived in 1832 and 39 left, while in 1833, 143 left and only fourteen arrived.

In 1834 the colony received only a handful of settlers, among them, Mrs Frances Bussell and her daughter Mary, who arrived at Fremantle in August, aboard the *James Pattison*. Frederick Ludlow, who had walked from Augusta via the Vasse, met the last two members of the Bussell family to migrate to Australia. He told Mrs

Bussell he wished to leave the Molloys and enter the Bussell family's service. He also told her that her sons were progressing at the Vasse. Mrs Bussell concluded, 'I think ultimately the whole of the Augusta settlement will be transferred to the Vasse.'[35]

1 3

MAKERS OF FORTUNE

WHEN MRS BUSSELL MIGRATED TO WESTERN AUSTRALIA SHE brought all the family's remaining English possessions, including heirlooms, linen, and the family silver. She arranged to ship the goods from Fremantle to Augusta aboard the *Cumberland*, captained by James McDermott. Mrs Bussell wanted to sail with her effects but Governor Stirling warned her that the puny *Cumberland* was unsafe and persuaded her to wait for the *Ellen*. Stirling's caution proved warranted. Shortly after the *Cumberland* left Fremantle in August 1834, a sudden storm wrecked the boat. McDermott and three sailors drowned and the cargo scattered along the coast.

Unaware of the *Cumberland*'s fate, Mrs Bussell and Mary sailed south on board the *Ellen* in October. The ship anchored briefly at the Vasse, and Mrs Bussell met her sons after a separation of five years. On the same day, the long-lost cow, Yulika, and calf, walked onto the farm. Yulika's arrival seemed propitious, and the Bussells decided to name their property Cattle Chosen. Because there was no accommodation at the Vasse and because her daughters were still at Augusta, Mrs Bussell sailed on to Flinders Bay with Mary.

The personal attention she received from Governor Stirling and the reunion with her children filled Mrs Bussell with a sense of the family's importance. When she reached Augusta she wrote to relatives in England that 'with all our barbarity we are very considerable people. Every possible distinction is shown us and the Bussells are as well known in every part of Australia as the Governor.' She was particularly proud of the role adopted by her daughters. 'My dear girls are perfect wonders in their new life,' she wrote. 'They mend every article for their five brothers and you will see their little hands sewing canvas trousers and making coarse cloth jackets, kneading bread, etc.' Anxious lest the relatives form a view of life in the colony as all mind-numbing labour, she added, 'We do not neglect the elegant occupations. We have our music and reading and dancing.' There was but one liability. 'Emma is our only drawback,' Mrs Bussell continued. 'She is the most depraved of girls. There is no truth in her. She is dishonest and a common courtesan. She has three times gone through the ceremony of being in the family way and is now playing the same trick, for a trick I do suspect.' But Emma was not deceiving; she was now six months pregnant with the child of Mrs Bussell's son Charles.[1]

After the *Cumberland*'s departure from Fremantle, months passed with no word of its fate. The Bussells began to assume the worst. By the time of Mrs Bussell's arrival at Augusta, the family accepted the boat and their possessions as irretrievable. 'Our losses have been incalculable,' Fanny told Capel Carter.[2]

Georgiana Molloy sympathised with the loss of the Bussells' property but thought Mrs Bussell was partly to blame. Molloy had looked forward to Mrs Bussell's arrival, 'as she will be like a mother to me, from age and experience', but she found the woman a fool. 'None but herself would have ventured property of value in such a vessel,' she remarked acidly, 'as it was only a boat built on.'[3]

Georgiana Molloy's mother had shipped several boxes of toys and other gifts for her grandchildren, daughter, and son-in-law by the *James Pattison*. On arrival at Fremantle these were placed aboard the *Cumberland* and were therefore lost along with the Bussells' goods. Georgiana Molloy, however, refused to dwell on her own loss and instead reserved her sympathy for McDermott's widow, the former Ann Turner, who had a two-year-old child and was pregnant but 'without a *penny* to support themselves owing to her husband's inadvertent speculations. I am in hopes she will come down here after her confinement and if she does not feel comfortable at her father's, we intend offering her an Asylum at our house.'4

Molloy confided her opinion and her intention in a very long letter to Helen Story that she commenced in December 1834. After nearly five years at Augusta, she told Story, she was still uneasy with the spiritual incompleteness of her Australian life. She still felt tension between body and soul, between the demands of daily living and duty towards God. 'Spiritually speaking,' she told Story, 'this is a most seductive life—even though we are only occupied with cares and necessaries, not the pleasures of life.' Colonial life was corrupting because of its incessant physical and material demands. As an example Molloy offered the self-centred contents of her letter, 'thus far occupied with egotistical details'. In a settler's life, work came before contemplation. 'You will be able fully to believe me when I say I must either leave writing alone or some useful requisite needlework undone. . . . I never open a book and if I can read a chapter on Sundays, it is quite a treat to have so much leisure.'5

In September Molloy had learned of her sister Elizabeth's death. They had long been estranged. Religious differences separated them. Georgiana regarded duty towards God as paramount; Elizabeth, although she had married a clergyman, concentrated on the joys of this life. Nevertheless, Molloy reacted with disbelief at the news. Death at such a distance seemed unreal. Her sister's passing, she wrote, 'I can scarcely believe, remote as we are from the land in which it occurred.' But the fact was, 'my poor dear sister Eliza has passed the awful limits of time and began neverending Eternity'. 'Oh! Helen,' she continued, 'would that I could see and speak to you on this.' She worried about Elizabeth's spiritual repose and wished 'that the dead might be recalled to retrace those heedless steps which were so prematurely and suddenly arrested'. But she felt 'great consolation that we were good friends on leaving England and even better since I was out here'. They had written regularly, Elizabeth had sent presents of seeds, books, and clothes, and Molloy had sent her Australian seeds and other bush curiosities. Molloy also consoled herself with the information that, in her last days, Elizabeth became more serious than formerly, that she read the Scriptures daily and consulted other religious works. But Molloy was still unconvinced that her sister was prepared for death and worried how Elizabeth would be judged in heaven. 'Write to me what you think her case will be,' she urged Helen Story. Molloy also feared for her sister Mary and asked Story to intervene, to write to her, 'and urge the folly of remaining so long buried in this world's wiles'.[6]

Elizabeth's death compounded Molloy's sense of isolation. She was too far removed to mourn and too remote to seek counsel for her own spiritual afflictions. The perpetual and merciless battle between the spirit and the flesh, she felt, could have been more fruitfully waged in Scotland, among friends. She confessed to Story, 'You may remember my reluctance to come out to Australia and I wish I never had.' Her regrets, however, were not only spiritual. 'We enjoy health and our children will have perhaps more than a competency,' she conceded, 'but Molloy and I have to work as hard and harder than our servants will.' Their servants' indentures expired in March 1835, and Molloy expected she and her husband would be entirely without help. She could not imagine how they would cope:

> I know I cannot do without a woman servant, however bad she may be, especially when there is no one to be got to wash even, and I have to carry baby, so fat she is, she makes my back quite ache. As to Molloy, he is a perfect slave; up by daybreak and doing the most menial work sometimes—so that all the former part of our lives was all lost time—even reading and writing, there is not time for here.[7]

Molloy also felt a pedagogical responsibility towards her children. She wanted them educated, literate, numerate, and taught good habits. Sabina was growing up and was learning to act wilfully. Her premeditated behaviour presented her parents with new challenges. In Molloy's plain Presbyterian upbringing, sin did not count; what mattered were the failings people must try to overcome. Deceitfulness, especially, was to be deplored, and Molloy expected truthfulness at all times, in all subjects. She confided to Helen Story, 'I never knew Sabina to tell a direct untruth till last Saturday when she was whipt for the first time, but still insensible to her fault.' As a mother, Molloy was unsure of her proper response. She questioned whether the infliction of pain could ever throw new light on the differences between parent and child. Whipping would not make up for the deficiency in truthfulness, and she asked, 'Tell me how you act when you are given to untruth.'[8]

Mary Dorothea, not quite six months old, was still too young to lie and subject her parents to moral dilemmas. Molloy described her as

a very large fat child and remarkably healthy. With great thankfulness I avow she has never had even infantine illness. Everyone says she is a beautiful child and, though it may appear very vain, I coincide with them. She is very fair—I call her *French white*—and her flesh is so hard and plump that her arms and legs are like polished marble. Her face is more like mine than dear Sabina is. Her eyes are rather dark blue.

Although she had breastfed Sabina for eighteen months, she planned to wean Mary Dorothea much sooner, 'before the servants go, as I am sure I shall not be equal to nursing her and all the other work'.[9]

Molloy continued her letter through January 1835 and on the new year resolved, 'I shall never be happy till I have less to do and think of than at present.' Relief, however, would have to be found in Australia. For despite her homesickness, her longing for Scotland, and her regrets, and despite her physical and spiritual burdens,

Molloy never thought of leaving Augusta. She accepted the consequences of her emigration. Indeed, she felt committed to Augusta's future and urged Helen Story to advise anyone contemplating emigration to consider southwestern Australia. The climate was perhaps more healthy than anywhere else in the world. For those who suffered from heat and for those who suffered from cold, Augusta was perfect. The southwest wanted immigrants, for at present 'we suffer materially from this place being as little known, as it makes our numbers so small we have no opportunity of progressing'.[10]

The Bussells made their own opportunities. They believed their own progress depended on rigid parsimony and family exclusiveness. Accordingly, they expected outsiders to accommodate themselves to, and accept the primacy of, Bussell family needs. Except where benevolence might serve their own interests first, they shunned reciprocity, compromise, and charity.

For several years the Molloys had felt importuned by Bussell family demands; they decided to end the Bussells' unilateral appropriations. In February 1835, while Captain Molloy toured King George Sound with Governor Stirling, Georgiana Molloy confronted Charles and Lenox Bussell about their cows, which grazed on the Molloys' grant. She told the brothers she intended to impose an agistment charge, the same as levied on James Turner, whose cows also grazed the property. Lenox objected and refused to pay. Despite, or perhaps because of, the Molloys' previous generosity, the Bussells viewed the agistment request as malicious and mean. Relations cooled, and the two families spoke only from necessity.

At the end of February Captain Molloy returned from King George Sound. Unable to put in at Flinders Bay, his ship sailed around to Geographe Bay and he disembarked at the Vasse. He spent a night with the Bussells and next morning borrowed a horse for the journey to Augusta. During the first night's bivouac, the horse escaped into the bush; Captain Molloy walked the rest of the way. Bessie commented acidly, 'We lent our horse to Captain Molloy to return home.

The stupid creature tied a slip knot and lo, it left him in the night as he slept. Of course he is responsible for it, but out here, it is an almost irreparable loss.'[11]

When Molloy reached Augusta he promised Lenox, who was visiting from the Vasse, that he would defray all reasonable charges incurred in looking for the missing horse. Lenox returned to the Vasse to notify his brothers of the animal's escape. He and Vernon then spent five days in the bush in a vain search. In the meantime, John was irate; ploughing season had begun but with a horse missing he could not harness his team. He wrote to Charles at Augusta, 'Ploughing for ourselves is at an end and the profit arising from their employment by others. Two hands and two horses have been employed five days, in a useless search when their services were wanted beyond everything.' Furthermore, the Bussells had expected Captain Molloy to organise a search party from Augusta to join Lenox and Vernon in the bush. Molloy, however, thought pursuit from Augusta unnecessary and left the search to the Bussells. The Bussells found his omission derelict and were incensed.[12]

Six weeks later the horse wandered back to the Vasse. John Bussell sent Captain Molloy a bill for each day the horse had been missing, plus a charge for the labour of the searchers. Captain Molloy thought the charges excessive and niggardly. He reminded the Bussells of his past generosity and asked for a fairer assessment. John Bussell visited Augusta in August and suggested the Bussells' loss be balanced against the hire of Molloy's bullocks, previously employed at the Adelphi for two weeks. Captain Molloy interpreted Bussell's proposal as a ploy and accused him of 'getting up his bib for the purpose of discharging an account which had not before troubled his memory'. His patience exhausted, he escalated the dispute and submitted a separate and exaggerated bill for the bullocks' use. Bussell refused to pay; the two men then resolved to place their quarrel before arbitration.

The Bussells were confident the court would rule in their favour.

In the meantime, they accepted strained relations. Lenox wrote to Capel Carter, 'The character of the Molloys is so notorious for meanness that we can scarcely reject the complete estrangement which now exists between us.' A few months later Fanny wrote to Capel, 'We have been following the colonial pattern of quarrelling with our neighbours, but Captain Molloy is unfortunately, rather extortionate in his charges, and objections and recriminations have been followed up by an angry correspondence.' Fanny was less circumspect in her opinion of the captain when she wrote to John, 'I look upon Captain Molloy as a dangerous and merciless enemy but I trust we have nothing to apprehend from him.'[13]

The Bussells may not have feared Captain Molloy, but other people in the little Augusta community felt the wrath of the Bussells. The family's truculent morality strictly rationed their compassion, and they judged others harshly. In January 1835, when Emma Mould's pregnancy became too obvious to be disregarded, the Bussells dismissed her from their employ. 'She is the most abandoned creature,' Mrs Bussell declared. 'She has violated every commandment.' Mrs Bussell refused to believe that the father was her own son and accused Emma of breaking the seventh commandment. Nearly eight months pregnant at the time of her dismissal, Emma Mould had no one and nowhere to turn to at Augusta.[14]

Georgiana Molloy, whose piety often made her a severe judge of other people, nevertheless accepted forgiveness and charity as her first duty and took the young woman into her service. A month later, on 17 February 1835, Emma Mould gave birth to Charles Bussell's son, Henry John. The illegitimate circumstances of the birth rankled with the Bussells. They wanted mother and child separated and, though they continued to deny the child's paternity, they took Henry John to bring up themselves. Emma Mould left Augusta with a recommendation of employment, from Molloy, to a woman at King George Sound. Mould later moved to Perth and in December 1836 married settler Thomas Sweetman. She had eight more children, including a son she named Charles.

Henry John's was not the first birth at Augusta in 1835, nor was the unmarried state of his mother the only case of scandal. On 27 January the 41-year-old Mary Smith, wife of labourer Andrew Smith, gave birth to a daughter, Mary Ann. Two months later the mother was dead. An inquest, presided over by Magistrate Molloy, determined that Smith had died after drinking a bottle of brandy. Blows from her husband had contributed to her death. Witnesses testified that Smith regularly mistreated his wife. The jury returned a verdict of death by apoplexy. No charges were laid against Andrew Smith.

Georgiana Molloy was appalled at Smith's conduct and thought him 'a brutal and wicked man' and 'so depraved a character' that she determined to adopt Mary Ann. As she explained to her mother, 'I was unwilling that a helpless, innocent child should be ushered into the Walks of Vice when the Path of Virtue might be thrown open to her.' With Captain Molloy's permission she took Mary Ann, or Polly, as she called her, into her home, with the intention of 'bringing her up as a servant and especially as a handmaid'. Polly, she found, was 'an uncommonly good child and sits and plays the whole day'. 'Of course,' she added, 'I have no great affection for so plebian a child and have never yet kissed her.' But she never got the chance, for shortly after, Andrew Smith claimed back his daughter.[15]

On 6 April 1835 Anne Dawson delivered another child, a daughter, Maria, barely nine months after she had previously given birth. The Dawsons were now no longer indentured to the Molloys. They aspired to own property. To ascertain opportunities at the Vasse, Elijah Dawson had arranged to work for the Bussells for six months in 1834. He had since returned to Augusta but hoped eventually to bring his family to the Vasse and take up land.

Amidst new life there was also death. On 29 April Robert Heppingstone drowned when a wave washed him out to sea while he was fishing from rocks in Flinders Bay. Heppingstone had originally been indentured to the Molloys, but he and his wife were among the first servants to leave and become independent landholders. Ann Heppingstone was 31 at the time of the drowning; she had six children and was barely able to make a living on their small Augusta allotment. Captain Molloy extended her credit from the government store.

Sinners or saints, the pregnant women at Augusta were never alone. Pregnancy and childbirth were collective experiences. The simultaneous and permanent presence of pregnancy was a central feature of the settlement. Being with child was a state of normalcy that women did not think to avoid. On 25 May Mary Ann Layman, wife of smallholder George Layman, gave birth to a daughter, Harriet.

Georgiana Molloy turned 30 in May and, as she predicted to Helen Story, facing the loss of domestic help, she weaned Mary Dorothea. By July she was pregnant. Pregnancy coincided with another winter of privation at Augusta.

Governor Stirling had promised relief but none came. The Bussells and Turner believed the governor's neglect was deliberate. 'We are all of an opinion,' Bessie wrote to Capel Carter, 'that the governor intends to oblige the people to leave Augusta.' Augusta, Mrs Bussell wrote to Capel, was 'suffering from dearth of provisions'. In contrast, at Cattle Chosen, 'Cabbages, carrots, turnips, onions, cucumbers, melons, etc., they have in abundance of prodigious size and quality.' Fanny also reported optimistically on progress at the Vasse and wrote to Capel that 'one year in the fertile regions of Cattle Chosen has effected more in the way of agriculture than ages could have produced upon the vast forest of the Blackwood'.[16]

The men at the Vasse had expected even greater progress than that celebrated by Fanny. Building and agriculture had advanced less rapidly than anticipated. John Bussell decided the farm was not yet ready to receive his mother and sisters. The planned family reunion was repeatedly delayed. John wrote of his disappointment to Capel:

'Had we had fair play and means of progressing with the outlay we have made we should by this time have been opulent.' Nevertheless, he still looked forward to future abundance, and continued, 'Such is for the best, we have served a long apprenticeship and after the various losses and retrograde movements perhaps we shall appreciate with greater gratitude the prosperity that is now dawning.'[17]

Sunrise, however, still lay in the future. In the meantime, want continued to prevail at both the Vasse and Augusta. By the end of the winter of 1835, the brothers rationed themselves to a quarter of a pound of rice a day and depended on their dogs and guns to procure fresh meat. At Augusta the Bussell family rationed themselves to half a pound of bread a day. 'We are all quite well under our short allowance,' Fanny assured John, 'but sometimes very hungry.' The family supplemented their provisions with fish from the river and went out almost daily with the net. 'Catching, cleaning, scaling and drying fish,' Bessie wrote to Capel, was their constant occupation, and as a consequence, 'our chimney has been filled with drying fish, our room with tubs for pickling and the beams hung with those ready for exportation.' When ships called, the women sent the smoked and salted fish to the Vasse. They also embarked clothes they had made. They were anxious for their brothers' well-being and Fanny looked forward to the time when 'female industry and foresight will soon make affairs [at the Vasse] wear an orderly and comfortable look'.[18]

By September 1835 Cattle Chosen had been established for seventeen months, yet the family remained separated. Bessie, the most pertinacious and impatient of the Bussell women, could stand the temporary life at Augusta no longer. She wanted to participate in the colonising adventure her brothers had pioneered at the Vasse. Eventually she persuaded John to take her overland to the new settlement. In mid-November she, John, Vernon, Alfred, and Dawson rode over to the Vasse from Augusta.

As soon as she had recovered from the trip, Bessie wrote a long account of her two-day journey—of rivers crossed, hills ascended, camp fires kindled, meals consumed, of saddle fatigue, sunburn, and the night spent under the southern sky. To pioneer the Vasse was, she understood, the family's manifest destiny. As the party neared Cattle Chosen, she later wrote to her mother and sisters, 'I put on my spectacles that I might see the house immediately it opened upon us from among the beautiful peppermint trees. You can form no idea of my sensation on beholding our dwelling for the first time.' But she was so tired she 'could hardly bestow a look upon our beautiful sleek cattle as they lay ruminating beneath the trees'.[19]

Despite her fatigue Bessie experienced unbounded delight. After travelling through the undifferentiated bush, 'through a country so exactly familiar to the woods of Augusta' that only amnesia resulted, she came upon a land where the imposition of civilisation rendered nature agreeable and intelligible. Sleek cows lay, as ordained, under properly spaced trees. The Vasse did not support the wild vegetative profusion of Augusta. Nature at the Vasse was controlled. Those features associated with European activity—cows, grassy fields, spreading trees, houses, smoke curling from chimneys, men on horse-back—dominated. At the Vasse Bessie perceived domesticated nature, nature tamed and imaginatively possessable.[20]

Bessie commenced farm chores. She milked the cow, Yulika, daily, churned the milk, and assisted Phoebe in making butter. She also cared for the farm animals. To the women at Augusta she wrote of 'our really splendid garden' and detailed the animals' habits and fecundity—Fan, Ness, and Ranger, the kangaroo-hunting dogs, winded and wounded from the chase; the turkey hen, Molloynie, incubating seven duck eggs; fillies, mares, fowls, cows and calves, the pig, Indy, and its litter. Everyone was busy. Lenox was clearing, Alfred and Vernon were planting potatoes, John was making a staircase, and 'I find plenty of work; I Mrs Morganize a great deal.' 'My toilet,' she assured her mother and sisters, 'I manage better than I expected having *never been so much alone before.*' 'Alone' meant without family female company.[21]

Mother and sisters admired Bessie's pioneering spirit and applauded her civilising efforts. They believed women were moral police, agents responsible for banishing barbarity and establishing order. Women were responsible for securing those social and domestic virtues inseparable from successful colonisation. Chastity, obedience, and domesticity were essential to subdue the wilderness. Mary Bussell wrote of Bessie's work to Capel Carter: 'She is indeed an admirable girl and equal to anything. We hear from the boys that she is working wonders, reducing our savage brothers into some kind of order.'[22]

In December 1835 John Bussell and Captain Molloy went to Perth for the arbitration of their dispute over the lost horse. The court ruled in the Bussells' favour. 'Strange to say,' Mary wrote to Fanny, 'they returned friends, which again places all parties on speaking terms.' The judgemental Bussells, who assessed others according to their own standards, had not expected the loser to concede so gracefully. In her triumph, Mary detected that Georgiana Molloy 'now courts a greater intimacy than has existed since we came out'. This was unlikely. Molloy thought the Bussells unconscionably avaricious, but she understood that in a small, mutually dependent community, neighbours, regardless of personal feelings, still had to cooperate and communicate. She preferred amicability, however forced, to open enmity.[23]

Little time remained, however, for socialising with the Bussells at Augusta. Ever since Bessie's departure, her mother and sisters thought only of the time when they would join her and the boys at the Vasse. On 15 January 1836 the *Sally Anne* put in at Flinders Bay. The Bussell women stowed aboard their goods, their journals and letters, and embarked for Geographe Bay, where they landed on 19 January.

Over the preceding year a steady migration of smallholders and labourers had already left Augusta for the Vasse. On the day his mother and sisters arrived, John wrote to Capel Carter, 'Augusta is, I think, on the eve of dissolution. It will be deserted by everyone except Mr Turner, who feels himself bound to the spot by the costly nature of his improvements, consisting of fences, buildings, etc.' Even the Molloys would leave eventually, he predicted. In the meantime,

> Captain Molloy is dark and mysterious in his actions. He upholds the prospects of a devoted settlement in the presence of one or two labourers who cling with hopeless perseverance to the small improvements they have effected with great labour; but like a skillful general he has provided for his own retreat.

Bussell explained that Molloy had arranged for his jurisdiction as resident magistrate to include the Vasse, so that he might 'move to his grant without incurring the odium of absenteeism and on that account forfeiting his government salary'.[24]

Unlike Molloy, James Turner had made no contingency plans in case of Augusta's failure. He had not taken his 5000 extra acres at the Vasse. While his Augusta neighbours and labourers continued to leave, he clung stubbornly to his grant. Turner was now 56 years old, and most of his labourers had left him. His eldest son had also struck out on his own.

In January 1833 Thomas Turner had taken land six kilometres up Hardy Inlet, adjacent to Molloy Island. With the help of a brother, he felled trees, dug waterways, fenced paddocks, and built a small cottage, several outbuildings, a barn, and a jetty. He called the property Turnwood. Mrs Bussell, who took tea there one day in April 1835 with her daughters, described the estate as one 'with which we could not be otherwise than highly delighted. Roads, entrenchments, fencing, buildings, clearances, etc. The labour and industry must have been intense and if ever a young man deserved success it is he.' Bessie also admired Turner's industry, but since everyone was leaving for the Vasse she thought his efforts in vain. 'It is wonderful the progress Mr Thomas Turner has made,' she wrote to Capel Carter, 'but it is very melancholy to think there is a probability of its not answering.'[25]

While Thomas Turner laboured on at Turnwood, the Bussell women assumed their respective domestic duties at Cattle Chosen. Fanny explained the arrangements to Capel: 'Phoebe [Bower] undertakes the greater part of the washing, but the assistance of one of us is constantly requisite. She makes and bakes our bread and butter at present, with the aid of one of us in churning.' Phoebe also cooked for herself and Frederick Ludlow, the Bussells' only male servant. 'Everything else,' Fanny explained,

> devolves upon ourselves, and our duties are divided into three departments: Cook, Housemaid and Chambermaid, which offices we change monthly. Add to this the care of the poultry, making and mending [clothes] for the boys, the household and ourselves and you will not call us idle.[26]

With the household and farm functioning as he desired, the family patriarch, John Bussell, began plans to visit England. The long-delayed family reunion had frustrated his desire to take leave to marry Sophie Hayward, an heiress, whom he had known since childhood. Hayward, however, was wary of the match and had expressed reservations. Friends warned her that Bussell was a fortune hunter. Additionally, Bussell's insistence, repeated in letter after letter, that his mother remain in charge of domestic affairs caused Hayward to doubt future happiness in Australia as a subordinate. As early as 1832 he told her, 'In domestic affairs, in her own circle, my mother must be paramount. In general external affairs, such as are not the province of women, as expediency demands, I might assume the control.' He insisted he command 'any income that a wife may bring'. There was, he protested, no ulterior motive to this arrangement; this was simply the way of things.[27]

As John planned his departure, the reunited family continued to effect progress and transform rude nature. 'Improvements are daily springing up around us,' Fanny reported to relatives in England. 'The garden, well fenced and productive in all English vegetables, would almost make you forget that you are in Australia.' Stock throve and multiplied. Chimneys vented all the buildings and a 'well-sized and well-proportioned' sitting room in the main house was rendered comfortable and civilised by books and furnishings. Upstairs, 'the windows command on one side a pleasant view of the river, with the country in its unredeemed state, which is so completely park-like that you would scarcely believe that a year and ten months only have elapsed since the improving hand of the European was first extended over its glades'. From here one could also view the bush, which, although 'full of beauty', was not as interesting as the prospect from the windows on the other side. There one apprehended a more comprehensible, domesticated nature, a framed picturesque composition where Bussell industry had obliterated the Australian character of the landscape. Fanny wrote, 'I dwell with more interest and delight on the opposite scene where we view the little hamlet, our garden, our hayrick and our stock-yard. It is more essentially English, and it bears the marks of daily improvements.'[28]

Fanny's preference reflected the Bussells' utilitarian ideal of beauty. A land compelled to usefulness and to perform an active and remunerative part in the drama of life, a land well-stocked for human profit, was a beautiful land. The familiar and reassuring sights and sounds of the farmyard almost made Fanny forget she was in Australia.

England was the standard of measure for settlers and visitors who wished they were elsewhere. Early in March 1836 the young Charles Darwin, aboard the *Beagle*, arrived at King George Sound. Near the end of a five-year voyage of global circumnavigation, Darwin was homesick and wrote disparagingly of his eight-day visit, 'We did not during our voyage pass a more dull and uninteresting time.' Earlier Darwin had spent several weeks in New South Wales. He disliked Australia and when he sailed from King George Sound wrote, 'Farewell, Australia! you are a rising child, and doubtless some day will reign a great princess in the South; but you are too great and ambitious for affection, yet not great enough for respect. I leave your shores without sorrow or regret.' Notwithstanding the monotony and disappointment of Australia, Darwin later reflected on the global changes induced by the philanthropic spirit of the British nation and concluded, 'To hoist the British flag, seems to draw with it as a certain consequence, wealth, prosperity, and civilization.'[29]

Wealth and prosperity, however, eluded settlers at King George Sound, Augusta, Swan River and Busselton, as the Vasse settlement was now known. Food supplies were precarious, ships infrequent, and the future uncertain. Aborigines continued to raid public and private stores. Migrant numbers remained static, although population grew slightly through natural increase. In April 1836 Georgiana Molloy gave birth to her fourth Australian child, a boy, John.

As Molloy nursed her newborn, John Bussell thought ever more urgently of starting a family of his own. In November he left Busselton for Swan River, and in December he sailed for England.

In the same month the colonial schooner *Champion*, with Governor Stirling aboard, called at Augusta. Goods and mail were unloaded. Molloy received a box of gifts from her mother and an entirely unexpected letter and box of seeds from a stranger in London. Her correspondent, Stirling informed her, was Ellen Stirling's cousin, Captain James Mangles, RN. Mangles, a horticulturalist interested in the plants of the Australian southwest, asked Molloy to accept the English seeds as a gift. In exchange, he requested her to refill the box with native seeds and specimens and return them to him. Mangles made no promises and offered no inducements. Fulfilment of his request augured neither wealth, nor prosperity, nor status. Botanising had no utilitarian purpose. Molloy immediately accepted the challenge.

1 4

LIFE AND DEATH

THE MAN WHOSE BOTANICAL REQUEST GEORGIANA MOLLOY FOUND so appealing and so irresistible was, like her husband, a veteran of the Napoleonic Wars. James Mangles had served in the Royal Navy, which he entered in 1800 at age fourteen. He served off France and South Africa and rose through the ranks to receive promotion to captain in 1815. A short time later he left the navy on half-pay.

In 1816 Mangles and fellow Royal Navy commander Captain Charles Leonard Irby commenced a grand tour of the continent. Together they walked 900 miles through Switzerland and then journeyed to Egypt, Syria, and Asia Minor. They sought a rigorous regime of discipline, application, challenge, and manly discovery. Travel was also an intellectual pleasure. Mangles, in particular, was a conscious and disciplined observer; he measured ancient buildings and tombs, took notes, and collected specimens and antiquities.

In Egypt Mangles and Irby supervised refractory and treacherous workers while excavating ancient tombs. Next they journeyed to the Holy Land, travelled among banditti, employed armed escorts, faced down hostile tribes and cheating guides, and endured hunger and thirst. In letters home Mangles projected firmness of character and a steely British resolve to resist all attempts at extortion and intimidation. Used to command, Mangles expected obedience, and commented about Egypt, 'It is a great inconvenience to a traveller in this country, that both servants and interpreters always think themselves wiser than their masters.'[1]

In Palestine Mangles sought out sites associated with Old and New Testament incidents. His religion, however, was conventionally Anglican, and he felt no need to proselytise. Rampant paganism and Mohammedism in the Holy Land did not trouble him. He accepted cultural differences and philosophically resigned himself to the conclusion that 'when all are rogues, and cheating and imposition are reckoned honourable and fair, and do not at all hurt the character of a man amongst his companions, one must not expect too much'. On the other hand, Mangles admired the pastoral, nomadic life of the Arabs: 'These people having few wants are unacquainted with many cares, and are thus ignorant of the greater part of the troubles and difficulties which are experienced in more civilized society.'[2]

Mangles's archaeological pilgrimage took four years; he and Irby returned to England late in 1820. In 1823 they published privately their descriptive letters of the trip under the title *Travels in Egypt and Nubia, Syria, and Asia Minor; During the Years 1817 & 1818.* Two years later Mangles was elected a fellow of the Royal Society. In 1828 he and Irby published an archaeological monograph, *Account of the Necropolis of Petra, a city in Palestine*, and in 1830 Mangles became one of the first fellows and members of the council of the Royal Geographical Society.

Social and committee obligations, however, did not impose a sedentary life. In 1831 Mangles travelled to Swan River and stayed three months with his cousin Ellen Stirling and her husband, the governor. At Perth Mangles met George Fletcher Moore, who recorded his delight in his new acquaintance: 'I had the pleasure of meeting one of a most agreeable party, Captain Mangles, who published his Travels in Egypt. Any man of sense, who has travelled far and observed much is invaluable as a companion.'[3]

Moore presented Mangles with specimens of flowering plants and a bottle full of snakes, lizards, and scorpions. Like most naturalists who preceded and followed him, Mangles was fascinated and excited by the prolific diversity of the plants of Australia's southwest. To European observers, the southwest presented a paradox. How could a terrain so arid, with soil mainly sand over granite rock and containing none of the humus normally considered essential for plant growth, provide such a rich habitat for botanical production?

In 1801 François Peron, the naturalist aboard the Baudin expedition, had observed:

> Everywhere in the midst of burning sands, grow numerous plants; created for this wild continent, they seem to take pleasure in the heat and aridity that characterize it. Considered from this viewpoint, most of the plants of New Holland seem to me worth particular attention.[4]

Peron bestowed as much attention as he was able, and the Baudin expedition brought back many Western Australian wildflowers. Propagated under hothouse conditions, *Anigozanthos* (kangaroo paw), *Hardenbergia*, *Pimelea*, and *Hovea* throve in the Mons Cels Gardens in Paris and at Kew and Birmingham, as well as in the conservatories of wealthy families. These strange and colourful plants maintained and stimulated interest in the flora of Australia's southwest.

After his visit to Swan River, Mangles returned to London to lead the life of a wealthy, cultured, and leisured gentleman. He was not idle, however. He was dedicated to horticulture and to the promotion of gardens and their care and to the propagation of plants, particularly flowering varieties. Collectors worldwide supplied him with specimens of exotic plants and seeds, which he shared among a wide circle of interested horticulturalists and botanists. In the early 1830s the plants of Western Australia became his particular interest.

In 1835 Mangles sent George Fletcher Moore two cases of plants, seeds, and books and requested the return of indigenous plant specimens and seeds. Although impressed by Mangles's munificence, Moore felt unable to reciprocate fully and sought the help of James

Drummond. Drummond, who had been botanist at Cork Botanical Garden, seemed ideally suited to the task. He wanted to collect for money, however, and mercenary motives did not appeal to Mangles. Determined to keep his collecting enterprise on a nonpecuniary basis, he asked his cousin Ellen Stirling for the names of willing Western Australian collectors. She replied, 'I see you are as anxious as ever to collect seeds and plants from this colony, and I assure you I will with pleasure endeavour to promote your wishes.' She suggested Captain Richard Meares of Swan River, Mrs Mary Bull of Leschenault, and Georgiana Molloy of Augusta.[5]

Molloy was delighted with the acquisition of English seeds and thrilled with the prospect of collecting Australian flowers. Unlike Moore, who regarded Mangles's request as an unwelcome responsibility, and unlike Drummond, who regarded the request as an economic opportunity, Molloy looked on the prospect of collecting with pleasure. Even though Mangles was a stranger, he had been well introduced by Governor Stirling, and Molloy wanted to oblige and to please. Moreover, as one of Mangles's worldwide collectors, Molloy would be participating in an undertaking that transcended parochial and frequently insipid colonial concerns. Nevertheless, she felt inadequate. She felt handicapped by a lack of botanical knowledge and skill.

Mangles's request, however, arrived at a fortuitous season—the beginning of summer, when plants, after spring flowering, began seed production. The hot drying days of December and January made seed-collecting conditions ideal. With the assistance of the now fourteen-year-old Charlotte Heppingstone, Molloy immediately began her search. Because she did not know the names of the plants from which she collected seed, she decided to enclose a leaf with each packet and, where known, a description of the flower, for purposes of identification.

By the end of March 1837 Molloy had enough seeds to fill a small box. She included some dried plants given to her by visitors from the Vasse. She now replied to Mangles and began her note self-effacingly: 'I much fear you have bestowed your liberality on one whose chief pleasure is her Garden, but who does not enter the lists as a Florist, much less a Botanist.' Indeed, if Augusta were closer to London, she would 'hesitate to accept so magnificent a present of so many long wished for seeds'. She feared that the 'peremptory' demands of her children and 'domestic drudgery' would never allow her sufficient time to return the favour. Nevertheless, she hoped for more free time in the future when she could return Mangles's large box filled with 'Australian productions'. In the meantime, she had asked acquaintances, of whom she confessed to having very few, to help in collecting. As another possible impediment to seed collecting, she mentioned her family's approaching removal to the Vasse. She did not want to leave, and she closed her note with a lament: 'It is with much regret I leave Dear Augusta, our climate is so heavenly, and the scenery is superior to other settlements, the flowers scentless but minutely beautiful.'[6]

Ever since 1832 Molloy had known she would eventually have to leave Augusta. Captain Molloy's major grant was at the Vasse, which everyone, except James Turner, agreed represented the future. Nevertheless, the Molloys had set no date for their departure.

Meanwhile, the Vasse began to receive greater government attention. In December 1836, at the time Molloy received Mangles's request at Augusta, Lieutenant Henry William St Pierre Bunbury arrived at the Vasse to take charge of the military outpost.

The 25-year-old Bunbury, an officer in the 21st Regiment, arrived in Perth in March 1836 after three years in the eastern Australian colonies. The procacious lieutenant found Perth 'a most dismal place, duller than anything imaginable'. Military duties, however, soon provided excitement. In May he helped two settlers establish a sheep station on the Williams River, east of the Vasse, and he founded a military station there. In June, while on duty in the Avon district, east of Perth, he boasted of shooting a 'few' Aborigines and hoped his forceful presence would induce quiet. After four months in the colony he felt he understood the Aborigines and pronounced them 'extremely cowardly, but very revengeful, never forgiving an injury; they take life for life but are not particular whom they spear. Any White man will do or else a Native of another tribe.'[7]

Bunbury was only partially correct in his observation of Aboriginal vengefulness. Aborigines were indeed appalled by death but not because they were especially vindictive or unforgiving. Just as the Christian idea of absolution had no place in the Aboriginal world, neither did the idea of chance. Death, sickness, even falling in love were never accidental, exterior to human being; someone, somewhere, either dead or alive, caused the event. Therefore the affected persons could take appropriate and direct action in their turn, including injury and killing. Contrary to what Bunbury and the other settlers believed, however, Aboriginal countermeasures did not lead to an endless cycle of revenge killing. Self-limiting customs intervened long before hostility became general.

After service at the Avon, Bunbury received a posting to the Vasse. He travelled overland from Perth and followed 'well-beaten' native paths. En route he encountered large numbers of Aborigines who, introduced to him by his guide, Monang, volunteered to accompany him to the Vasse Estuary. Bunbury found his companions amicable and concluded, from the plentiful supply of fish, the numerous and distinct paths, and the many huts, that the area supported a large Aboriginal population. Personal encounters confirmed his supposition. 'Seldom during the day had I fewer than one hundred Blacks about me, and often nearer two hundred,' he noted.[8]

When he arrived at the Vasse he found the Bussells' house still unfinished:

> only one room on the ground floor being habitable which serves as both kitchen and parlour in bad weather, when the cooking cannot go on in the open air. The large chimney is made of rammed earth, but all the rest of the building is of what is

colonially termed wattle and daub, the quickest and easiest method of building, but not very substantial.

He did, however, admire the Bussells' garden, which grew 'excellent vegetables, especially potatoes', and he was optimistic about future prospects. He predicted the Vasse would

> become a thriving and important part of the Colony. The climate is both milder and moister than at Swan River, there is abundance of excellent land, water to be obtained in plenty by digging only about three or four feet down . . . timber is abundant, large and good quality . . . cattle and horses look better and fatter than anywhere else in the Colony.[9]

During his five-month tour of duty at the Vasse, Bunbury discussed the Aboriginal problem with the Bussells. As a soldier he admired Aboriginal stealth, bush skills, and facility at eluding pursuit. As an imperialist, however, he contended it was useless to attempt to Christianise Aborigines. In their present state of degradation Aborigines were beyond redemption; far better first to make labourers of them. Bunbury also boasted of how settlers at York had dealt with Aboriginal thefts of grain: one night in September 1836 Arthur Trimmer and Ned Gallop armed themselves and hid in their barn. When natives appeared, Gallop fired, shot one dead, and badly wounded two others.

The Bussells approved of such summary justice. They had believed that the slaughter at Pinjarra in 1835 was the best thing that ever happened in the colony. 'No one circumstance,' Charles claimed, 'has been productive of greater benefit.' He supported the delivery of a shock of such force it could 'never be erased from their memory!' He advocated, like his brothers and most of the settlers, 'that the smallest infringement by them on the property of the European be punished by DEATH'. But Charles did not believe this penalty should be confined only to the actual perpetrators. Aborigines, by dint of being savages, were collectively guilty of any and every transgression committed by any individual. 'Is the spearing of a bullock or a horse, or the driving off of a flock of sheep the act of one man?' he asked. 'Common sense, unbiased by timidity, would answer No!' If one was guilty, all were guilty. Charles's opinions were not idle speculations; he and his brothers found ample opportunity to put theory into practice.[10]

In the southwest the Nyungar continued to assert their claim to the land and its produce. They resented the settlers' disruption of the landscape and the wholesale killing and disappearance of native animals. Distance from settlements conferred no protection. The external structure of every Nyungar cohort—its necessary dependence on others, often at several removes, in matters of marriage, trade, food gathering, and ceremony—ensured that contact with invaders anywhere would have quick repercussions everywhere over the region. The British settlements at Albany, Augusta, the Vasse, Swan River, York, and Williams fragmented the network of relations hundreds of miles away. Every Aboriginal in the southwest was adversely affected.

Thus disruption and dispossession did not depend solely on direct contact with the settlers. British settlement changed the very nature of the country and precipitated a marked environmental reversal in which a less demanding ecosystem replaced a collapsing complex one. Uniformity replaced diversity. Settler activity—clearing, cropping, grazing stock, and hunting—destroyed the material basis of a Nyungar culture inextricably bound to topography, flora, and fauna. The explorer George Grey noted that whether Europeans directly interfered with the Aborigines or not, their presence nevertheless disturbed the country: 'The mere circumstance of Europeans residing there does the Aboriginal, on whose land he settles, the injury of depriving him of his ordinary means of subsistence.'[11]

Driven from the bush, deprived of their familiar patterns of subsistence, and with the customary balances between themselves and their environment broken, the situation of the Nyungar became desperate and their reaction inevitable: lacking other means, they sought their food from the stock and stores of the colonists.

In December 1836, coincident with Bunbury's arrival at the Vasse, two Aboriginal men approached the Bussells and offered to look after their cows in exchange for food. Thereafter, they took the cows out to pasture early in the morning and brought them back at night. The Bussells gave them three pounds of flour a day. Other Aborigines turned to more direct methods of subsistence.

In April 1837 Aborigines at Augusta stole flour from the public store and raided potato gardens. Later in the same month Aborigines burned down Thomas Turner's establishment on the Blackwood. Resident Magistrate Molloy reported, 'On 28 April the whole of the Turner buildings were wilfully set fire to and destroyed by the natives at Turnwood.'[12]

Meanwhile, on 16 April at the Vasse, the Bussells caught some Aborigines stealing damper and next day dismissed their cow-keepers. A week later the Bussells' servant William and Aboriginal elder Gaywal argued. Gaywal threw a spear, but he aimed to frighten, not injure, and the spear missed. Nevertheless, William's anxiety and discomfiture unsettled the rest of the household. For the time being, however, Lieutenant Bunbury's presence reassured the Bussells.[13]

But Bunbury did not remain much longer. After he had established a second military garrison at Wonnerup, to the north of the Vasse, he left the area and returned to Perth. The Bussells were now on their own. Alerted by Bunbury's reports of the hundreds and hundreds of natives who lived in the vicinity of the Vasse, the Bussells, over the several weeks following William's altercation with Gaywal, became increasingly tense. Stock went missing and potatoes disappeared from the garden. The Bussells suspected theft and kept all-night vigils. They caught no thieves but, convinced of Aboriginal barbarity and treachery, they defamed Aborigines at every opportunity.

When a whale floundered on the local beach and some Aborigines took advantage of the unexpected food source, Bessie recorded their feasting with disgust: 'The men and two women tearing off immense pieces of the whale, putting it in the fire and setting it alight, then beating the flames out with boughs and devouring it, putrid as it was, with all possible gusto. . . . They continued their feast through the night, eating to satiety and then sleeping.' Alfred, who reported this wanton spectacle to his family, stressed he was able to stomach the sight only because he had fortified himself with a bottle of rum.[14]

In contrast to the ill-mannered savages, the commercially minded Bussells wished no more of the whale than that it yield a profit. Lenox began preparations to flinch the blubber for boiling down to oil; later, however, he realised the whale would yield an insufficient return and he abandoned the enterprise.

The Bussells' larger enterprise, Cattle Chosen—indeed, the very possibility of settlement at the Vasse—had been acquired from the Nyungar. The best Aboriginal land, the land most prolific with game and wildlife, was also the best area for European stock. But usurpation led directly to Aboriginal hunger. And while the Bussells expropriated the land, they expected Aborigines not to steal. The connection between their own thievery and Aboriginal hunger and dislocation never occurred to them. Members of High Church, they never felt the pangs of an unquiet conscience. With a hubris born of the assumption of progress, they convinced themselves that people on the lowest scale of humanity had performed their divinely allotted task of clearing the land and preparing it for occupation by more progressive, civilised people.

Vasse settlers expected Aborigines to accept European superiority. When Aborigines refused, the settlers reacted with surprise and indignation, which they expressed by labelling even the slightest display of resistance as 'aggression', 'depredation', or 'outrage'.

Aboriginal resistance continued throughout the first half of 1837. Towards the end of June the Chapmans discovered a calf missing. Lenox Bussell helped in the search, and while in the bush he met

Nugundung and Boobingoot, who told him that Gaywal and his son Kenny had speared the missing beast. Next day Alfred Bussell and five other armed men forced Nugundung and Boobingoot to lead them to Gaywal and Kenny. Upon the discovery of a group of encamped Aborigines, the settlers commenced firing. Gaywal and Kenny escaped, but the avengers, cognisant of Charles Bussell's aggressively stated principle that when one Aborigine was guilty, all were guilty, shot nine dead. They wounded two.

That evening, while Bessie recorded in her diary—with no more elaboration or comment than that accorded the slaughter of a pig— the number of Aborigines killed at nine, Lenox wrote to Resident Magistrate Molloy at Augusta to report three deaths. He asked Molloy to send additional troops.[15]

This was war. At Augusta the Bussells had imagined themselves metaphorically at war with the forest. Now, at the Vasse, they understood themselves to be literally at war with the Aborigines. On Sunday, 2 July 1837, Bessie recorded in her diary, 'The natives announced that a hostile tribe is making a descent upon us. How will all these wars and rumours end!' Later she observed, 'One might almost as well be campaigning. We live now in a council of war.' The invocation of war helped clarify matters, since war must end in either conquest or defeat. War permitted no ambiguity and abolished the patience necessary for negotiation, compromise, and accommodation. For the Bussells and for other colonists, the question was simple: were they or the natives to be masters? Framed in such a way, the problem could, of course, be solved only one way—by death.[16]

The declaration of war spurred the Bussells to prosecute their offensive. They assembled an arsenal, and Lenox ordered a cannon built and made ball cartridges. The cannon, made of wood, blew up on the first test firing.

Belligerence, cruelty, hatred, destruction, and an impulse to murder have existed in all civilisations, but the modern age placed these urges under an increasingly strong social control anchored in the state. The modern state demanded a monopoly of physical force and took away the right to private violence and private vengeance. Thenceforth, acts of killing required state sanction and justification of a particular kind, usually specious, but justification nonetheless. Previously, murder had been accompanied by little extenuation beyond the satisfaction or reason of the deed. Modernity, however, demanded excuses, and excuses necessitated a particular kind of sophistry.

From the moment of annexation, the British government had declared that all indigenous inhabitants of Western Australia were British citizens, subject to British law and entitled to lawful protection. Settlers, however, were uncomfortable with the implications of those entitlements. In practice, they dealt with the Aborigines largely as they considered circumstances demanded and not according to British law.

Colonial government officials, all of whom were also settlers, sympathised with settler justice yet were conscious of the necessity to uphold the law and the state's monopoly on violence. Thus, when Resident Magistrate Molloy replied to Lenox's urgent request, he was mindful of the policy of the day. This had been enunciated by Governor Stirling in 1831 when he cautioned against 'any combination on the part of the settlers for the purpose of vengeance unless previously authorised and commanded by the magistrates'. As authority's representative, Captain Molloy insisted that government policy receive respect. While he agreed to Lenox's request for reinforcements and temporarily dispatched two soldiers from Augusta to the Vasse, he expected Bussell to furnish depositions regarding the Aboriginal deaths.[17]

At the Vasse on 8 July, one of Gaywal's sons, Wooberdung, who had served the Bussells as a guide and tracker at Augusta, attempted to make peace. He appeared on the opposite side of the river from Cattle Chosen and signalled to the Bussells. The family, however, dismissed him coldly. The next day Lenox, with more vehemence than coherence, wrote to Captain Molloy to refuse his request for depositions. He offered several reasons for noncompliance.

First, he claimed, too strict a scrutiny of settler relations with Aborigines was unjust. Second, what the Aborigines had done—spear the Chapmans' calf—was not 'a mere breach of the law' but an act of war, which called for 'steps prompt and decisive'. The consequences, as in war, lay beyond the purview of the law. Third, the deaths were appropriate punishment and called for no inquiry. The alternative to deadly violence—capture and imprisonment of the offenders—he considered impractical. To Lenox, prisoners were a burden: their existence would serve only as a reproach to himself. It was much more conclusive to shoot them. Besides, incarcerated Aborigines could not plead to charges of which they were ignorant. Moreover, as non-Christians, they were unable to swear an oath and appear as witnesses. All things considered, Aboriginal savages were incapable of understanding the law. They must first be convinced 'of their inferiority' before any entitlement to due process.[18]

Lenox's argument reflected the commonplace opinions of his fellow colonists. British settlers responded to Aboriginal assertiveness on the basis of two interlinked ideas: punishment and correction. They measured the success of this disciplinary regime by the number of deaths inflicted on the offenders. The greater the number of Aboriginal lives extinguished, the greater the reformatory and pedagogic consummation.

The Bussells accepted brute force and violence as part of the nature of things. There was nothing fundamentally wrong with killing; killing was the inescapable logic of conquest. Ultimately, Lenox realised, the prosperity of his family—indeed, that of all the colonists—was made possible only by force of arms, by intimidation, terror, and murder. When the family's continued occupation of the land and conquest of the bush seemed threatened, the Bussell brothers did not hesitate to respond with violence.

A few days after Lenox defended his refusal to supply deposi-tions to Captain Molloy, the family's native cow-minders—who had been reinstated because the Bussells could not do without Aboriginal labour—failed to report for work. The Bussells interpreted their absence as ominous and remained apprehensive all morning. At midday they 'heard great shouting on the estuary' and then 'a terrible scream', followed by two shots in the direction of the Dawsons' hut.

A group of about seven Aboriginal men had surrounded the hut. Two men appeared at the window and each threw in a spear. One spear struck Elijah Dawson in the left arm, while the other grazed his wife on her elbow. Dawson grabbed his gun and confronted the attackers outside but did not fire, as he knew the Aborigines were aware that he must load again and thus expose himself to retaliation. The raiders ran off. The neighbouring Chapmans fired two shots to raise the alarm. That afternoon the Dawsons and the Chapmans abandoned their huts and moved in next to the Bussells.[19]

In the evening, Charles, Lenox, Alfred, and the servant William concealed themselves in the Dawsons' hut in the hope of ambushing and shooting any Aborigines who returned to plunder the vacated building. But the subterfuge failed; no Aborigines appeared, and the brothers returned next morning exhausted and consumed with anxi-ety.

Two days later a group of Aborigines again appeared opposite Cattle Chosen to seek peace. The Bussells suspected treachery and brought out their guns. Although they held their fire, their intentions were not peaceful; they had already implemented a larger strategy for war. The previous evening six armed settlers left the Vasse and marched up the coast to the military outpost at Wonnerup. They secured military reinforcements and official sanction for the existence of a state of war—implied by the deployment of Her Majesty's soldiers. The augmented force quickly captured an Aborigine named Dr Miligan, who, the war party hoped, would lead them to Gaywal, whom they suspected of being the ringleader of Aboriginal resistance.

Next day, Monday, 17 July, while Dawson and Alfred maintained a sentinel at Cattle Chosen, Charles, together with the additional troops from Augusta, set off in pursuit of 'Gaywal and sons'. With Dr Miligan forced into the lead, the search party found tracks but no Aborigines. Instead they shot three kangaroos. On Tuesday Lenox, Dawson, Alfred Green, and four soldiers continued the pursuit. This time they captured four women and a child, whom they intended holding hostage. Next day the Bussells, who feared their hostage-taking might provoke a mass attack, released the prisoners.

Amidst the self-generated war hysteria, the Bussells erected a sign on the beach, where passing ships off-loaded cargo, cautioning mariners of local hostilities. The warning functioned to keep the Bussells themselves in a high state of alert and stimulated their own aggressive proclivities. Recent experience made them receptive to the stern, repressive, and updated views of Governor Stirling, published in the *Government Gazette* of 22 July 1837. Shipped aboard the *Lady Stirling*, the latest *Gazette* reached the Vasse on 24 July. The only effective method of Aboriginal control, Stirling asserted, was 'an early exhibition of force, or, if the evil has already gained strength, such acts of decisive severity as will appall them as a people for a time and reduce their tribe to weakness'. His resolute recommendation of wholesale slaughter did not go unheeded.[20]

The following Sunday, 30 July, the Vasse settlers heard the shouts of natives at the estuary, near the Dawsons' and the Chapmans' deserted huts. The Bussell brothers grabbed their guns, formed the settlers into a troop, and advanced in the direction of the noise. As soon as they saw the Aborigines—a group of men, women, and children—the settlers opened fire, shot five dead (three women, a man, and a boy), and mortally wounded an unknown number of others. The survivors fled, and the attackers left the bodies where they fell.

Two days later, when Vernon and Alfred returned to the estuary, they found the bodies as they had fallen, unclaimed by the Aborigines, who feared to return to the scene of the massacre. The Bussells and other Vasse settlers dug graves, spread grass over the bottoms, lowered the bodies, sprinkled grass over them, threw in dirt, and, according to Bessie Bussell, 'laid the sods carefully over like an English grave'. This solemn ceremony, however, did not mark the end of hostilities. The Bussells were determined on further vengeance.[21]

On 18 August two armed parties left the Vasse in search of Aborigines. They camped overnight, encountered a group of natives, fired, and wounded several, one of whom dropped a young child, whom the pursuers quickly seized. With their fourteen-month-old hostage, the parties returned to the Vasse. Ten weeks later the Bussells returned the captive child to its parents.[22]

In the meantime, Governor Stirling, appraised of the June killings at the Vasse, pressured Lenox for depositions. Lenox, in turn, temporised; he pleaded the absence of the individuals concerned and lack of means to convey the documents to Perth. He promised the depositions at some future time and continued to rationalise the killings. In Lenox's mind, the end justified the means: as a result of his family's unequivocal exhibition of force, the natives were now quiet. 'I can only appeal to the effects produced,' he pleaded. Lenox thus artfully shifted his own attention, and that of the governor, from the individuals killed to a larger encompassing vision of the Aboriginal threat diminished. To have ceased actions against the natives, he continued, simply because he was unable to apprehend those actually responsible for the disappearance of the Chapmans' calf, 'would have been most impolitic. It became therefore necessary to visit the offence upon the whole of the party implicated.'[23]

All the Bussells were keenly aware of the power of language to deflect and marginalise; they understood language's ability to render even the most heinous act insignificant. Thus, while Lenox described the disappearance and death of a calf as a 'slaughter', he dismissed the killing of natives as an 'affray'. In his letters of self-justification,

Lenox rendered the wartime acts of injury and killing invisible; his official and personal correspondence neatly escorted the war against the Aborigines out of view.[24]

Under then-prevailing British law, justice demanded some relation between the penalty and the offence. While the taking of a murderer's life for that of his victim might be considered just, the taking of the lives of fourteen witnesses went beyond justice. Justice required that proof of the identity of the culprit should be reasonably complete and that mere suspicion was insufficient. Justice neither anticipated the commission of crime nor punished a person for something he or she might do in the future.

The highly literate Bussells understood the law and the principles of justice. Charles Bussell, in fact, had considered entering the legal profession before his emigration to Western Australia. In the matter of Aboriginal deaths, however, and under the circumstances created by the family's declaration of war, Lenox considered his actions beyond the jurisdiction of the British legal code. He appealed to a more personal sense of justice. Legal, impartial, abstract justice did not apply at the Vasse. What mattered were those means that the Bussells considered best served their own interests.

Murder is ageless, but Lenox's casuistry, his concatenation of justifications, is chillingly modern. What was particularly modern about the Vasse killings was Lenox's way of talking about them, of embedding them in history—Aboriginal deaths were necessary in order for progress to proceed. If progress demanded the slaughter of human beings, then progress must be satisfied.

1 5

GLORY IN THE FLOWER

THROUGHOUT THE WINTER OF WARFARE AT THE VASSE, GEORGIANA Molloy at Augusta thought of her commitment to James Mangles. She thought of flowers, the splendours of spring, and the myriad plant species that awaited her discovery. She determined that her future collecting would be systematic and thorough. When the spring of 1837 came and wildflowers blossomed, Molloy journeyed into the bush, to locate, observe, and mark plants that she hoped would provide seeds. But she did not seek alone; she enlisted her family's help. During September and October the Molloys took three trips up the Blackwood to a landing known as the Granite Rock to search for flowers—the first time in three years that Georgiana Molloy had been out in the family boat. In fact, in the eleven months since Mangles's letter had arrived, Molloy had been absent from her house for longer and had spent more time in the bush than in the whole of the previous nearly seven years she had lived at Augusta.

In November her excursions came to a sudden, brutal hiatus. On the eleventh of the month, at breakfast, Molloy, her husband, and two of the children, nineteen-month-old John and daughter Mary, played together, as was their custom. The family then retired to their separate chores. Molloy prepared to bake bread and churn milk and left the boy in the charge of the servant girl, Charlotte Heppingstone. Charlotte, however, believed John to be with his sister and father. Later in the morning Mary appeared in the house alone, and Charlotte prepared to place her in the cot alongside her brother. He was not there. Suddenly, all realised that no one knew John's whereabouts. Fear gripped Molloy, and she asked if anyone had been near the well, hidden behind a mimosa tree close to the house. 'The fatal truth stole over me,' she confided in her next letter to Mangles, and she described how, when pulled out of the well,

> that darling precious child, lifeless, his flaxen curls all dripping, his little countenance so placid he looked fast asleep but not dead, and we do not believe he really was so until some minutes after, but the medical man was at The Vasse and we knew not what to do. We tried every means of restoration but to no effect and that lovely, healthy child who had never known pain or sickness and who had been all mirth and joyousness five precious hours ago, the last time we beheld him together, was now a stiff corpse, but beautiful and lovely even in death.[1]

The shock of death debilitated Molloy, her malaise compounded by discomfort from the early effects of another pregnancy. For a month she grieved, withdrawn and indifferent. How could she love life when it was full of pain and suffering, heartbreakingly short, and bordered on either side by darkness? Christianity proposed that only the light of belief could banish darkness. Only growth in grace and an increasing attachment to spiritual things would bring peace and relief from suffering. She must pray to be weaned from the things of time, from allegiance to this parched and weary world. Incorporeity was the message of Robert Story, Isabella Campbell, and Henry Martyn.

But the world—the living world, the corporeal, material world— beckoned with other answers. The claims of life and the needs of her family demanded Molloy's participation. She grieved and did not pretend the loss was other than it was. Something had been cut out of her life that could be neither restored nor compensated. But she faced her loss consciously and thoughtfully, as a test of maturity that required a proper show of fortitude. Fortitude required one to labour and endure.

Molloy's labours could no longer be restricted to her homestead, however. Life there was cloistered, too potent with reminders of her son: the mimosa tree, the well, the cot—all suggested John. She must break out, burst the boundaries that focused her grief. Only the unbounded wilderness, the bush, the world beyond the fence, offered consolation. The forest sanctuary offered refuge, an asylum from the sorrows of the human world.

By 15 December, a month after the drowning, Georgiana Molloy had begun collecting again. She prosecuted her enterprise with vigour and determination and exerted herself as never before, gathering ripened seed during daily rambles through the bush. The family revisited the Granite Rock to gather seeds from the plants previously noted in bloom. Now the instigator and active participant in worldly affairs, she did not seek solace for her son's death in the Bible and religious literature. Instead she turned to the beauty of the living world. After the drowning Molloy grew more and more attached to worldly existence. Life, she realised, continued, and she wanted to live for life. Collecting, being in the bush, affirmed life.

Molloy kept up her daily bush excursions throughout the first trimester of her new pregnancy. Late in January 1838, after a day in the bush, she returned home and began a letter to Mangles, her first since her March 1837 note, in which she had agreed to collect for him. But she could not talk of botany until she first unburdened herself of the dreadful story of her and her husband's bereavement. 'Under the afflicting but inscrutable decree from all-wise Providence,' she began, 'we have been recently overwhelmed with the most bitter loss of our darling infant. Painful as it is to record, distance of place compels me.'[2]

In grief, Molloy narrated the painful details of the death of her only son. She addressed a complete stranger—a man whom she had never met and from whom she had heard but once, for Mangles had yet to reply to Molloy's March note. But something in his single communication suggested a worldliness, an ability to rise above the prejudices of the time, and a receptiveness to personal confession. Molloy also felt that distance permitted a degree of intimacy not normally accepted among strangers, especially those of the opposite sex. Only by communicating her grief to someone abroad, someone immersed in the objects and human commerce of a civilised and distantly familiar society, could she relieve herself. Augusta seemed too isolated, too confined, to give proper scope to the scale of her loss. Nevertheless, Molloy was aware that she might have breached convention and apologised for writing so intimately:

> Forgive me, my dear sir, for thus using towards a stranger, the freedom and minute detail that friendship warrants and desires. Our children and our necessary occupations, fraught as they are with uncontemplated interest, engross the sole attention and exertions of myself and my excellent husband. Acute indeed was the blow and when you reflect, how dead we are to the world and completely weaned from that sphere of pursuits, actions and modes of life in which we used to move, I trust you will pardon and excuse my entering thus egotistically and minutely on our present affliction.[3]

Less than three months had passed since Molloy's son's death, but she now closed the subject and wrote of botany and beauty. She described how September and October were the most delightful months at Augusta. 'The purple creeper begins to bloom in July,' she told Mangles, 'the red in August, but in these months the Wilderness indeed "begins to blossom as a Rose".' Just as the flowers of September and October had begun turning into the pods of November, her son had drowned. But the cycle of life continued and flower seeds ripened, potent with new life.[4]

By the end of January 1838 Molloy had collected enough seeds and specimens to fill Mangles's *hortus siccus*, received in December 1836, with 'every flower we have worth sending and many I fear you will esteem unworthy'. She still felt meritless and wondered, 'What could have led you, my dear Sir, to have selected me as a collector, much more to imagine I had botanical knowledge, I cannot divine.' Molloy could not conceive how anyone, anywhere, could consider her sufficiently skilled and observant to perform the duties of a conscientious collector. But when she put the indulgence of self-deprecation aside, she was eager to reassure Mangles of her willingness to continue to collect on his behalf, 'to comply with your laudable desire and curiosity to possess a knowledge of our floral productions'. The task of collecting, she assured him, had been 'discharged faithfully and jealously'. Moreover, she was delighted to have him as a correspondent. The intimacy she presumed over her son's death testified to her lack of local confidants. If she could find no one to confide in about such a personal matter, neither could she discuss the newly discovered love of her life, botany:

> In the limited society of south western Australia . . . very few bestow a thought on flowers . . . grubbing, hoes, beef, auctions and anchorage, whaling, harpooning, potatoes and onions are the chief topics of conversation, therefore I am well persuaded any observation affecting a flower garden would be ill timed and not agreeable to the generality of my guests.[5]

Molloy compensated for her self-imposed silence with a detailed description of her botanising to Mangles. She justified her loquaciousness with the reasoning that Mangles himself was partly responsible for her discovery of the wider world of the Australian bush—a world in which she rejoiced and of which she was compelled to speak. Until his offer of seeds for seeds, she told him, she had 'always avoided the tedious operation of gathering seeds'. But the work of collecting, carried on with all her body, mind, eyes, and fingers, inspired her with 'ardour and interest'. The bush proved a source of unexpected joy. She had never imagined such favour in this parched and weary world, and she thanked Mangles for being the agent who ignited her enthusiasm for the bush: 'but for your request, I should never have bestowed on the flowers of this Wilderness any other idea than that of admiration'.[6]

Molloy was grateful to Mangles not only for herself; her two surviving children—Sabina, six, and Mary, three and a half—willingly and joyfully participated in her bush rambles as well. They were, she said, 'of great utility, as their eyes being so much nearer the ground, they have been able to detect many minute specimens and seeds I could not observe'. Collecting also served a pedagogic function. At Augusta 'the children are bereft of most of the amusements of a highly civilized country and such a pursuit is highly delightful to their young Minds'. She also thought that walking, in and of itself, was of value to the children.[7]

Molloy and her daughters pursued their quest methodically. First, they rambled through the bush in search of flowering plants. They would note and number the location of each particular specimen and then revisit the plant as many times as necessary through flowering and seed production until the seed was ripe and ready for collecting. Sabina, Molloy found, was more '*au fait*' than herself at discovering and remembering the abode of different specimens. Moreover, possessed of 'unexhausted patience', Sabina sometimes went three to five times a week to monitor plants.[8]

Although Molloy bestowed great care on her collection, she still felt inadequate and apologised to Mangles for her inexperience. Her collection, she wrote, had not been 'as cleanly and neatly executed as I could desire'. Her ignorance concerning the ripening regimes of different seeds often confounded her collecting attempts. Some days she found seeds already shed from their pods, while others remained enclosed, still green. Other days high temperatures accelerated ripening, or a native fire would sweep the area and scatter the seeds. 'The manifold duties of domestic drudgery' also kept her from the quest.

This, she assured Mangles, was as unsatisfactory to her as it must be to him; she would much rather spend her time in the more congenial environment of the bush.

'The universal badness of seed' also contributed to the incompleteness of Molloy's collection. Contaminated seed, she recognised, resulted from the peculiar ecology of the southwest. 'In this uncultivated land and temperate climate,' she explained, 'insects and reptiles have unrestrained license, and the seeds of each plant afford sustenance to some of the animal creation.' She disputed the common belief that seeds kept best in their pods. On the contrary, seed vessels hosted large numbers of worms and grubs, and one unopened silique might spoil the contents of the entire box of seeds. She therefore felt constrained to examine each seed minutely. Out of a huge quantity collected, only a small number passed scrutiny. This accounted for the small packages within the *hortus siccus*. But these packages, she assured Mangles, contained seeds that were 'sound and fresh'.

As inferior as she often felt, Molloy could not help admitting some pride, both in the collection itself and in the knowledge she had acquired in the course of her bush rambles. She announced to Mangles:

> I have no hesitation in declaring that, were I to accompany the box of seeds to England, knowing as I do their situation, time of flowering, soil and degree of moisture required with the fresh powers of fructification they each possess, I should have a very extensive conservatory, of no plants but from Augusta.

Molloy quickly reconsidered what she had written. Her claim, while true and expressive of her newfound loyalty to Australian flowers, sounded boastful. She added a qualifier and wrote that she did not mean to speak 'vauntingly' but only in the hope of inspiring her correspondent to share the enthusiasm she felt towards the flowering flora of Australia's southwest.[9]

Molloy's collection included dried flowers from the Vasse gathered by her husband. These specimens, however, were not accompanied by an account of their growing conditions, locale, and other description necessary to positively identify the species. She promised to restitute the deficit and collect the corresponding seeds when the family moved to the Vasse. She feared, however, that employment 'in the odious drudgery of cheese and butter making' might preclude future collecting. In fact, she thought she might not even have time to attend to her own garden as, in addition to being dairy maid, she was her children's 'sole instructress and sempstress'. Nevertheless, lest Mangles doubt her commitment, Molloy doubly assured him that in future seasons she would readily transmit duplicates of any imperfect specimens.[10]

Molloy was additionally concerned that Mangles would not find the box and *hortus siccus* ordered exactly as he had suggested. She had devised her own arrangement, for which she apologised, and suggested that specimens packed her way would be more easily removed. She numbered each seed package against the dried leaf and flower to which the seeds belonged and then mounted the ensemble in the *hortus siccus*. Molloy found Mangles's *hortus siccus* too small, however, and she added her own larger one, which she had originally bought in London, but which, before the stimulus of Mangles's request, had lain unused at Augusta. She recommended the seeds be sown immediately they arrived in England, as the long sea voyage might impair their vitality.

At this point in her letter Molloy calculated she had covered all matters relevant to Mangles's concerns. She henceforth intended to continue with her own. She begged for a 'patient hearing' and apologised for her 'prolixity' but asked that Mangles himself accept at least partial responsibility for her 'voluminous epistle':

> You, I doubt not, have often heard of the inexhaustible properties of a Lady's pen; and as you have brought this infliction from an unknown person on yourself, I shall have less compunction in visiting you, although etiquette would demand the reverse.[11]

In matters of botany Molloy looked on Mangles as 'the highest source' through whom she would be 'enlightened'. She therefore asked him to send her the Latin name of each specimen according to the number she had assigned it. She kept her own copy of the numbers and duplicates of the specimens dispatched. Names were important to Molloy. To feel at home in the southwest, she had to index and inventory her surroundings and assign flora to their proper classification.

Floral names were based on the classificatory system devised by the eighteenth-century Swedish naturalist Carolus Linnaeus. Before Linnaeus, naturalists lacked a plan in which to fit the many kinds of things in nature. They lacked a system that all naturalists would accept and understand. But a universal system was essential if people were to make any sense of the world around them. Linnaeus devised a classificatory system for the whole of the natural world. He divided both zoological and botanical realms into classes, then subdivided these into orders, the orders into genera, and finally genera into species. The canonical tenth edition of Linnaeus's *Systema Naturae*, published in 1758, recorded some 9000 species of plants and animals. Each species received a binomial Latin name. The first part referred to the genus to which the organism belonged, while the second part denoted the particular and unique species. Linnaeus's hierarchy was not arbitrary but based on a conception of a plan in nature. All natural organisms formed a ladder, a *scala naturae* or 'great chain of being', grading from lower to higher, with man at the summit, although several degrees below God.[12]

Georgiana Molloy's primary relationship, however, was not to taxonomy or to the general idea of the great chain of being but to the particular, to southwest Australia. She collected to strengthen the sense of place she was beginning to feel in her new homeland. She collected for the joy and pleasure of being in the bush, for the individual beauty of each flower, and for the satisfaction of participating in a larger undertaking—an enterprise that transcended the circumscribed and insular activities of the colonists.

Molloy wanted to share her pleasure and her wonder. She asked Mangles to allow her brother George Kennedy, now living in Exeter, to inspect the collection. George had originally asked his sister to collect for him, but Molloy had never found time. She hoped his access to the Mangles collection would provide him with some recompense.

Molloy next asked Mangles to send cuttings of flowering shrubs. She suggested he wrap them in tanner's bark before enclosing them in a sealed metal box. Most of the seeds that arrived in December 1837 had failed. She had planted them in her recently enlarged garden and given them much attention. In fact, she favoured her new plants and neglected other concerns. 'Often has Molloy looked at a buttonless shirt,' she wrote, 'and exclaimed with a woe-begone visage, "When will Captain Mangles's seeds be sown?" ' Molloy also asked Mangles for rhubarb for tarts, tansy for puddings, lemon thyme, lavender, sage, sorrel, and borage, as well as melon seeds, apple and pear pips, raspberry and gooseberry seeds, and a variety of medicinal herbs.

Molloy made her request with her husband's permission. Since the receiver of goods paid the freight, the Molloys had to consider the cost of the request. Captain Molloy consented to the shrubs and seeds because his wife reminded him that 'he had no Milliner's bill to pay, therefore he may very well spare me a little indulgence in what is more beautiful and durable'. 'You must not imagine from this that Captain Molloy is at all parsimonious,' she assured Mangles, 'quite the reverse, but great prudence in luxuries is required where heavy and uncontemplated losses have been experienced.'[13]

Many of Molloy's original vegetables and herbs, brought from Britain, had hybridised and lost their vigour. Only plants from new seeds, she told Mangles, would survive and thrive. She was, she wrote, convinced that Augusta provided a superior environment for almost all vegetation: 'No situation can be preferable or more congenial to the vegetation of all countries than our present locality.' English flowers bloomed with a greater brilliancy of colour than in their homeland. Nasturtium flowers, for instance, radiated a deeper orange than was ever seen in England. Peaches and melons tasted stronger and possessed a more exquisite flavour than those at the Swan or the Vasse.

The Bussells would have disagreed about the flavour at the Vasse. Forward-thinking and progressive, they never regretted leaving Augusta. The six-month war against the Nyungar had not retarded their advancement, and they viewed 1837 as a year of progress. The Bussells were obsessed with progress. During John Bussell's absence in England, his brothers and sisters maintained a regular correspondence that itemised every measurable improvement, every material advance.

As early as January 1837, only a few weeks after John's departure, Charles began a long letter that detailed the family's accomplishments and prospects. The brothers had voted to end the regular employment of soldiers—working illegally as tradesmen and labourers—whose labour at the Vasse was performed in a 'desultory manner'. The money saved could be invested 'to treble advantage'. 'A postponement of comfort will be the consequence,' Charles admitted, 'but the comforts that will spring up will be such as will repay so short a delay.' He wrote also of acquiring more land and expanding the family estate.

Charles reported that his mother and sister Mary were not as tolerant of colonial conditions as the rest of the family. They were, he wrote to John, 'uncommonly fastidious . . . A clay floor gave them rheumatics. The sugar tasted of treacle and the viands, a treat to Fanny and Bessie, were left by them untasted.' Nevertheless, Charles was hopeful. His mother's and sister's queasiness was temporary; circumstances would change, improvement was inevitable. 'Every day,' he maintained, 'brings with it additional comfort, our march is forward, not backwards and happiness, as far as a mortal can possess it, is within reach of all.'[14]

Lenox also wrote to John in January 1837. He too was optimistic and enumerated the manifold progressive changes: Vernon and a labourer had cleared the banks of the river for a garden extension, the corporal had finished the upstairs window, the cow shed was nearly complete, shingling had continued, one cow had calved, and another was expecting.[15]

Mary Bussell never shared her siblings' total involvement in the family's colonial enterprise. She was too sceptical to fully embrace their optimism. Although she had not arrived in Western Australia until 1834, and therefore had not participated in the disappointments and frustrations of the Augusta settlement, she was nevertheless doubtful about the move to the Vasse. To a relative in England she had argued that while the colonial government felt some responsibility for Augusta, it was indifferent towards the Vasse. Without government support the Vasse settlers would progress very slowly, if at all.[16]

Mary did not stay long enough at the Vasse to confirm the accuracy of her prediction. In April 1837, fifteen months after she and her mother arrived, she, Vernon, and Fanny took an extended trip to Swan River. There Mary renewed her acquaintance with Patrick Taylor, a young man she had met on the *James Pattison* during her and her mother's original emigration. Taylor and Mary became engaged and married later in the year. Most of the Bussell family disapproved of Taylor. To avoid their censure, the newly married couple moved to King George Sound, as far away from the Vasse as it was possible to go within the colony of Western Australia.

The brothers expected all their sisters to marry eventually, but they also expected the family to stay together at Cattle Chosen. Charles and John especially dreaded the dissipation of property that their sisters' marriages might entail. But with the marriage of Mary, whose links to the rest of the family were least strong, a division of wealth became unavoidable. The brothers blamed Taylor's greed and Mary's selfishness for the looming partition of property.

At the end of 1837, a year during which the Bussells had warred with the Aborigines and Mary had left the family home, Charles wrote to John, 'The longer I live the more apparent is the abominable selfishness that governs the human race.' But Charles also understood that self-interest was becoming the one universal measure of the merit of humanity's actions.[17]

Western Australia's settlers had had their outlooks and behaviour shaped by the evangelical movement. But the émigrés from early industrial Britain had also been touched and shaped by utilitarian social philosophy. Frequently parallel, the two dominant currents of contemporary opinion enjoined similar types of social behaviour. Evangelicals urged the individual to take advantage of the dispensa-tions of Providence. Utilitarians urged the individual to take advantage of the dispensations of nature. In Britain and the colonies, piety and empiricism reinforced each other. Most Christians and all utilitarians believed in progress: material advance would lead to moral improvement.

For utilitarians, egoistic motives must predominate: could humanity survive for a single moment if each person were engaged in promoting the interest of his neighbour at the expense of his own? Just as the physical universe was subject to the laws of motion, so the moral universe, the world of human action, was subject to the laws of self-interest.[18]

Christians may not have regarded utility as the universal measure of merit, but economic self-interest propelled all emigrants—Christian and utilitarian—to Western Australia. Once settled, however, many colonists besides Charles Bussell began to bemoan the self-interest of their neighbours. They were shocked to discover that where individ-ual interests were concerned, people could be completely unscrupulous. Emigration, critics contended, had liberated greed. In settled, established countries the pursuit of self-interest was moderated by family, friends, and connections. But in a new colony, cut free from all such attachments and restraints, colonists had 'no feelings to consult beyond their own personal wishes and interests'. In a new colony, a Western Australian immigrant wrote, settlers

> find themselves suddenly emancipated from all those restraints which formerly acted with a salutary influence upon their natural inclinations; and having no one near them whose opinion they regard, or whom they care to conciliate, they fall rapidly into the belief that they have no one to live for but themselves, and, consequently, make self the sole guide of all their actions, and sole god of their idolatry.[19]

Faced with 'The accursed Spirit of Trade—that insidious spirit which undermines the truth of the heart, which destroys its most generous impulses, and sneers at every manifestation of disinterestedness,' moral improvers attempted to build up the family as a counterweight to the acquisitive spirit. The early nineteenth-century faith in the civilising power of women made it possible for people to believe that enlightened self-interest would express itself not in the ruthless pursuit of the main chance but in family feeling. Mary Bussell's rejection of the family, her decision to marry and leave the Vasse, equalled apostasy in the eyes of her brothers and sisters.[20]

But Charles's castigation of his fellow settlers' motivations was not provoked by Mary's behaviour alone. He believed that Governor Stirling too had acted in an unacceptably self-interested manner. Stirling had recently stocked his land at Leschenault with sheep and had placed a shepherd and an overseer in charge. To protect his investment, Stirling ordered Lieutenant Bunbury to establish the military barracks at Wonnerup and authorised the transfer of some of the soldiers stationed at Busselton to the new outpost. Smallholders from Busselton and Swan River moved onto grants adjacent to Stirling's. They were grateful for the governor's decision. George Layman wrote to Stirling, 'I am very much obliged to you for the military protection, as it has enabled me to remove to my grant. I have erected a hut and brought my things over.'[21]

The Bussells, however, opposed the dispersion. They feared for their safety and decried the loss of a local market and labour supply. Charles wrote to John, 'I have addressed a very strong letter to Peter Brown [colonial secretary] upon the subject of the proposed removal of the soldiers from the Vasse River and have requested an answer, but it does not appear to be forthcoming.'[22]

Charles Bussell understood that only the state could guarantee security in the possession of property. Property was a form of authority created by government, a set of rights to control assets: to refuse use of them to others, to hold them intact, or to use them up. Without government protection the Bussells' rights would not exist and their property would be worthless.

When the Bussells thought about property ownership they pictured the land as a region, a geographical object, treatable in isolation, as a legal or economic unit. The Nyungar thought in none of these terms. They could not understand how deeds, how a mark on paper, converted land to property. Property required boundaries, but the Aborigines knew no boundaries between wild and tame, vacant and possessed, barbaric and civilised. They wandered incessantly over the land they hunted and had no use for boundary fences. For the Aborigines, home was the entire habitat. For most British settlers in Australia, home was restricted to the farm, the house, or even faraway England, but mostly to what was legally and personally owned.

Although Charles Bussell did not understand the Aboriginal view of the land as sacred and inviolable, he did appreciate that for the settlers' view of property to prevail over the land of Australia, the settlers must employ force. Accordingly, they must have the protection of the military. Charles's fears were unfounded, however. The government was not about to abandon any of the scattered settlements of Western Australia. Troops remained stationed and on alert in each district. Moreover, the colonial schooner, loaded with supplies, personnel, news, and government directives, and symbolic of unity under the British flag, still sailed along the coast.

In March and April 1838 the colonial schooner again ventured south from Fremantle. Perth Magistrate G. F. Moore stepped ashore at both the Vasse and Augusta. As on a previous visit, he noted Augusta's pretty situation and remarked on the potential of Flinders Bay for whaling. But he found the settlement forlorn and wrote, 'Most of the settlers have deserted it and gone to the Vasse district.'[23]

Of the settlers who remained at Augusta, most were thinking of leaving. After the fire of April 1837, which destroyed Turnwood, Thomas Turner stayed on at his Blackwood property for seven months but in December returned to his father's house. Later he moved to his father's recently acquired grant, The Spring, at Cape Leeuwin. He was restless, however, and began to think of moving again.

A month after Moore's visit, the Augusta settlers celebrated the eighth anniversary of the landing of the *Emily Taylor* and the founding of the settlement. By now the Molloys had become established, even habituated, to Augusta. Georgiana Molloy, in particular, was attached. The family house, fences, cleared land, and the farm on Molloy Island evidenced tangible accomplishments and even provided a certain sufficiency. But shortage of labour, Captain Molloy's age (he was now 57), and his official duties limited the amount of work time available to advance development. Although he frequently visited his major grant at the Vasse, Captain Molloy effected little improvement beyond the erection of a small cottage. He wanted to move there permanently, but, partly at the insistence of James Turner, who repeatedly demanded of the government that the resident magistrate remain at his Augusta post, the Molloys kept postponing their departure.

But James Turner's objections were not the only obstacle to relocation. During the first half of 1838 Georgiana Molloy's advancing pregnancy made any imminent move impractical. In June she gave birth to her fifth child and fourth daughter, Amelia. The birth was difficult, Molloy haemorrhaged and fell ill, and recovered slowly.

The baby demanded care, and Molloy's two other daughters required attention. Apart from the young Charlotte Heppingstone, Molloy had no assistance. The exodus from Augusta had left the family with fewer and fewer neighbours, who formerly dropped by with gifts of food and offers of help. Molloy felt harassed and terribly pressed for time, but she did what she could. She nursed Amelia and continued instructing Sabina and Mary. Sabina could already read, and by the beginning of August, four-year-old Mary had begun to read.

But her children were not Molloy's only concern. Almost no ships came into Flinders Bay during 1838. The box of seeds and specimens Molloy had collected for Mangles over the previous spring and summer, and that had been soldered shut in April, had not left Augusta. She worried about the delay and early in September added another page to the long letter begun the previous January: 'I am quite grieved, my dear Sir, that you have not long ere this received our collection of seeds. I lament every day I have them in my possession.'[24]

1 6

PARADISE LOST

SPRING'S ARRIVAL IN 1838 DISTRESSED GEORGIANA MOLLOY. Blossoming bush flowers reminded her that Mangles remained deprived of the beauty that specimens from Australia's southwest would afford. She was anxious that he germinate the seeds she had collected and behold the floral riches himself. In the meantime, she reported on her own horticultural accomplishments. Some of the seeds Mangles sent, which had arrived in December 1836, had germinated the previous spring and summer. The young plants survived the winter and Molloy successfully transplanted them into her garden.

Botanical and horticultural matters were not the only concerns Molloy expressed in her September 1838 postscript to her January letter. Family affairs were also mentioned, even to a stranger. 'In June Baby [Amelia] was born and she engrossed so much of my time, I have scarcely leisure to teach Sabina and Mary,' she wrote. Mary had just begun to read, and to foster the skill, Molloy spent time with her every day. But three children and domestic duties so insistently demanded attention that she did not know what to do first. In addition, she still felt disquieted by the death of her son and enfeebled by her more recent difficult childbirth. Drained of energy she wrote, 'I am scarcely able to exert myself in either body or soul.'

But exert herself she did. For she cared, and cared passionately, for her home, her children, and for the flowers of the southwest.

What mattered were the vanities and allurements of this world, transitory yet strangely enduring, and above all, beautiful. Mangles's request had awakened her to the splendours of the bush and she ardently sought his sanction and support for her endeavours. She wanted him to form a favourable impression of her character, civility, and reliability. She asked him to excuse the very long delayed departure of the boxes and concentrate instead on the contents, which, she wrote, 'I hope will give you such a pleasing impression of Captn. and Mrs Molloy, but especially the latter, as an active and obliging person, that any derogatory feeling may be removed.' With this hope, she closed her letter.

A few weeks later Molloy added a second postscript. A ship had called at Augusta with sad news from England. She wrote to Mangles, 'I have received most melancholy news, namely, my poor brother George's Death. He has for some years been suffering, and now at the early age of 25 years had bade adieu to all the painful vicissitudes entailed upon Mortality.'[1]

But Molloy was too far removed to be involved in her brother's death. She did not dwell on George's heavenly fate as she had once dwelt on her sister's. The worldly fate of the boxes of botanical specimens and their reception was now her paramount concern. Fears and hopes were as bound to the *hortus siccus* as the seeds, pressed flowers, and leaves. Botanising had required great physical and emotional exertion, and she wrote, 'So much of the *hortus siccus*'s contents were collected under the extremes of joy and acute sorrow; it has beguiled many a moment and I hope you will receive much success and satisfaction in looking over and sowing your seeds.'[2]

Weeks passed and the boxes remained at Augusta. Meanwhile, spring advanced and the bush burst into a brilliancy Molloy could not describe. Collecting season had returned. Although, with baby at her breast, she found her time 'very much absorbed', she could not resist venturing into the bush with her children, 'running like butterflys from flower to flower'. She wanted, above all, to ship the boxes, but she took the opportunity to complete her collection and search for specimens omitted the previous season. Her rambles were tinged with regret, for she associated each familiar flower with the specimens she had already collected; the 'galling remembrance' that the seeds were still at Augusta made her 'quite sad'.[3]

Molloy's own flower garden also blossomed. Tall white lily (*Lilium candidum*), pink gladiolus, oleander, single pinks, sweet peas, crimson mignonette, geraniums, and many more burst into glorious flower. Between the flower beds she had planted grass plots to 'give solace to the eye' and to provide a contrast between the dark green of the grass and the flowers—their English colours heightened, she believed, by the warmer sun of Augusta. The yucca lilies her mother had given her had thrived and reproduced. Molloy formed them into a hedge and thought the 'white bell shaped pendulous flowers tipped at the end with faint purple', which covered the stalks, 'truly beautiful'. Orange nasturtium grew on either side of the veranda. First planted in 1833, the vigorous trailing plant now formed an impervious, cool shade, profuse with showy blossoms, resplendent against a gay light green foliage. Two creeper plants, one native with purple flowers (*Hardenbergia comptoniana*), and the other, from Mauritius, with pink flowers, covered one side of the veranda and entwined the window that looked out over Hardy Inlet.

By November 1838 the two specimen boxes had not moved. Worse still, Molloy had yet to receive a reply from Mangles to her March 1837 note. She feared she had squandered the intimacy with which she had endowed the correspondence—all one-way—and felt reluctant to address him again. Her chagrin at the delay and her anxiety to acquit herself of seeming disregard for his requests 'so handsomely made', however, caused her to write again on 1 November. Previous letters went in one of the boxes; this time she used the mail.[4]

She wrote that she 'trembled' lest the seeds, after all her particular care, should fail. She could not stand to look at the stationary boxes, as every passing hour rendered their contents more precarious. But she kept her letter short: 'I write with Baby on my knee and my time is very much absorbed.' She did, however, mention her family's imminent departure for the Vasse, now planned for February 1839. Again she disclosed that she would prefer not to move; she did not want to forsake Augusta's 'heavenly clime'. Augusta was so attractive that she wanted to share the region's charms. Anyone of sensibility who visited would immediately understand her reluctance to leave. She wrote, 'I wish very much, both on your account and on ours, you had visited us when you were at Swan River [in 1831], then you could have *really condoled* with me.' The family was leaving, Molloy suggested, not because they wanted to, but because the abandonment of Augusta by most of the other original settlers made their own continued residence untenable. She hoped the move was not irreversible and mused, 'I look forward to visiting Augusta in the evening of life, and very much regret all the rest of the world have abandoned it.'[5]

At the time Molloy wrote, Captain Molloy was at the Vasse. A week later he returned with some flowers his wife had not seen before. Although she doubted they were sufficiently dry to ship, she wanted Mangles to see them, so she pressed them and arranged them in one of the boxes. She also checked the contents for insects and found a very small fly. She sprinkled some pepper as a repellent and preservative.

On 16 November the colonial schooner unexpectedly called in at Augusta. James Turner disembarked some supplies, but the ship's main purpose was to take on board the first of the outdoor and farming gear the Molloys intended transferring to the Vasse. Although unwell, Georgiana Molloy struggled to place Mangles's two boxes aboard. The vessel sailed for Fremantle after unloading at the Vasse, and Molloy consigned the boxes to Ellen Stirling for reshipment to England on the first available ship.

A week later Molloy felt better and wrote to Mangles to

announce the dispatch of the boxes. She reminded him of her desire to be acquainted with the proper names of all the plants she had sent. Even if the seeds failed, she hoped he would at least appreciate her efforts on his behalf. She still felt self-conscious 'at throwing aside the garb of formal etiquette usually worn by those not personally known to each other' but explained that she felt acquainted from having written so frequently and at length, even though she had yet to hear from him. Indeed, without any encouragement from Mangles, Molloy's epistolary style became noticeably easier and more colloquial in the course of her correspondence from March 1837. Behind even the early formality of Molloy's prose there lay an ever-present eagerness, a genuine expression of the pent-up intellectual romanticism that defined her life.[6]

When the colonial schooner arrived at Fremantle, Ellen Stirling placed the boxes from Augusta aboard the *Joshua Carroll*, which sailed direct for England at the end of November. The ship made a fast trip and arrived in England early in 1839. Mangles received the boxes but held no great expectations for their contents. Previous collections from Western Australia had all disappointed him.

Mangles had sent his first inquiries for native plants and seeds to G. F. Moore and Captain Richard Meares in 1835. The requests arrived late in the season, and opportunities to gather seeds did not occur until December 1836 and January 1837. Owing to the infrequency of shipping, the first specimens—seeds and seedlings—collected by Meares did not leave Swan River until November 1837 and did not reach England until 1838. When Mangles opened the boxes he found all the seedlings dead. The mortality and the poor order of the collection convinced Mangles that Meares could not be relied on. Mangles wrote of his frustrated hopes to Moore. He lamented his failure to secure good specimens and find a dependable collector from Western Australia. As he was ill, he announced his intention to retire from all concerns with respect to the young colony. Molloy's boxes and letters changed his mind.

But Molloy's boxes were not the only packages for Mangles aboard the *Joshua Carroll*. First, he opened a box containing a letter and specimens from Moore's proxy, James Drummond. Drummond wrote that the box contained 'a collection of upwards of 220 sorts of seeds' for Mangles's personal use and '44 one-pound packages each containing 20 papers of seeds' for Mangles to sell on Drummond's behalf. Drummond also included 'a very large Bale of specimens of dried plants . . . but for want of paper fit for the purpose I have not been able to divide them into sets.' The jumble of unspecified dried plants, the 44 pounds of seeds to sell, and the careless labelling—Drummond had neglected to note the locality and date of collection of each specimen—convinced Mangles that Drummond was irresponsible.[7]

Next Mangles opened Molloy's two boxes. Out of one he retrieved two *horti sicci*, including the one he sent in 1836, and another larger one. They both contained pressed plants, finely and meticulously arranged, annotated, and carefully numbered. Most of the specimens were new to Mangles. The second box contained packages of seeds numbered to correspond with the specimens in the two *horti sicci*. The seeds, Mangles noted, were clean and had been sorted and packed with precision. The seed box also contained Molloy's letters of January and September 1838, with the account of her son's death, descriptions of colonial life, and a request for seeds and gardening articles, together with a cheque. Mangles tore up the cheque.

Mangles was delighted with the collection and with Georgiana Molloy's charm and enthusiasm. He sent the two *horti sicci* and Molloy's letters to John Lindley, former assistant to Joseph Banks, and Fellow of the Royal Society, Professor of Botany at University College, London, author of *Ladies' Botany*, and organiser of Britain's first flower show in 1830. Lindley replied:

> Your friend Mrs Molloy is really the most charming personage in
> all South Australia, and you the most fortunate man to have such

a correspondent. That many of the plants are beautiful you can see for yourself, and I am delighted to add that many of the best are quite new.[8]

Mangles next sent the specimens and correspondence to Joseph Paxton. Paxton, a gardener and architect, was superintendent of the gardens at Chatsworth, where he oversaw the construction of the greenhouse and orchid house and the formation of an arboretum. In 1836 he began the great conservatory, which became the model for the Great Exhibition Building in 1851. He wrote to Mangles that he had read Molloy's letters

> with considerable interest. They have been written by one who is devoted to the promotion of Botanical interest in this country and zealously able to fulfil the task of collecting seeds. . . . There are some splendid things in the *Hortus Siccus* of Port Augusta.

Paxton pointed out that most attempts to raise unknown seed were fraught with disappointment. In this case, however, the great care lavished on packaging gave an assurance of the good condition of the seed, while the attractiveness of the dried plants provided an added stimulus to try. Thus encouraged, Mangles rearranged the seeds from Molloy's and Drummond's boxes and sent the packages to fifteen horticulturalists around the country—private gardeners and public botanical gardens.[9]

Molloy's collection arrived in Britain during a period of acute concern regarding the relationship of natural history to religious belief. Before the nineteenth century, theologians allowed the earth no very great antiquity. In the Christian view, sacred history embraced a plan of salvation and a record of the steps along the road to redemption. Nature was only a setting for this movement towards grace. According to Genesis, God brought nature into existence in completed form. Animal and vegetable species were thus absolutely immutable and permanent, and each was created in its present image.

But in the nineteenth century, investigation of nature accelerated, and natural records, particularly fossils, indicated that the earth and the life upon it had undergone alterations in the past. Nature appeared to change over the course of time. Great debates arose, first over biblical chronology, then over the Noachian Flood, the dispersion of peoples, and the confusion of tongues at Babel. The sheer flux of questioning and explaining threatened to destroy the reputation of the Bible as a revealed world.

In the face of possible heresy, most natural historians sought to bring revelation into harmony with nature—to make the word of God agree with the works of God, or at least to find in the works a verification of the word. Truth was indivisible; its two branches—natural and revealed—must eventually coincide. Accordingly, investigation into natural history continued. Evidence that supported the idea of a long succession of time in the history of the earth continued to accumulate. Geologists could no longer avoid considering the question of the great age of the earth. But the consequences were disturbing. As long as the scale of time was brief and events few, Mosaic history could carry conviction. But how could epoch after epoch, creation after creation, be fitted to the teleology of man's redemption? And if Moses were wrong on cosmogony and history, then what could be relied upon? If the earth and its productions had existed for millions of years, were they then created for man?[10]

Some of the answers came from Australia—the source of some of the world's most primitive and grotesque forms of botanical and zoological life. In 1822 Australian marine surveyor and naturalist Phillip Parker King wrote, 'No country ever produced a more extraordinary assemblage of indigenous productions—no country has proved richer than Australia in every branch of natural history.' Indeed, in the 50 years after first settlement, Australian collectors shipped to Europe thousands upon thousands of specimens of plants, animals, and rocks, as well as Aboriginal skeletons, skulls, and pickled heads. Collectors generated a flood of facts that overburdened traditional taxonomies and challenged existing theories of natural history.[11]

In the face of the evidence, natural historians abandoned the doctrine of the fixity of species; forms of life *did* change, unquestionably. And subtly, slowly, inexorably almost, but certainly unintentionally, the spirit of patient empirical inquiry worked to undermine the very idea of a creator. At the same time as they believed they were in the service of God, natural historians, astronomers, geologists, and botanists were constructing a universe that excluded Him. Moreover, as a corollary, the fact of organic evolution appeared to demolish the idea of humans as specially created to be lords of the earth. But evolution lent credence to a new doctrine, the doctrine of progress. Species changed but always changed for the better. The history of life was about improvement, and the most improved species was man. Natural progress reinstated humans as lords of the earth, who rightfully exercised authority over the world.

The exposition of Charles Darwin's theory of evolution, or, descent with modification, in *The Origin of Species* (1859), lay two decades beyond Mangles's reception of Molloy's boxes of southwest specimens. By then, the southwest was known, and Darwin cited the species endemism and floristic richness of the southwestern corner of Australia several times in the course of his argument in support of the theory of natural selection. Darwin argued that the characteristics that naturalists—including botanists—considered as showing true affinity between species were those that had been inherited from a common parent; all true classification was genealogical. Community of descent, not some unknown plan of creation or great chain of being, was the bond that naturalists had been unconsciously seeking.

During the years when Molloy collected, however, botanists concerned themselves exclusively with description and classification of species. Finding new species was the highest goal. Theory was shunned. How species got the way they were was of little interest.

Some months after viewing Molloy's collection, John Lindley submitted *A Sketch of the Vegetation of the Swan River Colony* as an appendix to *Edward's Botanical Register*, a compendium of the world's botany that sought to classify and name every known plant species. The *Sketch* was based largely on Mangles's herbarium of about 1000 species, which included Molloy's specimens. Lindley wrote, 'The frequent arrival of seeds from this colony, the excellent state in which they are received, and the facility with which further supplies can be procured, appear to render some Botanical account of this remarkable country a desirable appendage to [*Edward's Botanical Register*].'[12]

Lindley's Swan River *Sketch* was possible because Mangles's colonial collector, Georgiana Molloy, possessed qualities that ideally suited her to the task, namely, dedication and an active and attentive intelligence. As an unwitting agent of modernity, Molloy helped bring Western taxonomy to the Australian bush, to the sacred landscape of the Aborigines. The imposition of the science of order intruded yet another boundary between the settlers and the world around them, a boundary not at all apparent to the Aborigines.

Although Molloy enjoyed her participation in a global undertaking, she did not contemplate the universal implications. At Augusta human life responded to necessity; people lived in the service of immediate interests and needs. And in the early months of 1839 the overwhelming fact of existence at Augusta was the Molloys' imminent departure.

After shipping farming gear aboard the colonial schooner in November 1838, Captain Molloy made several trips to and from the Vasse. Georgiana Molloy stayed at Augusta to look after the household, children, and farm. Even though abandonment was near, she still tended her garden.

As small as Augusta had become, the settlement's remaining inhabitants carried on with their lives. In January 1839 the widowed Ann Heppingstone, now remarried to the settler Samuel Bryan, gave birth to a daughter, Hannah. Visitors still arrived. Early in the new year a party of sealers, hunting along the coast from King George Sound, called at Augusta and were there when Alfred Green and

Charles Bussell walked down from the Vasse. Danger and crisis were apprehended: Aborigines set fire to the bush at the back of the town, and the flames burnt close to the Bryans' house. Gossip spread and conflict erupted: the Molloys' colt went missing and was found by Ann Turner and Green, out on a romantic walk. They penned it in an empty stockyard, but the horse panicked, leapt over the fence, impaled itself on a stake, and died. When Ann Turner visited Georgiana Molloy a few days later, Molloy admonished her for her precipitous act.

Other sources of tension soured the relationship between the Turners and the Molloys. James Turner resented the Molloys for leaving. The imminent departure of the next-to-last of the original Augusta settlers left Turner, or so he believed, in an impossible position. In 1838 he wrote to the colonial secretary to protest against the likely removal of the military from Augusta consequent upon the resident magistrate's relocation. He himself could not leave. His investments, worth several thousand pounds, entailed too great a sacrifice; he had to stay, and the government had to encourage and even subsidise settlement at Augusta. Turner's special pleading failed to convince the governor. Stirling instructed the colonial secretary to reply that military forces would be located according to the wants and numbers of settlers in each district. In the meantime, government would not interfere in the pursuit of private enterprise:

> The removal or anticipated removal of all the settlers from Augusta to another part of the district, with the exception of your own family, is doubtless the true cause of all the inconveniences alleged. Upon this point the governor is desirous to point out to you that it is not in his power to prevent individuals from consulting and pressing their own interests and views in that respect. It is equally out of his power to maintain at Augusta those public officers which in the present reduced state of its population are not required.[13]

But Turner was unconvinced. He wrote to Lord Glenelg, at the Colonial Office in London, to plead the need for a permanent military force at Augusta: the government must support that which it had founded. Glenelg, however, agreed with Stirling: Turner's claims for compensation and military protection were unwarranted.

Turner's case appeared hopeless. But in 1838 the unsympathetic Stirling resigned as governor, and Turner's protests reached the new Western Australian governor, John Hutt, who arrived at Swan River on 1 January 1839. Hutt subscribed to Edward Wakefield's theories of systematic colonisation, which called on government to carefully control the sale of land to capitalists in order to raise sufficient revenue to sponsor the emigration of labourers. Hutt opposed dispersed settlement and supported consolidation of existing settlements. He took an immediate interest in James Turner's circumstances. Within weeks of his arrival, he instructed the colonial secretary to write to Resident Magistrate Molloy and request him 'to state, as you are about to remove to the Vasse, in what way you propose to perform the duties of Resident at Augusta to which you were appointed'.[14]

On 20 February 1839 the *Lady Stirling*, en route from King George Sound, called in at Flinders Bay and delivered Hutt's directive. Captain Molloy postponed his reply. Meanwhile, he embarked the rest of the family possessions aboard the *Lady Stirling* for the voyage to the Vasse. Six days later he himself left for the Vasse. He was gone nearly a month, and while there he responded to Hutt's inquiry. Indignant that his decision to move should be questioned, he told Hutt that following the 1837 'disturbances that had taken place here [the Vasse] with the natives', Governor Stirling advised him to relocate as soon as possible. He had not, therefore, abandoned Augusta from whim but proposed moving to the Vasse from prudence, 'this being the most frequented port with the greatest number of settlers, the greatest quantity of livestock and the most numerous native population in the district'. The Vasse was, he concluded, 'the point at which I could be the most service to Her Majesty's Govt'. Molloy suggested a compromise: once settled at the Vasse, he would make periodic visits to Augusta. Hutt eventually agreed to this arrangement, over Turner's continued objections.[15]

In the meantime, Georgiana Molloy was content to stay at Augusta. Although her relationship with the Turners was formal and strained, her life was sufficient. Her children kept her occupied, she worked in her garden, and she collected for Mangles. The town of Augusta continued to receive visitors who attracted her interest.

In February an American whaler, *America*, anchored in Flinders Bay. The crew planned to spend the season bay whaling. Captain Cole and his brother introduced themselves to the settlers, dined with the Turners and the Molloys, and, in turn, invited settlers aboard ship. The Americans also rowed their whaleboat up the Blackwood to fish and sightsee.

Early in May the Molloys made final arrangements for their departure. They asked Captain Cole to ferry them and their goods up the Blackwood to the landing, where travellers began the overland trip to the Vasse. A few days before leaving, Georgiana Molloy planted a cutting of the dark crimson China rose on her son's grave. On the evening before departure, she visited her Augusta garden for the last time. She pulled up her favourite plants and shrubs and placed them in a basket.

Early next morning all the birds of the bush trilled, called, and whistled on the perfect chill of the air. The sky filled with a dazzling pink, and a pale shade of green came over the trees as the sun rose beyond the forest, on the western shore of Hardy Inlet. Georgiana Molloy, her husband, and the children boarded Captain Cole's whale-boat. Molloy sat in the stern with the basket of plants and shrubs cradled in the folds of her skirt. With her back towards her destination, she looked down at the lovely Blackwood, 'that Magnificent and peaceful River'. The water was dark and still; the trees and shrubs of the Australian bush overhung the river's banks. White pelicans floated at a distance and waterbirds careened overhead.

Departure from the natural beauty she had uncovered in what to others was, and had once been for her, an unadorned wilderness, filled Molloy with profound sadness. She likened her life at Augusta to Eve's life in the Garden of Eden. She now felt she had been expelled from paradise. 'My feelings on leaving my much loved retreat,' she later wrote, 'are best expressed in those beautiful lines of Milton, where he represents Eve driven from her garden in paradise':[16]

O unexpected stroke, worse than of Death!
Must I thus leave thee Paradise? thus leave
Thee Native Soil, these happy Walks and Shades,
Fit haunt of Gods? where I had hope to spend,
Quiet though sad, the respite of that day
That must be mortal to us both. O flow'rs,
That never will in other Climate grow,
My early visitation, and my last
At Ev'n, which I bred up with tender hand
From the first op'ning bud, and gave ye Names,
Who now shall rear ye to the Sun, or rank
Your Tribes, and water from th'ambrosial Fount?[17]

For Milton, paradise was a singularly treacherous place—the scene of the Fall of Man. Adam and Eve lived there enveloped by warnings of approaching catastrophe. But for Molloy, paradise was filled with joy, not foreboding. In Milton's paradise, Eve sinned and was cast out. Molloy felt condemned, but she had not sinned. Moreover, she identified with the strong-willed Eve, not with the weak, vacillating, meekly obedient Adam.

Molloy placed a strikingly secular and organic interpretation on Milton's verse. For her, his lines expressed her passionate attachment to the particular—to the bush, soil, flowers, air, and climate of Augusta, southwest Australia. 'At Augusta,' she wrote to Mangles,

'we suffered much in every way [but we] also enjoyed much undis-
turbed happiness.' She then dropped the plural pronoun, reverted to
the singular, and added, 'I was reluctant to leave.'[18]

At Augusta Molloy had discovered the earth was alive. Whereas
her neighbours had seen a wilderness in need of taming, she had
uncovered a natural beauty beyond compare. She found that the most
uninhabited parts of the earth were just as loaded with God's bounties
as the inhabited parts. In the midst of privation, Molloy found
joy—an acute sense of the willingness to live, the wish for more
life—in the productions of nature.

Augusta had been a revelation. Through the cultivation of her
domestic garden, Molloy encountered the greater garden of the bush.
Gradually, hesitantly at first, but with increasing confidence from the
safety of her garden path, Molloy approached the forbidding immen-
sity of the bush. In the Garden of Eden, God created order out of
natural chaos, created a civilised clearing at the centre of the cosmos,
and pushed the old chaos back to the edges, where it remained a
persistent threat. Molloy had also created order in her garden, but
when she botanised, when she ventured out of her garden, the
boundaries between order and chaos broke down. The wilderness
beyond her garden was the bush she had come to understand and
love.

The once-pious Molloy found that no religious creed, however
much it etherealised human experience, could exclude the vitality of
organic existence forever. Whereas once she had shared Henry
Martyn's view of the world 'as a mere wilderness through which the
children of God are passing to a better country', she now understood
that the world, the wilderness, had its own beauty and purpose,
independent of its role as a vale of tears or a staging ground to a
higher plane of existence. Unlike Martyn or Isabella Campbell,
Molloy did not find that with the passing of the years, 'the ways of
the world appear more insipid and vexatious'. On the contrary, the
world—the physical world, the material world of nature—had

become ever more piquant, pungent, and delightful. The once-dreary southwest was full of life.[19]

Being in the bush provided a dimension of existence not available to people living in the tamed and overcultivated garden of Britain, where only tiny remnants of the original wild forests remained, from which all wild animals had been banished. Being in the bush called forth an accentuated consciousness. A heightened feeling of life pervaded existence on the Australian continent. Even the sky was different. At night, southern stars shone with an extra brilliancy and copiousness. Unlike Wordsworth's northern England, where a 'little lot of stars' twinkled in a 'little patch of sky', in Australia the luminous expanse of the Milky Way shrieked and blazed across the southern sky. In Britain, stars twinkled; in Australia, billions of nighttime suns ignited in a great shining welt.

Georgiana Molloy had left Britain with her husband. She now followed him from Augusta. Like Milton's Eve, she felt bound to her man, to obey him, and to accompany him on his journey to the Vasse:

> My Author and Disposer, what thou bidd'st
> Unargu'd I obey; so God ordains,
> God is thy law, thou mine: to know no more
> Is woman's happiest knowledge and her praise.[20]

Prudence, Molloy wrote to Mangles, forbade her return.[21]

Captain Cole and his crew rowed the Molloys 30 miles up the Blackwood to a prearranged staging, where Alfred Green, who had set out from Augusta in the morning on horseback with a soldier and native guides, joined them. The whole party camped overnight.

For Molloy, the camp in the bush evoked an awareness of what a remote corner of the world she inhabited and what a strange but eventful life she led. She lay down to sleep. Only the occasional thud of a kangaroo, the nocturnal scurrying of some small swift marsupial, the shriek of an owl, and the heavy breathing of the men in their blankets by the fire interrupted the stillness of the night.

Next morning Captain Cole and his crew returned to Augusta. The rest of the party started for the Vasse. But with two young children and a baby, the normal two-day, one-night trip took longer, and the travellers spent two more nights in the bush. The clear, mild May days turned wet before the Molloys reached the Vasse on Friday, 10 May.[22]

Four days' travel had heightened expectations. The reality shocked Molloy. 'A terrible change,' she wrote to Mangles. The new homesite was on the banks of the river, but the Vasse was a narrow and sluggish stream, not much more than a chain of stagnant pools, and a poor substitute for the broad compass of the Blackwood. Upon arrival Molloy immediately looked around for a moist spot in which to place the plants she had dug up at Augusta and nurtured during the journey to the Vasse. She feared they would not survive and wrote, 'Torn from their native soil, they seemed to participate in the feelings of their Mistress, trying through the aid of Water to keep up their natural vigour, but evidently had met with some terrible reverse.'[23]

1 7

EFFLORESCENCE

SHORTLY AFTER THE MOLLOYS ARRIVED AT THE VASSE, JOHN BUSSELL returned to Western Australia. He brought a wife. Charlotte Bussell, however, had not been his intended bride when he left for England in 1837. He had quarrelled with his original fiancée, heiress Sophie Hayward, about money, and they had agreed to annul the engagement. Bussell's health then broke down, and in convalescence he met Charlotte Cookworthy, a 29-year-old widow and mother of three children. They married, sailed for Fremantle in December 1838, and arrived on 22 May 1839. Impatient to be at the Vasse, John Bussell hired a boat for the trip south and reached Busselton next morning.

A few days later Georgiana Molloy invited the couple to spend an evening at Fairlawn, the Molloys' new house. Cattle Chosen lay just across the Vasse River, and on the appointed day Charlotte and John took a boat across. Georgiana Molloy stood on the opposite bank with baby Amelia in her arms. Charlotte, three months pregnant with her first Australian child, noted that Molloy's 'complexion was very fair, [and that] she had a quantity of fair hair. She was dressed in a dark blue print very plainly made.' Molloy escorted the couple to her house. 'In the parlour,' Charlotte continued, 'was a bright fire. Tea was ready, and on the table was a beautiful bunch of wildflowers, for her garden was not in order and she could not be without flowers in her room.' While the adults ate at the table, Molloy's daughters seated themselves on low seats on either side of the fire. Afterwards, Molloy played the small piano that stood in the room.[1]

Despite her new acquaintance and the socialising that followed, Molloy still believed that in moving to the Vasse, she had met with some terrible reverse. The Vasse country was flat, the bush was dull, and even the climate was inferior: less temperate than at Augusta, hotter during the day, and colder at night. But, as at Augusta, the circumstances of pioneering necessarily involved Molloy in life. Life at the Vasse demanded a response, and she could not long maintain feelings of separation and detachment. Winter came, and the rains stimulated vegetative growth, both in her newly established garden and in the greater bush. Late in June Captain Molloy and Henry Ommanney, the Vasse surveyor recently married to Bessie Bussell, led a three-week expedition overland to Swan River. In her husband's absence Molloy assumed responsibility for the farm.

In July Captain Molloy returned to the Vasse, and in August Georgiana Molloy became pregnant again. Towards the end of the month, spring came and the bush began to bloom. The Vasse, Molloy quickly discovered, possessed a beauty of its own, a beauty that banished her initial unfavourable impressions. She discovered new wildflowers and 'was astonished at their loveliness, much finer than at Augusta'. She confirmed, however, that as at Augusta, the Vasse floral display generally took the form of great numbers of small flowers, showy in the mass, rather than of fewer large flowers, showy in the individual blossom. In September Molloy commenced collecting again for Mangles and was delighted to find so many varieties she had never before seen. She wanted to send them all to Mangles, but without a *hortus siccus* she had nowhere to place dried specimens. She thought of making her own book but could not find sufficient paper.[2]

Lack of time also inhibited collecting. Although Molloy always found time to put both cultivated and wild flowers on her table, she did not always have time to dry them. In the spring she became particularly attracted to 'a very elegant plant' with blue flowers that grew in moist places. She kept bunches in the house, but as she later wrote to Mangles:

> At that time I really had not one moment's leisure, and have often turned away from the vase on the table with regret saying, 'Shall I dry these or do my work?' Duty prevailed and I much regret it on your account, as you would have been lost in amazement at such uncontemplated beauties—they surpass all description.[3]

Molloy, however, had not abandoned collecting, even at Augusta. Before her departure she had arranged for Charlotte Heppingstone to collect in her absence. They kept in touch by letter, and Heppingstone sent specimens and seeds to the Vasse. Molloy also wrote to, and exchanged flower seeds with, the Turner sisters.

The last of the original settlers still at Augusta, the Turners, did not spend 1839 without company. Two American whaling vessels, *Pacific* and *America*, spent the entire season in Flinders Bay. The ships' crews set up bay whaling operations to hunt the Right whales (*Balaena australis*) that frequented the bay. These whales were part of an annual winter migration, when tens of thousands of Right whales swam north from Antarctica to mate and calve in the bays and estuaries along the coasts of New Zealand, Van Diemen's Land, and southern Australia. They congregated so thickly and so close to shore in Flinders Bay that Augusta settlers could stand on the beach and count the barnacles on their backs.[4]

Whales were not the only prey. Hunters discovered a cornucopia of valuable marine life along the southwest coasts. And despite 30 years of steady persecution by itinerant sealing gangs, the rocky promontories and islands around Cape Leeuwin and Flinders Bay still teemed with rookeries of seals at the time the British founded Augusta. As John Bussell wrote of his four years in the vicinity of Flinders Bay:

> There was scarcely a rock upon which man may set his foot, that

I have not frequented with sealing-club or fishing-line, or ransacked for sea-bird's eggs; nor a creek or bay within Hardy Inlet, that I have not persecuted with nets and guns in time of dearth.[5]

The seals, for a time at least, even survived John Bussell's club. In 1833 G. F. Moore reported large seal colonies 'of the most valuable species' inhabiting the rocky islands in the vicinity of Augusta.[6]

By the end of the 1839 whaling season, the Americans at Flinders Bay had taken over three dozen whales. The activity attracted large numbers of Aborigines, who feasted on the beached carcasses and the blubber discarded after flensing and boiling. The Turners felt uncomfortable with so many natives around.

Late in September Thomas Turner's garden was robbed of potatoes. Turner, his younger brother George, Thomas Salkild, their father's servant, John Herring, the constable, and two soldiers went in pursuit of the suspected native thieves. On the beach of Flinders Bay, four miles east of Augusta, Turner's men came upon a group of Aborigines feasting on a whale carcass. At the sight of the armed settlers, the Aborigines fled but not before the soldiers apprehended three men. Upon interrogation the prisoners denied stealing the potatoes. Soldier Richard West claimed, however, to have seen the three in Augusta on the day of the robbery, and so Turner ordered them shackled and marched back to Augusta. Two of the men, Wondabirt and Dundap, attempted to escape. West fired; Dundap fell, and died within a few minutes.

When Captain Molloy heard of the shooting, he and two soldiers walked down to Augusta from the Vasse to investigate. He stayed two weeks, took depositions, and escorted the two surviving Aboriginal captives back to the Vasse, where he and John Bussell, now a magistrate, considered the evidence and submitted a report to the government. They concluded that the prisoners 'were not the guilty party'. But Dundap's death, the death of an Aboriginal in custody, almost escaped their notice. 'The loss of life,' they commented obliquely and in the passive voice, 'in the attempt of Dundap to escape is lamented deeply.' The grammar and syntax they employed served to distance the killing and absolve the killer. This was especially important considering that the victim was innocent. By rhetorical means, Captain Molloy and John Bussell relegated a human death to a marginal, incidental position and attenuated their own expression of remorse.[7]

The Turners feared Aboriginal retaliation for Dundap's death. For protection, they concentrated their forces. Thomas and George came down from The Spring to stay at the main house; Ann Bryan moved temporarily into the Molloys' abandoned house, and, for the next several weeks, settlers grazed their stock close to the barracks. Although the two Aboriginal men released at the Vasse vowed revenge when they returned to Augusta, none came. Instead, Aborigines— individually and in small groups—visited Dundap's grave to mourn. The Turners, however, expressed no regret. Thomas Turner submitted a bill to the government for compensation for the time he spent in aiding the capture of the Aborigines. The government refused payment.[8]

In November Governor Hutt visited the Vasse and stayed with the Molloys. Georgiana Molloy discovered that she and Hutt shared an interest in natural history. Hutt informed her of the presence in the colony, since the previous year, of the German naturalist and collector Ludwig Preiss. Although interested in natural history specimens of all kinds, Preiss primarily collected plants. Molloy promptly invited him to visit the Vasse and stay at Fairlawn. Preiss arrived in December.

Keen to visit all the known parts of southwest Australia and to assemble a comprehensive collection of specimens, Preiss bought plants from other collectors in addition to collecting his own. In fact, John Gilbert, a collector employed by John Gould, who arrived in the colony three months after Preiss, complained that his rival bought practically everything offered and paid too high a price.

Monetary reward, however, did not interest Molloy. She hoped only that in the younger Preiss's company she might learn some botany that would augment her understanding of bush plants and increase her competence as a collector. She was soon disappointed. She and Preiss rambled together through the Vasse bush, where Molloy discovered that she learned less from him than he learned from her. Preiss, however, was oblivious to the inequality of the exchange. When he left he presented his hostess with some of the results of his work. Molloy noted he had given her but few specimens in comparison to what he took away. Moreover, she found his collecting habits and his presentation of specimens so 'rough and ungainly' that she 'could not deface the *hortus siccus* with them'. She decided to mount Preiss's specimens separately from her own.

Although Preiss supplied names for many of the Vasse plants, many more remained unclassified. He promised to furnish appellations in future correspondence, but he never wrote. His delinquency irritated Molloy. She felt his omission was inexcusable, for his time in the colony afforded him many 'excellent opportunities' to communicate. His failure to reciprocate the hospitality he had enjoyed at Fairlawn caused Molloy to reflect on the selfishness of residents and visitors in Western Australia: 'how easily persons in this colony lay aside the common rules of Society'.[9]

But if Preiss's conduct was dilatory and negligent, Molloy soon rejoiced in evidence of Old World mindfulness. Preiss's December 1839 visit coincided with the receipt of the first communication from Mangles since his original request had arrived at Augusta in December 1836. Shortly before Christmas, Mangles's response to the letters and two boxes of seeds and specimens that he opened in London early in 1839 reached the Vasse. His letter and an unexpected box of gifts constituted Molloy's 'long-wished-for' confirmation of her efforts. Mangles's generous acknowledgement of his antipodean collector assured Molloy that she was appreciated, that her efforts had not been in vain, and that her colonial confessions were not found embarrassing. Mangles proved to be a gentleman. He was not interested in exploiting either her eagerness or her vulnerability. His magnanimity was astonishing. With relief and gratitude, Molloy replied:

> Words fail me when I attempt to return you my many many grateful thanks and acknowledgements for [your box's] useful, beautiful and handsome contents. I stood quite amazed when Captn. Molloy took out the different things, wondering at your disinterested liberality and kindness to those you have never seen, and who are not able to make you any adequate return.[10]

As well as three *horti sicci* and collecting materials, the box contained books, periodicals, gardening manuals, soap, and cloth, including silk. Molloy regarded all the gifts as luxuries for which she felt 'very inefficient in conveying to you a sense of my gratitude'. The soap she found 'a fragrant and pleasant acquisition' but, she was happy to say, not an article for which she felt great need. There was no dearth of soap in Australia, nor of anything essential. She did not feel deprived, and added, 'I have never wanted for any single necessary of life since we have been out in Western Australia.' Settlers made do with what they had and in times of shortage, did without. 'I may have little,' she stated confidently, 'but still that little will keep, or else we can for a while deny ourselves.'[11]

Nevertheless, the family appreciated the gifts, especially the printed matter. Molloy delighted in the floral illustrations in *The Greenhouse*, which, 'after a day spent in servile drudgery', she would spread out before her and look at with 'unwearied pleasure'. Her husband, she wrote, enjoyed the periodicals, which informed him of current events. His restricted leisure afforded him time to read only 'what is really useful and interesting'. Included in this category was the recently published *Three Expeditions into the Interior of Eastern Australia* by Major T. L. Mitchell, which helped satisfy Captain Molloy's curiosity about the rest of Australia. The children too took pleasure in the books and magazines, and Molloy related how, 'When leave is granted for Captn. Mangles's Books to be looked at, a clean cloth is laid, and Sabina and Mary are permitted to regale themselves with the sight.'[12]

Mangles also sent a copy of the Reverend Alexander Keith's *Sketch of the Evidence from Prophecy: Containing an Account of those Prophecies which were Distinctly Foretold, and which have been Clearly or Literally Fulfilled.* First published in 1823, the volume was principally directed at unbelievers, to those who had closed their minds to the truth of Christianity but might be persuaded by evidence of the fulfilment of biblical prophecy. But Keith also sought to convince a doubting mind and to confirm a Christian one more strongly in belief. Christianity, according to Keith, appealed to reason and submitted its credentials to scrutiny. The Bible contained unambiguous predictions, the accuracy of which had been confirmed through historical and archaeological investigation in Egypt and Palestine. Indeed, Mangles's own journey through the Middle East was, in part, an attempt to verify biblical events. Biblical prophecies, Keith claimed, were as clear as the facts were visible. Christianity had nothing to fear from inquiry. Belief founded on reason was a positive proof that became fixed and immovable.

In an age that appealed to empiricism and granted increasing authority to verifiable evidence, Keith's book proved popular and ran through several editions. Mangles had sent a copy to G. F. Moore in 1835. Moore had read the book in England and was interested in another perusal. In the colony, however, Keith's urgency and piety seemed somehow removed and even irrelevant to the necessary occupations of settlers.[13]

Molloy wrote that she had always wanted Keith's *On Prophecy* but had considered the book too expensive. Unlike the botanical books, however, to which she often referred, she never mentioned the Reverend Alexander Keith again. Her rugged faith transcended Keith's empirical and superficial evidence. The larger prophecy of the Bible— the narrative of Creation, the Fall, God's judgement and redemption through Christ—Molloy accepted as the true account of the human condition, one that did not require ancillary proof.

The British evangelical movement had believed that appeals to facts concealed a childish and unworthy desire for certainty. The truth or falsity of biblical prophecy could never serve as a guide to the conduct of life. The agnostic rules for truth seeking, as laid down by empiricists, betrayed a timorous state of mind, a suspension of judgement that ignored the whole field of religious experience and its testimony to the power of faith. Molloy found that the prophecies to which Keith attested were Old Testament prophecies, revelations of death, ruin, decay, and desolation. Such dark foreboding now seemed distant and unrelated to life in the southwest of Australia, where the bush provided immediate, vibrant, and copious confirmation of life, testimony that required no independent verification.

Molloy appropriated all three *horti sicci* that arrived in the December box, even though Mangles had clearly addressed one to Mrs Mary Bull of Leschenault. Preiss pointed out the error, and Molloy reluctantly forwarded the third *hortus siccus*. She believed she was the more competent collector. Moreover, Molloy now had such a large botanical collection that she needed as much *hortus siccus* space as possible.

Molloy had organised others to collect on her behalf. Besides Charlotte Heppingstone at Augusta, whom she asked to collect seeds specifically requested by Dr John Lindley, she had importuned the military. 'The soldiers who used to pass between this and Augusta unmolested and unencumbered with anything but their knapsacks, are now seen to bring from thence specimens of all sorts of Plants under their arms,' she wrote. Molloy also convinced Aborigines to bring her flowers. She had learned that, owing to their custom of placing wreaths on graves, the Nyungar associated flowers with death. Nevertheless, she overcame their dislike of flowers, obtained their cooperation in collecting, and reported: 'the native Herdsmen are also employed bringing in some desired Plant or Fruit'. She also discovered that the Nyungar especially disliked flowers placed on their heads. On one occasion, however, she persuaded the man Battap to allow her 'to place a large piece of the crimson Anterrhinum in his Wilgied Locks'.[14]

In an earlier letter to Mangles, Molloy had wondered how she would dispatch future boxes of plants and seeds once the dependable Ellen Stirling left the colony. In January 1840 the arrival of the whaling ship *America* solved her problem. Captain Cole had spent the season whaling in Flinders Bay, where he became good friends with the Molloys. He had assisted their departure from Augusta, and he now agreed to carry Molloy's box of specimens with him on his return to New England. Once home, he promised to freight the box from New York, by steamer, across the Atlantic to Mangles in London.

After enlisting Captain Cole's cooperation, Molloy gave her daughters a week's holiday from schooling and commenced full-time organising of the *hortus siccus* and specimens. While she could not predict the time of the box's arrival in England, she wrote to Mangles that she hoped the dried flowers and leaves would 'afford amusement to your botanical Friends'. She believed these specimens would be the first in Britain from the Vasse country. The prospect that Mangles would be the first to examine these new southwest species 'roused all my energy'. Every day for a week, Molloy worked from breakfast till midnight to affix the specimens in the *hortus siccus*, paste on labels, write descriptions of each plant, and make paper-bag seed containers.[15]

The seeds, she assured Mangles, in a letter begun on the evening of the day she finished packing, had all been gathered during the last two months and were guaranteed fresh. Molloy resumed her long letter—over 3500 words—the next morning and through the following day. She thanked Mangles profusely for his gifts, narrated the family's departure from Augusta, which she reminded him she had 'left with much regret', described the weather at the Vasse, mentioned the visits of Governor Hutt and Ludwig Preiss, and detailed her collecting and arranging.

So many specimens had arrived at Fairlawn that Molloy found the packaging materials Mangles had sent were inadequate. In future she wanted more paper, bags for seeds, and pink tape to tie the packages. She 'could not bear' the pack thread she currently used: 'it cuts the papers and looks unseemly and inelegant!!' She also wanted different-coloured papers, so as to mount the different grasses, leaves, and white flowers to greater 'effect'. She explained her fastidiousness with respect to presentation as the natural expression of 'what I feel towards so kind a Friend'.[16]

Mangles had told Molloy he was the author of *The Floral Calendar*, a little book that argued for the beauty, usefulness, and possibilities in window and town gardening. She hoped he would send her a copy. But even more, she hoped the frontispiece contained a lithographic portrait of the author. Mangles's letters evinced an attractive personality—worldly, learned, and articulate—and Molloy longed to 'see face to face the person whom Fate has so capriciously veiled from sight, but made so instrumental in bestowing kindness and gratification at so remote a part of the Globe'. Frustrated at their continued and likely perpetual separation, and filled with curiosity about her correspondent, Molloy confessed:

> Our Acquaintance is both singular and tantalizing, and somewhat melancholy to me, my dear Sir, to reflect on. We shall never meet in this life. We may mutually smooth and cheer the rugged path of this World's Existence, even in its brightest condition, by strewing Flowers in our Way, but we never can converse with each other, and I am sincere when I say, I never met with any one who so perfectly called forth and could sympathize with me in my prevailing passion for Flowers.[17]

On the evening after she confessed her sweet melancholy, the six-months-pregnant Molloy proposed a final collecting expedition

before the departure, next morning, of the *America*. She asked
Captain Molloy to accompany her in a search for *Isopogon* seeds.
After nine months at the Vasse, she had learned to take every possible
opportunity to get out into the bush, for she had discovered that
'being in the Bush was one of the most delightful states of existence,
free from every household care'.[18]

Freedom from every household care did not mean a breaking of
connection. Rather, being in the bush was a liberation into a sense
of participation in a larger life. The earth abideth forever, and human
travail counted for little in the larger context of the natural world:
the endless cycles of birth and death and decay, the ever-changing
seasons, the bursting into blossom, the formation of seeds, and
regeneration. Being in the bush stimulated Molloy's perception and
enlarged her awareness. The irrevocable brilliance of Australian light
filled her collecting days and expanded her sense of self. Strewn with
flowers, the bush drew her into a consciousness of the sensuousness
of existence, of the vitality of organic life. She felt the breeze on her
face, the sun burning on her skin, and heard the cries of the magpie
and the Australian raven.

Freedom from domestic routine also meant freedom from the
tyranny of industrial, mechanised time that the settlers had brought
with them to Western Australia. As Molloy became more fully alive
to the life of the Australian bush, she became more fully aware of
organic time, time that inhered in the course of day into night: the
coming of dawn, the steady advance of morning, the length of the
afternoon, the cooling down of the evening, and the passage into the
starry night.

On the occasion of Molloy's last-minute attempt to collect
Isopogon seeds, she and Captain Molloy were unable to catch their
horses, which had run into the bush, and she abandoned the search
for the seeds. She promised Mangles she would send them later. In
a note written just before the box was sealed and placed aboard ship,
she apologised for what she regarded as a small quantity of seed. In

fact, the box contained 106 numbered specimens collected during December 1839 and January 1840, 64 identified by genus and species, 39 labelled 'sp. nova', to indicate a new species, and three unidentified, being completely unknown.

The dispatch of the box of specimens in February 1840, per the *America*, neither reduced Molloy's passion for flowers nor abated her commitment to Mangles. In fact, over the following twelve months, she wrote to him in every month but two. On 14 March, as her husband worked outside erecting a small cottage, which she planned to use as a dormitory and nursery and around which she intended planting the seeds Mangles had sent, she wrote to recapitulate the contents of her January/February letter. She estimated Mangles would receive the new box in July or early August at the latest.

In the meantime, Molloy continued collecting. To accommodate a future shipment of specimens, she asked her husband to construct a large shallow box, six feet by three feet. The size looked forbidding and the freightage promised to be alarming, but Molloy was determined to justify the expense. She vowed to fill every cubic inch with specimens. Among the first seeds she placed in the box were those of the yellow drumstick *Isopogon*, omitted from the February shipment. By 14 March, she told Mangles, she 'had a whole bag full'. She had also discovered other unknown plants. She hoped Preiss would furnish her with their names.[19]

Preiss's Vasse visit inspired Molloy to suggest to Mangles that he and his botanical associates combine to engage the services of a qualified British collector to come to Western Australia and collect on their behalf. She offered to host any nominated collector. He would, she wrote, 'be welcome to any accommodation as an inmate of our House, so that he might traverse the district yet untrod in these Floral beauties, which have been so long concealed to the rest of the Globe'.[20]

Mangles and his associates, however, had no need to engage a special collector from Britain. Georgiana Molloy already supplied them with excellent specimens. Experience taught Mangles that no one in the Swan River Colony collected with more care and attention than Molloy. A male collector—and Molloy unquestionably assumed an appointed collector would be male—might not prove as reliable. But Molloy was blind to her own value. She could not imagine, dare not even hope, that her own efforts were so highly rated.

Mangles appreciated more than Molloy's exactitude. Her evident and abundant joy gave him pleasure, and he delighted in corresponding with someone so intelligent and articulate. Few collectors provided such powerful and personal description. On one occasion, she wrote:

> I beheld a Tree of great beauty. . . . The flowers are of the purest white and fall in long tresses from the stem. Some of its pendulous blossoms are from three to five fingers in length and these wave in the breeze like snow wreaths; they are of such a downy white feathery appearance, and emit a most delicious perfume resembling the bitter almond; and like all human, or rather mortal, delicacies, how quick these lovely flowers fall from the stalk on being collected. I, however, was able to gather a good many, and on nearer view found the buds much more beautiful than the full blown flower. I regret they have assumed a yellow hue, but are lovely and elegant even in Death. The native name is 'Danja', and I rather think it will turn out to be a Hakea.[21]

In her March letter Molloy mentioned the possibility of Captain Molloy visiting England on business. She and her husband had discussed the subject for several years, and they both expected his departure at any time. She had prepared herself for his long absence and thought not of deprivation but of the opportunity his going would afford her and the children to 'repair to dear Augusta (this I will delight in)'. The Vasse, she conceded, was a fine country, very rich, 'but give me my lovely "thatched cottage" again, and my *sweet flower garden* on the magnificent Blackwood'. In January Molloy had written to Mangles of the 'prudence' that forbade her ever returning to Augusta. But, given the present likelihood of her husband's departure, she felt so certain of her return that she reserved some of the seed Mangles had sent, for planting at Augusta. Her garden there, she imagined, would be 'more beautiful than ever, as Sabina and Mary are so much older, they can assist me greatly'.[22]

In the letter received in December 1839, Mangles had asked Molloy for more seeds of *Nuytsia floribunda*. Although two of his associates, including Joseph Paxton, had successfully raised some young *Nuytsia* seedlings, all the plants died after a year. Known in Western Australia as the Christmas Tree, the endemic *Nuytsia* grows to about thirteen metres in sheltered places. Brittle stems expose most large trees to wind damage. In November and December the tree flowers profusely; great masses of bright yellow-orange racemes cover the crown and provide a vivid contrast against the endlessly blue summer sky. Seeds ripen some three months after flowering and are borne in papery, winged fruits. They quickly lose viability and, if collected, must be sown immediately. Early colonists were struck by the massive display of brilliant colour, and their descriptions made English nurserymen eager to grow *Nuytsia*. The tree is a semi-parasite, however, a member of the mistletoe family, and draws nourishment from surrounding trees and shrubs, even grass. Unless provided with a host, seedlings soon fail. English nurserymen were unaware of the tree's parasitism. They kept trying to grow the tree in isolation, and so they needed large quantities of seed.

Mangles also asked Molloy for seeds of *Kingia australis*, another species endemic to Western Australia. An odd, ancient-looking plant, *Kingia* rises in a single slim column of three or four metres and is crowned with a spiky foliage from which emerge, at flowering season, several sticks with round heads, like drumsticks, covered in small white flowers.

The seeds of both *Nuytsia* and *Kingia* appear in March, and Molloy, although about to bring her seventh pregnancy to term, promised Mangles she would collect them. *Nuytsia*, she informed him, 'grows here in great abundance, and splendid it is. It looks so rich among all the sombre Eucalyptus.' She still thought Augusta superior to her present habitation, but the sight of *Nuytsia* on the Vasse plains reminded her of 'the rich and luxurious trees which adorn paradise'.

According to Milton, the flowers of paradise were: laurel and myrtle, acanthus, iris, rose, jessamin, violet, crocus, and hyacinth. Their pastel prettiness hardly compared with the uncompromising vividness and robustness of Australian flowering plants. In any case, comparisons no longer interested Molloy. Australian flora possessed its own special beauty and significance. In fact, Molloy discovered in the southwest that all parts of the earth were as abundantly beautiful as any other. God had bestowed His gifts indiscriminately: 'It strikes me so forcibly in riding through the surrounding wilderness that the "hand of God" is indeed impartial, for the uncultivated parts of the earth are as much loaded with his bounties as are the most frequented parts.'[23]

Georgiana Molloy was not the first to note the special providence of the southwest. Every organism, every feature of the terrain held special meaning and significance for the Nyungar. To prepare the land for life and for human habitation, the Dreamtime Ancestors had invested each rock and animal and tree with spiritual significance. The *Nuytsia floribunda* too was part of the Dreaming. According to the Nyungar, the soul of the newly dead (*kanya*) departed the body and rested in the *Nuytsia floribunda* (*moojarr* or *moodurt*) before reaching *Kurannup*, the home of the Bibbulmun dead located beyond the western sea.

The western sea, and much more besides, also separated Molloy from Mangles; the likelihood that she would never meet him continued to frustrate her. The lost opportunity of meeting during Mangles's visit to Swan River in 1831 constantly tormented her. She expressed her desideratum: 'If we had only met at Augusta what time we should have redeemed.'[24]

1 8

HELICON

LATE IN MARCH 1840 GEORGIANA MOLLOY'S SISTER MARY KENNEDY
arrived at the Vasse. Molloy had not seen any of her family for ten
years. She had long urged them to migrate, or at least to visit.
'Nothing,' she told her mother, 'would tempt me to undertake
another voyage.' Therefore, any family reunion must take place in
Australia. Molloy had but one reservation: 'poor Mary's dereliction'.
Mary Kennedy's consumption of alcohol, Molloy confided to her
brother, made her an unwelcome visitor. Molloy continued, 'We
should be quite appalled at the idea of Mary becoming our inmate,
not only as regards our own respectability, but as an example to my
children.'[1]

Of all Georgiana Molloy's family, however, only Mary visited
Australia. At the Vasse Molloy introduced her to their neighbours,
and visits were exchanged. But Mary Kennedy was unimpressed with
Vasse society. She found colonial life repellent. Participation in the
domestic and childbearing trials of her sister confirmed her adverse
opinion.

On 7 May the Molloy family cook abruptly left to work for
the Bussells. Next day, assisted by her sister and Ann McDermott,
also recently arrived at the Vasse, Georgiana Molloy gave birth to
her sixth child, another daughter, named after her prevailing passion,
Flora. The confinement left Molloy exhausted and ill.

Few European women in the nineteenth century could expect to pass through childbearing without contracting at least one infection. In fact, infections were so common that most midwives and doctors dismissed them as unimportant, nothing more than 'milk fever', caused by the milk rising in the mother's breasts. But postdelivery sepsis was potentially fatal. Bacteria, introduced into the mother's vagina by a midwife's or a doctor's unwashed hands or by contaminated instruments, could spread to the uterus and then enter the bloodstream, to infect the whole body. Septic shock, or septicaemia, a dramatic and fatal drop in blood pressure, was often the consequence.

Molloy's latest delivery left her with a low-grade, debilitating infection. She could scarcely leave her bed, but when the colonial schooner arrived a week later, she made sure that her March/April letter to Mangles was put aboard for dispatch from Swan River. For the rest of the month she could not, to her intense frustration, exert herself.

Molloy particularly fretted about her inability to botanise. As she had learned, there was no suspension of life in winter in Australia. Winter, in fact, vivified life. As she lay in bed, early-season wildflowers were blossoming without her notice. She could not let this pass, so she organised her children to collect for her. She instructed five-year-old Mary Dorothea to take Amelia out and gather as many flowers as they could find. When the specimens came in, Molloy directed their drying and pressing from her bed. Sabina attended the sick chamber, and Captain Molloy and neighbours brought bouquets. Georgiana Molloy also received a visit from an Aborigine who, aware of her 'floral passion', presented her with a nosegay. She kept the floral tributes for Mangles.

Although it left her incapacitated, Molloy's infection remained relatively mild throughout May. But early in June she became highly feverish and delirious. Mary Kennedy later told her sister that in her delirium she would call out, three times out of every four when visited at her bed, 'Oh Poor Captain Mangles! I cannot go on with his collection, and the seeds of the *Nuytsia floribunda* will all be shed!' During the day of 5 June Molloy began to haemorrhage badly—probably owing to the infection of a retained fragment of placenta—and by evening was desperately ill. Fanny Bussell, who was at her side during the day, thought she was going to die. Over the next few days, however, Molloy's condition stabilised, and she rested.[2]

But Molloy's precarious health was not the only cause of alarm in the little community of Busselton during May and June 1840. On the same day Molloy gave birth to Flora, settlers received news of the death of Henry Campbell, a young labourer who worked on a property a few kilometres up the Collie River. Campbell had raped a young Aboriginal woman, the daughter of tribal elder Gaywal. Three of her kinsfolk, Nugundung, Duncock, and Gerback—obliged to revenge the offence—speared Campbell to death. Settlers were outraged, not at the rape, but at Aboriginal justice. This assertion of Aboriginal sovereignty was as unexpected as it was unwelcome, especially by the Bussells. They had thought the Aborigines cowed beyond response.

At the end of 1837 Lenox was convinced that, as a result of the recent killing of fourteen Aborigines, 'a lasting peace has been established without the loss of a single European'. Charles had written to John to confirm this felicitous outcome and observed, 'You have heard of our row with the natives. The whole affair was admirably conducted and by the blessing of God no European suffered. It did not meet with the entire approbation of the Government but it was not the less well done on that account.' Lenox's prognostication proved premature, and Charles's derisive braggadocio proved misplaced.[3]

The British had come to Western Australia to own land. Like the other colonists, the Bussells viewed the southwest as land in need of ploughing by profit-pursuing private enterprise. Land was a commodity. But to the Nyungar, the land was their Dreaming, their past, their present, and their being. British and Nyungar views were incompatible. Conflict was inevitable between a community that regarded alienable property as the only rational and natural arrangement and a community that thought of land not as property but as sacred life. For most of the colonists, and particularly for the Bussells, to deprive Aborigines of their land by fraud, robbery, murder, and any other suitable kind of pressure was as moral as it was profitable.

But Aborigines resisted ejection. While they sought accommodation with the settlers, they were not prepared to abandon their kinship with the land nor indefinitely tolerate outrages against their own laws. Nugundung, Duncock, and Gerback could not ignore Campbell's rape of their sister and cousin.

Shortly after the spearing, the Leschenault resident magistrate, Henry Bull, seized the three men responsible, flogged them, and set them free. Governor Hutt considered the punishment inadequate and demanded the men be recaptured. In the meantime, Bull resigned. Bull's replacement, George Eliot, accepted the logic of his predecessor's limited response and convinced Hutt of the inexpedience of a second punishment. He warned that further retribution would provoke further Aboriginal revenge; the spiralling violence would be disastrous.[4]

But if the governor accepted Eliot's argument, the Bussells did not. News of Campbell's spearing, according to Fanny Bussell, had convulsed Cattle Chosen in 'great consultation about the natives'. John Bussell, in particular, was incensed. His fury only increased when Hutt decided to drop the matter. The Aborigines were guilty of moral turpitude and deserved the most severe penalty. They lived in a state of nature not yet dignified by the idea of progress. Only severe punishment, even death, could advance the cause of civilisation. John Bussell refused to consider the case of Campbell's death closed, and he waited for an opportunity to deliver further punishment.[5]

Georgiana Molloy withdrew from the rage and violence manifest in the Bussells. Close to death herself, she did not wish to lend moral support to killing. Her husband, while broadly sympathetic to his fellow settlers, carried the memory of carnage and warfare from his years in the Peninsula War. A cautious man, Captain Molloy favoured bureaucratic, rather than military, solutions. In the meantime, he was preoccupied with his wife's illness.

Molloy believed her poor recovery was due to the Vasse being a less healthy place than Augusta. But with no prospect of return, she trusted for convalescence in kangaroo soup, porter, and port wine. At least the diet made her no worse. Less than two weeks after her haemorrhage, she began a letter to Mangles to assure him that, 'In all my illness and real suffering I did not forget you.' Molloy repeated information included in previous letters. And although distracted and slightly incoherent from continued pain, she outlined some of her latest collecting enterprises. As she explained: 'Scarcely a day passes [when] I am not thinking of what I can do or how in any way I could promote your cause.' She had other regrets. Her indisposition and the general lack of labour—her gardener Staples had quit—meant that her flower garden had not been fenced or prepared. The seeds Mangles had sent in December 1839 remained unsown. Even worse, cattle had eaten the *Cobea scandens* she had sown in pots.[6]

A greater health restorative than kangaroo soup arrived on 20 June. An overland party from Swan River brought a letter from Mangles. Originally in company with another box of seeds, gifts, and a *hortus siccus*, now at Fremantle awaiting transshipment to the Vasse, the letter reinforced Molloy's determination to get well and pursue her botanical interests. She resumed the letter begun earlier in the month, acknowledged receipt of Mangles's letter, and thanked him for the gifts to follow. She felt humbled at 'such uncommon instances of friendship and liberality'. 'We are really overpowered,' she continued, 'when we think of our impotent and circumscribed exertions in your behalf. Would that I could do more.'[7]

Mangles's letter contained a list of the contents of the boxes still at Fremantle. Among other items, he had sent two microscopes, which he suggested Molloy use to examine seed for insects. She agreed these would prove very useful. For Captain Molloy, Mangles sent a telescope that he himself had used when in the navy. Molloy passed on her husband's gratitude. The box also contained some recently published maps of Western Australia. Molloy looked forward to reviewing them; she felt she needed to orient herself as, 'I feel so little familiar with our present situation as scarcely to know where we are.' For the children, Mangles promised a mouth organ. This prospect, Molloy reported, was regarded with general excitement for, 'We are all passionately fond of music.' She described her own small upright organ and reminisced about when, on evenings

> at dear Augusta, I used to take it out on the Grass plot and play till late by Moonlight, the beautiful broad water of the Blackwood gliding by, the roar of the [ocean over the sand] Bar, and ever and anon the wild scream of a flight of Swans going over to the Fresh Water Lakes. The air perfectly redolent with the powerful scent of Vergilla, Stocks, and *Oenothera biennis*, Cloves, Pinks and never fading Mignonette. We used always to have Tea outside, and for our amusement and interest I had sown the *Oenothera tetraptera* and *Oenothera biennis* profusely in the borders adjoining this plot, so that we might watch their expanding blossoms.[8]

The imminent arrival of English seeds made the bedridden Molloy feel impotent. She prevailed upon her husband to fence and prepare a flower garden outside the windows of her and her sister's rooms. By the end of June she was well enough to assist: 'the only pleasure (and that not an uninterrupted one) I can avail myself of'.

Despite the attention of her neighbours and the presence of her sister during her illness, or perhaps because of their very solicitude, Molloy began to feel her loneliness more acutely than ever. None of her acquaintances shared her interest in literary conversation or in matters of the mind, and no one, neither neighbours nor family, shared her passion for the bush. In the absence of a proximate confidant, she transferred all her impounded fervour and eloquence onto the absent Mangles. She found him sympathetic and understanding, or, at least, imagined him so. He was a stranger but he did not spurn or squander her intimacies. Although he was someone she had never met and never would meet, he supported her passion.

In contrast, Molloy's family, at least her husband and sister, did not take her seriously and found her botanical interests amusing. They indulged her. 'Both Molloy and my sister,' she confided to Mangles, 'cannot forbear frequently from smiling at the unparalleled devotion of all my spare moments to this all engrossing concern, and the very frequent mention made of Captn. Mangles and the specimens.' But what to others was a frivolous, if harmless, hobby, was to Molloy of central importance to her life. Botanising gave her an independence that did not require family and community endorsement. She had discovered an intrinsic justification for her bush rambles. 'When I sally forth on foot or Horseback,' she explained, 'I feel quite elastic in mind and step; I feel I am quite at my own work, the real cause that enticed me out to Swan River.'[9]

Although the immediate benefits were personal, Molloy never regarded botanising as a strictly individual enterprise. She recognised the collective nature of botany and knew she was one of many collectors. Moreover, she believed the collectors of Western Australia ought to cooperate rather than compete. She had never met Captain Richard Meares of Swan River but knew he collected for Mangles and hoped he would contact her. But Meares kept his own counsel, and although Molloy felt the impropriety of taking the initiative in the matter, she promised Mangles she would write to Meares, 'as I think our cooperation might effect more for you than working separately'. She was also curious as to how Meares packed his boxes and suspected his arrangements were superior to her own. She thought that she and Meares ought to exchange enclosures, so as to maximise the use of space and not swell freightage: 'as it is, we are perhaps impeded by acting separately not conjointly'.[10]

Mangles asked Molloy to write an article on southwest flora for his *Floral Calendar*. She was honoured by the request, but feminine modesty and a lingering sense of inferiority gave her reservations. Mangles, she was sure, had exaggerated her literary skills. She thought she was inadequate, but she would try:

> I shall with unfeigned pleasure attempt to gratify you in writing in the 'Floral Calendar', but really feel you have over-rated my poor exertions in a former description, and now I shall only, I fear, exhibit my impotency. But I will glean all I can, and pray my health may be so recruited as to permit of my making those much enjoyed Floral excursions.[11]

At the end of June the boxes from Fremantle had still not arrived. Molloy waited expectantly. In the meantime, she continued her letter and reiterated her exasperation at not being well enough to collect. She recalled previous collecting expeditions, particularly for *Isopogon* and *Petrophile*, 'beautiful beyond description'. The genus *Petrophile* contains 40 species, 30 of which are restricted to the southwest. Molloy's particular quest had been for *P. linearis*, a small shrub common on the Vasse plains, with softly hirsute, ravishingly pink, cone-shaped flowers. Molloy lived in awe of the varied forms, colour, and beauty of the southwest flora, and wrote: 'such flowers of imagination; I am now in raptures when I think on them; in searching to come suddenly on such gems and be surrounded by them, makes you for a time think you are in fairy land'.[12]

Dedicated to improving her collection and to perfecting methods of preservation and shipment, Molloy asked Mangles for advice on the best way to ship really large specimens. The present *hortus siccus* was too small, and she wondered if an artist's portfolio might suffice. She also asked for some pots. The perforated raisin boxes she presently used for growing seedlings were insufficient.

On 6 July the *Lady Stirling*, with the boxes from Fremantle, arrived at Busselton. At the sight of the ship, Molloy resumed her letter. She announced the ship's appearance in the bay and then maintained a running commentary, a record of disembarkation, throughout the day. The *Lady Stirling* had put in at the Vasse during a midwinter storm. 'It blows really a hurricane,' Molloy observed. 'The ground is strewn with branches.' The storm lashed several American whaling ships at anchor in Geographe Bay. High winds damaged the *North American* and *Samuel Wright* and drove the *Governor Endicott* onto the beach. No lives were lost.

Heavy seas hampered unloading of the *Lady Stirling*. Molloy watched from the sandhills as the sailors, to save effort, threw boxes directly onto the beach. She was appalled and insisted the boxes be moved above the high-water line. Despite her vigilance, which, as she reported to Mangles, at least prevented the boxes from being washed away, heavy surf overnight drenched the contents. The first box the Molloys opened contained cuttings and fruit trees: magnolia, lily of the valley, hyacinth, myrtle, double violet, and camellia, as well as peach, almond, and black mulberry. Molloy immediately had the plants placed 'in the genial earth just before my windows'.[13]

By the following evening the Molloys had unpacked another box. They found many articles water-damaged. Books and the new *hortus siccus* were soaked. Georgiana Molloy, however, was undaunted. She refused to be discouraged. She cleaned off the sand and spread out the wet articles to dry. A small book, John Lindley's *A Sketch of the Vegetation of the Swan River Colony*, caught her attention. The *Sketch* included descriptions of specimens contained in the first two *horti sicci* Molloy sent Mangles. Lindley's identification of many southwest plants, Molloy wrote, 'has quite inflamed my ardour; and instigated me to greater exertion. To think how small an aid I lent to your cause.' She hoped to be of continuing assistance 'but am so fully aware of my own inability and real want of time; but nothing shall be wanting on my part'.[14]

Despite the small amount of time available between the dispatch of her previous box and the onset of her illness, Molloy had managed nearly to fill the long shallow box her husband had built in February. By midyear she had packed seeds of *Nuytsia floribunda, Isopogon*, and *Petrophile*, as well as plant specimens. The box was ready to ship, but she did not want to send it to Fremantle until the next sailing for England. She could not abide the thought that her precious box might sit neglected at the port awaiting reshipment. She preferred to wait till September, when American whaling vessels returned to Geographe Bay. She was certain that, aboard an American vessel, 'the plants will be well attended to'. She was not so sure she could similarly trust the English.

Molloy did, however, intend mailing her latest letter via Swan River. She closed in time for the *Lady Stirling*'s departure. She asked Mangles to write 'immediately' and signed herself, as in previous letters, 'your sincere and attached friend, Georgiana Molloy'.[15]

On 17 July, nine days after the *Lady Stirling* sailed, Molloy received another letter from Mangles. Two more boxes followed. They contained vegetable seeds, English fruits, an edition of Shakespeare, other literary works, and several books and magazines on gardening. Mangles's demonstrable interest in his southwest antipodean collector flattered Molloy. She determined to recommence botanising as soon as she recruited her health.

One Sunday, at the end of July, Molloy felt well enough for a bush excursion. Escorted by Vernon Bussell, she rode out into the Vasse country. Formerly, Molloy had forsworn all activity, especially active, pleasurable activity, on the Sabbath. She had not even dared to write letters on Sunday. She kept the Sabbath holy not out of unthinking habit but because she understood the real reason for Sabbath observation: that while man ruled the world for six days, albeit with God's will, on the seventh day God forbade man to fashion anything for his own purpose. In his observation of the Sabbath, man acknowledged that he had no rights of ownership or authority over the world. Even the smallest work done on the Sabbath was an arrogant assumption of man becoming his own master. But the Australian bush had enlarged Molloy's sense of the sacred. Sunday rambles could not possibly profane the Sabbath. To the contrary, immersion in the bush exalted Creation. On this Sunday excursion, Molloy discovered the bush was again pregnant with new growth. She knew she must soon begin another season of observation and collection.

In early August Molloy resumed her search for flowers. Sometimes she brought her children; often she rambled in company with an Aborigine named Calgood. Sometimes she rode, sometimes she walked. She also began another letter to Mangles, which, like previous letters, she added to over successive days. She described the daily collecting excursions and the pleasure they gave her. She found the season, early spring, most felicitous, a time that 'inexpressibly inspires me with my pleasant and consonant work'. The bush was so refreshing and her activity so enjoyable that she was always reluctant to return home. 'I should like nothing better,' she declared, 'than to kindle a fire and lay all night as I should be ready for my work early in the morning without again coming so far.'[16]

First at Augusta and now at the Vasse, Molloy recognised that being in the bush was an escape from the domestic captivity within which men sought to imprison her and from the servitude that Milton, Pollok, and the whole weight of her culture sought to impose. The freedom Captain Molloy and other male settlers experienced on the new shore—the freedom to claim land and transform it, the freedom to make a new order out of the wilderness—required the confinement and emplacement of their wives, daughters, and sisters. Male freedom depended on female bondage. Men needed partners who were cooks, seamstresses, cleaners, wives, and mothers. Georgiana Molloy obliged all these roles; she never directly challenged patriarchy. But Molloy also discovered and created her own world, even though the disclosure of that world came through the agency of a man. James Mangles's request, the summons of male authority, brought Molloy into intimacy with the bush and provided the setting for her own liberation. During her plastic season of passage from the confines of domesticity to the freedom and refuge of the bush, during her passage from the homestead hearth to the camp fire, Molloy developed a sense of independent relationship to the world. In physically separating herself from the scene of her domestic travail, she discovered a world independent of the male construct at the Vasse.

But Molloy believed her wish to camp out all night could never be; domestic claims were too insistent. Nevertheless, she stayed out as late as possible, so as to prolong the joyous self-forgetfulness that comes with immersion in some all-absorbing activity. She no longer viewed the country as merely picturesque. At the moment of forgetfulness, the once-sharp boundary between observer and observed dissolved. Instead Molloy felt only life and herself in life.

Late one afternoon, while looking for *Nuytsia*, she saw in the distance a spot distinguished by different bright colours. She turned in that direction. On the way she passed through a swamp of *Hakea:*

> the sunny evening and the perfect stillness which everywhere prevailed, with the total absence of other beings besides ourselves and a single native, and recollecting I was employed in the delightful service of so kind a friend made me really feel singularly happy and free from care.[17]

Molloy spent much of August looking for *Nuytsia* and *Kingia*. At first the difference between *Kingia australis*, commonly known as the grass plant, and *Xanthorrhea preissii*, or common blackboy, equally unusual in appearance, confused her. But one day she discovered a grove of *Kingia* and at once perceived the difference. She was 'quite exhilarated' by the discovery. On another occasion, towards evening when she had turned home, she discovered a grove of *Nuytsia floribunda*. She wrote to Mangles, 'I thought myself truly blest that these desiderata should place themselves before me, and going up to the trees I unhappily found I was too late. I should but for my long illness have had the seed.' Alternatively, she thought she might dig some seedlings. She looked, but the light had failed and she could not find any. A few days later she discovered that most juvenile *Nuytsia* seemed to grow from suckers, not from seed. She pulled up some shoots and transplanted them to her garden to keep them alive for shipment to Mangles; she awaited the arrival of a ship whose captain she could depend upon. In the meantime, she discussed plants with the Aborigines at the Vasse and sent them in search of flowers and, as the season advanced, seeds.

In September the *Mentor*, an American whaler, anchored in Geographe Bay. The ship had sailed around from Augusta with Ann Bryan aboard. Bryan, the former Ann Heppingstone, intended settling at the Vasse with her family. Only John Herring and the Turners now remained at Augusta. The *Mentor* planned to sail direct for North America. Mary Kennedy, who had taken only a short while to decide she did not like colonial life, booked passage aboard the ship. Her sister's embarkation gave Molloy an opportunity to dispatch her box. The *Mentor*, however, stayed in Geographe Bay; departure was indefinitely delayed.

On Sunday, 18 October, Molloy continued her letter to Mangles. She thanked him for a gift 'beauteous and elegant beyond description': a copy of Mrs Loudon's *The Ladies' Flower-Garden of Ornamental Annuals*, recently published in London. Mangles knew Mrs Loudon, and he had arranged for an early copy of the book to be sent to Georgiana Molloy in Western Australia.

A large folio edition of 272 pages, *The Ladies' Flower-Garden* contained 48 full-page colour plates, an index, and a glossary of ornamental flowers grown in British gardens. The text advised on the cultivation of each plant. Jane Loudon and her husband, John, were crusading advocates for the suburban garden. They were the first writers to insist that it was not merely proper but positively moral for ladies and gentlemen to dig and plant their own gardens. The garden was a defence against the moral degradation of cities.

Mrs Loudon explained to her readers a garden's pedagogic value and its connection to divinity. Flower gardening was a particularly worthwhile feminine pursuit, where the exertion did not exceed the reward:

> The pruning and training of trees and the culture of culinary vegetables, require too much strength and manual labour; but a lady, with the assistance of a common labourer to level and prepare the ground, may turn a barren waste into a flower-garden with her own hands.[18]

Molloy had learned her aesthetics in Britain, and in her own garden she strove to follow Loudon's advice that 'flowers must be arranged as to harmonize in their colours and habits of growth'. But the Australian bush had opened her eyes to a much wider and manifold beauty. In the bush Molloy learned that nature had a life of its own, independent of human artifice and struggle. She was eager to communicate her discovery to Mangles. She considered the difference between cultivated flowers and wildflowers. The 'true character' of the wildflower, she claimed, lay in its being 'single, simple, elegant and unadorned'.[19]

While Molloy quietly and purposefully pursued her discoveries in the bush, John Bussell raged about the injustice and inadequacy of the flogging punishment of Nugundung, Duncock, and Gerback for the May spearing of Henry Campbell. Bussell looked upon Aborigines as children who required the severest discipline to instil obedience and surrender. He waited seven months to impose his pedagogic regime. On 7 December 1840, while travelling from Bunbury to the Vasse, he met Nugundung and immediately seized him. Without consulting Magistrate George Eliot, in whose judicial area the arrest occurred, Bussell removed Nugundung to the Vasse, imprisoned him at Cattle Chosen, and later sent him to Fremantle for trial. Bussell's disrespect for due process provoked Eliot's ire. Eliot protested to Governor Hutt that Nugundung's injudicious arrest had made the local Aborigines angry. Once again Eliot warned of possible trouble. 'I have had,' he wrote, 'great difficulty in appeasing the natives by almost promising them that Nugundung should be released.'[20]

Aware of Eliot's displeasure, John Bussell hastened to make his own case before the governor. Nugundung, he explained, was 'a very dangerous character', wanted for offences that predated the spearing of Campbell. Nugundung, Bussell asserted, had speared the Bussells' Aboriginal cow-keeper in May 1839 and had thrown one of the spears through the window of the Dawsons' hut in 1837. Considering the man's notorious character, the rule of law did not apply. 'That any steps can be taken to render the capture of such an offender as Nugundung unnecessary or illegal I have considered impossible,' he wrote. He dismissed the possibility that other Aborigines might feel obliged to avenge Nugundung's arrest. The government acquiesced in Nugundung's capture but upbraided Bussell for exceeding his authority.[21]

John Bussell's fury and paranoia had little effect on Georgiana Molloy. Although Bussell had branded all Aborigines as irredeemably treacherous, Molloy still employed Aboriginal guides, and she continued her excursions into the bush with them. To have forsaken her Aboriginal guide Calgood would have meant a return to domestic captivity and a capitulation to the rigid prohibitions demanded by the Bussells.

After the *Mentor*'s departure from Geographe Bay in December 1840, the colonial schooner visited the Vasse and picked up mail, including Molloy's latest letter to Mangles. Settlers, however, were no longer as dependent upon the colonial schooner for communication with the outside world. By the late 1830s, southwest Australia had been inducted into the world economy. American whalers, scouring the Southern and Indian oceans for sperm (*Physeter catodon*) and Right whales, came in increasing numbers to Geographe Bay. They took on water and wood, and the ships' crews traded with the Vasse's small farms. For molasses, knives, boots, rum, spirits, and cash, the whalers bought butter, cheese, chickens, and vegetables. In March 1840 Molloy had commented to Mangles, 'Since January we have had six American Whalers and they are charmed with the Bay—they are of great use to us.'[22]

The congregation of whalers in Geographe Bay and the income they generated revealed the settlement's dependence, not, as the colonists believed, on profit-pursuing private enterprise, or even on human labour, but on bountiful nature—in this case, on the existence of mighty herds of marine mammals.

Over the month of January 1841, seventeen American whaling ships arrived in Geographe Bay. They joined several already at anchor, including the *Montpelier*, *Hibernia*, and *Napoleon*, under Captain William Plaskett. Plaskett invited the Molloys aboard for a trip to Castle Bay, an inlet of Geographe Bay to the lee of Cape Naturaliste, where whalers sheltered to take on wood and water. Castle Bay fronted a valley bounded by high granite rocks and through which flowed, in winter at least, a rapid stream. Fish were abundant, and the water close to shore was deep enough for anchorage. Early on a Sunday morning the three ships set sail, under a light breeze from the east. The run up to the bay took only a few hours.

Once ashore, Georgiana Molloy found the outlook, which took in views of the 'boundless ocean' and the rich and luxuriant flora of the area—*Hovea*, *Kennedia*, *Kingia*, *Xanthorrhea*, golden *Helichrysum*—so enticing that she urged her husband to take up land there. She spent the day gathering seeds and looking for flowers. In the evening, 'a lovely, beauteous Sabbath evening', two more American whalers, the *Izette* and the *Uncas*, joined the ships already at anchor.

After three days at Castle Bay, Molloy walked and rode the 26 kilometres to Cape Naturaliste, which she described as 'a most bleak and barren headland'. She and her husband then took a boat across Geographe Bay to Toby Inlet, where they pitched a tent, kindled a fire, and lay all night and watched the stars till they fell asleep. Next day Molloy continued collecting and spent another night encamped under the stars. The constellations of the Southern Hemisphere, revolving in cloudless brilliancy above, reminded her that half the globe's expanse intervened between Western Australia and her native land. The following day she and her husband returned to Fairlawn.

Molloy had scarcely resumed domestic duties before she began a week of collecting, 'unremittingly occupied in your service', she wrote to Mangles. Dedication, however, did not provide as many specimens as she had hoped. Three *horti sicci* awaited filling. Acquaintances and fellow collectors, including botanist William Morrison and a Mr Northey, who stayed with the Molloys during January, promised assistance but proved unreliable. The capricious Ludwig Preiss promised a box of specimens, but they never arrived. Molloy found no one who shared her commitment and passion for flowers. For most settlers and visitors who collected, botany was a hobby, a part-time pastime; for Molloy, collecting had become her life, an all-consuming passion.[23]

On 20 January Molloy began another letter to Mangles and reported that *Nuytsia floribunda* were in flower. She pledged herself to watch the trees' progress and to send Mangles the first seed that ripened. By 6 February, when she took up her letter again, she had filled the small *hortus siccus* with *Nuytsia* and other seeds and specimens. The two large *horti sicci* would soon follow, she promised: 'Rest confident that I shall not suspend my exertions.' She would send as many seeds as she could collect. She had complained of lack of time. Captain Molloy's absences over the previous months had forced her to stay at Fairlawn. Now he had promised to stay at home, and she was determined to make up for lost time.[24]

Throughout January and February 1841, while Molloy pursued *Nuytsia floribunda*, the Vasse Aborigines remained angry at Nugundung's continued incarceration in Fremantle. Nugundung's kin, already antagonistic to British law, particularly as applied by the Vasse settlers, did not understand the notion of a second punishment for a single offence and warned of retribution. In the middle of January, Gaywal's sons Wooberdung and Kenny told James Chapman that if Nugundung did not return, the black fellows would spear a white man. Another native asked John Gill, a carpenter, what would happen to Nugundung. Gill said Nugundung would hang if found guilty of the murder of Campbell. If that happened, said the native, then the Aborigines would retaliate by killing one of the settlers.

19

VORTEX

ON SUNDAY EVENING, 22 FEBRUARY 1841, AT WONNERUP, THE LAYMAN family and their workers assembled for dinner. The Europeans ate inside the Laymans' cottage; outside, Aboriginal workers and their kin cooked damper at a camp fire. The elder, Gaywal—father of the girl raped by Henry Campbell, and father-in-law, by another daughter, of the incarcerated Nugundung—took some damper from Miligan. Miligan, who had worked for Vasse settlers for several years, felt robbed. He complained to George Layman. Layman, a quick-tempered man, confronted Gaywal, pulled his beard, and demanded the return of the damper. Gaywal was offended and replied indignantly that Miligan was undeserving. Gaywal agreed, however, to return a portion of the expropriated damper. Layman was unsatisfied by the offer of partial restitution and continued to pull Gaywal's beard. Finally he let go, turned, and walked back to the house. But Gaywal could not forget the insult. Enraged, he picked up a spear and hurled it at the retreating figure. Layman stumbled as the spear pierced his left side. A second spear, thrown by Gaywal's son Wooberdung, passed between Layman's legs. He staggered to the cottage, pulled the spear from his left side, and called for his gun. Before he could fire, he collapsed and died. The Aborigines dispersed.

Robert Heppingstone, Jr, one of Layman's workers, immediately mounted a horse and galloped over to Cattle Chosen and Fairlawn.

He reported the killing to the Bussells while the family was gathered for evening prayer. The brothers cursed the heathen black. But anger was not confined to Cattle Chosen. Most of the settlers responded, as they had many times before, with vengeful paranoia. They felt threatened. Their corporate identity as colonists, as civilised Britons, and as property owners depended on creating and acting against enemies. On a national scale, such consensual paranoia commonly erupts as warfare between states; on a local scale, the consequences are often no less murderous.

The Bussells and Captain Molloy quickly assembled a group of armed settlers and led them into the bush to engage the Aborigines. Shortly, the avengers heard noise from an Aboriginal camp. Recognising Gaywal's voice, they attacked. In a few minutes they shot dead seven Aborigines—men, women, and children. Gaywal escaped.

For years Gaywal had defied the hatred and savage intentions of the Bussells and other settlers. Ever since the first British settlements in the southwest, at Augusta and at the Vasse, Gaywal had responded with a mixture of accommodation and resistance. Either response was doomed. Faced with the combined punitive determination of the Vasse settlers, his luck ran out. Every night after Layman's death and the massacre that followed, armed parties scoured the bush in search of him. Finally, early on the morning of 6 March, a party led by Captain Molloy and including John, Charles, and Alfred Bussell, hunted him down. They shot him dead.[1]

Wooberdung and two of Gaywal's other sons, Kenny and Mungo, eluded the search parties. Tired of the impossible chase, Captain Molloy decided on a different stratagem. Because Nyungar did not think collectively, they did not understand the possibilities of European solidarity. They believed mistakenly that Aboriginal/settler disputes were confined to the people directly involved. Accordingly, Wooberdung, Kenny, and Mungo had fearlessly befriended the crew of the American whaler *Napoleon*, currently anchored in Geographe Bay. They visited the ship regularly throughout the hostilities that followed Layman's spearing. They could not imagine betrayal. Captain Molloy, however, was more sophisticated. He asked Captain Plaskett to lure the brothers aboard and seize them; subterfuge would be easy. He wrote to Plaskett:

> I take the liberty of the service of humanity and your actual love of justice to beg you would interest yourself in the apprehension of [the] three natives . . . Any movement from this quarter would lead to their immediate flight but as they suppose you are ignorant of their crimes they will not suspect you.[2]

Plaskett needed no further convincing; he quickly enticed and trapped one of the men aboard. The other two proved more wary. Plaskett then decided to become more actively interested in their apprehension. He sent a party of sailors ashore to search for the fugitives. The Americans were successful and confined all three men aboard the ship. When Captain Molloy heard of the men's capture, he offered Plaskett £5 to take the captives to the Aboriginal prison on Rottnest Island. Plaskett asked for £25; Molloy agreed.[3]

Nugundung's capture, the settlers' revenge of Layman's death, and Gaywal's execution made the Bussells colonial heroes. Fellow settlers lauded their leadership, and the Swan River press congratulated them on their example and decisiveness. In a 13 March 1841 editorial, the *Perth Gazette* dismissed the deaths of the seven innocent Aborigines as irrelevant: 'There cannot be a question that the salutary chastisement thus inflicted will be the means of saving much bloodshed and that the supremacy of power must be upheld, is equally indisputable.' Furthermore, the settlers' conduct had always been coupled 'with acts of kindness and consideration for their [the Aborigines'] situation'. Contrast the civilised life led by the colonists, the newspaper argued rhetorically, with that of the savagery of Aboriginal life and no one could doubt that 'the benefits we have conferred upon them far outweigh any loss they may have experienced from our occupation of their lands'.[4]

Such self-serving justifications did not convince everyone. The itinerant Quaker preacher James Backhouse, who visited the colony in 1838, deplored the common sentiment that the Aborigines ought to be destroyed whenever they made trouble. This opinion, he wrote, was based on the belief that the natives must be made to fear before they could be made to love. Backhouse proposed Christian charity instead: 'Persons who voluntarily settled in a country, which the British Government has usurped, ought, with that Government, to labour for the civilization of the Native Inhabitants, and to bear patiently the inconveniences resulting from their customs, until these could be changed.'[5]

Edward Landor, a lawyer who arrived at Swan River in 1841, rejected Backhouse's sentimentalising. But neither did he accept the 'Amiable sophistry!' of the press. The invaders, he wrote, had no moral right of occupation, only 'the right of power':

> We have seized upon the country and shot down the inhabitants, until the survivors have found it expedient to submit to our rule. We have acted exactly as Julius Caesar did when he took posses-sion of Britain. But Caesar was not so hypocritical as to pretend any moral right to possession. On what grounds can we possibly claim a *right* to the occupancy of the land? . . . We have a right to our Australian possessions; but it is the right of Conquest, and we hold them with the grasp of power.[6]

Throughout the violence and killings of early 1841, Georgiana Molloy kept watch on the *Nuytsia*. She was unmoved by the rage and demagoguery of the Bussells. Settler paranoia about dangerous Aborigines did not intimidate her. As the *Nuytsia* seeds began ripen-ing at the end of March, Molloy and her Aboriginal guides went out once a week to monitor their progress. Because she had found no botanical intimates among her European neighbours, Molloy relied on Aborigines as collectors, companions, and guides. Ever since she had begun collecting she trusted their enthusiasm and willingness to help, their keen sight, and their thorough familiarity with the bush. She wrote in praise:

> The natives are much greater auxiliaries than white people in flower seed hunting. They ask no impertinent questions, do not give a sneer at what they do not comprehend and above all are implicitly obedient, and from their erratic habits, penetrating every recess, can obtain more novelties.[7]

Aborigines did not find Molloy's passion strange. They recognised in her a familiar exuberance of step and a kindred lightness of touch in dealing with the surrounding world. Unlike most settlers, Molloy was not violently disposed either to them or to their home, the bush.

The arrival in Geographe Bay of an unusually large number of American vessels in the early months of 1841 gave Molloy an unprecedented transport opportunity. She doubled her efforts to complete the *hortus siccus* in time for shipment aboard one of the whalers. In April she began daily collecting expeditions. On 9 April she and three native guides discovered that a fire had ripened *Nuytsia* seeds sooner than expected. The next day she went out early, gathered seed, planted some in her garden, and then sat down to write to Mangles:

> It is a lovely luminous morning, cloudy and gently falling showers, the beauteous and gigantic Peppermint trees [*Agonis flexuosa*] in front of where I write drooping their graceful form. My window (or rather calico blinds stitched tight on square frames) down, my doors open, the children playing in the verandah, the songsters of the wood chanting it so merrily.[8]

At the end of April the rainy season began, and Molloy suspended collecting. The *hortus siccus*, however, remained at Fairlawn, and Molloy kept adding to her letter to Mangles. In May, while the memory was still vivid, she wrote a long description of her January trip to Castle Bay. By 4 June winter had 'commenced in earnest', and she sat before a large log fire to finish her letter. She thought about the coming spring and worried about her future usefulness to Mangles. Over the previous seasons she had collected so assiduously she feared she would not find anything new. 'I shall be at a loss to know what to send you of novelties in the coming season,' she wrote. 'I believe I have sent you everything worth sending far and near. Therefore what am I to do?' Seeds, she knew, would always be welcome, 'but they ripen at such a broiling season of the year it is almost Martyrdom to procure them'.[9]

Molloy knew that the southwest of Australia contained many, many more plant species than what could be found at the Vasse. So while the Vasse might be exhausted of new specimens, other regions remained unexamined. Acquaintances had invited her to visit King George Sound, and she hoped to be able to accept. A trip to the south coast would afford new collecting opportunities. 'Nothing would cause me sooner to go there than to be enabled to send you specimens from thence,' she wrote to Mangles.

But if, as Molloy believed, Mangles had already obtained a full complement of southwest plants and was not interested in more, she feared she would no longer be of use to him. She hoped other natural history specimens might interest him. She suggested birds. Ludwig Preiss had previously promised to help her begin ornithological pursuits. When he was at the Vasse he had offered, in exchange for the use of Molloy's preservative soap, to send her some stuffed birds. She waited in vain but not in hopelessness. She had learned not to depend on promises; she had seen too much of colonial life to expect sudden or disinterested bequests. Instead, she trusted in her own resources and obtained a treatise on skinning and preserving birds from Bunbury settler Thomas Thompson. Molloy was prepared to perform the procedure herself, if necessary.

But whether employed in botany or taxidermy, Molloy was still unhappy with residence at the Vasse. She continued to hope to return to Augusta. She did not think Fairlawn well situated, and the Vasse summers were so hot that 'all the labours of winter in the garden are burnt up'. Molloy told Mangles she had heard a rumour that Governor Hutt was about to purchase land at Augusta and establish a settlement there. 'How happy shall I be if this is really the case,' she wrote. New settlers would revive Augusta and enable the Molloys to return.[10]

As Molloy sat before her June fire, she concluded the letter begun in January. She had an ominous premonition. The manifold demands of domestic duty pressed so severely that she did not know when she would get another chance to write. Captain Molloy's patience was running out. He felt that his wife neglected her household responsibilities; she should spend more time at home and less in the bush. Captain Molloy had never taken his wife's passion, her botanical interests and love of the bush, seriously. At the end of a previous letter to Mangles, Georgiana Molloy had written, 'My husband and sister laugh at this all engrossing theme.' Behind their patronising indulgence lay impatience and the opinion that Molloy ought to devote her time to domestically useful pursuits.

Contrary to rumour, Governor Hutt had no intentions of purchasing land or encouraging settlement at Augusta. He did, however, endorse a settlement plan for Australind, at Port Leschenault, north of the Vasse.

Throughout the 1830s, the numbers of British settlers in Western Australia had hardly increased at all. In 1832 there were 1497 settlers in the colony; five years later there were still only 2032. The stagnant population alarmed the colonists. Desperate for immigrants, they needed labour, consumers, and a sufficiently large population to be able to defend themselves from an imagined Aboriginal attack. Everyone had an idea to encourage immigration. In England and in Western Australia, private citizens, entrepreneurs, and government officials suggested various settlement schemes designed to increase the population.

In England, ex-governor Sir James Stirling continued to champion the colony. In 1839 his friend Nathaniel Ogle published the grandiloquent *The Colony of Western Australia: A Manual for Emigrants 1839*. Ogle had never been to Western Australia but recommended the colony as a field for emigration above all others. Based on material supplied by Stirling, including an essay by John Bussell, Ogle concluded that the colony's soil could be made to yield riches that would justify an extensive British occupation. Moreover, there was no better time to emigrate than the present. Western Australia's discovery and colonisation had come during a most propitious period: just and rational principles now informed enterprise and industry, the sum of human knowledge had never been so extended, and colonial progress was inevitable. In Western Australia the migrant will, 'under the guidance of Providence, plant his name and his race, to increase and multiply, and to subdue the earth'.[11]

In the same year that Ogle's book appeared, Governor Hutt's London-based brother William, in partnership with Edward Gibbon Wakefield, formed an emigration and land development company, the Western Australian Company. In July 1839 the company paid some £11 500 each to James Stirling and Peter Lautour for 190 000 acres of land they owned at Port Leschenault. For Stirling and Lautour, the sale represented a return of over 350 per cent on their initial investment of 1s 6d an acre. After the transaction, the company directors issued a prospectus that showed, at Leschenault, the plan of a beautiful but mechanically designed city, Australind. Four thousand quarter-acre town sections and 500 rural blocks were offered for sale. Land sold quickly.

The first settlers reached Port Leschenault in May 1841. Though the scheme had attracted far fewer migrants than anticipated, those who did arrive represented a huge increase in the settler population along the coast of Geographe Bay. The newcomers provided labour and a market for the produce of the established colonists.

Shortly after the Western Australian Company began advertising, an impoverished Anglican curate from Cambridgeshire, the Reverend John Ramsden Wollaston, applied for the position of company chaplain. The directors accepted his application, but although they advertised Wollaston's ministerial services as an attraction for Australind settlers, they refused to pay him a stipend. Eventually the British government assured him an official allowance if he went to Western Australia. With his wife, five sons, and two daughters, Wollaston arrived at Fremantle in April 1841, a few weeks after his fiftieth birthday.

In May Wollaston and his family sailed south and bought land at Picton, near Bunbury. They built a house and began clearing and farming. Wollaston had been attracted to Western Australia, at least in part, by Nathaniel Ogle's *The Colony of Western Australia*. Within a few months of his arrival, however, Wollaston dismissed Ogle's praise of the colony as fraudulent. The book was full of 'positive falsehoods'. Contrary to Ogle's 'misrepresentations', the soil was nothing but sand, the rivers sluggish and pestilential, and annoying insects—fleas, mosquitoes, and flies—swarmed in plague numbers. Living was excessively expensive, labour incessant, and the heat oppressive.[12]

Wollaston, however, had a mission. Despite the demands of pioneering, he immediately began clerical work. He provided ministerial services for his Australind neighbours and for the settlers at Bunbury and at the Vasse, where he befriended the Bussells and the Molloys. He was especially attracted to the Molloys and confided in his diary that they would make the most desirable of colonial neighbours. They possessed an uncommon generosity and were motivated less by self-interest than anyone else in the colony.[13]

When the wet winter of 1841 was over, the bush burst into spring glory. Georgiana Molloy, however, rarely rambled about. She felt she had collected nearly all she could for Mangles. Mostly, though, domestic duties kept her at home. Four young daughters, the house, farm, and garden monopolised her time.

In the second week of December 1841, Governor Hutt called on Wollaston at Picton. Together they rode south to the Vasse, through a country that Wollaston thought looked dried up and arid. They reached Fairlawn on a Thursday morning, just in time for breakfast, which Molloy, assisted by ten-year-old Sabina, served outdoors under a sail cloth. The Molloys' alfresco hospitality extended to three American whaling captains, with whom Wollaston and the governor shared hot rolls and a round of beef.

Wollaston found Georgiana Molloy's household management astonishing, 'without servant of any kind'. The contrast between the crude domestic arrangements and the civility of his hosts impressed him:

> Although the dining room has a clay floor and opens into the dairy, the thatch appears overhead and there is not a single pane of glass on the premises (the windows being merely square frames with shutters) yet our entertainment, the style of manners of our host and hostess, their dress and conversation, all conspired to show that genuine good breeding and gentlemanly deportment are not always lost sight of among English emigrants.[14]

Wollaston recalled the degrading work that colonial life forced on his wife. And, 'as Mrs Molloy passed in our view from the house to the kitchen, with the dinner dishes in one hand and her youngest daughter without shoes or stockings, in the other', he remarked to Hutt that genteel women, torn from the common comforts and plain cleanliness of life in England, suffered a distressing and laborious life in the colonies. Although Georgiana Molloy agreed that domestic work was 'servile drudgery', subjection did not describe the rest of her colonial life. Wollaston soon discovered that Molloy was 'a perfect botanical dictionary'. Moreover, her attitude towards the bush differed greatly from his. Where he discerned an arid waste, she found beauty.[15]

Wollaston had left England with the desire 'to see a country in a state of primitive nature'. He recoiled in horror from what he found in Western Australia. 'Nothing can be more depressing than the loneliness of the bush,' he wrote:

I have been almost tempted to shed tears at the desolation of the scene, had I not called to mind the ubiquity of the God of Nature, who can make 'a wilderness like Eden and a desert like the Garden of the Lord'. Before, however, this happy time can come the moral wilderness of the world must be broken up and cultivated.[16]

Georgiana Molloy, in contrast, loved the bush and did not find it depressing. Neither did she find the solitude frightful, nor see any need to break up and cultivate the untamed bush. She found splendour, not utility, in the wilderness.

On the Sunday following his arrival at the Vasse, Wollaston performed divine service at the Bussells'. The Molloys attended, and Wollaston baptised Flora. In appreciation, Molloy sent the Wollastons a jar of preserved Vasse apples and some Indian mats. She also invited the Wollastons' 21-year-old son, John, who had an interest in botany, to stay at Fairlawn. The new year was the time to show off the flowering splendour of *Nuytsia floribunda*.

The new year was also the time when Governor Hutt's Protectors of Natives issued their annual reports on the state of Aboriginal/settler relations. Hutt had arrived in Western Australia with the hope of civilising the Aborigines. He had in mind a colony of agricultural and pastoral estates interspersed with small holdings and served by market towns. Hutt envisaged plenty of opportunity for Aborigines as servants and labourers in the households and on the farms of the upper classes. He hoped the Protectors of Natives would facilitate the transition from Aboriginal barbarism to civilised servitude. The Vasse district fell under the jurisdiction of Protector Charles Symmons.

Notwithstanding the massacre of eight Aborigines in February and March, Symmons declared 1841 a peaceful year. This was due, he reported,

> partly to fear, the hope of reward, or other such motives, but I have also reason to believe that our mild treatment, our undeviating good faith in all transactions with the natives and the conviction that neither time nor space can eventually avert the punishment of crime, have each and all combined to produce the beneficial effects here alluded to.[17]

Hutt, however, had not been so sanguine about events at the Vasse. In April 1841 he had instructed the colonial secretary to write to Resident Magistrate Molloy and outline the administration's native policy. Aborigines must learn to understand that British law—remote and unseen, exercised not so much by interested local authority but impartially by government—controlled and protected them. Accordingly, in future disputes, settlers must not immediately resort to arms or launch attacks on miscreants that risked innocent lives. At the same time, Aborigines must understand that offences against settlers would be prosecuted with the utmost severity.[18]

The impartial application of British law seemed a remote and incomprehensible abstraction to the Aborigines of Geographe Bay, however. Throughout 1841 and 1842 they remained resentful and hungry. The influx of new settlers, their occupation of land, clearing, grazing of domestic flocks, and hunting with firearms and dogs destroyed traditional foods. Aborigines continued to beg and steal.

In February 1842 Vasse Aborigines raided the Bussells' flour mill, took produce from local gardens, and abducted several goats. John Bussell, now a judicial magistrate, issued a warrant for the arrest of the suspects, who, shortly after being taken into custody, escaped. Notwithstanding Governor Hutt's recent injunction against immediate recourse to arms, the Bussell brothers pursued the fugitives to a swamp, where Charles shot and killed a man, Erigedung. A magisterial inquiry immediately pronounced the act 'justifiable homicide'.

Wollaston deplored the Bussells' violence and wrote in his diary that Erigedung's death was 'most unjustifiable homicide'.[19]

On the morning of 10 March the Bussells found a quantity of flour missing from their mill. In the afternoon two Aboriginal men, Teapot and Uglymug, brought in a seven-year-old girl, Cummangoot. The men expected a reward and told the Bussells they found the girl in the bush, with a boy, Barrbe, endeavouring to conceal about fifteen pounds of flour. Barrbe, however, escaped. The Bussells took Cummangoot and another prisoner, Booly, into custody. In the evening Charles separated the two, removed Cummangoot to John's bedroom, and began to question her. He demanded the names of her accomplices.

Although very frightened, Cummangoot denied all knowledge of the robbery. Charles took down a gun from the gun rack, clicked the lock several times close to Cummangoot's ear, and told her he would shoot her if she told a lie. In a fever of excitement, Charles began to stutter wildly and sent for Alfred, who renewed the interrogation. Cummangoot continued to deny all connection with the robbery. Charles told Alfred they must frighten her into telling the truth. He then pointed the gun at Cummangoot's stomach and pulled the trigger. The gun discharged; the ball pierced Cummangoot and passed through the carpet and the floor.

Charles's first reaction was to exculpate himself. The gun had been unloaded when he had earlier placed it on the rack, he exclaimed. Who had loaded it? he cried. On inspection, he and Alfred discovered that the gun belonged to John, who had placed it on the rack earlier in the morning. The Bussells then called the local medical officer, Robert Sholl. Sholl dressed Cummangoot's wounds but concluded they were mortal. She died next morning.[20]

The killing occurred at a time when the British government had come under the influence of reformers—known as the Exeter Hall movement—who were determined that native peoples in British colonies should be treated as British subjects with full rights of protection, on the same basis as every other subject of the Crown. All colonies came under Exeter Hall pressure. Accordingly, Western Australia's colonial government felt compelled to investigate Cummangoot's death as they would that of a European. Charles Bussell was indicted for manslaughter and summoned to appear at Quarter Sessions in Perth on 1 July 1842. Alfred was cited as an accomplice, though not charged.

The indictment pleased Wollaston. The Bussells' use of terror and their cavalier attitude towards Aboriginal lives had distressed him ever since he arrived in the colony. He particularly objected to their tactics of intimidation. He wrote in his diary:

> This threatening was perfectly illegal and unjustifiable and Mr C. Bussell, I am glad to find, is summoned to Perth that this affair may be properly investigated. All this slaughtering of blacks by the whites, although in great measure, accidental, is distressing and lamentable.[21]

But Wollaston was a lone dissenter. Most of the Vasse settlers cheered the Bussells' actions. When neighbours learned of Charles's indictment, they took up a petition to express their 'most sincere and fervent thanks for the liberal spirited and persevering manner with which you have constantly met the aggression of the natives upon the lives and property of the settlers'.

Charles Bussell was gratified. He and Alfred immediately drafted a reply to acknowledge their fellow settlers' understanding 'that we had not been entirely actuated by selfish principles in our last fatal attempt to bring certain native offenders to justice'. Unfortunately, their philanthropic enterprise had resulted in 'the family of which we are members [becoming] the injured party'. They complained that the government had neglected the Vasse settlement, and that when Aborigines committed 'murders—the slaughter of horses and kind', the perpetrators went unpunished. The brothers hoped, therefore, that their appearance in court might 'have the effect of causing the

Government to make a proper provision for the security of our united property'.[22]

Captain Molloy blamed the violence at the Vasse on the Aborigines. Settlers simply responded to Aboriginal provocation. The consequences were the responsibility of the government, which, he complained to Governor Hutt, had failed to provide sufficient military force to search for and apprehend native offenders. Furthermore, the lack of facilities for incarcerating prisoners meant that the apprehension and interrogation of suspects was impractical. Settlers were in an impossible situation:

> The settler under present circumstances, has the alternative either to suffer robbery or proceed with the constable and with his own hands and at his own expense, both alike uncongenial and inconvenient, to apprehend the party who has transgressed the law.[23]

Captain Molloy told Hutt he regretted the Aboriginal deaths, but he advocated all means possible 'to impress on the minds of the natives the inviolability of the settlers' property and the consequences that must follow any infraction of the laws'. Notwithstanding the shootings, he concluded that the natives at the Vasse 'generally are treated by each and all of the settlers, with more than common kindness and that, as far as I am able to form an opinion, civilization amongst them has progressed as rapidly as in any other part of the Colony'.[24]

Charles's defence counsel, Edward Landor, doubted that Aborigines were capable of civilisation. They were inferior human beings, possessed of small intellects and feeble physical structure.[25]

At the trial Landor told the court his client had pleaded guilty in the expectation that the justices, in consideration of the special circumstances of the case, would render a mild decision. Charles Bussell had resorted to intimidation only after the efficacy of the tactic had been proved by the Aborigines themselves. Teapot and Uglymug had forced Cummangoot to confess earlier in the day, and the accused had only followed their example in seeking the same confession. 'Among such a people,' Landor resolved, 'there was no other way of getting at the truth except through their fears.'[26]

The advocate general replied that the government never doubted the deceased's death was 'purely accidental'; the government had prosecuted only in the determination 'to enforce the principle that the natives should be treated in every way as British subjects', entitled to judicial protection. He reminded the court that intimidation was against the spirit of British law. In Bussell's case, however, 'extenuating circumstances' predisposed the court to leniency. Considering that Charles Bussell's own reflection 'on the fatal results of his indiscretion' would be sufficiently heavy punishment, the court 'had resolved to inflict on him a fine of one shilling'.[27]

Charles, however, experienced no remorse over Cummangoot's death. His conscience had hardened in step with the progress of colonisation. At the beginning of settlement in Western Australia, settlers were insecure in their tenure and unsure of themselves and the land. They depended on Aborigines for food, travel, and information, all of which the Aborigines gave freely and without restriction. Moreover, colonists depended on Aboriginal tracks, water holes, and fire-burned land for the possibility of their own settlement. The timidity, even meekness, of the migrants in earlier days had helped maintain a certain enforced equilibrium. But as the colonists' sense of self-definition cohered, their confidence enlarged, and their knowledge of the land increased, they came to disparage, despise, and resent Aborigines. Like the forests at Augusta, Aborigines were obstacles to progress. Settlers' early caution and unease in the presence of Aborigines gave way to belligerence. Growth in arrogance was considered progress.

By 1842 the settlers regarded their occupation of the Vasse and all the land along Geographe Bay as history, recorded in deeds of possession, certified by government, and lodged in the archives at Perth. In contrast, Aborigines were utterly indifferent to what the

British called history, that is, the series of irreversible events taking place in chronological order. Aborigines had no use for sequential time. They were concerned rather with their own sacred history, with the Dreaming, when all things began.

The Nyungar regarded the coming of the British, at least at first, not as a beginning—the start of a sequence of events, unrepeatable and leading to a unique future—but as coeternal, part of an existence that was continuous. Because they assimilated the British into their own world, they could not imagine that the settlers meant the end of that world. The irruption of terror into Nyungar life came from an invasion they found impossible to understand. Aborigines never suspected there was a world beyond their own, a world that understood the universe differently from the way they did.

The conflict that followed the invasion—the skirmishes, ambushes, battles, shootings, spearings, rapes, and killings—was about the meaning of the earth. For the Aborigines, the land was sacred, it was their home, their life, their Dreaming, the source of the mythical and creative acts that established the laws of Aboriginal society and bequeathed a culture, which, in constant renewal, bestowed meaning upon human existence. For the settlers, land, nature, the earth, was raw material to be turned to the purposes of human convenience. These outlooks were impossible to reconcile. One view had to prevail over the other. And progress, the promise of material abundance wrung from nature, triumphed.

The Aborigines lost because they were unprogressive. They lost because their lack of social hierarchy and lack of desire for possessions made them easy victims. The contented and satisfied Aboriginal way of life was a hideous embarrassment to the meliorist myth that animated the lives of the settlers. For the Aborigines, the ultimate goal of life was life itself; the day and the hour were ends in themselves, not a means to another day or another experience. For the settlers, the day and the hour existed as opportunities for profit and improvement, to be realised on the morrow. The thrusting, self-possessed British directed their efforts towards the future. The Aborigines lived in an eternal present, undeceived by notions of progress or improvement; past, present, and future folded into one another. Time and space were in flux.

Like the killings in 1837, Aboriginal deaths in 1841 and 1842 were not an aberration. Extermination was the logical outcome of an ideology of occupation and conquest. And through the violent way in which individual Nyungar met their end—usually a bullet in the back—Aborigines were irruptively incorporated into history, into European time. The recording of those particular deaths—in letters, diaries, and depositions—inducted Aborigines into the new order of things.

But still the Nyungar could not understand dispossession. They could not imagine how the Dreaming could ever be broken or lost, except by unthinkable disaster. But the unthinkable had happened. The Dreaming was destroyed—a catastrophe that plunged the Nyungar and the southwest into a maelstrom of change and death.

20

LILIES OF THE FIELD

IN THE MIDDLE OF JANUARY 1842 JOHN WOLLASTON ACCEPTED Georgiana Molloy's invitation to botanise at the Vasse for a few days. Molloy told Wollaston that her current collecting interest was in seeds of *Nuytsia floribunda*. In previous seasons she had found *Nuytsia* seeds very difficult to collect and felt she had never obtained enough for Mangles. This summer she was determined to put together a large package. While the trees were still in flower, Molloy and Wollaston rode out onto the Vasse plains to select and mark those specimens with blossom-laden crowns, which promised an abundance of seeds.

By the end of January *Nuytsia* flowering was finished. In February seeds began to form. In March Molloy became pregnant for the eighth time, a condition she had found inescapable. She had been pregnant for over one-third of her entire life in Australia. But, though childbirth had proved increasingly hazardous, actual pregnancy rarely interfered with what she referred to as her 'own work'—botanising. Accordingly, discomfort from the early effects of pregnancy did not distract her from her purpose.

In March and April Molloy collected *Nuytsia* seeds. From experience she knew the seeds scattered quickly and unexpectedly. To prevent dispersion, she wrapped the capsule-bearing branches in bags. To catch any seeds that escaped, she spread cloths under the trees. Nevertheless, she impounded few seeds. She found that if she was not present on the day the seeds ripened and sprang from their capsules, they would, despite the bags and the cloths, be so widely broadcast as to be uncollectible. The only way to gather any seed at all was to regularly monitor every tree. She resolved to go out every day. When she could not, she sent her Aboriginal helpers. On 11 April Molloy wrote her last letter to Mangles, a single paragraph. She apologised for the 'small, small harvest' of the elusive *Nuytsia* seeds, but they represented all she had been able to collect.[1]

At the end of April, winter rains began. The collecting season was over; Molloy returned to full-time household duties at Fairlawn. After the long dormancy of summer, the bush erupted into life: new leaves covered tree crowns, flowering annuals germinated, and perennials pushed out new shoots. Within Molloy's own body a new life quickened.

At the end of October 1842 the Reverend Wollaston and his son John visited the Vasse. They spent a night at Cattle Chosen, where Wollaston noted the Bussells ate well: butter, cheese, beef, and rabbit. They lived, however, 'in a sad, dirty muddle'. Next day, a Sunday, Wollaston performed divine service. Afterwards, father and son called at Fairlawn. John planned to continue on to Augusta, and he promised Molloy he would visit her old garden. He did not need directions or a guide. The Aboriginal *bidi* and the bush track pioneered by the Bussells between Augusta and the Vasse had been replaced by a clearly marked road.[2]

Although the Molloys had left Augusta early in 1839, James Turner, his immediate family, a few other settlers, and a small military detachment still lived there. Settlers and soldiers travelled regularly between Augusta and the Vasse, and in 1840 Captain Molloy had petitioned Governor Hutt to upgrade the track to a road. He provided two cost estimates submitted by Charles Bussell, one for rendering the track efficient for foot traffic and another, more costly, for rendering the track efficient for carts. Hutt accepted the lower of the two quotes, and work commenced. As he read the progress reports Hutt grew more enthusiastic about the road and he authorised additional expenditure. In February 1841 Hutt instructed Captain Molloy to 'Let public notice be given that a good road has been formed between Augusta and the Vasse whereby cattle may be safely driven.'[3]

Settlers considered roads a measure of civilisation. Progress was marked by the passage from the mere footfalls of the savage to the broader lanes and routes used by the horse under subjugation and in harness. Without roads, there could be little or no communication between communities and no opportunity for traffic and barter. Roads civilised the southwest.

John Wollaston, however, did not travel for trade but out of curiosity. He found Charles Bussell's road in a poor state—'a constant succession of swamps'—but he was pleased with Augusta, where he examined Georgiana Molloy's abandoned garden. Many of her introduced plants were growing wild 'but rapidly giving way to the exuberance of growth in the native plants'. The deserted tumbledown huts and overgrown garden seemed a 'melancholy sight', but the bush was beautiful and the Blackwood was a fine river. He also noted the timber-encumbered country that had defied clearing. When he returned to the Vasse he told Molloy he had delighted in all the strange and wonderful plants that grew there. He stayed two days at Fairlawn. When he left, Georgiana Molloy gave him some seeds she had obtained from a ship that had visited India.[4]

Unusually heavy rain fell along the shores of Geographe Bay from the end of November through the beginning of December. Despite the deluge, John Wollaston left Picton to botanise along the coast. As a result of his botanical interests he had become, according to his father, 'thick with Mrs Molloy, who is a perfect botanical dictionary'. On the first of December he sheltered at Fairlawn and resumed his botanical discussions. Molloy was now in the last days of her eighth pregnancy.[5]

On 7 December Molloy's labour began; the birth was difficult. Nevertheless, when finally delivered, the child, a girl, whom the Molloys named Georgiana, was fine. The mother, however, was not. She suffered exhaustion and was anaemic and generally disabled by a constitution enfeebled by successive pregnancies. Summer heat added to her discomfort. Additionally, she had contracted another uterine infection, and a few days after the birth she became feverish.

Captain Molloy was alarmed. Distressed by the ineffectual ministrations and drunkenness of the attending surgeon, Alfred Green, he sent Alfred Bussell galloping 48 kilometres to Australind for one of the Western Australian Company doctors. Alfred told the Reverend Wollaston that Mrs Molloy had been 'seized with shiverings and other dangerous symptoms'. Wollaston prayed that Molloy's five daughters would 'not be motherless in this moral wilderness'. Next day, surgeon Henry Allen, who, according to Wollaston, was 'an experienced *accoucheur*' [man-midwife], went down to the Vasse with Henry Ommanney. Allen dismissed the incompetent Green and prescribed his own treatment. Molloy's fever subsided and she passed out of danger. By the end of an abnormally wet and unsettled December, however, her condition had not improved. She lay 'in a weak and precarious state'.[6]

Rain fell again in early January. According to Wollaston, the wet weather revivified the grass and everywhere gave 'a powerful stimulus to vegetation'. A few days later the sky cleared and summer returned. *Nuytsia floribunda* blazed golden orange against the azure blue sky and the blossoms opened to the souls of the newly dead.

In the second week of January Wollaston and his son William visited the Vasse. Wollaston found Molloy's health critical. She had been ground down by repeated attacks of septicaemia, spiking fevers, recurring chills, and suddenly accelerated pulse. Wollaston despaired for Molloy's life. The days grew hotter and hotter, and Molloy grew no better. During a heat wave in early February, fires raced through the bush all along Geographe Bay and left blackened trees and charcoal-blackened sand in their wake. Smoke and ash added to the heat and suffocating closeness.

The leaping flames prompted the Reverend Wollaston to think of the Scriptures. After a conflagration at Australind in February 1842, he wrote in his diary: 'I was reminded of the scene Abraham witnessed on looking toward Sodom and Gomorrah after their overthrow; for I beheld and lo the smoke of the country went up as the smoke of a furnace.'7

For the Nyungar, fire meant life and renewal, not death and destruction. The Nyungar burned the bush to continue the cycle of life begun in the Dreaming. Episodic conflagrations—Aborigines burned every two or three years—cleared scrub, flushed the infertile biota with nutrients, and enabled regeneration. Heat from fires opened hardened seed capsules, which shed onto mineralised ashbeds. With winter rains, seedlings took root and grew rapidly, free from heavy shade and competition for space.

Burning had been maintained by, and in turn had maintained, the Nyungar for millennia. But with British settlement the cycle had to stop. For Aboriginal fires now burned not just the bush but also swept through farm holdings and damaged private property, consuming fences and buildings, destroying crops, and incinerating stock. Settlers were angry and vowed to prevent Aborigines from burning.

But thoughts of vengeance in the interests of worldly empires did not disturb the sick Molloy. During February her condition worsened. A blood clot paralysed one of her legs. From Picton Wollaston sent medicine and letters of comfort and encouragement. Molloy was too weak and in too much pain to reply. Another heat wave marked the end of February and the beginning of March. *Nuytsia floribunda* blossoms faded and seeds began to set.

Early in March a comet appeared in the western sky. The tail dipped below the horizon but appeared larger, brighter, and higher with each passing night. Wollaston hoped the comet was not a '*belli fera signa*'—a wild banner of war. He was 'startled by its great size and length'.[8]

Aborigines were also startled and ascribed the comet's appearance to an evil agency. The flame on the horizon, they said, was a sign, a portent of death, which foreboded, as one Aborigine told Wollaston, 'no good to blackfellow'. At Picton Aborigines stood in mute astonishment before the apparition in the west and then fell to the ground coughing and spitting in order to purge the evil spirit. Wollaston lamented their refusal to pay any attention to his assurances 'that all things are in the hands and under the superior control of a good Almighty and Beneficent Being'.[9]

But Aborigines had a better understanding of their own fate than Wollaston. For thirteen years the Nyungar had suffered direct assault on their lives and land. Now they faced an even more insidious and devastating scourge—introduced disease. In 1841 a disastrous influenza epidemic had swept through Nyungar camps in the southwest. Children and the elderly suffered the most. At the time, Wollaston nonchalantly noted the disease 'has carried off a great many of the old people'. Thereafter, outbreaks of infectious disease occurred annually. In 1843 Wollaston wrote, 'It is an ascertained fact that great numbers of Aborigines are carried off by epidemics.' By now the Nyungar realised they had made a fatal mistake in identifying the Europeans as the reincarnates of their own dead. They well understood the cause of the catastrophe that had overtaken them and commented, 'Meenya djanga bomungur'—the smell of the *djanga* kills us.[10]

As the comet blazed in the night sky during the early days of March, Georgiana Molloy's health declined. Henry Allen's intervention had failed to revive her. Wollaston thought Allen incompetent and on 7 March confided in his diary that Molloy's life was being sacrificed for want of proper medical attention. Meanwhile, John Ferguson, another Australind settler and surgeon, attended Molloy. He found her in a feeble condition. Painful bedsores covered her back; she was distressed and uncomfortable. On 18 March Captain Molloy sent a note to Wollaston with the news that Mrs Molloy was worse and in great pain. He urged Wollaston to continue to write to her for the sake of her peace of mind.

Wollaston thought the end was near but also unnecessary. He was no fatalist. God expected people to take all 'proper measures for the recovery from sickness'. Molloy's treatment and care were inadequate, and he angrily noted in his diary, 'Mrs Molloy will lose her life for want of nursing.'[11]

With her back now one mass of ulcers, Georgiana Molloy sought some practical relief. In a magazine she had seen directions for the construction of a water bed. The contrivance promised to lessen the painful pressure on her bedsores, and she asked her husband to build one. Captain Molloy and John Ferguson found a sealed trough, which they filled with water. Across the top they stretched an old mackintosh. But when they placed the bedding and the patient on the bed, the mackintosh leaked. The dampness caused Molloy greater discomfort than ever. Her hopes for relief were dashed, and the water bed's failure aggravated her distress. She thought she would never find ease.

Captain Molloy sent an urgent request to Perth for more mackintosh cloth. On 23 March he wrote again to Wollaston. He related the failure of the water bed and told Wollaston that Ferguson held no hope for Mrs Molloy's recovery. Molloy herself accepted the end and sent a message that she wished to receive the Lord's Supper.

For the sin of corrupting Adam and precipitating the expulsion from paradise, God cursed Eve with the fate of wifely submission and child giving. According to Milton, God told Eve:

> Thy sorrow I will greatly multiply
> By thy conception; Children thou shalt bring
> In sorrow forth, and to thy Husband's will
> Thine shall submit, he over thee shall rule.[12]

Yet, without the Fall, the Incarnation and the Redemption could never have occurred. For as death came into the world by a woman, so also did life. Without Eve, humans would never have known pain and death but also would never have known joy and rebirth. For Milton, the only response to the paradox was to accept gratefully the gift of life and to accept the inevitability of pain in all joy.

Georgiana Molloy went further. The world was indeed suffused with suffering, and the greater part of the world's suffering was borne by women. Moreover, women were not the sole authors of their misfortune. For men, a moment's passion had no lasting reminder and led to no monstrous catastrophe of body or soul. But women suffered the consequences, and Molloy understood she suffered not because she had done anything wrong, or shown insufficient faith, or performed few good works, but because she was a woman.

Gender was not all-determining, however. For the world was also suffused with meaningful, purposeful beauty. Though the world's meaning and purpose were not human, its joy was available indiscriminately to all humans. Therefore, Molloy did not despair. She knew that human beings—each individual, as well as the species— were not all-important, not at the centre of the world. Molloy witnessed and lived life in the biotically fecund southwest and understood that the cycle of life in the bush had nothing to do with her. Life existed independently of her and of the settlers' need for utility, even of their need for beauty. Nevertheless, she had found in Australia an intensity of existence she never imagined possible in Scotland. She had lived with an exuberance and an adroitness that grew from her love for the bush. Her life had been enriched by the myriad productions of nature, her senses stimulated by form, colour, and smell.

Molloy's own fertility, her very womanness, had weakened her to the point of death, but life in the Australian bush had strengthened her spirit and bestowed her life with passion. She found virtue in the grateful recognition of life as a gift. God, Molloy believed, did not intend life as a challenge to human power to shape the world to human purpose. Most settlers, however, engaged the challenge and were unmoved by the gift. They were determined to make the world fit their purposes and satisfy their desires.

But perhaps God was not first and foremost a god of history, with an obsessive interest in the human story alone. Perhaps God was not controlled by humans. Perhaps awareness of God did not reside in the preaching of certain individuals, or in the liturgy of Sunday sermons, but in the worship of the holy and in the presence of the sacred. Molloy's bush rambles, her encounter with the forest, flowers, plains, and night sky of the Australian southwest, gave her a sense of God much different from the vengeful, brooding presence in Milton's *Paradise Lost*.

Georgiana Molloy had shared the colonial hope of a better life in Australia. She never, however, accepted material improvement as the end of existence. She did not believe human ingenuity could triumph over fate. Life ended in death; there was no escape. Fate could be transcended only by wonder and virtue, by grateful acceptance of a world that was not made solely for human enjoyment.

Insatiable desire led only to frustration, unhappiness, and spiritual instability. And a society based on insatiable desire led to privation and despair. The Reverend Wollaston certainly thought so. Everywhere he travelled in the colony in the early months of 1843, he noted the depressed state of the economy. Business was at a standstill. Nothing could be sold. Poverty was general. Even the original colonists, such as the Bussells and the Molloys, suffered destitution.

Wollaston was despondent. His own family's real suffering through the early months of 1843 seemed without end. In January his wife, Mary, became 'so weak and worn' she could hardly eat. The rest of the family were 'unwell with bowel complaints'. In March Wollaston, Mary, and their two daughters contracted ophthalmia. Their eyes swelled, became inflamed, and discharged copiously. Next, Wollaston's son William became so ill with vomiting and pain that he required constant nursing. Son John also fell sick. Wollaston ascribed the various ailments to exposure to the sun, excessive hard work, and poor diet. 'A colonial life is very hard on persons like ourselves,' he wrote. 'The fatigue arising from the exertion necessary during the hot weather completely weighs down the spirits.'[13]

Wollaston visited Fairlawn again on 27 March. He found Molloy exhausted, wasted, and under the influence of opiates. She was comatose. He waited for her to regain consciousness, for an opportunity for conversation and prayer. He wanted to draw her mind to the consideration of the great changes that awaited her.

Captain Molloy concerned himself with his wife's physical comfort. He had found another plan for a water bed and engaged a ship's carpenter, from a whaler in the bay, to make a sturdy and watertight trough of sufficient length to accommodate his wife's body. Wollaston lent his new mackintosh for the covering. They filled the trough three-quarters full with water, stretched the mackintosh across, and laid on sheets and blankets, in which they rested the patient. Molloy felt immediate relief. Next day she said she was free from pain. She was so weak, however, she could barely eat. Wollaston conferred with her and reminded her of the all-important duty of 'setting her house in order'. On Wednesday he administered the Last Sacrament and next day returned to Picton. Molloy lapsed into unconsciousness.[14]

A week later, on 7 April 1843, Georgiana Molloy died. The life that had begun 37 years before in England at the violent dawn of the nineteenth century, that had been swept up in religion and emigration and crossed oceans to the far corner of the earth, that had borne seven children, and had found grace in the Australian bush, ended.

Georgiana Molloy was buried on 10 April, in a field near the house she knew as Fairlawn. Yucca lilies brought from her garden at Augusta surrounded the grave. John Bussell read the service.

ACKNOWLEDGEMENTS

ONLY BARBARIANS ARE NOT CURIOUS ABOUT WHERE THEY COME FROM and how the world came to be what it is. Culture, in contrast, permits and encourages questions about origins. In modern English-language culture, libraries are a chief means of inquiry into the past.

With respect to libraries, then, I owe greatest thanks to the eminently civilised Battye Library of Perth. The Battye's repository of Molloy and Bussell papers was indispensable for the writing of this book.

But documents alone do not make a library. Donors, curators, staff, and volunteers who spend untold hours sifting, cataloguing, and transcribing to make documents accessible and useful form the joy and public heart of a library.

I record here my thanks to the people of the Battye Library, whose labour, assistance, and cheerfulness testify to the persistence of civic virtue. In an age when publicly funded organisations suffer relentless assault from barbarian free marketeers and ideologues of minimal public life, Australian libraries stand for informed citizenship. May they continue.

I also wish to thank the archivists at the Cumbria Record Office, Carlisle, England, whose institution epitomises the very best Anglo-Saxon traditions of openness, access, and cooperation. Despite a decade and more of ignoble Thatcherite economic rationalism, which attempted to rob public life of its purpose and community of its bonds, the spirit and means of free inquiry endure.

I have incurred one other major debt of gratitude: to my companion and love, Carlotta Hartland. Through her conscientious and heroic engagement with the text, Carlotta raised sympathetic, cogent, and crucial questions of substance, style, and consistency. Without her contribution, *An All Consuming Passion* would have been a poorer book.

William J. Lines
Warrandyte, June 1993

ILLUSTRATION CREDITS

10   South-southwest view of Augusta, 1838. Pen and ink and watercolour by Thomas Turner. Collection, The Art Gallery of Western Australia, Presented by Mr J R Turner, 1929.

11   Albion House, Augusta, 1836. Pen and ink and watercolour by Thomas Turner. Collection, The Art Gallery of Western Australia, Presented by Mr J R Turner, 1929.

12   Albion House, Augusta, c. 1840s. Pen and ink and watercolour by Thomas Turner. Collection, The Art Gallery of Western Australia, Presented by Mr A W Pullan, 1987.

13   View of Fremantle. Pen and ink and watercolour by Richard Morrell. Collection, The Art Gallery of Western Australia.

14   Cattle Chosen. Pencil by Thomas Turner. Collection, The Art Gallery of Western Australia, Presented by Mr J R Turner, 1929.

15   James Mangles's inscribed title page. Author's collection.

16   Letter from Georgiana Molloy to Mrs Kennedy, 16 July 1832, CRO D/Ken/3/28/9. Photographed by the author, 12 January 1993, with permission.

17   John Bussell. Battye Library 4599B/60.

18   John Molloy. Battye Library 25863P.

NOTES

Abbreviations used in credits, notes, and bibliography

ANU   Australian National University
BL   Battye Library (Perth)
CRO   Cumbria Record Office (Carlisle)
CS   Colonial Secretary
CSF   Colonial Secretary Records (Forwarded), Battye Library
CSR   Colonial Secretary Records (Received), Battye Library
CUP   Cambridge University Press
HUP   Harvard University Press
JRWAHS   Journal Royal Western Australian Historical Society
MUP   Melbourne University Press
OUP   Oxford University Press
RM   Resident Magistrate
UWA   University of Western Australia
WAGG   Western Australian Government Gazette

BL citations conform as follows: accession number/specific document number.

1   GENESIS

1   The ideas for this chapter were suggested by and in turn based on
    several sources: Russell Banks, *Continental Drift: A Novel*, Harper &
    Row, New York, 1985; Peter Westbroek, *Life as a Geological Force:*

Dynamics of the Earth, Norton, New York, 1991; Reg and Maggie Morrison, *The Voyage of the Great Southern Ark*, Landsdowne Press, Sydney, 1988; Herbert Butterfield, *The Whig Interpretation of History*, Charles Scribner and Sons, New York, 1951; Stephen Jay Gould, *Time's Arrow Time's Cycle: Myth and Metaphor in the Discovery of Geological Time*, HUP, Cambridge, Mass., 1987, *Wonderful Life: The Burgess Shale and the Nature of History*, Norton, New York, 1989, and *Bully for Brontosaurus: Reflections in Natural History*, Norton, New York, 1991.

For specific information regarding Australia's biotic heritage I drew on: for the evolution of southwest flora, *Journal of the Royal Society of Western Australia*, no. 56, 1973 and George Seddon, *Sense of Place: A Response to an Environment—The Swan Coastal Plain of Western Australia*, UWA Press, Nedlands, 1972; for Australia's fire history, Sylvia J. Hallam, *Fire and Hearth: a study of Aboriginal usage and European usurpation in south-western Australia*, Australian Institute of Aboriginal Studies, Canberra, 1979 and Stephen J. Pyne, *Burning Bush: A Fire History of Australia*, Henry Holt and Company, New York, 1991; and for Aboriginal history and the Pleistocene, Josephine Flood, *Archeology of the Dreamtime: The Story of Prehistoric Australia and its People*, revised edition, Yale University Press, New Haven, 1990 and Paul S. Martin and Richard G. Klein, eds, *Quaternary Extinctions: A Prehistoric Revolution*, University of Arizona Press, Flagstaff, 1984.

To reconstruct the world of the first Australians I drew on: Mircea Eliade, *Australian Religions: An Introduction*, Cornell University Press, Ithaca, 1973; W. E. H. Stanner, *White Man Got No Dreaming*, ANU Press, Canberra, 1979 and *On Aboriginal Religion*, University of Sydney Press, Sydney, 1989.

For the nature of travel, Paul Carter, *The Road to Botany Bay: An Exploration of Landscape and History*, Knopf, New York, 1988.

2 AUTHORS OF THEMSELVES IN ALL

1 Adam Smith, *An Inquiry into the Nature and Causes of the Wealth of Nations*, The Modern Library, New York, 1937, pp. 324–25.

2 Ibid., p. 423.

3 Quoted in J. B. Bury, *The Idea of Progress: An Inquiry into its Origin and Growth*, Macmillan and Co., London, 1924, p. 221.

4 Smith, *Wealth of Nations*, p. 13.

5 The story of the Luddite revolt from E. P. Thompson, *The Making of the English Working Class*, Pantheon, New York, 1964, pp. 547–602. Byron quoted in Robert Reid, *Land of Lost Content: The Luddite Revolt, 1812*, Heinemann, London, 1986, p. 61.

6 Paul Johnson, *The Birth of the Modern: World Society 1815–1830*, Harper Collins, New York, 1991, pp. 165–285.

7 Quote from Susanna Moodie, *Roughing it in the Bush; or, Life in Canada* (first published 1852), Beacon Press, Boston, 1986, p. xvi.

8 In addition to the previously cited sources, the information and arguments in this chapter draw from: Elie Halevy, *A History of the English People: 1815–1830*, T. Fisher Unwin Ltd, London, 1926; Arthur Bryant, *Years of Victory: 1802–1812*, Collins, London, 1945 and *The Age of Elegance 1812–1822*, Collins, London, 1950; John Ashton, *The Dawn of the XIXth Century in England: A Social Sketch of the Times*, T. Fisher Unwin, London, 1898; William Leiss, *The Domination of Nature*, George Braziller, New York, 1972; J. L. and Barbara Hammond, *The Village Labourer, 1760–1832: A Study in the Government of England before the Reform Bill*, Longmans, Green, and Co., London, 1911; Charles E. Lindblom, *Politics and Markets: The World's Political Systems*, Basic Books, New York, 1977; and J. H. Clapham, *An Economic History of Modern Britain: The Early Railway Age 1820–1850*, CUP, Cambridge, 1959.

3 THE LANGUAGE OF HEAVEN

1 See G. Kitson Clark, *The Making of Victorian England*, HUP, Cam-

bridge, Mass., 1962 and Arthur Bryant, *The Age of Elegance: 1812–1822*, Collins, London, 1950.

2   The picture of Irving in London from Julian Symons, *Thomas Carlyle: The Life and Ideas of a Prophet*, Victor Gollancz, London, 1952, p. 76.

3   Quoted in William Charles Maughan, *Rosneath Past and Present*, Alexander Gardner, London, 1893, p. 266.

4   The above paragraphs on Rosneath and Irving draw on: Maughan, *Rosneath*; Mrs (Margaret) Oliphant, *The Life of Edward Irving*, Hurst and Blackett, London, 1862; and Andrew Landale Drummond, *Edward Irving and His Circle*, James Clarke & Co., London, 1937.

5   Robert Story, *Peace in Believing: A Memoir of Isabella Campbell of Rosneath, Dumbartonshire, Scotland*, Jonathan Leavitt, New York, 1830, p. 21.

6   See Charles Coulston Gillispie, *Genesis and Geology: A Study in the Relations of Scientific Thought, Natural Theology, and Social Opinion in Great Britain, 1790–1850*, HUP, Cambridge, Mass., 1951 and Lynn Barber, *The Heyday of Natural History: 1820–1870*, Jonathan Cape, London, 1980.

7   Keith Thomas, *Man and the Natural World: A History of the Modern Sensibility*, Pantheon Books, New York, 1983, pp. 181–83.

8   Georgiana Kennedy to John Molloy, 11 December 1828: BL 3278A/3, Typescript 501A/1.

9   John Harris, *Recollections of Rifleman Harris*, ed. Henry Curling, Robert M. McBride & Company, New York, 1929, p. 40.

10 Ibid., p. 161 and Captain J. Kincaid, *Adventures in the Rifle Brigade: In the Peninsula, France and the Netherland, from 1809 to 1815* (first published 1848), Peter Davies Limited, London, 1929, p. 161.

11 Kincaid, *Adventures*, p. 37.

12 Harris, *Recollections*, p. 90.

13 Kincaid, *Adventures*, p. 221.

14 DuCane, Lieut.-General Sir Edmund, 'The Peninsula and Waterloo: Memories of an old Rifleman,' *Cornhill Magazine*, vol. 76, July to December 1897, pp. 750–58.

4   CARPE DIEM

1   William Dampier, *Dampier's Voyages*, ed. John Masefield, two volumes, E. Grant Richards, London, 1906, vol. 1, p. 453 passim.

2   Biographical information on Stirling from *Australian Dictionary of Biography*, vol. 2, 1788–1850, I–Z, ed. Douglas Pike, MUP, Melbourne, 1967 and Malcolm Uren, *Land Looking West: The Story of Governor James Stirling in Western Australia*, OUP, London, 1948.

3   Quoted in Uren, *Land Looking West*, p. 283.

4   Susanna Moodie, *Roughing it in the Bush; or, Life in Canada* (first published 1852), Beacon Press, Boston, 1986, pp. xvi and xv.

5   Besides the sources quoted, the story of Stirling's original reconnoitre of Swan River, his negotiations with the Colonial Office, and Swan River Mania is drawn from: J. M. R. Cameron, 'Information Distortion in Colonial Promotion: The Case of Swan River Colony,' *Australian Geographical Studies*, vol. 12, no. 1, 1974, pp. 57–76 and *Ambition's Fire: The Agricultural Colonization of Pre-Convict Western Australia*, UWA Press, Nedlands, 1981; and R. T. Appleyard and Toby Manford, *The Beginning: European Discovery and Early Settlement of Swan River Western Australia*, UWA Press, Nedlands, 1980.

6   Reverend John Giles Powell, *The Narrative of a Voyage to the Swan River*, F. C. Westley, London, 1831, p. 40.

7   Lieutenant W. H. Breton, *Excursions in New South Wales, Western Australia, and Van Diemen's Land, During the Years 1830, 1831, 1832, and 1833*, Richard Bentley, London, 1834, p. 29.

8   T. B. Wilson, *Narrative of a Voyage Round the World*, Sherwood, Gilbert, & Piper, London, 1835, p. 198.

9   Ibid., p. 195.

10 Quoted in Cameron, *Ambition's Fire*, p. 89.

5   GODSPEED

1   Sempill quotes from J. M. R. Cameron, 'H. C. Sempill: The Western

Connection,' *Journal and Proceedings of the Armidale and District Historical Society*, no. 22, 1978, pp. 75–92.

2 Georgiana Molloy to Mary Dunlop, 29 August 1829: BL 3278A/2, Typescript 501A/1.

3 Ibid.

4 Ibid.

5 Georgiana Molloy to Helen Story, 12 September 1829: BL 3278A/2.

6 Walter Scott quoted in Fred Kaplan, *Thomas Carlyle: A Biography*, Cornell University Press, Ithaca, New York, 1983, p. 47.

7 Georgiana Molloy to Mary Dunlop, 29 August 1829: BL 3278A/2, Typescript 501A/1.

8 Georgiana Molloy to Helen Story, 12 September 1829: BL 3278A/2.

9 Ibid.

10 Ibid.

11 Hapgood quoted in Cameron, 'H. C. Sempill.'

12 John Bussell to Mrs Bussell, March 1829: BL 337A/457.

13 Bussell family background based on E. O. G. Shann, *Cattle Chosen: The Story of the First Group Settlement in Western Australia 1829 to 1841*, OUP, London, 1926, pp. 1–9.

14 Charles Bussell to Capel Carter, 14 August 1829: BL 337A/144.

15 Captain Molloy quoted in Cameron, 'H. C. Sempill'; Georgiana Molloy's journal, 19 and 20 October 1829: CRO D/Ken/3/28/2.

16 Diary of James Turner reproduced in Tom Turner, *Turners of Augusta*, Paterson Brokensha Pty Ltd, Perth, 1956, 18 October 1829, p. 37.

17 John Bussell to Mrs Bussell, 22 January 1830: BL 337A/460.

18 On the suggested names for Swan River see J. M. R. Cameron, *Ambition's Fire: The Agricultural Colonization of Pre-Convict Western Australia*, UWA Press, Nedlands, 1981, p. 34. Turner quote from Diary of James Turner, 24 October 1829, p. 39.

6 PASSAGE

1 Georgiana Molloy's journal, 23 October 1829: CRO D/Ken/3/28/2.

2 Charles Bussell's journal, 26 October 1829: BL 337A/171.

3   Diary of James Turner reproduced in Tom Turner, *Turners of Augusta*, Paterson Brokensha Pty Ltd, Perth, 1956, 28 October 1829, p. 41.

4   Charles Bussell's journal, 13 November 1829: BL 337A/171.

5   Georgiana Molloy's journal, 31 October 1829: CRO D/Ken/3/28/2.

6   Charles Bussell's journal, 13 and 14 November 1829: BL 337A/171.

7   Ibid., 10 November 1829; Georgiana Molloy to family, 23 November 1829: CRO D/Ken/3/28/9.

8   Charles Bussell's journal, 9 and 10 November 1829: BL 337A/171.

9   Ibid., 9 November 1829.

10 Diary of James Turner, 2 November 1829, p. 42.

11 Charles Bussell's journal, 18 October 1829: BL 337A/171.

12 Georgiana Molloy's journal, 18 November 1829: CRO D/Ken/3/28/2.

13 On the changing perception of mountains see Marjorie Hope Nicolson, *Mountain Gloom and Mountain Glory: The Development of the Aesthetics of the Infinite*, Norton, New York, 1963.

14 Charles Bussell's journal, 18 October 1829: BL 337A/171. For another contemporary traveller who commented on the Cape Verde Islands' sterility see Charles Darwin, *The Voyage of the Beagle*, Doubleday, New York, 1962, p. 2.

15 Fight description from Charles Bussell's journal, 19 November 1829: BL 337A/171.

16 Captain Molloy quoted in J. M. R. Cameron, 'H. C. Sempill: The Western Connection,' *Journal and Proceedings of the Armidale and District Historical Society*, no. 22, 1978, pp. 75–92; Georgiana Molloy's journal, 19 November 1829: CRO D/Ken/3/28/2.

17 Captain Molloy from Cameron, 'H. C. Sempill.'

18 Charles Bussell's journal, 23 and 24 November 1829: BL 337A/171; John Bussell to Mrs Bussell, 22 January 1830: BL 337A/460. Charles's *Warrior* journal covers the period from departure, in October 1829, to arrival at Swan River, in March 1830, to subsequent events, and totals some 12 500 words. He devoted over a quarter of the journal (3500 words) to the two days spent at St Jago—a testament to the novelty and stimulus of land after four weeks at sea.

19 Georgiana Molloy's journal, 24 November 1829: CRO D/Ken/3/28/2.

20 Ibid.

21 Georgiana Molloy to family, 23 November 1829: CRO D/Ken/3/28/9; Georgiana Molloy to Mrs Kennedy, 4 December 1831: CRO D/Ken/3/28/9.

22 Georgiana Molloy's journal, 10 December 1829: CRO D/Ken/3/28/2; Charles Bussell's journal, 12 December 1829: BL 337A/171.

23 Georgiana Molloy's journal, 25 December 1829: CRO D/Ken/3/28/2.

24 John Bussell to Mrs Bussell, 22 January 1830: BL 337A/460; John Molloy to Mrs Kennedy, 25 January 1830: CRO D/Ken/3/28/9.

25 Georgiana Molloy to family, 15 April 1831: CRO D/Ken/3/28/9.

26 Georgiana Molloy to Helen Story, 25 January 1830: BL 3278A/2 and Typescript 501A/1.

7   TO THE BUSH

1 Letter of James Turner, March 1831: BL 315A/2.

2 Mary Ann Friend from 'The Diary of Mary Ann Friend,' *JRWAHS*, vol. 1, part x, 1931, pp. 1–11.

3 Vernon Bussell to Capel Carter, August 1832: BL 337A/524.

4 Georgiana Molloy to family, 15 April 1831: CRO D/Ken/3/28/9; Georgiana Molloy to Mrs Kennedy, 4 April 1830: CRO D/Ken/3/28/9.

5 Georgiana Molloy to Mrs Kennedy, 4 April 1830: CRO D/Ken/3/28/9.

6 Ibid.

7 Letter of James Turner, March 1831: BL 315A/2.

8 See Joseph Cross, ed., *Journals of Several Expeditions Made in Western Australia, During the Years 1829, 1830, 1831, and 1832*, J. Cross, London, 1833, pp. 35–50.

9 Ibid.

10 Ibid., 'Government Notice relative to Port Leschenault,' pp. 80–88.

11 Ibid.

12 Quotes from Reverend John Giles Powell, *The Narrative of a Voyage to the Swan River*, F. C. Westley, London, 1831, pp. 52 and 54. See also Lieutenant W. H. Breton, *Excursions in New South Wales, Western*

Australia, and Van Diemen's Land, During the Years 1830, 1831, 1832, and 1833, Richard Bentley, London, 1834, p. 34.

13　E. W. Landor, *The Bushman; or, Life in a New Country*, Richard Bentley, London, 1847, p. 266.

14　Breton, *Excursions*, pp. 15–16.

15　Quote from Landor, *The Bushman*, pp. 98–99.

16　Georgiana Molloy to Mrs Kennedy, August 1830: CRO D/Ken/3/28/9; Georgiana Molloy to family, 15 April 1831: CRO D/Ken/3/28/9.

17　Cross, *Journals*, 'Government Notice relative to Port Augusta,' pp. 89–91.

18　John Boultbee, *Journal of a Rambler: The Journal of John Boultbee*, ed. June Starke, OUP, Wellington, 1986, pp. 125–26.

19　Cross, *Journals*, pp. 89–91.

20　Vernon Bussell to Capel Carter, August 1832: BL 337A/524.

8　WILDERNESS

1　Above based on Georgiana Molloy's account of the birth and death of her first daughter, Elizabeth Mary: CRO D/Ken/3/28/3; Georgiana Molloy to Mrs Kennedy, August 1830: CRO D/Ken/3/28/9; Georgiana Molloy to family, 15 April 1831: CRO D/Ken/3/28/9.

2　Georgiana Molloy to Helen Story, 1 October 1833: BL 3278A/2.

3　Ibid.

4　Georgiana Molloy to Mrs Kennedy, August 1830: CRO D/Ken/3/28/9; Georgiana Molloy's account of the birth and death of her first daughter, Elizabeth Mary: CRO D/Ken/3/28/3.

5　Georgiana Molloy to Mrs Kennedy, August 1830: CRO D/Ken/3/28/9.

6　On the history of British forests see Keith Thomas, *Man and the Natural World: A History of the Modern Sensibility*, Pantheon Books, New York, 1983, p. 192; J. H. Clapham, *An Economic History of Modern Britain: The Early Railway Age 1820–1850*, CUP, Cambridge, 1959, p. 9; and John Perlin, *A Forest Journey: The Role of Wood in the Development of Civilization*, HUP, Cambridge, Mass., 1991, chapter 10. On the literary history of civilisation and forests see Robert Pogue

Harrison, *Forests: The Shadow of Civilization*, University of Chicago Press, Chicago, 1992.

7   William Howitt, *The Rural Life of England*, two volumes, Longman, Orme, Brown, Green, & Longmans, London, 1838, vol. 2, pp. 30 and 370.

8   John Bussell to Mrs Bussell, 29 August 1830: BL 337A/461.

9   Charles Bussell to Capel Carter, 1 November 1832: BL 337A/153.

10   Reverend John Giles Powell, *The Narrative of a Voyage to the Swan River*, F. C. Westley, London, 1831, p. 95.

11   Quote from Charles Bussell's *Warrior* diary: BL 337A/171.

12   RM to CS, 29 August 1830: CSR 8.

13   John Bussell to Mrs Bussell, 19 August 1830: BL 337A/461.

14   Tom Turner, *Turners of Augusta*, Paterson Brokensha Pty Ltd, Perth, 1956, pp. 76–78.

15   For an example of the 'servant problem' at Swan River see Pamela Statham, ed., *The Tanner Letters: A Pioneer Saga of Swan River & Tasmania, 1831–1845*, UWA Press, Nedlands, 1981, pp. 23 and 55.

16   See William Paley, *Reasons for Contentment: Addressed to the Labouring Part of the British Public*, R. Faulder, London, 1793.

17   Charles Bussell to Mrs Bussell, 16 October 1830: BL 337A/145.

18   John Bussell to C. Wells, July 1831: BL 337A/788. In other correspondence Bussell referred to the area as 'beautifully picturesque and fertile': John Bussell to Capel Carter, 6 April 1831: BL 337A/462.

19   For a discussion of the picturesque and wilderness see Paul Shepard, *Man in the Landscape: A Historic View of the Esthetics of Nature*, Knopf, New York, 1967, p. 124; Paul Carter, *The Road to Botany Bay: An Exploration of Landscape and History*, Knopf, New York, 1988, pp. 252 and 290; and John Passmore, *Man's Responsibility for Nature: Ecological Problems and Western Tradition*, Charles Scribner and Sons, New York, 1974, p. 37.

20   John Bussell to C. Wells, July 1831: BL 337A/788.

21   Georgiana Molloy to Mrs Kennedy, August 1830: CRO D/Ken/3/28/9.

22   John Bussell to C. Wells, July 1831: BL 337A/788. Bussell quoted the

lines in Greek. My translation is by Philip Vellacott, from Aeschylus, *Prometheus Bound*, Penguin Books, London, 1970.

23 Georgiana Molloy to family, 15 April 1831: CRO D/Ken/3/28/9.

24 John Bussell to Capel Carter, 6 April 1831: BL 337A/462.

25 BL Exploration Diaries, vol. 1, PR 5441, J. G. Bussell, 'Account of the Country Intervening Between Augusta and Swan River,' pp. 110–13.

26 'Report of an Excursion in a Whale Boat, from Six Miles to the Eastward of Rame Point to Six Miles to the N.W. of Point d'Entrecasteaux, and from thence to the Murray River by Land,' in Joseph Cross, ed., *Journals of Several Expeditions Made in Western Australia, During the Years 1829, 1830, 1831, and 1832*, J. Cross, London, 1833, pp. 114–31.

27 BL Exploration Diaries, vol. 1, PR 5441, J. G. Bussell, 'Report of an Excursion to the Northward from Augusta by Mr. J. G. Bussell,' pp. 348–57.

28 John Bussell to Capel Carter, 11 December 1831: BL 337A/464.

29 Vernon Bussell to Capel Carter, December 1832: BL 337A/525.

30 Georgiana Molloy to Mrs Kennedy, August 1830: CRO D/Ken/3/28/9.

9   SPIRIT AND NECESSITY

1   On flowers and gardening see Paul Shepard, *Man in the Landscape: A Historic View of the Esthetics of Nature*, Knopf, New York, 1967, chapter 3, 'The Image of the Garden' and Keith Thomas, *Man and the Natural World: A History of the Modern Sensibility*, Pantheon Books, New York, 1983, chapter 5, 'Flowers'.

2   Georgiana Molloy to Mrs Kennedy, 4 December 1831: CRO D/Ken/3/28/9.

3   Charles Bussell's journal, 10 November 1829: BL 337A/171; John Bussell to Capel Carter, 11 December 1831: BL 337A/464; Charles Bussell to Capel Carter, 1 November 1832: BL 337A/153.

4   John Bussell to C. Wells, July 1831: BL 337A/788.

5   John Bussell to Capel Carter, 6 April 1831: BL 337A/462.

6   Hanson quotes from Alexandra Hasluck, *Portrait with Background: A Life of Georgiana Molloy*, OUP, Melbourne, 1955, pp. 84–85.

7   Georgiana Molloy to Mrs Kennedy, 4 December 1831: CRO D/Ken/3/28/9.

8   Georgiana Molloy to Margaret Dunlop, 12 January 1833: BL 501A/1.

9   Georgiana Molloy to Elizabeth Besly, 7 November 1832: BL 3278A/2.

10   Ibid.

11   See Keith Thomas, *Man and the Natural World*, p. 237.

12   Georgiana Molloy to Elizabeth Besley, 7 November 1832: BL 3278A/2.

13   Ibid.

14   Ibid.

15   The contents of John Bussell's library from E. O. G. Shann, *Cattle Chosen: The Story of the First Group Settlement in Western Australia 1829 to 1841*, OUP, London, 1926, p. 43. Quote from John Bussell to Capel Carter, March 1832: BL 337A/466.

16   Georgiana Molloy to Helen Story, 1 October 1833: BL 3278A/2.

17   Robert Pollok, *The Course of Time: A Poem, in Ten Books*, ninth edition, William Blackwood, Edinburgh, 1829, p. 288.

18   John Milton, *Paradise Lost*, book ix, lines 232–34.

19   Georgiana Molloy to Helen Story, 1 October 1833: BL 3278A/2.

20   Georgiana Molloy to Elizabeth Besly, 7 November 1832: BL 3278A/2.

21   Georgiana Molloy to Helen Story, 1 October 1833: BL 3278A/2.

22   John Sargent, *A Memoir of Rev. Henry Martyn, B.D.*, American Tract Society, New York, c. 1870, p. 126.

23   Ibid., p. 84.

24   Georgiana Molloy to Helen Story, 1 October 1833: BL 3278A/2.

10   A WORLD OF READY WEALTH

1   John Bussell, Reports: BL 337A/521.

2   Ibid.

3   Ibid., and John Bussell to C. Wells, July 1831: BL 337A/788.

4   On the collecting of word lists see Ian and Tamsin Donaldson, *Seeing the First Australians*, George Allen & Unwin, Sydney, 1985. On taking

versus talking see Paul Carter, *The Road to Botany Bay: An Exploration of Landscape and History*, Knopf, New York, 1988, p. 327. For colonial consensus on Aboriginal language see the appendix 'A Descriptive Vocabulary of the Language of the Aborigines' in George Fletcher Moore, *Diary of Ten Years Eventful Life of an Early Settler in Western Australia*, M. Walbrook, London, 1884. The Bussells contributed to Moore's word list.

5   See R. M. W. Dixon, *The Languages of Australia*, CUP, Cambridge, 1980.

6   John Bussell to C. Wells, July 1831: BL 337A/788.

7   Vernon Bussell to Capel Carter, January 1833: BL 337A/526.

8   Ibid.

9   Moore, 'Descriptive Vocabulary,' Preface.

10 Piero Sraffa, ed., *The Works and Correspondence of David Ricardo*, vol. 2, 'Notes on Malthus's Principles of Political Economy,' CUP, Cambridge, 1952, p. 428.

11 George Grey, *Journals of Two Expeditions of Discovery in North-West and Western Australia, during the Years 1837, 1838, and 1839*, two volumes, T. and W. Boone, London, 1841, vol. 2, p. 262.

12 From Deborah Buller-Murphy, *An Attempt to Eat the Moon; And other stories recounted from the Aborigines*, Georgian House, Melbourne, 1958, pp. 42–44.

13 John Bussell, Reports: BL 337A/521. The relationship between naming and possession is the subject of Carter's *Botany Bay*.

14 Ibid. For those whose memories were intact, Bussell offered, from Book I of the *Aeneid*:

> Ac primum silici scintillam excudit Achates,   (174)
> suscepitque ignem foliis, atque arida circum   (175)
> nutrimenta dedit, rapuitque in fomite flammam   (176)
> illi se praedae accingunt dapibusque futuris;   (210)
> tergora deripiunt costis et viscera nudant;   (211)
> pars in frusta secant veribusque trementia figunt;   (212)

For the location of these lines, I am grateful to Dr Fernando M. S. Silva of Berkeley, California, who provided me with a literal translation that I could compare to John Bussell's.

15 Ibid., and John Bussell to Sophie Hayward, November 1832: BL 337A/469.

16 For general insight into this aspect of exploring and settling I drew on Carter, *Botany Bay*, p. 36.

17 Nicolas Baudin, *The Journal of Post Captain Nicolas Baudin*, trans. Christine Cornell, Libraries Board of South Australia, Adelaide, 1974, pp. 173–74.

18 Quote from J. B. Bury, *The Idea of Progress: An Inquiry into its Origin and Growth*, Macmillan and Co., London, 1924, p. 167.

19 Peron quote from Frank Horner, *The French Reconnaissance: Baudin in Australia 1801–1803*, MUP, Melbourne, 1987, p. 198.

20 Ibid., p. 205.

21 Fremantle quote in R. T. Appleyard and Toby Manford, *The Beginning: European Discovery and Early Settlement of Swan River Western Australia*, UWA Press, Nedlands, 1980, p. 124.

22 John Bussell to Sophie Hayward, November 1832: BL 337A/469.

23 John Bussell, Reports: BL 337A/521 and 520.

24 William Cronon makes a similar point with respect to the occupation and settlement of the western United States in *Nature's Metropolis: Chicago and the Great West*, Norton, New York, 1991. See especially pp. 149–50.

25 Vernon Bussell to Capel Carter, January 1833: BL 337A/526.

11 BLUNDERING PLOUGH

1 John Bussell to Capel Carter, 11 December 1831: BL 337A/464.

2 Georgiana Molloy to Helen Story, 8 December 1834: BL 3278A/2.

3 Shaw quoted in Mary Durack, *To Be Heirs Forever*, Constable, London, 1976, p. 93.

4 George Fletcher Moore, *Diary of Ten Years Eventful Life of an Early Settler in Western Australia*, M. Walbrook, London, 1884, p. 124.

5   John Bussell to C. Wells, 30 May 1832: BL 337A/468.

6   Ibid.

7   Georgiana Molloy to Margaret Dunlop, 12 January 1833: BL 501A/1.

8   Ibid.

9   Georgiana Molloy to Elizabeth Besly, 7 November 1832: BL 3278A/2.

10 Ibid.

11 Georgiana Molloy to Margaret Dunlop, 12 January 1833: BL 501A/1.

12 Vernon Bussell to Capel Carter, December 1832: BL 337A/525.

13 Quoted in Alexandra Hasluck, *Portrait with Background: A Life of Georgiana Molloy*, OUP, Melbourne, 1955, p. 118.

14 Moore, *Diary*, p. 166.

15 Fanny Bussell to Mrs Bussell, 5 April 1833: BL 337A/332.

16 Ibid.

17 Georgiana Molloy to Mrs Kennedy, 28 February 1833: CRO D/Ken/3/28/9; Fanny Bussell to Mrs Bussell, 5 April 1833: BL 337A/332.

18 Fanny Bussell to Mrs Bussell, 5 April 1833: BL 337A/332.

19 Ibid.

20 Georgiana Molloy to Mrs Kennedy, 29 May 1833: CRO D/Ken/3/28/9.

21 Georgiana Molloy to Helen Story, 1 October 1833: BL 501A/1.

22 Ibid.

23 Ibid.

24 Diary of Fanny Bussell: BL 294A/12.

25 Georgiana Molloy to Helen Story, 1 October 1833: BL 3278A/2.

26 Ibid.

27 Ibid. and to Mrs Kennedy, 24 July 1833: CRO D/Ken/3/28/9.

28 Georgiana Molloy to Elizabeth Besly, 13 November 1833: BL 3278A/2.

29 Bessie Bussell to Fanny Bussell, 5 November 1833: BL 337A/264.

30 Journal of Bessie Bussell, 1834: BL 337A/274.

31 Ibid.

32 Georgiana Molloy to Elizabeth Besly, 13 November 1833: BL 3278A/2.

33 John Bussell to Mrs Bussell, 9 July 1834: BL 337A/475; John Bussell to Capel Carter, November 1833: BL 337A/473.

12 POSSESSION

1 Georgiana Molloy to Elizabeth Besly, 13 November 1833: BL 3278A/2.

2 Georgiana Molloy to Mrs Kennedy, 29 May 1833: CRO D/Ken/3/28/9; Georgiana Molloy to Elizabeth Besly, 13 November 1833: BL 3278A/2. For the story of Gyallipert in Perth see entry in Sylvia Hallam and Lois Tilbrook, eds, *Aborigines of the Southwest Region, 1829–1840: The Bicentennial Dictionary of Western Australians, Volume VIII*, UWA Press, Nedlands, 1990, pp. 154–55.

3 Georgiana Molloy to Mrs Kennedy, 29 May 1833: CRO D/Ken/3/28/9; Georgiana Molloy to Elizabeth Besly, 13 November 1833: BL 3278A/2.

4 The story of this encounter from Georgiana Molloy to Helen Story, 8 December 1834: BL 3278A/2.

5 Diary of Fanny Bussell, 1834: BL 294A/12.

6 Georgiana Molloy to Helen Story, 8 December 1834: BL 3278A/2.

7 Ibid.

8 Georgiana Molloy to Elizabeth Besly, 13 November 1833: BL 3278A/2; Georgiana Molloy to Helen Story, 8 December 1834: BL 3278A/2.

9 Georgiana Molloy to Helen Story, 8 December 1834: BL 3278A/2.

10 Ibid.

11 Ibid.

12 Ibid. and to Elizabeth Besly, 13 November 1833: BL 3278A/2.

13 Bessie Bussell's journal, January 1834: BL 337A/274.

14 Georgiana Molloy to Mrs Kennedy, 29 May 1833: CRO D/Ken/3/28/9; Georgiana Molloy to Mrs Kennedy, 24 July 1833: CRO D/Ken/3/28/9; Georgiana Molloy to Elizabeth Besly, 13 November 1833: BL 3278A/2.

15 Georgiana Molloy to Helen Story, 8 December 1834: BL 3278A/2.

16 Jane Porter, *Sir Edward Seaward's Narrative*, Longman, Rees, Orme, Brown, and Green, London, 1831.

17 Georgiana Molloy to Helen Story, 8 December 1834: BL 3278A/2.

18 Ibid.

19 Bessie Bussell to Capel Carter, 13 April 1834: BL 337A/266.

20 John Bussell to Fanny Bussell, July 1834: BL 337A/483.

21 Lenox Bussell's journal, 1834: BL 337A/544.

22 Above paragraph based partly on Judith Wright, *The Cry for the Dead*, OUP, Melbourne, 1981, p. 22.

23 Alfred Bussell's journal, June 1834: BL 337A/119.

24 John Bussell to Mrs Bussell, 9 July 1834: BL 337A/475.

25 Georgiana Molloy to Elizabeth Besly, 18 May 1834: BL 3278A/2.

26 Ibid.

27 Georgiana Molloy to Mrs Kennedy, 26 June 1834: CRO D/Ken/3/28/9.

28 Georgiana Molloy to Helen Story, 8 December 1834: BL 3278A/2.

29 For Stirling in England see Malcolm Uren, *Land Looking West: The Story of Governor James Stirling in Western Australia*, OUP, London, 1948, chapter XXVII.

30 Joseph Cross, ed., *Journals of Several Expeditions Made in Western Australia, During the Years 1829, 1830, 1831, and 1832*, J. Cross, London, 1833, pp. x, xii, and xix.

31 Neville Green, *Broken Spears: Aborigines and Europeans in the south-west of Australia*, Focus Education Services, Perth, 1984, p. 97.

32 Stirling quoted in Uren, *Land Looking West*, p. 283.

33 George Fletcher Moore, *Diary of Ten Years Eventful Life of an Early Settler in Western Australia*, M. Walbrook, London, 1884, p. 237.

34 Surveyor-General to John Bussell, 6 April 1833: BL 337A/406.

35 Mrs Bussell to Capel Carter, 18 September 1834: BL 337A/786.

13 MAKERS OF FORTUNE

1 Mrs Bussell quoted in Rodger Jennings, *Busselton: '. . . outstation on the Vasse,' 1830–1850*, The Shire of Busselton, Western Australia, 1983, p. 86.

2 Fanny Bussell to Capel Carter, 21 October 1834: BL 337A/344.

3 Georgiana Molloy to Mrs Kennedy, 28 February 1833: CRO D/Ken/3/28/9; Georgiana Molloy to Helen Story, 8 December 1834: BL 3278A/2.

4 Georgiana Molloy to Helen Story, 8 December 1834: BL 3278A/2.

5 Ibid.

6 Ibid.

7   Ibid.

8   Ibid.

9   Ibid.

10 Ibid.

11 Letter of Bessie Bussell, February 1835, quoted in Alexandra Hasluck, *Portrait with Background: A Life of Georgiana Molloy*, OUP, Melbourne, 1955, p. 136.

12 John Bussell to Charles Bussell, 29 May 1835: BL 337A/477.

13 Lenox Bussell to Capel Carter, July 1835: BL 337A/541; Fanny Bussell to Capel Carter, 12 September 1835: BL 337A/349; Fanny Bussell to John Bussell, 27 August 1835: BL 337A/348.

14 Mrs Bussell to Capel Carter, 1 February 1835: BL 337A/786.

15 Georgiana Molloy to Mrs Kennedy, 22 December 1833: CRO D/Ken/3/28/9.

16 Bessie Bussell to Capel Carter, 20 April 1835: BL 337A/268; Mrs Bussell to Capel Carter, April 1835, quoted in Jennings, *Busselton*, p. 108; Fanny Bussell to Capel Carter, 12 September 1835: BL 337A/349.

17 John Bussell to Capel Carter, 19 January 1836: BL 337A/479.

18 Fanny Bussell to John Bussell, 27 August 1835: BL 337A/348; Bessie Bussell to Capel Carter, 13 September 1835: BL 337A/270; Fanny Bussell to Capel Carter, 12 September 1835: BL 337A/349.

19 Bessie Bussell to family at Augusta, November 1835: BL 337A/277.

20 Ibid.

21 Ibid.

22 Mary Bussell to Capel Carter, 24 December 1835, quoted in E. O. G. Shann, *Cattle Chosen: The Story of the First Group Settlement in Western Australia 1829 to 1841*, OUP, London, 1926, p. 47.

23 Mary Bussell to Fanny Bussell, 26 December 1835, quoted in Jennings, *Busselton*, p. 113.

24 John Bussell to Capel Carter, 19 January 1836: BL 337A/479.

25 Mrs Bussell to Capel Carter, April 1835, quoted in Jennings, *Busselton*, p. 108; Bessie Bussell to Capel Carter, 20 April 1835: BL 337A/268.

26 Quoted in Jennings, *Busselton*, pp. 94–96.

27 John Bussell to Sophie Hayward, November 1832: BL 337A/469.

28 Fanny Bussell to family at Henley, 6 February 1836: BL 337A/346.

29 Charles Darwin, *The Voyage of the Beagle*, Doubleday, New York, 1962, pp. 448, 449, and 502.

14   LIFE AND DEATH

1 Charles Leonard Irby and James Mangles, *Travels in Egypt and Nubia, Syria, and Asia Minor; During the Years 1817 & 1818*, privately published, London, 1823, p. 103.

2 Ibid., pp. 475 and 279.

3 George Fletcher Moore, *Diary of Ten Years Eventful Life of an Early Settler in Western Australia*, M. Walbrook, London, 1884, p. 39.

4 Peron quoted in Frank Horner, *The French Reconnaissance: Baudin in Australia 1801–1803*, MUP, Melbourne, 1987, p. 291.

5 Mangles Letterbooks: BL 479A/1–2.

6 Mrs Molloy to Captain Mangles, 21 March 1837: BL 479A/1–2.

7 H. W. Bunbury, *Early Days in Western Australia*, OUP, London, 1930, pp. 26 and 27–28.

8 Ibid., p. 79.

9 Ibid., pp. 108 and 103.

10 Draft of a letter from Charles Bussell [n.d.], reprinted as Appendix 7 in E. O. G. Shann, *Cattle Chosen: The Story of the First Group Settlement in Western Australia 1829 to 1841*, OUP, London, 1926.

11 George Grey, *Journals of Two Expeditions of Discovery in North-West and Western Australia, during the Years 1837, 1838, and 1839*, two volumes, T. and W. Boone, London, 1841, vol. 2, p. 298.

12 RM to CS, 15 May 1837: CSR 53.

13 Bessie Bussell's journal, 23 April 1837: BL 337A/795.

14 Ibid., 5 May 1837.

15 Ibid., 28 June 1837; Lenox Bussell to RM, 28 June 1837: CSR 54.

16 Bessie Bussell's journal, 2 and 17 July 1837: BL 337A/795.

17 Stirling quoted in Paul Hasluck, *Black Australians: A Survey of Native*

Policy in Western Australia, 1829–1897, second edition, MUP, Melbourne, 1970, p. 47.

18   Lenox Bussell to RM, 9 July 1837: CSR 54.

19   Bessie Bussell's journal, 13 July 1837: BL 337A/795.

20   Stirling quoted in Hasluck, *Black Australians*, p. 49.

21   Bessie Bussell's journal, 18–19 August 1837: BL 337A/795.

22   George Layman to CS, 27 September 1837: CSR 55.

23   Lenox Bussell to CS, 10 November 1837: CSR 57; Lenox Bussell to CS, 27 December 1837: CSR 59.

24   Lenox Bussell to CS, 27 December 1837: CSR 59.

15   GLORY IN THE FLOWER

1   Mrs Molloy to Captain Mangles, 25 January 1838: BL 479A/1–2.

2   Ibid.

3   Ibid.

4   Ibid.

5   Ibid.

6   Ibid.

7   Ibid.

8   Ibid.

9   Ibid.

10   Ibid.

11   Ibid.

12   See Lynn Barber, *The Heyday of Natural History 1820–1870*, Jonathan Cape, London, 1980, especially pp. 47–57 and Arthur O. Lovejoy, *The Great Chain of Being: A Study in the History of an Idea*, HUP, Cambridge, Mass., 1942.

13   Mrs Molloy to Captain Mangles, 25 January 1838: BL 479A/1–2.

14   Charles Bussell to John Bussell, 6 January 1837: BL 337A/161.

15   Lenox Bussell to John Bussell, 30 January 1837: BL 337A/543.

16   Mary Bussell to Fanny Bowker, 21 September 1834: BL 337A/791.

17   Charles Bussell to John Bussell, 22 January 1838: BL 337A/162.

18 Based on Elie Halevy, *The Growth of Philosophic Radicalism*, Faber & Faber, London, 1934, p. 15.

19 E. W. Landor, *The Bushman; or, Life in a New Country*, Richard Bentley, London, 1847, p. 108.

20 Quote from ibid., p. 111.

21 George Layman to CS, 20 May 1837: CSR 53.

22 Charles Bussell to John Bussell, 22 January 1838: BL 337A/162.

23 George Fletcher Moore, *Diary of Ten Years Eventful Life of an Early Settler in Western Australia*, M. Walbrook, London, 1884, p. 341.

24 Mrs Molloy to Captain Mangles, 25 January 1838: BL 479A/1–2.

16   PARADISE LOST

1 Mrs Molloy to Captain Mangles, 25 January 1838: BL 479A/1–2.

2 Ibid.

3 Mrs Molloy to Captain Mangles, 1 November 1838: BL 479A/1–2.

4 Ibid.

5 Ibid.

6 Mrs Molloy to Captain Mangles, 21 November 1838: BL 479A/1–2.

7 James Drummond to Captain Mangles, November 1838: BL 479A/1–2.

8 John Lindley to Captain Mangles, 1839: BL 479A/1–2.

9 Joseph Paxton to Captain Mangles, 1839: BL 479A/1–2.

10 See Charles Coulston Gillispie, *Genesis and Geology: A Study in the Relations of Scientific Thought, Natural Theology, and Social Opinion in Great Britain, 1790–1850*, HUP, Cambridge, Mass., 1951 and Francis C. Haber, *The Age of the World: Moses to Darwin*, The Johns Hopkins Press, Baltimore, 1959.

11 King quoted in Ann Moyal, *A Bright and Savage Land*, Collins, Sydney, 1986, p. 37.

12 John Lindley, *A Sketch of the Vegetation of the Swan River Colony*, in *Edward's Botanical Register*, Appendix to the first 23 volumes.

13 Quoted in Alexandra Hasluck, *Portrait with Background: A Life of Georgiana Molloy*, OUP, Melbourne, 1955, p. 182.

14 CS to RM, 21 January 1839: CSF 12.

15 RM to CS, 30 March 1839: CSR 74.

16 Mrs Molloy to Captain Mangles, 31 January 1840: BL 479A/1–2.

17 John Milton, *Paradise Lost*, book xi, lines 268–79.

18 Mrs Molloy to Captain Mangles, 31 January 1840: BL 479A/1–2.

19 John Sargent, *A Memoir of Rev. Henry Martyn, B.D.*, American Tract Society, New York, c. 1870, pp. 181 and 288.

20 Milton, *Paradise Lost*, book iv, lines 635–38.

21 Mrs Molloy to Captain Mangles, 31 January 1840: BL 479A/1–2.

22 Diary of Ann Elizabeth Turner reprinted in Tom Turner, *Turners of Augusta*, Paterson Brokensha Pty Ltd, Perth, 1956, 7 and 8 May 1839, p. 134.

23 Mrs Molloy to Captain Mangles, 31 January 1840: BL 479A/1–2.

17 EFFLORESCENCE

1 *JRWAHS*, vol. 1, part iv, 1929, p. 68.

2 Mrs Molloy to Captain Mangles, 31 January 1840: BL 479A/1–2.

3 Ibid.

4 John Bussell, Reminiscences [n.d.]: BL 337A/518.

5 Ibid.

6 George Fletcher Moore, *Diary of Ten Years Eventful Life of an Early Settler in Western Australia*, M. Walbrook, London, 1884, p. 167.

7 RM to CS, 15 December 1839: CSR 74, Depositions and reports relating to the death of Dundap.

8 Diary of Ann Elizabeth Turner reprinted in Tom Turner, *Turners of Augusta*, Paterson Brokensha Pty Ltd, Perth, 1956, 2 October–1 December 1839, pp. 138–41.

9 Mrs Molloy to Captain Mangles, 14 March 1840: BL 479A/1–2.

10 Mrs Molloy to Captain Mangles, 31 January 1840: BL 479A/1–2.

11 Ibid.

12 Ibid.

13 Moore, *Diary*, p. 290.

14 Mrs Molloy to Captain Mangles, 31 January 1840: BL 479A/1–2.

Wilgie was a mixture of red ochre and mud with which the Nyungar adorned their hair.

15 Ibid.

16 Ibid.

17 Ibid.

18 Ibid.

19 Mrs Molloy to Captain Mangles, 14 March 1840: BL 479A/1–2. *Isopogon* is an Australian genus of about 35 species, 25 of them endemic in Western Australia. To Molloy's yellow drumstick species John Lindley gave the name *Isopogon sphaerocephalus*.

20 Ibid.

21 Ibid.

22 Ibid.

23 Ibid.

24 Ibid.

18   HELICON

1 Georgiana Molloy to Mrs Kennedy, 4 December 1831: CRO D/Ken/3/28/9; Georgiana Molloy to George Kennedy, 13 September 1835: CRO D/Ken/3/28/9.

2 Mrs Molloy to Captain Mangles, June 1840: BL 479A/1–2.

3 Lenox Bussell to CS, 10 November 1837: CSR 57; Charles Bussell to John Bussell, 22 January 1838: BL 337A/162.

4 For the governor's opinion see CS to George Eliot, 1 April 1841: CSF 13.

5 Fanny Bussell's diary, 8 May 1840: BL 294A/12.

6 Mrs Molloy to Captain Mangles, June 1840: BL 479A/1–2.

7 Ibid.

8 Ibid.

9 Ibid.

10 Ibid.

11 Ibid.

12 Ibid.

13 Ibid.

14 Ibid.

15 Ibid.

16 Mrs Molloy to Captain Mangles, August 1840: BL 479A/1–2.

17 Ibid.

18 Mrs Jane (Webb) Loudon, *The Ladies' Flower-Garden of Ornamental Annuals*, William Smith, London, 1838, Introduction.

19 Mrs Molloy to Captain Mangles, August 1840: BL 479A/1–2.

20 George Eliot to CS, 25 December 1840: CSR 85.

21 John Bussell to CS, 26 December 1840; John Bussell to CS, 10 March 1841; and John Bussell to CS, April 1841: all BL Transcript 337A/788. For the government's position see CS to John Bussell, 11 January 1841 and CS to John Bussell, 25 March 1841: CSF 13.

22 Mrs Molloy to Captain Mangles, 14 March 1840: BL 479A/1–2.

23 Mrs Molloy to Captain Mangles, 20 January 1841: BL 479A/1–2.

24 Ibid.

19 VORTEX

1 Fanny Bussell's diary, entries for 26 February–7 March 1841: BL 294A/12.

2 Captain Molloy to William Plaskett, 9 March 1841: CSR 100.

3 Ibid., 11, 16, and 18 March 1841.

4 *Perth Gazette*, 13 March 1841.

5 James Backhouse, *A Narrative of a Visit to the Australian Colonies*, Hamilton, Adams, and Co., London, 1843, p. 531.

6 E. W. Landor, *The Bushman; or, Life in a New Country*, Richard Bentley, London, 1847, p. 187.

7 Mrs Molloy to Captain Mangles, 20 January 1841: BL 479A/1–2.

8 Ibid.

9 Ibid.

10 Ibid.

11 Nathaniel Ogle, *The Colony of Western Australia: A Manual for Emigrants 1839*, James Fraser, London, 1839, pp. 6 and 36.

12   John Ramsden Wollaston, *Wollaston's Picton Journal (1841–1844)*, ed. Percy U. Henn, Paterson Brokensha Pty Ltd, Perth, 1948, p. 26.

13   Ibid., p. 43.

14   Ibid., p. 30.

15   Ibid., p. 112.

16   Ibid., p. 5.

17   Report of the Protector of Natives, 21 January 1842: WAGG 288.

18   CS to RM, 23 April 1841: CSF 13.

19   RM to CS, 28 February 1842: CSR 114; Report of the Protector of Natives, 13 January 1843: WAGG 338; Wollaston, *Picton Journal*, p. 59.

20   The account of Cummangoot's arrest and death based on depositions relating to Regina v. Chas Bussell, July Sessions, 1842, Record of conviction: BL 3422/271 and draft of a letter by John Bussell, 11 March 1842: BL 337A/788.

21   Wollaston, *Picton Journal*, p. 59.

22   The settlers' petition and the Bussells' reply published in the *Perth Gazette*, 16 July 1842.

23   RM to CS, 11 May 1842: CSR 114.

24   Ibid.

25   Landor, *The Bushman*, p. 189.

26   *The Inquirer*, 1 July 1842.

27   Ibid., 13 July 1842.

20   LILIES OF THE FIELD

1   Mrs Molloy to Captain Mangles, 11 April 1842: BL 479A/1–2.

2   John Ramsden Wollaston, *Wollaston's Picton Journal (1841–1844)*, ed. Percy U. Henn, Paterson Brokensha Pty Ltd, Perth, 1948, p. 110.

3   CS to RM, 12 February 1841: CSF 13.

4   Wollaston, *Picton Journal*, p. 112.

5   Ibid.

6   Ibid., pp. 126–31.

7   Ibid., p. 56.

8   Ibid., p. 157.

9   Ibid., pp. 157–59.

10   Ibid., pp. 26 and 199. Nyungar quote from Neville Green, *Broken Spears: Aborigines and Europeans in the southwest of Australia*, Focus Education Services, Perth, 1984, p. 186.

11   Wollaston, *Picton Journal*, p. 166.

12   John Milton, *Paradise Lost*, book x, lines 193–96.

13   Wollaston, *Picton Journal*, pp. 141, 158, 161, and 55.

14   Ibid., pp. 158–71.

BIBLIOGRAPHY

WESTERN AUSTRALIA

Appleyard, R. T. and Toby Manford, *The Beginning: European Discovery and Early Settlement of Swan River Western Australia*, UWA Press, Nedlands, 1980.

Australian Dictionary of Biography, vol. 1, 1788–1850, A–H, ed. Douglas Pike, MUP, Melbourne, 1966.

Australian Dictionary of Biography, vol. 2, 1788–1850, I–Z, ed. Douglas Pike, MUP, Melbourne, 1967.

Backhouse, James, *A Narrative of a Visit to the Australian Colonies*, Hamilton, Adams, and Co., London, 1843.

Barrow, John, 'State of the Colony of Swan River, 1st January, 1830,' *The Journal of the Royal Geographical Society of London*, vol. 1, no. 1, 1831.

Bassett, Marnie, *The Hentys: An Australian Colonial Tapestry*, OUP, London, 1954.

Baudin, Nicolas, *The Journal of Post Captain Nicolas Baudin*, translated by Christine Cornell, Libraries Board of South Australia, Adelaide, 1974.

Beard, J. S., *Vegetation Survey of Western Australia: The Vegetation of the Swan Area*, UWA Press, Nedlands, 1981.

Berndt, Ronald M. and Catherine H., eds, *Aborigines of the West: Their Past and Their Present*, UWA Press, Nedlands, 1980.

Berryman, Ian, *A Colony Detailed: The First Census of Western Australia, 1832*, Creative Research, Perth, 1979.

Boultbee, John, *Journal of a Rambler: The Journal of John Boultbee*, ed. June Starke, OUP, Wellington, 1986.

Breton, Lieutenant W. H., *Excursions in New South Wales, Western Australia, and Van Diemen's Land, During the Years 1830, 1831, 1832, and 1833*, Richard Bentley, London, 1834.

Buller-Murphy, Deborah, *An Attempt to Eat the Moon; And other stories recounted from the Aborigines*, Georgian House, Melbourne, 1958.

Bunbury, H. W., *Early Days in Western Australia*, OUP, London, 1930.

Byrne, J. C., *Twelve Years' Wanderings in the British Colonies from 1835 to 1847*, Bentley, London, 1848.

Cameron, J. M. R., 'Information Distortion in Colonial Promotion: The Case of Swan River Colony,' *Australian Geographical Studies*, vol. 12, no. 1, 1974, pp. 57–76.

——, 'H. C. Sempill: The Western Connection,' *Journal and Proceedings of the Armidale and District Historical Society*, no. 22, 1978, pp. 75–92.

——, *Ambition's Fire: The Agricultural Colonization of Pre-Convict Western Australia*, UWA Press, Nedlands, 1981.

Cross, Joseph, ed., *Journals of Several Expeditions Made in Western Australia, During the Years 1829, 1830, 1831, and 1832*, J. Cross, London, 1833.

Crowley, F. K., *Australia's Western Third: A History of Western Australia from the First Settlements to Modern Times*, Macmillan & Co., London, 1960.

Dampier, William, *Dampier's Voyages*, ed. John Masefield, two volumes, E. Grant Richards, London, 1906.

Durack, Mary, *To Be Heirs Forever*, Constable, London, 1976.

Erickson, Rica, A. S. George, N. G. Marchant, and M. K. Morcombe, *Flowers and Plants of Western Australia*, Reed, Sydney, 1988.

Gentilli, J., ed., *Western Landscapes*, UWA Press, Nedlands, 1979.

Green, Neville, *Broken Spears: Aborigines and Europeans in the southwest of Australia*, Focus Education Services, Perth, 1984.

——, ed., *Nyungar—The People: Aboriginal Customs in the southwest of Australia*, Creative Research, Perth, 1979.

Grey, George, *Journals of Two Expeditions of Discovery in North-West and Western Australia, during the Years 1837, 1838, and 1839*, two volumes, T. and W. Boone, London, 1841.

Hallam, Sylvia J., *Fire and Hearth: a study of Aboriginal usage and European usurpation in south-western Australia*, Australian Institute of Aboriginal Studies, Canberra, 1979.

Hallam, Sylvia and Lois Tilbrook, eds, *Aborigines of the Southwest Region, 1829–1840: The Bicentennial Dictionary of Western Australians, Volume VIII*, UWA Press, Nedlands, 1990.

Hammond, J. E., *Western Pioneers: The Battle Well Fought*, ed. O. K. Battye, Imperial Printing Co., Perth, 1936.

Hasluck, Alexandra, *Portrait with Background: A Life of Georgiana Molloy*, OUP, Melbourne, 1955.

Hasluck, Paul, *Black Australians: A Survey of Native Policy in Western Australia, 1829–1897*, second edition, MUP, Melbourne, 1970.

Horner, Frank, *The French Reconnaissance: Baudin in Australia 1801–1803*, MUP, Melbourne, 1987.

Jennings, Rodger, *Busselton: '. . . outstation on the Vasse,' 1830–1850*, The Shire of Busselton, Western Australia, 1983.

Journal of the Royal Western Australian Historical Society, vol. 1, 1927–31.

Landor, E. W., *The Bushman; or, Life in a New Country*, Richard Bentley, London, 1847.

Lindley, John, *A Sketch of the Vegetation of the Swan River Colony*, in *Edward's Botanical Register*, Appendix to the first 23 volumes.

MacDermott, Marshall, *A Brief Sketch of the Long and Varied Career of Marshall MacDermott*, Adelaide, 1874.

Marchant, N. G., 'Species diversity in the southwestern flora,' *Journal of the Royal Society of Western Australia*, no. 56, 1973.

Moore, George Fletcher, *Diary of Ten Years Eventful Life of an Early Settler in Western Australia*, M. Walbrook, London, 1884.

Norris, William, *Annals of the Colonial Church Diocese of Adelaide*, The Society for the Propagation of the Gospel, London, 1852.

Ogle, Nathaniel, *The Colony of Western Australia: A Manual for Emigrants 1839*, James Fraser, London, 1839.

Powell, Reverend John Giles, *The Narrative of a Voyage to the Swan River*, F. C. Westley, London, 1831.

Roberts, Jane, *Two Years at Sea: Being the Narrative of a Voyage to the Swan River and Van Diemen's Land During the Years 1829, 1830, 1831*, Richard Bentley, London, 1834.

Seddon, George, *Sense of Place: A Response to an Environment—The Swan Coastal Plain of Western Australia*, UWA Press, Nedlands, 1972.

Shann, E. O. G., *Cattle Chosen: The Story of the First Group Settlement in Western Australia 1829 to 1841*, OUP, London, 1926.

Stannage, C. T., *The People of Perth: A Social History of Western Australia's Capital City*, Perth City Council, Perth, 1979.

——, ed., *A New History of Western Australia*, UWA Press, Nedlands, 1981.

Statham, Pamela, compiler, *Dictionary of Western Australians, 1829–1914: Volume 1, Early Settlers, 1829–1850*, UWA Press, Nedlands, 1979.

——, ed., *The Tanner Letters: A Pioneer Saga of Swan River & Tasmania, 1831–1845*, UWA Press, Nedlands, 1981.

Stokes, J. Lort, *Discoveries in Australia*, T. and W. Boone, two volumes, London, 1846.

Taylor, Jan, *Australia's Southwest and Our Future*, Kangaroo Press, Kenthurst, NSW, 1990.

Turner, Tom, *Turners of Augusta*, Paterson Brokensha Pty Ltd, Perth, 1956.

Uren, Malcolm, *Land Looking West: The Story of Governor James Stirling in Western Australia*, OUP, London, 1948.

Wilson, T. B., *Narrative of a Voyage Round the World*, Sherwood, Gilbert, & Piper, London, 1835.

Wollaston, John Ramsden, *Wollaston's Picton Journal (1841–1844)*, ed. Percy U. Henn, Paterson Brokensha Pty Ltd, Perth, 1948.

GENERAL

Aeschylus, *Prometheus Bound*, translated by Philip Vellacott, Penguin Books, London, 1970.

Ashton, John, *The Dawn of the XIXth Century in England: A Social Sketch of the Times*, T. Fisher Unwin, London, 1898.

Banks, Russell, *Continental Drift: A Novel*, Harper & Row, New York, 1985.

Barber, Lynn, *The Heyday of Natural History 1820–1870*, Jonathan Cape, London, 1980.

Bell, Douglas, *Wellington's Officers*, Collins, London, 1938.

Berlin, Isaiah, *The Crooked Timber of Humanity: Chapters in the History of Ideas*, Knopf, New York, 1991.

Briggs, Asa, *The Age of Improvement: 1783–1867*, Longmans, London, 1960.

Bryant, Arthur, *Years of Victory: 1802–1812*, Collins, London, 1945.

——, *The Age of Elegance: 1812–1822*, Collins, London, 1950.

Burleigh, J. H. S., *A Church History of Scotland*, OUP, London, 1960.

Burroughs, Peter, *Britain and Australia, 1831–1855: A Study in Imperial Relations and Crown Lands Administration*, OUP, Oxford, 1967.

Bury, J. B., *The Idea of Progress: An Inquiry into its Origin and Growth*, Macmillan and Co., London, 1924.

Butterfield, Herbert, *The Whig Interpretation of History*, Charles Scribner and Sons, New York, 1951.

Campbell, Colin, *The Romantic Ethic and the Spirit of Modern Consumerism*, Basil Blackwell, Oxford, 1989.

Carlyle, Thomas, 'Signs of the Times,' *The Edinburgh Review*, London, vol. XLIX, 1829, pp. 439–59.

Carrothers, W. A., *Emigration from the British Isles*, P. S. King & Son, London, 1929.

Carter, Paul, *The Road to Botany Bay: An Exploration of Landscape and History*, Knopf, New York, 1988.

Catton, William R., Jr, *Overshoot: The Ecological Basis of Revolutionary Change*, University of Illinois Press, Urbana, 1980.

Clapham, J. H., *An Economic History of Modern Britain: The Early Railway Age 1820–1850*, CUP, Cambridge, 1959.

Clark, G. Kitson, *The Making of Victorian England*, HUP, Cambridge, Mass., 1962.

Creighton, M., *Carlisle*, Longmans, Green, and Co., London, 1889.

Critchett, Jan, *A Distant Field of Murder: Western District Frontiers, 1834–1848*, MUP, Melbourne, 1990.

Cronon, William, *Nature's Metropolis: Chicago and the Great West*, Norton, New York, 1991.

Crosby, Alfred W., *Ecological Imperialism: The Biological Expansion of Europe, 900–1900*, CUP, Cambridge, 1986.

Darwin, Charles, *The Origin of Species: By Means of Natural Selection*, The Modern Library, New York, n.d.

——, *The Voyage of the Beagle*, Doubleday, New York, 1962.

Dixon, R. M. W., *The Languages of Australia*, CUP, Cambridge, 1980.

Donaldson, Ian and Tamsin, *Seeing the First Australians*, George Allen & Unwin, Sydney, 1985.

Drummond, Andrew Landale, *Edward Irving and His Circle*, James Clarke & Co., London, 1937.

Drummond, Andrew Landale and James Bulloch, *The Scottish Church 1688–1843*, Saint Andrews Press, Edinburgh, 1973.

DuCane, Lieut.-General Sir Edmund, 'The Peninsula and Waterloo: Memories of an old Rifleman,' *Cornhill Magazine*, vol. 76, July to December 1897, pp. 750–58.

Dunlop, John Graham, *The Dunlops of Dunlop and of Keppoch*, Frome, London, 1939.

Eddy, J. J., *Britain and the Australian Colonies 1818–1831: The Technique of Government*, Clarendon Press, Oxford, 1969.

Ehrenfeld, David, *The Arrogance of Humanism*, OUP, New York, 1981.

Eliade, Mircea, *Australian Religions: An Introduction*, Cornell University Press, Ithaca, 1973.

Elias, Norbert, *The History of Manners*, Pantheon, New York, 1978.

Figes, Eva, *Patriarchal Attitudes: Women in Society*, Faber and Faber, London, 1970.

Flood, Josephine, *Archeology of the Dreamtime: The Story of Prehistoric Australia and its People*, revised edition, Yale University Press, New Haven, 1990.

Foucault, Michel, *The Order of Things: An Archeology of the Human Sciences*, Pantheon, New York, 1970.

Gelis, Jacques, *History of Childbirth: Fertility, Pregnancy and Birth in Early Modern Europe*, translated by Rosemary Morris, Northeastern University Press, Boston, 1991.

Gifford, Don, *The Farther Shore: A Natural History of Perception, 1798–1984*, Atlantic Monthly Press, New York, 1990.

Gillispie, Charles Coulston, *Genesis and Geology: A Study in the Relations of Scientific Thought, Natural Theology, and Social Opinion in Great Britain, 1790–1850*, HUP, Cambridge, Mass., 1951.

Glover, Michael, *Wellington's Army in the Peninsula, 1808–1814*, David and Charles, London, 1977.

Gordon, Barry, *Political Economy in Parliament, 1819–1823*, Macmillan, London, 1976.

——, *Economic Doctrine and Tory Liberalism, 1824–1830*, Macmillan, London, 1979.

Gould, Stephen Jay, *Time's Arrow Time's Cycle: Myth and Metaphor in the Discovery of Geological Time*, HUP, Cambridge, Mass., 1987.

——, *Wonderful Life: The Burgess Shale and the Nature of History*, Norton, New York, 1989.

——, *Bully for Brontosaurus: Reflections in Natural History*, Norton, New York, 1991.

Greenblatt, Stephen, *Marvelous Possessions: The Wonder of the New World*, University of Chicago Press, Chicago, 1991.

Haber, Francis C., *The Age of the World: Moses to Darwin*, The Johns Hopkins Press, Baltimore, 1959.

Hadfield, Miles, *A History of British Gardening*, third edition, John Murray, London, 1979.

Halevy, Elie, *A History of the English People: 1815–1830*, T. Fisher Unwin Ltd, London, 1926.

——, *The Growth of Philosophic Radicalism*, Faber & Faber, London, 1934.

Hammond, J. L. and Barbara, *The Village Labourer, 1760–1832: A Study in the Government of England before the Reform Bill*, Longmans, Green, and Co., London, 1911.

Harris, John, *Recollections of Rifleman Harris*, ed. Henry Curling, Robert M. McBride & Company, New York, 1929.

Harrison, Robert Pogue, *Forests: The Shadow of Civilization*, University of Chicago Press, Chicago, 1992.

Himmelfarb, Gertrude, *The Idea of Poverty: England in the Early Industrial Age*, Vintage Books, New York, 1985.

——, *The New History and the Old*, HUP, Cambridge, Mass., 1987.

Hobsbawn, E. J., *The Age of Revolution: Europe 1789–1848*, Weidenfeld and Nicolson, London, 1962.

Howitt, William, *The Rural Life of England*, two volumes, Longman, Orme, Brown, Green, & Longmans, London, 1838.

Irby, Charles Leonard and James Mangles, *Travels in Egypt and Nubia, Syria, and Asia Minor; During the Years 1817 & 1818*, privately published, London, 1823.

——, *Account of the Necropolis of Petra, a city in Palestine*, T. Cadell, London, 1828.

James, Patricia, *Population Malthus: His Life and Times*, Routledge & Kegan Paul, London, 1979.

James, William, *The Varieties of Religious Experience*, HUP, Cambridge, Mass., 1985.

Jennings, Humphrey, *Pandaemonium 1660–1886: The Coming of the Machine as Seen by Contemporary Observers*, The Free Press, 1985, New York.

Johnson, Paul, *The Birth of the Modern: World Society 1815–1830*, Harper Collins, New York, 1991.

Kaplan, Fred, *Thomas Carlyle: A Biography*, Cornell University Press, Ithaca, New York, 1983.

Keen, Sam, *Faces of the Enemy: Reflections of the Hostile Imagination*, Harper & Row, San Francisco, 1986.

Keith, Rev. Alexander, *Sketch of the Evidence from Prophecy: Containing an Account of those Prophecies which were Distinctly Foretold, and which have been Clearly or Literally Fulfilled*, Waugh and Innes, Edinburgh, 1823.

Kincaid, Captain J., *Adventures in the Rifle Brigade: In the Peninsula, France and the Netherland, from 1809 to 1815* (first published 1848), Peter Davies Limited, London, 1929.

Lasch, Christopher, *The True and Only Heaven: Progress and its Critics*, Norton, New York, 1991.

Leed, Eric J., *The Mind of the Traveler: From Gilgamesh to Global Tourism*, Basic Books, New York, 1991.

Leiss, William, *The Domination of Nature*, George Braziller, New York, 1972.

Lindblom, Charles E., *Politics and Markets: The World's Political Systems*, Basic Books, New York, 1977.

Loudon, Mrs Jane (Webb), *The Ladies' Flower-Garden of Ornamental Annuals*, William Smith, London, 1838.

Lovejoy, Arthur O., *The Great Chain of Being: A Study in the History of an Idea*, HUP, Cambridge, Mass., 1942.

Martin, Paul S. and Richard G. Klein, eds, *Quaternary Extinctions: A Prehistoric Revolution*, University of Arizona Press, Flagstaff, 1984.

Maughan, William Charles, *Rosneath Past and Present*, Alexander Gardner, London, 1893.

Milton, John, *Paradise Lost*.

Moodie, Susanna, *Roughing it in the Bush; or, Life in Canada* (first published 1852), Beacon Press, Boston, 1986.

Morris, R., *Time's Arrows: Scientific Attitudes Toward Time*, Simon and Schuster, New York, 1985.

Morrison, Reg and Maggie, *The Voyage of the Great Southern Ark*, Lansdowne Press, Sydney, 1988.

Moyal, Ann, *A Bright and Savage Land*, Collins, Sydney, 1986.

Nash, Roderick Frazier, *The Rights of Nature: A History of Environmental Ethics*, Primevera Press, Sydney, 1990.

Nicolson, Marjorie Hope, *Mountain Gloom and Mountain Glory: The Development of the Aesthetics of the Infinite*, Norton, New York, 1963.

Nisbet, Robert, *History of the Idea of Progress*, Basic Books, New York, 1980.

Oliphant, Mrs (Margaret), *The Life of Edward Irving*, Hurst and Blackett, London, 1862.

Paley, William, *Reasons for Contentment: Addressed to the Labouring Part of the British Public*, R. Faulder, London, 1793.

Passmore, John, *Man's Responsibility for Nature: Ecological Problems and Western Tradition*, Charles Scribner and Sons, New York, 1974.

Perlin, John, *A Forest Journey: The Role of Wood in the Development of Civilization*, HUP, Cambridge, Mass., 1991.

Petersen, William, *Malthus*, HUP, Cambridge, Mass., 1979.

Pollok, Robert, *The Course of Time: A Poem, in Ten Books*, ninth edition, William Blackwood, Edinburgh, 1829.

Porter, Jane, *Sir Edward Seaward's Narrative*, Longman, Rees, Orme, Brown, and Green, London, 1831.

Pyne, Stephen J., *Burning Bush: A Fire History of Australia*, Henry Holt and Company, New York, 1991.

Reid, Robert, *Land of Lost Content: The Luddite Revolt, 1812*, Heinemann, London, 1986.

Sargent, John, *A Memoir of Rev. Henry Martyn, B.D.*, American Tract Society, New York, c. 1870.

Shepard, Paul, *Man in the Landscape: A Historic View of the Esthetics of Nature*, Knopf, New York, 1967.

Shorter, Edward, *A History of Women's Bodies*, Basic Books, New York, 1982.

Smith, Adam, *An Inquiry into the Nature and Causes of the Wealth of Nations*, The Modern Library, New York, 1937.

Smith, Harry, *The Autobiography of Lieutenant-General Sir Harry Smith*, ed. G. C. Moore Smith, two volumes, E. P. Dutton & Company, New York, 1902.

Sraffa, Piero, ed., *The Works and Correspondence of David Ricardo*, vol. 2, 'Notes on Malthus's Principles of Political Economy,' CUP, Cambridge, 1952.

Stanner, W. E. H., *White Man Got No Dreaming*, ANU Press, Canberra, 1979.

——, *On Aboriginal Religion*, University of Sydney Press, Sydney, 1989.

Story, Robert, *Peace in Believing: A Memoir of Isabella Campbell of Rosneath, Dumbartonshire, Scotland*, Jonathan Leavitt, New York, 1830.

Strachan, Gordon, *The Pentecostal Theology of Edward Irving*, Darton, Longman & Todd, London, 1973.

Symons, Julian, *Thomas Carlyle: The Life and Ideas of a Prophet*, Victor Gollancz, London, 1952.

Thomas, Keith, *Man and the Natural World: A History of the Modern Sensibility*, Pantheon Books, New York, 1983.

Thompson, E. P., *The Making of the English Working Class*, Pantheon, New York, 1964.

Trevelyan, George Macaulay, *British History in the Nineteenth Century (1782–1901)*, Longmans, Green and Co., London, 1922.

Turner, Frederick, *Beyond Geography: The Western Spirit Against the Wilderness*, The Viking Press, New York, 1980.

Virgil, *The Aeneid*.

Westbroek, Peter, *Life as a Geological Force: Dynamics of the Earth*, Norton, New York, 1991.

Wilberforce, Reverend S., ed., *Journals and Letters of the Rev. Henry Martyn, B.D.*, R. B. Seeley and W. Burnside, London, 1837.

Wilson, Alexander, *The Culture of Nature: North American Landscape from Disney to the Exxon Valdez*, Blackwell, Cambridge, Mass., 1992.

Wright, Judith, *The Cry for the Dead*, OUP, Melbourne, 1981.

INDEX

Preston, Lieutenant William, 100–1,
125–6, 147
Preston River, 100
progress: and biological evolution, 5–6,
261; no Aboriginal notion of, 13;
as the aim of travel, 14; as the
goal of Napoleonic War
antagonists, 18; in the *Wealth of
Nations*, 20, 21; Enlightenment
formula for, 20; and the Industrial
Revolution, 23; threatened by
worker protest, 25; identified with
clearing, 116; reported at Augusta,
120, 132; at the Adelphi, 127; bias
and hubris of, 151, 228; supposed
innateness of, 152; against the
forest, 163; tangibility of, 176; and
restlessness, 192; documents
measure, 193; dependence on, 207;
murderous demands of, 235;
general belief in, 241; Bussells'
obsession with, 246–7; colonial
inevitability of, 312; coterminous
with hardening attitudes, 320;
triumph of, 321; as measured by
roads, 325
Prometheus Bound (Aeschylus), 123
property: nature of, 250
Proteaceae, 8
Protectors of Natives, 315

Quarterly Review, 50

Raffles Bay, 49
rainforest, 7
religion: in postwar Britain, 27, 29–30;
Romanticism, and Edward Irving,
31; deficit of in Britain, 67;
immortality and temporality, 84;
attitude of to travel, 89; and
natural history, 259–61; could not
exclude organic existence, 267; *see
also* Bible; God
restlessness: of James Turner, 74;
among servants and masters in WA,
120; of the Bussell brothers, 147;
of industrial Britain, 153; at
Augusta, 172; source of, 192; of
Thomas Turner, 251
Rifle Brigade, 39, 91

Right whales, 272, 301
Roe, John Septimus, 56, 101, 108,
124, 134
Roe, Matilda, 99
Romanticism: and Edward Irving, 31;
of GM, 81; exalts mountains,
83–4; opposes utilitarianism, 85;
and awe, 85
Rosneath: Georgiana Kennedy's life at,
and natural surroundings of, 32–4;
marriage of the Molloys at, 63;
GM's homesickness for, 89, 93,
128, 179
Rottnest Island, 48, 95
Royal Geographical Society, 220
Royal Society, 220, 258
Rugby: Kennedy family moves to and
Georgiana Kennedy detests, 28;
George Kennedy attends school at,
29; GM visits before departure
from England, 63–4

Saint Alouarn Islands, 107
St Leonard, 56, 57
Salkild, Thomas, 273
Sally Ann, 214
Samson Agonistes (John Milton), 142
Samuel Wright, 295
Sargent, John, 144
scala naturae, 244
Scotland: migration of people from,
16, 22; religious revival in, 35;
original home of the Stirlings, 46;
GM's thoughts of, 89, 93, 206; as
a better site for spiritual struggle,
205; existence in compared to
Australia, 330
Scott, Walter, 66
scurvy: breaks out at Swan River, 57;
debilitates travellers to Swan River,
102, 106
seals: James Stirling's reports
inaugurate hunting of, 102; hunters
of report river discovery, 105; on
the Saint Alouarn Islands, 107;
hunters of abduct Aboriginal
women, 151; hunters of visit
Augusta, 262; former abundance of
along WA coast, 272–3
self-interest: drives economic machine,

76; starts journey, 77; attends
Sunday service aboard *Warrior*, 78;
the sceptic, 79; on voyage's
neverending prospect, 83; animals
of die, 86; rheumatism of, 90;
purchases stock at Cape Town, 92;
servants desert, 93; writes less in
journal, 94; at Fremantle, 96, 97;
journeys to Perth, 99; initial land
grant of, 103–4; agrees to settle at
Flinders Bay, 106; disembarks at
Augusta, 109; initial Augusta land
allocation of, 110; pioneering at
Augusta, 114; servant problems of,
114, 119; dissatisfaction of with
land grant, 118; daughter of
marries James McDermott, 165;
claims land, 167, 168; pays
agistment fee to the Molloys, 207;
alleges Stirling's neglect, 211; fated
to remain at Augusta, 215; objects
to Captain Molloy's relocation to
the Vasse, 251, 263–4; disembarks
supplies at Augusta, 256; remains
at Augusta, 324
Turner, Maria, 74
Turner, Thomas: establishes Turnwood,
215; Turnwood burned, 227;
restlessness of, 251; pursues
Aborigines, 273
Turnwood, 215, 227
Twiss, Horace, 52, 71

Uglymug, 317, 319
Uncas, 302
usurpation: leads to Aboriginal hunger,
228
utilitarianism: and Romanticism, 85;
not relevant to GM's botanising,
218; influence of, 248

Van Diemen's Land: migration to, 51;
tainted by convicts, 54; fated
Cumberland left from, 107; Baudin
in, 159; supplies sought from, 166;
whales around, 272; *see also*
Tasmania
Vasse (French seaman), 160
Vasse, the: explored by Collie and
Preston, 100; explored by Preston,

125–6; explored by John Bussell,
125, 147–63; surveyed, 167;
applauded by Bessie Bussell, 190;
settled by the Bussells, 190–2, 193;
grants of land at concentrated for
defence, 200; progress at, 211;
John Bussell's reports of, 221;
Molloys plan to move to, 223,
256; Lt Bunbury at, 224–5, 227;
settlement at fragments Nyungar
life, 226; possibility of settlement at
inherited, 228; dried flowers from,
242–3; Captain Molloy's
improvements at, 251; GM arrives
at, 269; new life of GM at, 271;
regarded as less healthy than
Augusta by GM, 291; GM's
continued unhappiness at, 311; *see
also* Busselton
Vasse estuary: wildlife and exploration
of, 100–1
Vasse River: reached by John Bussell,
149; classical setting of, 157;
named, 160; explored by Bussells,
192; compared to the Blackwood
River, 269
Vimiera, 40
Vincent, Sir Francis, 50
violence: in everyday British life, 27,
29–30; British willingness to use,
197; monopolised by the state,
230; accepted by the Bussells, 231;
repels GM, 290; of the Bussells
deplored by Rev. John Wollaston,
318
Virgil, 77, 157

Wakefield, Edward Gibbon, 264, 312
war: mobilisation for, 17; for progress,
18; expansive effects of, 21, 24;
opposition to, 23; exhilaration of,
40; and the habit of dichotomising,
41; and sex, 41; of 1812, 46;
against the bush, 132; Nyungar
unpreparedness for, 198; idea of
structures settler thought, 198; at
the Vasse, 229; Lenox Bussell's
view of, 231; consequences of, 231;
hysteria of, 233; *see also*
Napoleonic Wars